THE

IN

ER

Page
In T
figur
Page
that
Page
elect
Page
town
Page
insistence on the need to fight for

Page 282, line 4: the dates should be 1871-1945.

THE FEMINIST MOVEMENT IN GERMANY 1894-1933

Richard J Evans

SAGE Studies in 20th Century History
Volume 6

SAGE Publications   London and Beverly Hills

For information address

SAGE Publications Ltd.
44 Hatton Garden
London EC 1

SAGE Publications Inc.
275 South Beverly Drive
Beverly Hills, California 90212

International Standard Book Number
0 8039 9951 8 Cloth
0 8039 9996 8 Paper

Library of Congress Catalog Card Number
75-31571

First Printing

Printed and Bound in Great Britain by
Biddles Ltd., Guildford, Surrey.

To my mother and father

CONTENTS

LIST OF TABLES

ABBREVIATIONS

ABDF	Archiv des Bundes Deutscher Frauenvereine
ADEFB	Archiv des Deutsch-evangelischen Frauenbundes
ADLV	Archiv des Allgemeinen Deutschen Lehrerinnenvereins
AStA	Allgemeines Staatsarchiv
BA	Bundesarchiv
BDF	Bund Deutscher Frauenvereine
BNN	Berliner Neuste Nachrichten
BT	Berliner Tageblatt
BVZ	Berliner Volkszeitung
CSU	Christlich-Soziale Union
DDP	Deutsche Demokratische Partei
DF	Die Frau
DHV	Deutschnationaler Handlungsgehilfenverband
DP	Die Post
DNVP	Deutschnationale Volkspartei
DSB	Deutsch-soziale Blätter (Deutsches Blatt)
FB	Die Frauenbewegung
FDP	Freie Demokratische Partei
FES/ASD	Friedrich-Ebert-Stiftung/Archiv der Sozialen Demokratie
FS	Frauenstimmrecht!
FZ	Frankfurter Zeitung
GA	General-Anzeiger (Hamburg)
GL	Die Gleichheit
GStA	Geheimes Staatsarchiv
HA	Heeresarchiv
Hbg	Hamburg
HC	Hamburgischer Correspondent
HE	Hamburger Echo
HF	Hamburger Fremdenblatt
HLA	Helene Lange Archiv
HN	Hamburger Nachrichten
HNN	Hamburger Neueste Nachrichten
HStA	Hauptstaatsarchiv
IISG	Internationaal Instituut voor Sociale Geschiednis
JB	Jahrbuch der Frauenbewegung (from 1927: Jahrbuch des Bundes Deutscher Frauenvereine)

LVZ	Leipziger Volkszeitung
NAZ	Norddeutscher Allgemeine Zeitung
NSDAP	Nationalsozialistische Deutsche Arbeiterpartei
PP	Politische Polizei
RT	Stenographische Berichte über die Verhandlungen des Deutschen Reichstags
SB	Die Staatsbürgerin
SCPC	Swarthmore College Peace Collection
SPD	Sozialdemokratische Partei Deutschlands
StA	Staatsarchiv
UB	Universitätsbibliothek
VW	Vorwärts
ZFS	Zeitschrift für Frauenstimmrecht

PREFACE

This book is a history of the feminist movement in Germany, a movement that in its heyday claimed over a million adherents. Historians know a great deal about feminist movements in England and America, but there have been no scholarly studies of feminism on the European continent. This is a first attempt at filling this gap in our knowledge of what is rapidly coming to be regarded as one of the most important and significant of all movements of social reform and human emancipation. It seeks to contribute to the comparative study of feminism by showing, among other things, that feminism cannot be properly understood unless it is seen as an integral part of the social and political system within which it sought to achieve its aims. The closest ties of feminism in the 19th and early 20th centuries, it suggests, were to bourgeois liberalism, and it is to the success or failure of this creed, itself dependent on wider political and social circumstances, that its fate was linked. Too often, histories of feminism proceed as if feminists everywhere meant the same thing when they spoke of the emancipation of women, and assume that undifferentiated male prejudice was all that stood between them and the achievement of their aims. This book hopes to contribute to the new and rapidly expanding field of women's history by demonstrating the inadequacy of these assumptions.

When this study was originally undertaken in 1970 however it was for quite another reason, and it is this that forms the major purpose behind the present work. In the first place this book is intended as a case-study in the development of German liberalism from the fall of Bismarck to the advent of Hitler. Historians such as John Vincent and Brian Harrison have recently shown that liberalism in Victorian England rested on a complex infrastructure of social institutions and social movements.[1] The present work seeks to examine the history of one particular social movement which formed part of the infrastructure of German liberalism. Such studies, it seems to me, are badly needed.

Because of their concentration on the forces of right and left German historians have neglected the political groupings in the middle, among them the liberal and progressive movements. The result is a very confused picture in which some historians see a revival of liberalism taking place after the turn of the century, culminating in the foundation of the Weimar Republic under liberal auspices,[2] while others trace the roots of Nazism to the decay of liberal values and liberal politics in the years before the First World War.[3] The present work hopes to clarify at least part of this confusion through a close study of the changing aims and structure of one large liberal movement of social reform across the whole period from the 1890s to the 1930s.

That there was a genuine liberal revival at the turn of the century there can be, at least in the case of the feminist movement, no doubt. The whole nature of German feminism, it is argued in this book, was radicalised between 1894 and 1908. There were many reasons for this: the upsurge of pressure-group politics after the lapsing of the Anti-Socialist Law in 1890; the rapid changes in social structure brought about by the continuing process of Germany's headlong industrialisation; the growth of the tertiary sector of the economy with its expansion of employment opportunities for middle-class women, associated with the general economic upturn after the end of the Great Depression in 1896; a rapid expansion – with the spread of urbanisation, the growth of the population and the spread of economic pressure-groups – of the numbers and the professional consciousness of women schoolteachers, generally recognised as a mainstay of the feminist movement. More significantly from a political point of view, the emergence of radical feminism was part of a general movement within German liberalism towards a greater and more active concern for the peaceful solution of the many social problems and tensions created by industrialisation.

However, the radicalisation of the feminist movement was superficial and short-lived. From 1908 onwards it became rapidly more conservative. Once more, this development, it is argued in the present work, reflected changes in the nature of German liberalism as a whole. The radicals and reformers, though active and vocal, were always in a minority. Their activities stimulated a defensive reaction on the part of the mass of the middle ranks of the bourgeoisie, who feared that they would lead to too many concessions to the working class. Despite the continued numerical growth of feminist support, that support was itself becoming rapidly less liberal in character by 1914. This retreat from liberalism was a process of great complexity, and the analysis of its many causes forms the core of the present work. Recent research has stressed the weakness and fragility of liberal institutions in the Weimar Republic;[4] this book argues that their foundations were shaky long before then and suggests that the liberal revival of the early years of the 20th century was at best a short-lived affair, at worst specious and superficial, appealing only to a small minority among the middle classes.[5]

Yet a word of caution is also needed; like many other issues, female emancipation to some extent cut across party lines and elicited unfamiliar responses from party politicians. Political liberalism in Wilhelmine Germany may ultimately have rejected female suffrage, but so too did its counterpart in Edwardian England. An extreme conservative such as Stumm could be more enthusiastic about female emancipation than a dedicated liberal such as Haussmann. The final lesson of this book, therefore, is that society and politics in Wilhelmine Germany were more complicated perhaps than many historians find it convenient to imagine; and that some caution is needed in assessing the nature of its structure, its development and its constituent parts.

A word is necessary about the scope of this study. It concentrates in the first place on the Federation of German Women's Associations, founded in 1894 and dissolved in 1933, and organisations which either belonged to it or tried to influence its programme. In keeping with its purpose, it focuses on the political aims and development of the Federation. The analysis of the social, economic and legal status of German women, the history of the Social Democratic women's movement and other women's organisations, the policies of the SPD towards women's emancipation – these and other topics not central to the concerns of the present work have been relegated to a strictly subordinate position or omitted altogether. This is not to say, however, that they do not urgently require to be investigated; simply that the whole field of the history of German women is so new, the mass of available material so great and our ignorance so general, that I have had to concentrate much – though I hope not too much – of my effort on piecing together a basic narrative of the development of German feminism from the primary sources.[6] Elsewhere I have attempted to deal at greater length with some of the issues only briefly touched on in the present work.[7] As for the rest, if this book stimulates someone else to undertake the task of further investigation it will have served its purpose.

Most of the research for the present volume was carried out in Germany between September 1970 and October 1971, and additional research was undertaken at intervals during 1972 and 1973. The research was financed by a Studentship from the Social Science Research Council, a Studentship of St Antony's College Oxford, a Hanseatic Scholarship of the Stiftung FVS, and grants from the General Purposes Committee of the Board of the Faculty of Modern History in the University of Oxford, the Warden and Fellows of St Antony's College, Oxford, and the Department of History in the University of Stirling. I am indebted to all the bodies concerned for their generosity. I also wish to express my gratitude to the following libraries and archives for allowing me access to the material upon which this book is based: Archiv des Deutsch-evangelischen Frauenbundes, Hanover; Bayerisches Hauptstaatsarchiv Munich; Berliner Frauenbund 1945 e.V.; British Museum; Bundesarchiv, Koblenz; Deutsches Zentralarchiv, Potsdam; Deutsches Zentralinstitut für Soziale Fragen, West Berlin; Fawcett Library, London; Friedrich-Ebert-Stiftung, Bonn; Internationaal Instituut voor Sociale Geschiednis, Amsterdam; Niedersächisisches Haupstaatsarchiv, Hanover; Schweizerisches Sozialarchiv, Zürich; Staatsarchiv der Freien- und Hansestadt Hamburg; Swarthmore College Peace Collection, Swarthmore, Pennsylvania, USA; Universitätsbibliothek, West Berlin; Staats- und Universitätsbibliothek, Hamburg; Württembergisches Hauptstaatsarchiv, Stuttgart. I am particularly obliged to Klaus Stukenbrock of the Staatsarchiv Hamburg for his patience and helpfulness in guiding me through the voluminous files of the political police and other organs of the Hamburg Senate; to Friedrich Kahlenberg for allowing me access to the Adele Schreiber papers in the Bundesarchiv Koblenz; to Ingeborg Richarz-Simons, Munich, for lending me a copy of the autobiography of Helene Stöcker, her aunt; to Annelise Glaser, of the Deutscher Frauenrat, Bonn, for supplying me with information about the Archiv des Bundes Deutscher Frauenvereine; to Amy Hackett, Columbia, for lending me her notes on the Käthe Schirmacher papers in Rostock; to Doug Skopp, Peggy Anderson, Richard Grassby and Bernice Nichols, who helped me obtain material from the Swarthmore College Peace Collection; and to all those who have kindly provided me with references and suggestions in the course of my work. The present manuscript was completed in April 1975. An earlier and rather different version of this book was submittèd in October 1972 for the degree of Doctor of Philosophy in the University of Oxford. I am most grateful to the examiners, Francis Carsten and Agatha Ramm, for their helpful comments, and to the many friends and colleagues who read various drafts of this book, especially Terry Cole, Amy Hackett, Steve Hickinbotham, Tim Mason, Tony Nicholls, Hartmut Pogge-von Strandmann and Peter-Christian Witt. They saved me from many errors and suggested improvements too numerous to mention. My debt to Tony Nicholls extends far beyond this; for three years he was an ideal supervisor, and without his constant help and encouragement this book would most probably never have been written. I would also like to thank the Warden and Fellows of St Antony's College, Oxford, and my many friends in Berlin, especially Alex and Irmgard Latotzky, Karin Hausen and George Raptis, and Martyn and Jutta Phillips, for providing me with a congenial and stimulating environment in which to write and research. Finally I would like to express my gratitude to Margery McNaught, Brenda Wilson and Doreen Davy for typing successive drafts of this volume, and to the many other people who have helped me in countless ways in the task of research and preparation. None of them of course, nor anyone else except myself, bears any responsibility for anything that follows.

Stirling
December 1975

NOTES

1. John Vincent, *The Formation of the Liberal Party 1857-1868* (London, 1966); Brian Harrison, *Drink and the Victorians. The Temperance Question in England 1815-1872* (London, 1971); Brian Harrison, 'The British Prohibitionists 1853-72. A Biographical Analysis', *International Review of Social History*, 1970. See also Patricia Hollis (ed.), *Pressure from Without in Early Victorian England* (London, 1974).

2. Peter Gilg, *Die Erneuerung des demokratischen Denkens im Wilhelminischen Deutschland* (Wiesbaden, 1965); S. T. Robson, 'Left-Wing Liberalism in Germany 1900-19' (Oxford, D.Phil., 1966).

3. George L. Mosse, *The Crisis of German Ideology. Intellectual Origins of the Third Reich* (London, 1966); Fritz Stern, *The Politics of Cultural Despair* (Berkeley/Los Angeles, 1961).

4. Modris Eksteins, *The Limits of Reason. The German Democratic Press and the Collapse of Weimar Democracy* (Oxford, 1975); Larry E. Jones, ' "The Dying Middle": Weimar Germany and the Fragmentation of Bourgeois Politics', *Central European History*, 1972, 23-54.

5. I hope to discuss this argument at greater length and in a more general way in a forthcoming article. A parallel study of the illiberal aspects of an apparently liberal social movement can be found in Daniel Gasman, *The Scientific Origins of National Socialism. Social Darwinism in Ernst Haeckel and the German Monist League* (London, 1971).

6. One publication based on primary sources has so far appeared: Amy Hackett, 'The German Women's Movement and Suffrage, 1890-1914: A study of National Feminism', in Robert J. Bezucha (ed.), *Modern European Social History* (Lexington, Mass., 1972), 354-386; this touches only on one aspect of German feminism. The only scholarly work of any length based on primary sources is Irmgard Remme, 'Die Internationalen Beziehungen der deutschen Frauenbewegung vom Ausgang des 19. Jahrhunderts bis 1933' (phil.Diss., West Berlin, 1955). By far the best overall survey is 'Die bürgerliche Frauenbewegung' in Dieter Fricke (ed.), *Die bürgerlichen Parteien in Deutschland 1830-1945. Handbuch*, Bd. I (Leipzig, 1968). I have attempted to discuss recent and current work in my article 'Feminism and Female Emancipation in Germany 1871-1945: Sources, Methods and Problems of Research' (forthcoming).

7. The reader should refer in particular to my articles 'Prostitution, State and Society in Imperial Germany', *Past and Present* 70 (February, 1976), and 'German Women and the Triumph of Hitler', *Journal of Modern History,* March 1976. In work currently under preparation I hope also to discuss some social and social-psychological aspects of German feminism, and the problem of female domestic servants in Germany. I have also completed a book-length manuscript on Women and Social Democracy in Imperial Germany 1871-1918, which I hope will shortly be published.

1

THE GERMAN FEMINISTS

INTRODUCTION

Nineteenth-century feminism, in all parts of the world, had two major characteristics: it was liberal and it was middle-class. The basis of the feminist creed was the doctrine of liberal individualism, whose roots lay partly in Protestant sectarianism and partly in the rationalism of the Enlightenment. Liberal individualism regarded the world as composed of a mass of individual human atoms, all competing with one another for their own individual benefit. Competition, free and unrestricted, would not only benefit the individual, however, it would also benefit society as a whole. Only if the interference of the State were reduced to a minimum, all inequalities between individuals abolished, and all barriers to their free competition one with another removed, could a truly just and equitable society come into being. The most consistent exponents of this doctrine realised that it could not logically be confined in its application to men alone. Thinkers such as John Stuart Mill whose work *The Subjection of Women,* published in England and America in 1869 and issued in French and German translations in the same year, was probably the most widely-read and influential of all

feminist tracts, demanded equal rights for women, or rather the removal of all legal restraints on their ability to act as free individuals in a
society based on economic and social competition, as the final step in
the creation of a perfect laissez-faire society.[1] Mill did not intend his
remarks to be applied to any other women than those of the middle
class, however; and the ideology which he and those who agreed with
him propounded served as a legitimation for the economic, social and
political aspirations of the bourgeoisie.

Yet Mill was only stating in a characteristically clear and logical way
what all the great feminist movements of the 19th century believed. No
feminist movement wanted equal rights merely for their own sake. No
feminist movement desired equality in the strict sense of the word and
the last thing any female suffrage society anywhere wanted was for
women simply to be absorbed into the existing political system without
changing it in the process. Female suffrage was a weapon in the fight
for moral improvement. Feminism was a means by which the individual
woman was to become, in the words of the American feminist Eliza-
beth Cady Stanton, 'the arbiter of her own destiny'; but this necessarily
involved the triumph throughout the whole of the social and political
structure of what Stanton called 'our Protestant idea, the right of
individual conscience and judgement; our republican idea, individual
citizenship'.[2] It was not surprising then that the supporters of female
suffrage in America 'consisted' as Alan P. Grimes, the most perceptive
student of American feminism, has written, 'mostly of white, middle-
class Protestants who were in the main native-born and sought purifica-
tion, according to their lights, of the social and political order'.[3] The
liberal individualist feminist movements of the later 19th century, in
sharing these beliefs thus aimed at far more than merely securing
employment for middle-class widows and spinsters, or even gaining full
civil and political equality for women. They aimed at nothing less than
the moral regeneration of society in conformity with the ideals of
bourgeois liberal morality. The classical programme of feminist demands in every country included not only the right to vote, the right to
control property and earnings within marriage and the right to enter the
professions; it also included everywhere the introduction of an equal
moral standard for men and women by persuading men to exercise
self-control, the imposition of temperance or even prohibition in the
question of alcohol, and the improvement of standards of private,

public, political and international morality. Feminists everywhere commonly shared the ideals of bourgeois, Protestant-based liberal individualism; they were pacifists, temperance enthusiasts, crusaders against the State regulation of prostitution and opponents of prize-fighting, duelling and cruelty to animals, as well as campaigners for equal rights for women.

In this sense feminism can be seen as an extension of the liberal individualist ideology of the middle classes, part of their attempt to ensure that the society that was in the throes of creation proved to be a society based on free competition; a competition they themselves would win because they possessed the virtues of self-respect, self-help and self-discipline that provided the key to economic and social success. It follows, then, that the relative success or failure of feminism was largely determined by the success or failure of bourgeois liberal individualism, or in other words to the extent to which the social and political structure was dominated and controlled by the bourgeoisie. In bourgeois liberal states such as Australia and New Zealand, and some of the Western States of the USA, almost all of the feminists' demands including the vote had been conceded by the turn of the century.[4] In England women had been granted admission to the universities and the professions, equal property rights in marriage and the abolition of State-regulated prostitution well before 1900; and they were only prevented from getting the vote by the opposition of the landed aristocracy in the House of Lords after female suffrage bills had been passed by the House of Commons. In many countries, however, very few of these rights were granted to women. Other influences besides social structure decided the issue in the vast majority of cases; in Catholic and Islamic countries religion played a major role; in others economic, educational and political backwardness was the decisive factor. In one country, however, the relative failure of feminism and the continued restriction of women's rights well into the 20th century can be ascribed neither to the dominance of a certain religion, nor to illiteracy, nor to economic backwardness and the lack of a substantial middle class. This country was the German Empire, founded in 1871 under the guidance of Otto von Bismarck. Imperial Germany was a predominantly Protestant, highly industrialised country with high educational standards and a large and growing middle class. In the case of Germany, therefore, we have to seek the key to the subjection of women, the nature of feminism and the extent of the rights which German women enjoyed, in the social distribution of political power.

Unlike other industrialised countries, Imperial Germany was not governed by a parliamentary, constitutional political system. The powers of the Reichstag, the German Lower House, elected by universal manhood suffrage, were strictly limited. Government ministers were appointed by the Kaiser and were responsible to him and not to the Reichstag. Legislation was initiated in the Upper House, the Bundesrat; the Reichstag only had the power of debating and amending it, and even then it could be vetoed by the Upper Chamber. The Bundesrat itself consisted of delegates of the rulers of the various federal States that made up the German Empire – the King of Bavaria, the King of Württemberg, the Grand Duke of Baden, the City Senate of Hamburg and so on. Most of the important functions of government were reserved to these States, which also had their own Parliaments or Diets, their own governments, their own laws (except the Criminal Law), their own educational systems and their own police forces. Very few matters were dealt with at Reich level, the most important of these being perhaps financial and foreign policy and naval and colonial affairs. The federal States were very jealous of their prerogatives and often obstructed the extension of central authority.

What unifed this chaotic mixture of conflicting authorities was the Kingdom of Prussia. Prussia was by far the largest, richest and most powerful federal State. It also occupied a dominant position in the Bundesrat, where it could never be overruled by other States. Moreover the Constitution ensured that the King of Prussia would always be the German Emperor, and furthermore endowed the Kaiser with very extensive powers. He appointed the Reich ministers, who were responsible to him; he could summon and dissolve the Reichstag as he pleased; he could make war and peace; he was the supreme commander of all the armed forces in the event of war; he appointed the Reich civil servants. Although his powers were almost autocratic, however, it would be wrong to see him as some kind of crowned dictator. He was in reality an instrument of a wider ruling class: the Junkers, the landowning aristocracy of Prussia. They controlled the Prussian Diet, which was elected on a complicated franchise that divided the electorate into three classes according to the amount of taxes they paid, and gave most weight to the highest and smallest class, the Junkers themselves, who were thus able to control the Diet through their political wing, the Conservative Party. The Junkers occupied key positions in the army, the civil service, the judiciary and the government of Germany. Despite his wide powers the Kaiser hardly ever dared to go against the wishes of this ruling class; their fate and his were bound closely together.[5] The aristocratic agrarian élite that constituted the ruling class of the German Empire was conservative in the extreme. It maintained its position not only by rejecting all attempts to democratise the Prussian franchise, revise the Constitution or increase the powers of the Reichstag, but also through a number of social institutions all of which it imbued with its own feudal notions of honour and propriety, its own hatred of democracy, parliamentary institutions and social changes, and its own fear and contempt of the great mass of the population, from the workers in the fields and factories to the capitalists and industrialists in the cities and towns.[6] The most important of these institutions was the army. The army was legally empowered, if it so wished, to declare a state of siege in time of internal unrest, and by so doing establish military government, institute censorship of the press, arrest oppositional elements and curtail civil liberties. Beyond this the army's influence penetrated the whole of society. The army officer corps was strongly dominated by aristocrats; its social prestige made it a desirable career and its feudal ideology was transmitted to the middle classes through the institution of the reserve officer. Large numbers of middle-class civilians became officers in the reserve, and while this gave them the prestige of a uniform and a rank – both very considerable in Imperial Germany – it also filled them with the same reactionary ideas as the officer corps itself possessed.[7] The Naval Officer Corps, constructed on similar lines, fulfilled a similar function even though it was dominated by members of the middle class.[8]

The army was undoubtedly the most important institution through which the Junkers dominated the society of Imperial Germany. Others included the bureaucracy and the judiciary. The most interesting of these institutions for our purposes, however, is the Protestant Evangelical Church. Germany was divided in her religious affiliations, but to the East and North of the river Elbe, in East and West Prussia, Brandenburg, Pomerania, Schleswig and Mecklenburg, and in Central Germany, in Hanover, Anhalt, Brunswick and the Thuringian States, the great majority of the population was Protestant. Under the Empire the

Protestant Evangelical Church was everywhere governed, as it had been since the establishment of the principle of *cuius regio eius religio* in the age of the Reformation, by the temporal Head of State – in Prussia the King, in Mecklenburg the Grand Duke and so on. Often the government was direct and the involvement of the secular Head of State close. The culture of the Protestant Church was thus an official culture, and its values were strongly identified with those of the ruling élite. The vigorous Protestant sectarianism that played such a major part in the growth of political radicalism in Britain was absent in Germany. Perpetuating the political quietism of the Lutheran Church, German Protestantism – united in the Evangelical Church in 1814 – represented conservative values and indoctrinated its congregations into loyalty to the State and obedience to the social and political status quo. The only significant political deviations that occurred in the Evangelical Church were deviations to the right, such as the movement led by the Court preacher Adolf Stöcker in the 1870s and 1880s which tried – unsuccessfully – to wean the urban working classes away from subversive and democratic ideas by a combination of Anti-Semitism and populist demagoguery. Catholicism in Germany was also on the whole a conservative force. It was dominant in peripheral and subordinate States – Bavaria, Baden, the lower Rhine, Western Westphalia, Silesia, Prussian Poland. Only in the industrial Rhineland, the home of 'social Catholicism', did the Catholic Church compromise with the modern world. Elsewhere, especially in Silesia, it was reactionary.[9] Although the Catholic religion had been submitted to a considerable amount of persecution by the government in the so-called *Kulturkampf* of the 1870s, it was nevertheless in general socially conservative, and its political wing, the Catholic Centre Party, for most of the Imperial period the largest single party in the Reichstag, was – with occasional exceptions – one of the main parliamentary supporters of the government. It did little, therefore, to counteract the conservative influence of German Protestantism.

These two influences – the army and the Church – greatly weakened the allegiance of the German middle classes to liberal values and beliefs. Even more important as far as political liberalism was concerned was the fact that the liberal movement for a parliamentary constitution had met with a series of crushing defeats by the conservative Prussian State, first of all in the unsuccessful liberal revolution of 1848, then in the failure of the attempt by the liberals to establish Parliamentary control over the army in the early 1860s, and finally in the unification of Germany by Prussian military might in 1866 and 1870-71, which by achieving one major aim of the liberals – national unity – induced most of them to abandon the other – parliamentary rule. As a last blow Bismarck and the Junker élite, faced with the prospect of massive corn imports from the USA and Russia in 1878, abandoned the liberal policy of free trade and threw the liberal politicians into opposition. There they remained, weak, divided and few in number, for nearly thirty years, unable and often also unwilling to offer serious opposition to the Junker élite. The real opposition to the status quo came from the Social Democratic Party of Germany (Sozialdemokratische Partei Deutschlands or SPD), a working-class party founded in 1875 and adhering from 1890 onwards to the ideas of revolutionary Marxism. The rapid growth of the SPD, which drew its support from the working classes in the big towns and burgeoning industrial areas of Germany, its promise to establish parliamentary socialism if ever it obtained power, its constant and often harsh and telling criticism of the existing political order, its ceaseless propaganda and its opposition to all that the Junkers stood for,[10] greatly alarmed the ruling classes; and from 1878 to 1890 the Party was outlawed by an Anti-Socialist Law *(Sozialistengesetz)*. The rapid economic growth that had transformed Germany into an industrial society by the 1890s may have increased the resources available to her ruling class; it also increased its anxiety for their future dominance of the political and social structure.

It was indeed highly anomalous for one of the world's richest and most rapidly expanding industrial societies to be ruled by an élite whose source of wealth and power, ideology and whole outlook were essentially pre-industrial. No wonder that they viewed the great cities with alarm, despair and incomprehension. Here was a social milieu where their techniques of social control were often useless, particularly as far as the industrial workers were concerned. The army was so anxious to continue recruiting the bulk of its troops from agricultural labourers and peasants, easily controlled and indoctrinated into subservience by the Junkers and the Evangelical Church, that it stopped all expansion from 1893 to 1912 for fear of recruiting dissident urban workers and adherents of Social Democracy. While older and more conservative political and social ideologies found a strong basis in smaller towns and rural areas, the great cities were seedbeds of radicalism in every form. This applied not only to the division between conservatism and socialism but also the divisions within the more progressive creeds, socialism, liberalism and even, as we shall see, feminism; in all these cases, the radical party found its strongest support in the great cities. Arthur von Posadowsky-Wehner, the Secretary of the Treasury, was speaking for the whole ruling class when he complained in January 1896:[11]

> that Germany is becoming more and more an industrial State. Thereby that part of the population is strengthened upon which the Crown cannot depend – the population of the great towns and industrial districts, whereas the agricultural population provided the real support of the monarchy. If things went on as at present, the monarchy would either pass over to a republican system, or, as in England, become a sort of sham monarchy.

Clearly, the more industrialisation proceeded, the greater the strain would become.

Germany, then, was quite unlike other countries which boasted a strong feminist movement. It was not dominated by the middle classes. It did not have a parliamentary constitution. Its Protestantism stressed service to the State and community and subservience to the ruling class, rather than the development of the individual personality. Its liberal movement was weak and divided. Its middle classes were to a large extent 'feudalised', adhering to pre-industrialial notions of honour, social standards and moral codes, and were attracted at various times into co-operation with the feudal aristocracy in the control of the country. These peculiarities had important consequences for the legal and social position of women in Imperial Germany. The ideology of the ruling class, shared, as we have seen, by large sectors of the bourgeoisie, was extremely hostile to female emancipation. The dominant social institution of the Empire, the army, set the tone for society's attitudes towards women. To a great extent the army served as a vehicle for the antiquated world-view of the feudal aristocracy, but just as important as this was the way in which its values permeated much of the social and political thinking of all the politically influential groups in society. It was largely as a consequence of this that one objection to giving equal rights to women was raised more often than any other, whenever the subject was debated in Imperial Germany: men, it was alleged, had the vote – and other rights – because they had to defend their country. Women, it was presumed, did not have to sacrifice themselves to the nation by dying in battle. Proponents of equal rights for women retorted that women also risked their lives, and all too often sacrificed them, in giving birth to the soldiers of the future. Nevertheless, the notion remained very widespread and almost impossible to eradicate, at least in the minds of the classes that mattered, that men earned their rights because they served the nation in the armed forces while women did not deserve these rights because they did not so serve. It was a conviction that perhaps more than any other prevented the women's rights movement from being as successful in Germany as it was in other less militarised societies. Moreover, it was a conviction that, as we shall see, forced the women's rights movement in Germany to argue that women should be granted equal rights because they *did* serve their country – in welfare organisations and charitable institutions. In the 19th century feminists in Germany demanded rights because they served the community, not because they were entitled to them as a matter of natural justice.

MIDDLE-CLASS WOMEN AND THEIR RIGHTS IN IMPERIAL GERMANY

Under the Constitution of the German Empire women lacked the most basic and fundamental civil liberties. Although the Constitution of 1871 established universal manhood suffrage for the Reichstag, it was never a serious political prospect that women would get the vote as well. Indeed the ideas was hardly mentioned at all in Germany until the SPD leader, August Bebel, introduced into the Reichstag a motion to grant female suffrage in the various federal Diets on 13 February 1895. Women, he said, had the same interest in making laws as men did; most women, he added (correctly, as it eventually turned out), would vote for conservative parties in the first decade or so of their enfranchisement, so it was not necessarily – in the short run at least – in the interests of the Social Democrats to support the measure. Nevertheless, it was a question of social justice, and female suffrage would, he said, echoing a

classic feminist argument, improve the moral tone of public life. However, Bebel's speech was virtually ignored; only one speaker followed
him, and he hardly deigned to allude to the question at all except by
remarking that women did not want the vote.[1][2]

In their lack of voting rights German women were in roughly the
same position as women in other countries, though by the turn of the
century women had the vote in New Zealand and some States in the
American mid-West, and they were shortly to be enfranchised in
Australia. In England, too, some women had the right to vote in local
elections. The same was also true in Germany, though this right was
hedged about with so many restrictions that it was practically meaningless even for those who possessed it. In no part of the Empire did
women have the right to stand for election. However they could vote in
urban and rural communal elections in Hohenzollern, Bavarian territory
West of the Rhine, Saxe-Weimar-Eisenach, Saxe-Meiningen, Reuss of
the older and younger line, Waldeck and Schwarzburg-Rudolstadt, and
in rural communes in Prussia (except the Rhine province), the Kingdom
of Saxony, Brunswick, Saxe-Altenburg, Saxe-Coburg-Gotha for Coburg,
Lübeck, Bremen and the Knightly Office of Wredenhagen in
Mecklenburg-Schwerin. Even these voting rights were severely restricted,
however. In rural communes in Hanover, the Kingdom of Saxony,
Schaumburg-Lippe, Lübeck, Bremen and Wredenhagen they could vote
in person, but elsewhere the vote had to be given by proxy. According
to Sections 622ff. of the Civil Code which embodied earlier laws in this
respect and came into force in 1900, the agent entrusted with the
proxy, who had to be a man, was empowered to vote for a different
candidate from the one the voter had chosen, provided that he thought
the voter would change her mind if she knew the political circumstances fully. Even if the voter did not approve of the way in which the
proxy carried out the vote, this had no effect on the vote's validity. The
major limitation on the communal suffrage, however, was a high
property qualification. Loss of property, for example through marriage,
entailed the loss of the vote. The consequence was that very few
women indeed had real voting rights.[13] One contemporary authority
estimated their number in 1909 as no more than 2000,[14] most of
whom were probably rich spinsters or widows.

Not only did women in Germany lack the right to vote, however,
they were also deprived of the right to join political parties or attend

meetings at which political affairs were discussed in public. The Law of Association *(Vereinsgesetz)*, passed in Prussia in 1851, expressly forbade women to engage in politics in these ways, and similar laws in Bavaria and Saxony were even more severe. Only in the more liberal states of Hamburg, Bremen, Baden and Württemberg did women have full rights of participation in politics. This law, effectively barring women from expressing their political views in public in most parts of the Empire, was rigorously applied in Prussia, and political meetings at which women were present — even more, political meetings at which women dared to speak — were forcibly broken up by the police. Restrictions of this kind were unknown in England, America or Australasia. In these and many other countries, even if women did lack full political equality, at least they enjoyed freedom of expression, not to mention other civil rights that German women lacked. Attempts to reform the Law of Association foundered on the opposition of the federal States to the ideas of a national Imperial Law of Association (finally passed in 1908), and on the hostility of the Prussian Conservatives and Catholic Centre to the idea that women should take part in politics at all. Martin Schall, a Conservative Reichstag deputy, remarked during a debate on an SPD motion to extend freedom of assembly and association to women in 1896:

> In our age, which is really quite politically excited enough, and in elections, indeed, is almost mad with excitement, if one decided to admit women to political life as well, then one would bring trouble and strife into the last place where one can, thank God, find a haven of peace in times of political excitement. One would turn house and home, which under normal circumstances ought to be even these days a piece of Heaven on Earth, and family life too, into a living hell. (Quite right! on the right.)

He was strongly supported by Carl Bachem of the Catholic Centre Party, who quoted St Paul's phrase *mulier taceat in foro* and argued that laws governing public life had to take account of the fact that men and women were fundamentally different by nature.[15] It was the predominance of views such as these that prevented women from gaining basic civil liberties until well after the turn of the century. Political rights, too, were far from being the only ones which German women lacked to a greater degree than women in other countries. They were also discriminated against by the Civil Law.

Until 1900, when a new Civil Law Code came into effect for the whole German Empire, many different codes of Civil Law were in existence. There were, for example, over one hundred different local laws governing the division of property between husband and wife. The most influential of these various codes — influential because it was valid in the largest state in Germany and had been copied or adapted by several other German states since its promulgation in 1794 — was the Prussian Civil Code, the *Preussisches Allgemeines Landrecht.* The Allgemeines Landrecht firmly declared that the husband was the head of the family, and made him the legal guardian of his wife. Without his permission she could not take a job, sign a contract or engage in litigation; she was not a 'legal person' in Civil Law. Clearly, by the 1890s, when women were playing a large and increasingly independent part in economic life,[16] this was grossly anachronistic, although by then this law was no longer regarded as binding. As far as property was concerned this was left to local laws, but mostly all the wife's property passed to the husband on marriage. Even money earned by the wife during the marriage generally belonged legally to her husband. The law did allow people to regulate their property relations within marriage by a legal contract, however, for example if they wanted to separate their property; few can have made use of this clause.

Although it left the regulation of property relations to local custom, the Allgemeines Landrecht did deal in some detail with the rights of parents over their children. The father was given full control over his children; he alone had the right to make decisions about their education, to approve their marriage if they were under age, to allow them to work, even — when they were babies — to decide when they should be weaned. Over the daughters of the family his power was most complete. Until they married, he represented them in law and held their property as his. Even a spinster in her forties had no rights in Civil Law if her father was still alive. The *Personenstandsgesetz* of 1875 did allow women over 24 to marry without parental permission. Still, in these and other respects the Allgemeines Landrecht was extremely authoritarian. In one important respect, however, it was ahead of its time, pushed forward by the overriding concern of a military state to fill the ranks of its armies, and unimpeded by religious or moral scruples which Enlightened Despotism had long since cast aside. Frederick II was of the opinion that divorce helped population growth, and the Allgemeines Landrecht reflected this belief; 'It hinders population increase if one compels people to live together when they could create even more children for the State in better assorted partnerships.' The law therefore allowed childless couples to divorce by mutual consent or even, in the case of couples who had already had children, because of insurmountable dislike for one party by the other (i.e. the incompatibility did not even have to be mutual). Otherwise it allowed divorce on both sides on the ground of infidelity. If infidelity was proven on the part of the husband there were generous alimony provisions. The children went to the innocent party. In the cast of 'insurmountable dislike', the party who sued counted as guilty. All in all, these were very advanced provisions which demonstrated the determination of Enlightened Despotism to override custom in the interests of the State.

The Civil Code which replaced the Allgemeines Landrecht and other regional laws in 1900, the *Bürgerliches Gesetzbuch,* did little to improve the situation of women, and in some respects even worsened it. True, in form at least it appeared to accord women a position of greater equality within marriage than they had previously enjoyed. Women were now 'legal persons', and a husband was no longer regarded as the legal guardian of his wife. The word 'obedience' was removed, for 'paternal power' over the children 'parental power' was substituted, and some of the most anachronistic clauses of the Allgemeines Landrecht were deleted. If the form of the law was modernised, however, the content was not. Section 1354 Part 1 stated that 'the husband takes the decisions in all matters affecting married life.' Other paragraphs explicitly made over all the wife's property to her husband on marriage. Property which came to her during the marriage was also automatically made over to the husband. The only exception – and it was an important one – was that earnings the wife made from any job she took remained legally hers. Also, of course, she no longer required the legal consent of her husband before she entered employment. This was an important concession to the changing place of women in the economy, perhaps the only important concession in the entire Code. It gave working married women, for the first time in many parts of Germany, a certain amount of financial independence from their husbands. For most married women, however, the situation remained the same; indeed, since the Civil Code stipulated that special property relations (e.g. separation of property) could only be allowed by a legal contract concluded *before* the marriage (the Allgemeines Landrecht had allowed the validity of such contracts made *during* the marriage as well), their position was in some ways even worse.

Nor was the position really improved as far as a wife's control over the children of her marriage was concerned. All legal power remained in the hands of the husband. He could, for example, approve the marriage of a daughter if she was still a minor, even if the wife opposed it. The wife was not entitled to legally represent the children in their relations with third parties — she could not enrol them in a school, for example, or sign them away as apprentices. This right was reserved to the children's father. If a widow with children remarried, her new husband gained all legal powers over her children including the disposal of their property. True, the position of unmarried daughters in a family was somewhat better than before, but in general the last legal word always lay with the father; as Section 1634 of the new Code put it, 'If the parents disagree, the father's opinion takes precedence'.

It was in the matter of divorce, however, that the Civil Code was least satisfactory, and marked a retreat from the relative liberality of the Allgemeines Landrecht. Gone was the possibility of divorce by consent for childless couples, gone was the possibility of divorce on the grounds of 'insurmountable dislike'. The grounds for divorce were declared to be of two kinds — absolute (infidelity, bigamy, desertion, unnatural intercourse) or relative ('dishonourable and immoral conduct', 'serious neglect of marital duties' or 'serious maltreatment'). All these grounds involved proving the guilt of one party or another, and the full investigation of the circumstances by a judge, who was entitled to grant a divorce only if he was convinced that the guilty party (i.e. the party sued for divorce) 'has caused such a deep disruption of the marriage that the plaintiff cannot reasonably be expected to continue it.'[17] The Civil Code of 1900, which remained in force until after the Second World War, gave fewer rights to women than the corresponding laws in many other advanced countries. Indeed, in many ways the Civil Code of 1900 represented a step backwards for women. It replaced the single amoral standard of 18th-century *Staatsräson* with the double moral standard of 19th-century Christian ethics. It replaced a reliance on common law with a marked preference for Roman Law, generally more authoritarian, particularly in its attitudes to women. It represented a combination of the social conservatism of the Evangelical Church and the anachronistic and authoritarian familial ideals of the Prussian aristocracy. During the debates on the Civil Code in the Reichstag, the women's cause was championed once again by August Bebel and the SPD. The party demanded full equality of man and wife within marriage, and full economic freedom for women within the law. In particular they wanted a separation of possessions and incomes within marriage. The Social Democrats were supported by a few of the more progressive of the left-wing liberals. Albert Träger of the Liberal People's Party (Freisinnige Volkspartei), the party which − led by Eugen Richter − most closely adhered to the traditional ideals of liberal individualism, remarked that

> Women are now quite different from what they used to be. Even in the past, of course, individual women have gained eminence in certain particular fields. Even in the past, cases of women exerting a quite definite and positive influence even in the field of high politics have been known. But these were of course only rarities, only individual exceptions. But since then, gentlemen, women have conquered almost all fields of human activity. Let us not mention the fine arts, let us mention the sciences, let us mention the technical professions, in short, let us admit that women have shown themselves everywhere to be of equal ambition and equal worth to men. And how many marriages have we seen in all classes of society in which, gentlemen, it is the wife who bears the real burden of the marriage, not just with her property, but also, gentlemen, with her earnings, with her work! And how is it, gentlemen, that you then want to place such a wife under this unconditional control of her husband?

The proponents of the amendment of the Civil Code to give greater equality to women also received help from an unexpected quarter − from Baron von Stumm-Halberg, a leading conservative industrialist, who opposed the SPD amendments and insisted that the last thing he wanted was the emancipation of women. Nevertheless, he pointed out that the Civil Code worsened the legal position of women in many parts of Germany, and argued that since the Code allowed women to keep their earnings it should also allow them to keep their property. Clearly, in the class to which Stumm belonged women were more likely to bring property into a marriage than earnings. Whatever the rationale behind Stumm's support of the separation of property within marriage however he was, like his Free Conservative colleague Prince von Schönaich zu Carolath, one of the Reichstag's most persistent and vociferous champions of more educational, professional and legal rights for women, a rather isolated figure on the right in this respect; most conservatives supported the original draft of the Code. It was characteristic too that the Catholic Centre Party also strongly opposed the amendments.[18] The combination of these various conservative forces ensured that the Married Women's Property Acts in England and the various legislative measures passed to the same end in Australia, New Zealand and the USA had no real equivalent in Germany until the 1950s.

Women were also discriminated against in Imperial Germany by the Criminal Law. Cases of women being treated as unreliable or inferior witnesses simply by virtue of their being women were not unknown. Judges would argue that women were too easily swayed by their emotions to be relied upon as sober and impartial observers of criminal or violent acts.[19] Women were not only discriminated against in the application of the law, they were also discriminated against by the law itself. The Criminal Code of Imperial Germany was based on the Prussian model and introduced shortly after the foundation of the German Empire. As in most countries, it made abortion illegal. Section 218 of the Code provided for imprisonment of up to five years for women performing or assisting in an abortion, for whatever reason it was being carried out, even in cases of rape. Women were thus denied the physical freedom enjoyed by men to dispose over their own bodies as they wished. In a situation where 180,000 illegitimate births occurred every year, the effects of this law were not to be underestimated. It not only affected in the first place working-class women, who could not afford the discreet but expensive abortions of which middle- and upper-class women were able to avail themselves; it also had a strong influence in maintaining the double standard of sexual morality, according to which women were responsible for the consequences of sexual intercourse but men were not.

So too did Section 361/6 of the Criminal Code, which stated that the police could arrest any woman they suspected of being a prostitute and subject her to a compulsory medical examination which — if she were found to be suffering from a venereal disease — could result in her being registered as a prostitute and forced to live in a police-controlled brothel. Despite the fact that Section 180 of the Criminal Code made the maintenance of brothels illegal, the police generally used Section 361/6 as a pretext for establishing a form of State regulation of prostitution, based on a wide interpretation of the powers of the police and not (as in England) on legislative acts specifically empowering them to do so. Attacks on the regulation of prostitution were thus, as we shall see in Chapter 2, attacks on the police's claim to control public morality, and ultimately, therefore, attacks on the whole method of social control employed by the ruling class. In many German cities prostitutes were strictly controlled by the police, restricted to certain areas, certain streets or even (as in Hamburg) certain specified brothels, and forced to submit to regular medical examinations. Section 361/6 was used to threaten and punish those who did not obey; it was not applied to those who did. The prostitutes' male customers were subjected neither to a medical examination nor to the social contempt and ostracism that went with it. Indeed in the circles most strongly influenced by official morality — the army, student corporations and parts of the middle class — a visit or two to a brothel was as necessary a *rite de passage* into the moral world of the adult ruling class as was the duelling scar; both were marks of honour, proofs of manhood. The regulation of prostitution, which affected only a small minority of women actually engaged in vice, was the device used by the authorities to provide, as far as they were able, relatively safe means by which young men could make easy sexual conquests, just as the duelling club or student fraternity provided them with the means by which they could gain scars without risking wounds. Institutions of this sort did not exist in countries such as England and the USA.[20]

The same differences between Germany and these other countries existed in the field of education. In Germany, unlike England, America and Australasia, women were not admitted to universities as full-time students until after the turn of the century. As the historian Heinrich von Treitschke remarked:[21]

Many sensible men these days are talking about surrendering our universities to the invasion of women, and thereby falsifying their entire character. This is a shameful display of moral weakness. They are only giving way to the noisy demands of the Press. The intellectual weakness of their position is unbelievable . . . The universities are surely more than mere institutions for teaching science and scholarship. The small universities offer the students a comradeship which in the freedom of its nature is of inestimable value for the building of a young man's character . . .

Views such as these were widespread in the German academic community. The tone of student life was set by the student duelling corps,
whose communal life, gaudy uniforms, mediaeval code of honour,
aristocratic pretensions, social irresponsibility and political conservatism made them into youthful imitations of the Prussian officer
corps and ensured that the values and standards of the ruling élite
would be transmitted to a fresh generation of upper- and middle-class
German males. This was what Treitschke meant by the 'character-
building' function of the universities; and this is what he and his
fellow-professors thought would be endangered by the admission of
women as full-time students. The Academic Senate of Erlangen University, for example, was really defending these values against the
introduction of the gentler and less martial values that women (it was
thought) would favour, when it declared in 1898 that the admission of
female students was a 'measure that would overthrow all academic
order'.[22] Government and education ministries, especially in Prussia,
also played a part in refusing women entry to universities even on
exceptional grounds until the very end of the 1890s.

When women eventually were admitted to German universities, it
was for a combination of reasons which had little to do with the
pressure exerted by women's organisations. The first universities to
admit women were in South Germany, where the influence of Prussian
militarism was less strong than in the North. Governments such as those
of the liberal State of Baden did not object in principle to women
students. The Catholic Church also acquiesced, albeit reluctantly, because it feared it would fall behind in the struggle to influence the
people. As the conservative Catholic newspaper *Kölnische Volkszeitung*
remarked on 18 March 1898:

> If we adhere, as we have done hitherto, to the principle of *non-involvement* (in
> women's higher education), then the next practical consequence of this is that
> those posts for which scientific, professional or scholarly training for women is
> required cannot be filled by Catholic women. Women's education will carry
> on developing, and we need not wonder if one day a regrettable inequality
> between religious groups emerges in this sphere too, and towns and cities are
> soon filled with Jewish or Protestant women secondary school teachers or
> women doctors in large numbers, while Catholic women of this kind will
> simply not exist anywhere.[23]

The antifeminism of the Catholic Church in South Germany was thus modified in this respect at least, just as the hostility of the Catholic Centre Party to women in politics was also eventually to be modified, by socially competitive attitudes encouraged by the religious division of Germany and the experience of the *Kulturkampf*. Perhaps it was for this reason, as well as the weaker influence of militarism and the presence of a long-established tradition of liberalism in South German States such as Baden and Württemberg, that a leading Hamburg feminist once remarked that 'whoever has spent some time in South Germany will have discovered that the war between the sexes is carried on there in a much more peaceful way than here in the North, where men and women confront each other with such stark hostility.'[24]

By the turn of the century, too, German education ministries, who liked to think that Germany's educational system was one of the most advanced in the world, were painfully aware that other countries had long since admitted women to their universities — England since 1878, America since 1853 and even France since 1861 — and that Germany was beginning to look something of an anachronism in this respect. The attitude of education ministries thus underwent a gradual change on the issue. In December 1896 the Prussian Minister of Education dropped the requirement that all women who wanted to attend lectures at Prussian universities had to obtain his permission first (such permission had invariably been refused). The universities and lecturers could now decide for themselves. Individual professors were still reserved the right to refuse women admission to their lectures; many did so, although the more progressive ones, particularly in the social sciences, strongly encouraged women to attend. Once this move had been made others followed. The admission of women to the universities and the medical profession was frequently debated in the Reichstag in the 1890s, and sentiment seemed generally in favour of admission. On 1 February 1898 the Secretary of State in the Reich Office of the Interior Count Posadowsky, sent a memorandum to the federal education ministries referring to these debates and pointing out that speakers had generally favoured admitting women to the medical profession, even though the profession itself opposed this. The general feeling seemed to be that women had a right to be treated by women doctors if they so wished. Admission to a university was necessary in order to qualify for medical practice, however. Posadowsky declared that 'In these circumstances I am prepared to do what I can, as far as it lies within my competence, to remove the hindrances that stand in the way of the admission of women to the medical profession.'[25] Once the Reich government had thus given its blessing, the Universities of Baden (Freiburg and Heidelberg) admitted women as full-time (matriculated) students to all faculties in 1901, and other federal States followed suit, ending with Prussia which finally took the plunge in 1908. In 1905 there were already 80 full-time women students at German universities; by 1910, the figure was 1867; by 1914, 4126.[26]

These reforms could not have failed to have had an effect on the structure of elementary and secondary education. Most girls' schools, particularly at the primary level *(Volksschule)*, gave their pupils an education geared to their supposed future position as housewives and mothers, concentrating on practical household tasks and supposedly 'feminine' subjects such as art and music, to the neglect of subjects such as mathematics and the natural sciences which might be useful to the growing number of girls entering employment. As a result of this and other factors, the expansion of female labour was an expansion of unskilled labour; skilled female employees and apprentices were a rarity. The lack of proper training and education ensured, too, that prospects of promotion for women were extremely small. Such reforms as there were concentrated on the upper end of the scale. Here indeed it was most necessary. State secondary education for girls was almost non-existent and most girls' secondary schools were private. They were all generally confined to 'aesthetic' subjects and household skills. The reforms of the 1890s and onwards, culminating in the reorganisation of the Prussian girls' schools system in 1908, increased to some extent the amount of teaching of subjects more relevant to university entrance and paid employment. Nevertheless, the girls' curriculum was a nine-year course, compared with the 12-year course that boys' schools found necessary to prepare for university. Until 1894, too, there was no State-controlled girls' equivalent of the boys' grammar school, the *Gymnasium.* The first such school was opened in that year in Baden, and a few others were subsequently opened in other States. Despite the large-scale reorganisation of girls' schools in Prussia in 1908, however, the situation remained more or less the same well into the 1920s. Girls' education concentrated on domestic science, elementary pedagogy and the care of children, with perhaps religious instruction and 'aesthetic' subjects thrown in. The Prussian government did little to encourage girls to prepare for university or professional life. Co-education was considered immoral and avoided in Prussia, though a more liberal State such as Baden did admit a limited number of girls to boys' grammar schools. The grammar school, like the university, was in many ways a means of perpetuating the values and standards of the ruling élite, and in Prussia at least care was taken to ensure that its discipline and character were not affected by the introduction of female pupils. In 1914, therefore, girls had still not attained a position even of relative equality to boys in the educational system of Imperial Germany.

If the system did produce any women qualified to enter the professions, then it was generally the teaching profession which they entered. Here again they were in a position of marked inferiority. Most women teachers remained in the primary schools. When they did teach in secondary education, then it was usually in the lower forms. The Prussian decree of 1908 ruled that at least a third of the teaching staff of girls' schools had to be male, and at least a third of the science teaching had to be done by men. Once more the authorities revealed their adherence to the idea that women were incapable other than in exceptional cases of teaching subjects where reason rather than emotion was the criterion of competence. Women were not allowed to assume the headship of girls' schools. As for the boys' schools, women teachers were unheard of. The inadequacies of women's education erected a further barrier to women teachers taking over science teaching and assuming a leading role in the secondary schools. The major institution for training women teachers was not the university or any kind of mixed teacher training college but the *Lehrerinnenseminar,* the Women's Teacher Training College, which until the turn of the century formed the only widely available means by which women could obtain any form of higher education. It offered a two-year or in some places a three-year course which only sufficed to train women to teach at an elementary level. Opposition to any change in this situation was widespread, and it was strongest among the male teachers. As a conference of men teachers working in girls' schools resolved:

The Girls' School can only fulfil its task in a satisfactory manner if men and women teachers work together in the school, just as father and mother work together in the family, with the male influence predominant at the higher level, the female at the lower level, but neither influence lacking at any level. *The Leadership of the State Higher Girls' School belongs to men.*

This kind of reasoning, drawing an analogy between the family, the school and the State and prescribing a subordinate place for women in each of them, drove many male teachers into antifeminist organisations after the reforms of 1908 had led to fears – groundless, as it proved – that women would be allowed to assume the headship of girls' schools. Their hostility also ensured that little was done to bring the level of women teachers' pay up to that of their male colleagues, even when they were teaching at the same level. Economic independence was thus not accompanied by economic equality. The many other inferiorities of the woman teacher's position in her profession help to explain why women teachers provided by far the largest body of support for the feminist movement in Germany.[27]

Middle-class woman's place in Imperial Germany was in the home. If she ventured outside it, it should merely be to duplicate in other social institutions the subordinate role and secondary functions she performed within the family. She could venture into girls' schools to teach the pupils – much as she was expected to teach her own daughters – how to be a good housewife and mother. She could tend the sick, much as she was supposed to tend the sick within the family. She could look after the poor, the needy and, in time of war, the wounded, much as she might look after her own children. She could join charitable associations designed to fulfil the noble end of mothering social outcasts and unfortunates – provided of course that like the largest of all women's organisations in the German Empire, the Patriotic Women's Association (Vaterländischer Frauenverein), it was run by men.[28] But she could not perform the tasks for which the supposed masculine martial virtues of hardness, aggressiveness, toughness, boldness, devotion to duty, strict obedience to command, sense of honour, ability to think dispassionately and so on, were felt to be necessary. Nor could she disturb with her presence the institutions which inculcated these virtues. The family, the school, the State and the nation, it was felt, were analogous institutions all based upon the same aims and principles, and in each case the role of each sex was clearly defined; men were to rule, women were to obey; men were to think, to create, to develop their own personality, women were to lead a life of emotion and feeling, to sacrifice their individuality and potential to the interest of the larger social unit to which they belonged. The place that women should occupy in society was clearly outlined by the most eminent of all spokesmen for the official ideology of the German ruling class, Kaiser Wilhelm II himself, when he declared in a speech delivered at Königsberg in 1910 that:

our women . . . should learn that the principal task of the German woman lies not in the field of assemblies and associations, nor in the achievement of supposed rights, with which they can do the same things as men, but in quiet work in the house and in the family. They should bring up the younger generation above all else to obedience and respect for their elders. They should make it clear to their children and their children's children that what matters today is not living one's life at the expense of others, achieving one's own aim at the expense of the Fatherland, but solely and exclusively committing all one's mind and strength to the good of the Fatherland.[29]

It was the predominance of ideas such as these with which the German feminist movement had to contend. In addition middle-class women were directly subjected to this ideology through the practice of the military and naval officer corps in requiring officers and reserve officers to obtain their permission before marrying. The granting of this official consent depended on the social acceptability of the prospective bride, not only on her social antecedents (which had to be respectable, non-Jewish and preferably wealthy but not necessarily aristocratic) but also on her conformity to the mores of the upper classes. Young officers were discouraged from marrying too soon; they were expected to lead a communal, masculine life in the army camp or the officers' mess where, as the most recent historian of the Naval Officer Corps puts it, 'the young executive officers, like their counterparts in the Prussian army, talked of women, horses, dogs, and hunts, and lost their contacts with other members of society'.[30] As they moved up the ladder of promotion, however, they were encouraged to get married. Since the social prestige of an officer was very considerable, the pressure on unmarried middle-class women to conform in behaviour and ideas to the model of what a regular or reserve officer's wife was expected to be was also very considerable. If they did not, the prospect of having their character examined by a military or naval officers' committee was in itself enough to deter them from making a good match.[31] Here then was an additional pressure on the middle-class woman encouraging her to remain in the role to which official morality assigned her.

THE WOMEN'S MOVEMENT IN GERMANY, 1848-1889

Under these circumstances the feminist movement in Germany took on, in its earliest stages from 1865 to 1889, a rather different aspect from feminist movements in other countries. The German feminist movement began in October 1865 with the foundation of the General German Women's Association (Allgemeiner Deutscher Frauenverein) in Leipzig. Characteristically, the foundation was inspired by a foreigner — one Captain Korn, a retired Hungarian cavalry officer who had become acquainted with feminist ideas during a stay in America. This pattern of new developments in the history of German feminism being inspired from outside was to repeat itself on many subsequent occasions. The General German Women's Association was quickly taken over by a group of women who had been active in the unsuccessful liberal revolution of 1848 in Germany, chief of them the social novelist Louise Otto-Peters (1819-1895) who became the President of the new society. During the revolution, as radical liberalism in Germany reached its high-water-mark, Louise Otto-Peters had engaged in feminist propaganda of the classical kind, demanding full equality for women in every sphere including the vote. The new foundation, particularly in its close relationship with the nascent democratic labour movement in Saxony among whose leaders August Bebel strongly favoured the women's cause, still retained some of the spirit of 1848. In most respects, however, like the liberalism to which it was so closely bound, it had already retreated from the radicalism of 1848, and in the following decades as liberalism in Germany — stunned by the successive blows of 1866, 1871 and 1878 — withdrew even further and compromised more and more with the existing order, the General Association followed suit.

The demand for equal political rights which had been raised by Louise Otto-Peters in 1848 was not repeated by the General German Women's Association. Its leader had not retreated from her belief in female suffrage, but now she declared that it was too early to begin working for it.[32] In 1869, she also rejected the suggestion that the Association's magazine, *Neue Bahnen* ('New Paths'), should include discussion of political activities.[33] In the reaction that followed the revolution of 1848, the General Association must have feared that any political activity on its part might bring about its dissolution by the police under the 1851 Law of Association which forbade women to involve themselves in politics. In this question too the General Association did nothing. Louise Otto-Peters criticised the Law of Association on one occasion at least,[34] but neither she nor the movement she led took any steps to bring about its repeal and give to women one of the most fundamental of all civil rights, the right of assembly and association.

A similar pattern could also be observed in the question of the repeal of other laws which discriminated against women. In 1873, two years after the foundation of the German Empire, it became clear that the government intended to codify the Civil Law. Although as we have seen the work was not finished until 1895-96, and the Code did not come into effect until 1900, nevertheless the proposal made in 1873 did give rise to widespread public debate. The General German Women's Association, which had sedulously avoided the topic up to that point, was persuaded by Henriette Goldchmidt, one of its more progressive members, to take the matter up; in 1876 it submitted a petition to the Reichstag asking for the separation of property and income within marriage, the granting to every woman of equal status as a fully independent legal person, and the prevention of a father from doing as he pleased with his children without the mother's consent. However, it was characteristic of the timidity of the General Association that it did its utmost to avoid provoking a public debate on these issues. When the Reichstag rejected the petition, the General Association simply sent it to the Reich Chancellor's office with the request that it be forwarded to the Commission charged with drawing up the new Civil Code. The General Association did not protest at the rejection of its petition, nor did it enclose the dossier of evidence it had gathered on the harmful effects the existing law often had on women. The evidence, wrote Louise Otto-Peters, should not be published 'because our pen declines to dip into this filth, and it is impossible for us to overcome our shame, repulsion and disgust to such an extent as we would have to if we wanted to publish what, after all, has been confided to us as women by women'.[35] Nor, when the publication of the first draft of the Civil Code in 1888 revealed the petition to have been in vain, did the General Association do any more than repeat its performance of 1876 and send a similar petition to the Reichstag, with predictably identical results.[36] Nor did the General Association dare even to mention, let alone tackle, the various kinds of discrimination that were exercised against women in practice and precept by the Criminal Law.

In fact, the women's movement in Germany, led in the 1870s and 1880s by the General German Women's Association, concentrated heavily on two issues: the improvement of women's education and the admission of women to the medical profession. By far the largest part of its activities took place in these fields; yet it is characteristic that even here the German women's movement, unlike feminist movements in other countries, did not aim at equality between men and women. Whatever the views of Louise Otto-Peters and her associates had been in 1848, from 1865 onwards they accepted almost without question the role which official social morality assigned to women. They accepted too for the most part the stereotype created by official ideology of the 'true German woman', emotional, subordinate and above all motherly. Like most middle-class liberals, they were by the late 1860s no longer independent-minded enough to resist the ideological assault launched by the victorious Prussian ruling class. Instead of arguing that this stereotyped view of women was false, they accepted it as valid and tried to ennoble it. Their enthusiastic acceptance of the role created for them and their attempt to use this acceptance to gain more privileges for themselves *within* the social and moral system which the Junkers had created, was a classic example of the 'feudalisation' of the German bourgeoisie in the later 19th century.

Thus Auguste Schmidt, one of the most influential educationalists in the General German Women's Association, a woman through whose Women's Teacher Training College in Leipzig a number of leading figures in the women's movement passed, declared that the girls' schools system must be improved to give women a really 'aesthetic, intellectual and moral education'. Only in this way could they develop 'true womanhood' which consisted, according to Auguste Schmidt, 'in the capacity for self-sacrifice and commitment, in serious work and the highest striving for her aims, in truth, and in fidelity'.[37] Here as in other respects the marked rightward shift of liberalism after the Prussian victory over Austria at Königgrätz in 1866 was reflected in a drastic scaling-down of the original objectives enunciated by the General Association in 1865, which in the field of education had even included co-education, regarded by the existing educational authorities as revolutionary and immoral. In the 1870s and 1880s, the practical proposals of the General Association boiled down to the addition to existing schools of grammar school type classes for girls to prepare them for university, and the admission of women to the universities to study medicine. Medicine, it was felt, was a discipline for which the motherly qualities of women were ideally suited, and a discipline which fulfilled a real need, as many women had too strong a sense of decency to let themselves be examined and treated by male doctors. They also argued for the improvement of the content of girls' education and the inclusion of subjects that would help prepare them for earning a living. In the 1880s, though, an even more conservative set of demands was rapidly gaining influence within the General Association; for the creation of special institutions to take girls who had already gone through the educational system through the last stages before entry to university. In effect, since a number of such institutions already existed, the most celebrated perhaps being the Viktoria-Lyzeum in Berlin, founded (predictably) by an Englishwoman, Miss Archer, this merely meant State support and recognition of these institutions, in the hope that this would lead the State to recognise the absurdity of a situation in which girls were being publicly financed to enter French or Swiss universities – which was where most German women who wanted higher education had to go – and open the German universities to women as well.

This scheme was advanced with a good deal of noise and publicity by Helene Lange, a woman who became prominent in the conservative wing of the Berlin feminist movement in the 1890s. Although her importance has been grossly exaggerated in later years, her growing influence was nevertheless an interesting symptom of the continued decline of the women's movement in the 1880s and early 1890s. Born on 9 April 1848 into a merchant family in Oldenburg, she lost her mother in early childhood, like many other leading feminists. She grew up in an intellectual but evangelical-conservative and authoritarian atmosphere.[38] She earned her living, in preference to getting married, as a teacher in a private girls' secondary school in Berlin, and from the mid-1880s she began to take an active part in the affairs of the General German Women's Association. What distinguished her from her colleagues in that body was not her views on politics, education and female emancipation, which were if anything even more conservative than theirs, but her energy. She was an ambitious, authoritarian woman with an extremely exalted opinion of herself who, unlike her gentler colleagues, was more than ready to use the weapons of sarcasm and invective at her command to put those who disagreed with her in their place. Like nearly all German feminists of the 1870s and 1880s, she fully accepted the role prescribed for women by the official social ideology of Imperial Germany. The educational system, however, according to Helene Lange, was not producing women capable of fulfilling this role to the best of their ability. The girls' schools, she argued, should stop teaching their pupils the mere dregs of masculine learning and institute the systematic education of girls into 'womanhood'. Girls, she thought, should be thoroughly imbued with the principles of 'morality, love, fear of God'. They should all be taught religion, German and history, and in girls' schools these 'ethical subjects' should always be taught by women because they were subjects 'in which not only humanity, but womanliness should be fostered'. Finally Lange demanded that girls' secondary schools should all have attached to them 'a Kindergarten, to give the young girls the opportunity of becoming acquainted with their later real profession'.[39]

The profession to which Lange was referring was of course that of motherhood. The German women's movement insisted that the natural impulse of women was towards motherhood, and this was therefore what education should equip them for. As far as they did anything else, it should be to extend their 'spiritual motherhood' beyond the family into the sphere of charity and good works. This was precisely what the official social ideology of Imperial Germany was prepared to allow. It was also one of the consequences of women's subordinate role in society that John Stuart Mill most strongly condemned: 'unenlightened and short-sighted benevolence', he argued, 'saps the very foundations of the self-respect, self-help and self-control which are the essential conditions both of individual prosperity and of social virtue.'[40] Yet in the 1870s and 1880s the bias of women's organisations in Germany was increasingly towards welfare and charity. A large part of the energy of the General German Women's Association was devoted to the erection of kindergartens, homes for unmarried working girls, and a number of small associations for the protection of girls which, copying the Girls' Friendly Society — a strongly maternalistic Tory organisation in

England – offered entertainment and protection to working girls to keep them from the moral (and political) dangers of the big city.[41] Here too the General Association was attempting to capitalise on the traditional motherly role of women and the general belief that women were the moral guardians of the family.

Above all, as time went on the General Association pressed its members to engage in poor relief *(Armenpflege)*, and to participate actively in official welfare institutions for the blind and the sick. The General Association attached paramount importance to voluntary welfare work of this kind which, it argued, would prove beyond doubt that women were serving the Fatherland in the same way as men were when they did their military service. The presence of large numbers of women in voluntary welfare work was used by the General Association, especially in the period 1890-1914, to argue that women should be allowed the right to sit on school and welfare boards and have an equal voice with men in determining their policy. The ultimate demand which the General Association put, under the influence of the radicalisation of the women's movement in the 1890s and 1900s, was for the vote in local council elections; because, it argued, since women played such a large part in local welfare services, they should have a say in deciding local council welfare policies. Even when it urged that women be granted the local suffrage as a reward for their services for the community, however, it seemed to regard the suffrage as a gift to be granted by the benevolence of the ruling élite rather than something that should be demanded of right. Indeed Helene Lange, in this respect as in others even more conservative than the General Association, did not even think that women were entitled to demand rights as a reward for services to the community; in her view they had yet to prove that they were really serving the community; and many of her efforts were devoted to devising new ways in which they could do this.[42]

The growing orientation of women's organisations towards welfare work gradually reduced the central role played by the General Association in the 1880s. More and more welfare societies and other women's organisations were founded in isolation from the General Association; and by the 1880s it lacked the energy to attempt to unite them under its aegis. The women's movement was becoming more fragmented and less coherent as well as more timid and less progressive. By the 1880s, too, the General Association was stagnating in other ways. Its membership, which had risen rapidly in the first five years of its existence, had reached a peak of about 11,000 by the mid-1870s; then it ceased to grow. By 1914 it had risen slightly to about 14,000; but an increase of 2000 members in 40 years did not compare favourably with the increase of 11,000 in less than a decade which the General Association experienced in the first years of its existence.[43] By the 1880s, too, the movement had lost the sympathetic contacts it had maintained with the labour movement in the late 1860s; apart from anything else the Social Democrats were officially illegal in Germany from 1878 to 1890, and their growing allegiance to Marxism also frightened off their sympathisers within the women's movement.

The German women's movement, then, was in a state of stagnation and decay by the late 1880s. It was numerically weak, fragmented, timid and conservative. Like the liberalism which inspired it, it had been bludgeoned into submission by the successive defeats of 1848, 1866, 1871 and 1878. It avoided public controversy, it fully accepted the role of housewife and mother laid down for women by society, it displayed a fawning subservience before royalty and titles, and it ignored all attempts by isolated radicals to persuade it to endorse the classical aims to which feminist movements in other countries adhered. Hedwig Dohm might raise the cry of votes for women in 1876 and urge the foundation of a German Women's Suffrage Society;[44] Gertrud Guillaume-Schack might attempt the foundation of a German branch of Josephine Butler's movement for the abolition of State-regulated prostitution in the early 1880s;[45] neither demand found an echo in the organised women's movement. Guillaume-Schack's society, indeed, was suppressed by the police, and its leader, despairing of any help from bourgeois women, joined the Social Democrats.[46] Feminism of the classical liberal individualist type had no place in the German women's movement before the 1890s. As the General Association, headed by its new leader Auguste Schmidt, told the International Council of Women in a letter refusing to join that most moderate of world feminist societies in 1888: 'In Germany we have to work with great tact and by conservative methods . . . The difference between our position and that of our American sisters is largely due to the fact that you live in a republic, we in a monarchy . . . in a land centuries old, where the ideas and habits of thought are . . . incrusted in the people.'[47] The reasoning was specious; but the sentiment that gave rise to it was deeply ingrained.[48]

NOTES

1. John Stuart Mill, *The Subjection of Women* (Everyman ed., London, 1929), 219-317.
2. Quoted in Aileen S. Kraditor, *The Ideas of the Woman Suffrage Movement 1890-1920* (Columbia, 1965), 46.
3. Alan Pendelton Grimes, *The Puritan Ethic and Woman Suffrage* (New York, 1967), 102, 78, 118.
4. Female suffrage was granted in Australia in 1902 and in New Zeland in 1893. For the USA, see Alan P. Grimes, op. cit.
5. Holger H. Herwig, *The German Naval Officer Corps. A Social and Political History 1890-1918* (Oxford, 1973), 28-9. See also, more generally, Barrington Moore, Jr., *Social Origins of Dictatorship and Democracy. Lord and Peasant in the Making of the Modern World* (Boston, 1966), esp. 435-442; V. R. Berghahn, *Germany and the Approach of War in 1914* (London, 1973); J. C. G. Röhl, *Germany without Bismarck. The Crisis of Government in the Second Reich 1890-1900* (London, 1967).
6. For a first attempt to delineate these informal but vital *Herrschaftstechniken*, see Hans-Ulrich Wehler, *Das Deutsche Kaiserreich 1871-1918* (Göttingen, 1973) Chapter 3 (105-141).
7. See M. Kitchen, *The German Officer Corps 1890-1914* (Oxford, 1968); W. Deist, 'Die Armee in Staat und Gesellschaft, 1890-1914; in Michael Stürmer (ed.), *Das Kaiserliche Deutschland. Politik und Gesellschaft 1870-1918* (Düsseldorf, 1970); Eckart Kehr, 'Zur Genesis des Königlich Preussischen Reserveoffiziers', in E. Kehr, *Der Primat der Innenpolitik. Gesammelte Aufsätze zur preussisch-deutschen Sozialgeschichte im 19. und 20. Jahrhundert*, ed. H. U. Wehler (Veröffentlichungen der Historischen Kommission zu Berlin beim Friedrich-Meinecke Institut der Freien Universität Berlin, Bd. 19, Berlin, 1965), 53-63.
8. See Herwig, op. cit., Chapters 3-4.
9. See Georges Castellan, *L'Allemagne du Weimar* (Paris, 2nd ed., 1972), which contains the best short summary of the religious structure of Imperial Germany.
10. There is a great deal of truth in Wehler's remark (op. cit., 88) that the SPD spent much of its political energies in fighting outmoded feudalistic structures rather than the newer structural institutions of bourgeois capitalism.
11. Quoted in H. Pogge-von Strandmann, 'Domestic Origins of Germany's Colonial Expansion under Bismarck', *Past and Present,* Feb. 1969, 142.
12. *RT,* 9. Leg. Per., 3. Sess., Vol. 1, 849-850.
13. Jenny Apolant, *Das kommunale Wahlrecht der Frauen in den deutschen Bundesstaaten* (Leipzig, 1918).
14. StA Hbg, PP, S9001/1: *BT,* 21 Oct., 1909.
15. *RT,* 9. Leg. Per., 4. Sess., Vol. 2, 8 Feb. 1896, 836, 839.
16. For a warning against assuming too simple a connection between women's

work and women's rights, however, see Louise Tilly and Joan Scott, 'Women's Work and the Family in 19th Century Europe', *Comparative Studies in Society and History*, Jan. 1975, 36 ff. See also Eric Richards, 'Women in the British Economy Since About 1700: An Interpretation', *History* 59/197, Oct. 1974.

17. Agnes von Zahn-Harnack, *Die Frauenbewegung-Geschichte, Probleme, Ziele* (Berlin, 1928), 39-43; Marianne Weber, *Ehefrau und Mutter in der Rechtsentwicklung*, (Tübingen, 1907), 331-341.

18. *RT*, 9. Leg. Per., 4. Sess., Vol. 4, 25 June 1896, 2910-2938.

19. StA Hbg, PP, S14139 (judgement in case concerning Anita Augspurg and Hamburg police).

20. See Abraham Flexner, *Prostitution in Europe* (New York, 1912).

21. Margrit Twellman, *Die Deutsche Frauenbewegung in Spiegel repräsentativer Frauenzeitschriften. Ihre Anfänge und erste Entwicklung 1843-1889* (Marburger Abhandlungen zur politischen Wissenschaft, herausgegeben von Wolfgang Abendroth, Bd. 17/1-2, Meisenheim am Glan, 1972), Vol. II, 194. For a critical but fair review of this book, see Ruth Schlette, 'Neue Veröffentlichungen zur Geschichte der Frauenbewegung', *Archiv für Sozialgeschichte* XIV, 1974, 531-6.

22. AStA Munich, MK 11116: Erlangen Senate to Kultusministerium, 20 May 1898.

23. ibid.: quoted in *Augsburger Postzeitung*, 27 March 1898.

24. StA Hbg, P, SA593/II: Versammlungsbericht, 8 Nov. 1906, 18 (speech of Lida Gustava Heymann).

25. AStA Munich, MK 11116, 1-2: Posadowsky to Bavarian Kultusministerium, 1 Feb. 1898.

26. Hugh Wiley Puckett, *Germany's Women Go Forward* (New York, 1930) 187, 200.

27. Zahn-Harnack, op. cit., 168.

28. The Patriotic Women's Association and its various branches (*Badischer Frauenverein*, etc.) was a German version of the Red Cross. There were smaller welfare associations in the big cities, mostly connected with the Churches and controlled by an all-male priesthood. From the turn of the century, the Catholics and Evangelicals began to found larger women's associations controlled by women. But there was no real equivalent of the active, conservative and women-controlled Girls' Friendly Society in England. Cf. Brian Harrison, 'For Church, Queen and Family: The Girls' Friendly Society 1874-1910', *Past and Present*, 61, November 1973.

29. Quoted in *GL*, 20/25, 12 Sept. 1910, 386.

30. Herwig, op. cit., 79-83.

31. For an example of threats of a social scandal arising from the marriage of a reserve officer to a feminist, see B. A. Koblenz, N. L. Schreiber, 3: P162: Protokoll der Vorgänge am Schluss der Vorstandssitzung der Berliner Ortsgruppe des deutschen Bundes für Mutterschutz am 10 Januar. 1910.

32. Twellmann, op. cit., Vol. I, 207.

33. ibid., 210.

34. ibid., 210-211.

35. ibid., 196.

36. ibid., 194-202.
37. ibid., 77.
38. Helene Lange, *Lebenserinnerungen* (Berlin, 1921).
39. Twellmann, op. cit., 88 ff.
40. J. S. Mill, op. cit.
41. Cf. Brian Harrison, op. cit.
42. Helene Lange, *Kampfzeiten. Aufsätze und Reden aus 4 Jahrzehnten.* (2 volls., Berlin, 1928).
43. *JB 1914*, 'Allgemeiner Deutscher Frauenverein'; Puckett, op. cit., 139-140.
44. Twellmann, op. cit., Vol. II, 535 ff.
45. ibid., Vol. II, 526 ff.
46. ibid., Vol. I, 191 ff.
47. Quoted in Irmgard Remme, *Die Internationalen Bezeihungen der deutschen Frauenbewegung vom Ausgang des 19. Jahrhunderts bis 1933.* (phil. Diss. West Berlin, 1955), 17.
48. For a detailed and well-researched study of one aspect of the problems discussed in this Chapter, see Helmut Beilner, *Die Emanzipation der bayerischen Lehrerin, aufgezeigt an der Arbeit des bayerischen Lehrerinnenvereins (1898-1933). Ein Beitrag zur Geschichte der Emanzipation der Frau* (Miscellanea Bavarica Monacensia, 40; Neue Schriftenreihe des Stadtarchivs München, Bd. 57), Munich, 1971.

2

THE RADICAL CHALLENGE

FROM SOCIAL WELFARE TO
SOCIAL REFORM, 1889-1899

The increasing concentration of the women's movement on social welfare may still, for all its lack of any real feminist impulse, have satisfied the aspirations of the great majority of those middle-class women who wished for a more active and useful life than that of the housewife,[1] at least up to the end of the 1880s. In the 1890s, however, this was no longer so, and many women made the politically vital transition from social welfare to social reform in the course of the decade. The enforced retirement of Bismarck in 1890, and the lapsing of the Anti-Socialist Law in the same year, created a freer political atmosphere. The transition of Germany at the beginning of the 1890s to a mature, predominantly urbanized industrial society brought with it a new consciousness of social problems and a new desire for social reform. The combination of these two influences made the 1890s into a decade of social and political ferment in Germany. Out of this ferment came a whole host of new pressure-groups and reform movements. Among the most important of these from our point of view was the German Society for Ethical Culture (Deutsche Gesellschaft für Ethische

Kultur) led by Ludwig Büchner, Georg von Gizycki, Friedrich Wilhelm
Förster and other 'Socialists of the Academic Chair' *(Kath-edersozialisten)*, which aimed to overcome social conflict through social
reform.[2] Another, with much the same aims but further to the
right, was the National Social Association (Nationalsoziale Verein),
led by Friedrich Naumann.[3] All these groups, initially at least,
occupied a position somewhere between the left wing of the liberals
and the right wing of the Social Democrats, and it was from this
intellectual background that a new, more active and radical wing of the
feminist movement began to emerge in the mid-1890s. This development was underpinned and perhaps even made possible by the slow
expansion of educational opportunities for women which took place, as
we saw in Chapter 1, in the late 1880s and early 1890s. However
unsatisfactory it might have been, it did at least mean that more women
could now lead a life of sufficient financial and intellectual independence to permit their involvement in feminist politics. At the same
time, as the mature industrial economy developed, new occupations
began to develop which offered further opportunities to middle-class
women – the white-collar, or *Angestellte* jobs. The growth of these
two types of occupation helped stimulate a new increase in support for
the women's movement in the 1890s; and a concentration on feminist
issues was further aided by the formation in 1889 of professional
associations to cater for those two expanding occupational groups –
the General German Women Teachers' Association (Allegmeiner
Deutscher Lehrerinnenverein) led by Helene Lange,[4] and the Commercial Union of Female Salarised Employees (Kaufmännischer Verband
für Weibliche Angestellte) led by Minna Cauer.[5] Finally, at the end of
the century, an attempt by Junker agrarians and heavy industrialists to
force up import tariffs led to a regrouping of the liberals and moderate
left, in which sectors of the middle class became for a period more
hostile to the Wilhelmine Establishment than they had been before. The
leftward move of the women's movement which took place at this time
also reflected this more general political process.[6]

   The first new development in the 1890s in the women's movement
was, however, organisational rather than political. The proliferation of
local women's organisations, mostly of a charitable nature, and the
emergence of new professional and educational organisations in the
1890s, were clearly creating the need for a new, central co-ordinating

body on the lines of the Federation of American Women's Clubs founded in 1890. Reform movements often internationalise themselves, and feminism was no exception. At Chicago in 1893 a World Congress of Representative Women was called by the International Council of Women, itself founded on American initiative in 1888. Germany was represented unofficially by Anna Simson and Auguste Förster, two leading members of the General Women's Association, Hanna Bieber-Böhm and Käthe Schirmacher. Together, spurred on by the International Council, they persuaded Auguste Schmidt — the leader of the General Association — to appoint a committee to prepare the foundation of a German national council of women.

The council was duly constituted on 29 March 1894, as the Federation of German Women's Associations (Bund Deutscher Frauenvereine, or BDF), uniting 34 women's associations of various sorts. By March 1895, after one year, there were 65 member associations with some 50,000 members; by 1901 the BDF contained 137 associations with about 70,000 members. The BDF's foundation also marked the beginning of a new era of growth for the women's movement; the largest of the established societies, the General German Women's Association, had remained static at about 12-14,000 members for nearly two decades; now, suddenly, stagnation was replaced by rapid growth. With this new growth and expansion came, ultimately, unprecedented changes in policy and ideology.[7]

Yet to begin with the BDF, whose leaders were largely drawn from the officialdom of the General Women's Association, did little to raise the German women's movement out of the doldrums into which it had sunk in the 1870s and 1880s. Most of the BDF's executive committee, led by August Schmidt, who became the first President, were mainly involved in social welfare work within the framework of the established welfare organisations, patronised by royalty and operating with modesty and discretion.[8] It was such charitable societies that first joined the BDF in largest numbers.[9] The BDF's first two manifestos, issued by Auguste Schmidt, Hanna Bieber-Böhm and the General German Women Teachers' Association, addressed themselves to charitable associations and presented the foundation of the BDF as a largely organisational step without any political significance.[10] In accordance with these ideas, the first programme of the BDF was narrow and welfare-orientated.[11] The leaders of the BDF, from Auguste Schmidt herself to other luminaries of the General German Women's Association such as Helene von Forster and Betty Naue, could hardly be called either dynamic or progressive.[12] As the SPD women's magazine *Die Gleichheit* ('Equality') reported on 6 March 1895, the bourgeois women's movement remained as socially timid and undemocratic as ever.[13]

It required political as well as organisational changes if the women's movement was ever to become feminist in the accepted sense of the word, and these changes came from two new organisations. The first was Hedwig Kettler's Women's Association 'Reform' (Frauenverein 'Reform'). Kettler's Association marked a new departure in that it aimed to give women the same education as men, instead of the 'separate but equal' policy hitherto adopted by Helene Lange and the General German Women's Association. Its manifesto, quoting copiously from John Stuart Mill, declared the intention of setting up by voluntary contribution a girls' grammar school in Karlsruhe. The school was actually founded in 1893 and taken over by the Baden authorities soon afterwards, thus becoming the first State Grammar School for girls in Germany. After this, however, the pressure-group ran into difficulties as it waited for the graduation of girls from the school in order to persuade universities to admit women by presenting them with suitable candidates in large numbers for the first time. The personality of its founder and leader, Hedwig Kettler, was idiosyncratic and domineering, and by 1895 it was creating serious problems for other members of her association. In 1895 all the executive committee save three honorary members (including Hedwig Dohm) resigned because of Kettler's failure to consult them, and there were also serious divisions of opinion in the management of the girls' grammar school in Karlsruhe. Anita Augspurg, who had represented Kettler at the opening ceremony of the school, and Marie Stritt, who had joined the association in 1891, finally managed to oust her in 1895 before her conduct caused the enterprise to collapse altogether.[14]

Meanwhile, however, another impulse for social reform was coming from the women's section of the German Academic Alliance (Deutsche Akademische Vereinigung), yet another pressure-group for educational reform, based in Berlin and founded in 1888. Renamed the Women's Welfare Association (Verein Frauenwohl) in 1889, its aims were at first confined to enlarging opportunities for women in education and the professions, like nearly all its contemporaries in the field of women's rights, and it soon began to establish branches in other parts of the country. As the political climate relaxed, however, and the government focused public attention on social questions by passing a fresh series of social reforms, particularly affecting women,[15] its leader Minna Cauer began to urge that the Association extend its work into the field of charity and social work. Early in 1893 it began organising voluntary work in homes for the blind, day-nurseries and similar institutions. In October the same year a special committee was formed to organise the work on a broader basis. A meeting called on 8 December 1893 revealed widespread support within the Association for this work, and some 50 to 60 women agreed to participate.[16] This development indicated Cauer's new concept of the role of the Frauenwohl. Influenced by the growing concern for social reform among Berlin intellectuals and academics, Cauer now regarded the major task of the Association as pioneering new kinds of social work for women. As Else Lüders,[17] for many years her closest associate and personal secretary, explained:

> It is well-known that propaganda societies pioneer ideas and pave the way for societies that work on a practical basis; it is obvious that these societies, because they work in the front line, have the most resistance on the part of the authorities and of public opinion to overcome, while societies working on a charitable basis almost always enjoy a greater measure of approval on the part of the authorities and also need above all else a calm atmosphere in which to do their work effectively.

The Frauenwohl, therefore, was to blaze the trail with propaganda and leave practical social reform to those who followed. This change in direction did not go unchallenged. Many members wanted the Frauenwohl to remain a women's educational and professional association of the old sort. The Frauenwohl General Assembly held on 30 December 1894 was a stormy one. Demands were made for Helene Lange to be elected President in Cauer's place, as a guarantee that the Association would return to the paths of respectability; but Cauer and her party emerged victorious, and were strengthened by the resignation of many members who formed a Berlin Women's Association (Berliner Frauenverein) under Helene Lange, and the addition of three new members, Jeanette Schwerin, Hanna Bieber-Böhm and Lily Braun (von Gizycki) to the committee.

The changes of 1894 were followed in due course by the extension of the pioneering reformism of the Frauenwohl into a number of new fields. In 1895 the Association held a meeting in Berlin at which the speaker raised the demand for votes for women. Cauer also, as we shall see, soon took up the cause of the reform of prostitution. Meanwhile she proceeded to found a new feminist magazine, *Die Frauenbewegung* ('The Women's Movement'), which became the major organ of the newly emerging 'radical' party within the women's movement, with articles advancing new demands for women's rights in many fields, reports of the activities of the various radical feminist groups, encouraging news of the progress of women's rights abroad, and, from 1899 onwards, a supplement edited by Anita Augspurg, devoted to reporting the treatment of feminist demands in the Reichstag and the provincial Diets. In 1896, too, the Frauenwohl Association chose the occasion of the Berlin Exposition to hold an international women's congress, attended by 1700 delegates from a number of countries. The congress fulfilled an important function in reassuring feminists abroad that some progress was being made in Germany, and in acquainting the international feminist movement with the ideas and personalities of the German radicals. The holding of the congress also demonstrated the close contacts established by the radicals with the women's movement outside Germany, their receptiveness to advanced ideas from abroad and their pronounced tendency to internationalism.[18]

It was not long before Minna Cauer, Anita Augspurg and Marie Stritt joined forces in attempting to persuade the BDF to adopt their more advanced ideas. Already in 1895 *Die Gleichheit,* reporting the second BDF Congress in Munich, noted that 'the opposition, represented in the main by the ladies von Gizycki, Cauer, Stritt, and Augspurg, has succeeded in pushing German bourgeois feminism just a little, a very, very, little, towards the left, and to a certain extent in democratising the character of the "Federation".'[19]

In 1896 they went further. They persuaded the BDF to launch an unprecedented public campaign against the provisions of the new Civil Code, which, as we have seen, were very disadvantageous to women, and were formally debated and ratified in the Reichstag in that year. On 29 June 1896 a large public meeting was held in Berlin. It was led by Minna Cauer and Anita Augspurg.[20] The *Hamburgischer Correspondent* estimated that there were 3000 people present, nearly all of them women. The paper's reporter on the occasion wrote that he had not previously had any firm opinions on the matter; but the meeting forced him to agree that women had been unfairly treated by the Reichstag in the Civil Code debates. The campaign seemed to him and to many others to herald the arrival of an important new force in the field of German social politics. The meeting of course could do little more than deplore the passage of the Code; it was too late to attempt any amendments. The speakers were unanimous in their condemnation of the measure. The final resolution labelled the Code as 'an expression of one-sided man's law *(Männerrecht)*'. Anita Augspurg accused the Reichstag of 'frivolity' and 'hypocritical sophistry'. Marie Stritt concluded ironically that one more such defeat would bring victory to the feminist cause.[21]

These statements, the radicalism of their tone and the unprecedented fact that they were made in a mass public meeting, signalled the beginning of a new, more active phase in the development of the women's movement in Germany. Indeed, during the course of the campaign the leadership of the BDF began to feel anxious about the radicalism it was encouraging. Some prominent members found the tone of the BDF's final resolution on the Civil Code, agreed at the mass public meeting on 29 June, too strident. 'It speaks the language of Frl. Augspurg', remarked one of the old-established women's leaders to Auguste Schmidt.[22] The independent initiative taken by the BDF's Legal Commission in organising the campaign was not appreciated by some;[23] and others such as Anna Simson, a long-standing member of the General Association's Committee, resented the element of controversy and dissension that the campaign brought into the affairs of the BDF.[24] Women such as Simson soon began to style themselves 'moderates', in contrast to the band of 'radicals' who were emerging as a new force in the women's movement. By 1898, indeed, the BDF had clearly divided into two opposing parties, and as the strength and self-confidence of the radicals grew, a major clash began to seem inevitable.

The specific issue over which the clash eventually took place was the problem of prostitution.[25] This was brought to prominence largely by the furious national debate sparked off by the government's proposals to control prostitutes more strictly. The pioneer of the discussion of the prostitution problem within the women's movement was Hanna

Bieber-Böhm, the founder in 1889 of an Association for the Protection of Young Persons (Verein Jugendschutz). Though her ideas were far from progressive, the very fact that she discussed the problem at all made her into a radical and controversial figure in the eyes of most contemporaries. The Frauenwohl Association for instance, before the events of December 1894, had voted on 8 and 14 June 1892 not to discuss her ideas at all.[26] However, with the changes in personnel and direction upon which the 1894 general assembly of the Frauenwohl set the seal, the way was open for the emergence of prostitution and morality as a major concern of the Frauenwohl group. Bieber-Böhm had a monopoly on this subject within the women's movement and had little difficulty in persuading the Association to adopt her ideas. She drew up a petition, which was approved by the Frauenwohl, and by other women's organisations, and presented it in person to the Berlin chief of police Count Pückler at the end of 1895. Among other things the petition demanded the abolition of police-controlled brothels, the deportation of foreign prostitutes and the imprisonment of all other prostitutes, including first offenders, for between one and two years. Women's prisons were to be reformed, and special departments established to deal with the prostitutes and educate them into moral conventionality. This was a programme which corresponded to a large degree with that of the conservative evangelical Men's Morality Associations, who believed that prostitutes were essentially evil and should be dealt with toughly by the police. The Morality Associations were led by Pastor Weber, an ex-army officer who regarded the defeat of Social Democracy as his life's work. He was a close associate of the Court preacher and anti-semitic demagogue Adolf Stöcker, and the aim of his movement — which sought to impose strict police control on prostitution, 'dirty' books, 'immoral' plays and 'obscene' advertisements — was to discipline the working classes, whose support of Social Democracy, which he ascribed to their lack of moral fibre, he viewed with the utmost alarm.[27] However radical they may at first sight have seemed in the context of the women's movement, Hanna Bieber-Böhm's ideas in fact corresponded quite closely to Pastor Weber's programme of moral repression.

Bieber-Böhm's ideas were at first accepted without question in the Berlin Frauenwohl. But three years later, in 1898, the issues of prostitution and morality came to the forefront of public discussion with the revival, this time in a more extreme form sponsored by the Catholic Centre Party, of the government's proposals to regulate prostitution and control 'immoral' art and literature, the so-called *Lex Heinze* .[28] Naturally the Frauenwohl Association felt that it had to make its voice heard on the subject, and the executive committee proceeded to consider the framing of a petition to the Reichstag formulating its views on the prostitution question. This time, however, Bieber-Böhm's views did not go unchallenged. For in the meantime some members of the Association had come into contact with the English movement for the abolition of State-regulated prostitution, led by Josephine Butler, who was now trying to extend her crusade to Europe.

evil and a danger to society and that they should be hounded out of existence by the law, Josephine Butler and her followers, who styled themselves 'Abolitionists' after their aim, thought that prostitutes were victims of a male-dominated society. True liberal individualists, they wanted the removal of all State interference in private morality, and especially (in Germany) the abolition of Section 361/6 of the Criminal Code on which the police control of prostitution rested.

In this their views were directly opposed to those of Bieber-Böhm, and rested moreover on strongly feminist attitudes. The legal punishment of prostitutes, they maintained, symbolised and legitimised the double standard of morality that society applied to men and women. It was wrong, they thought, that women engaging in prostitution should be punished and degraded while their male customers were not. The State regulation of prostitution was, they said, 'a formal crime against personal freedom'. The State must respect 'the individual's right of self-determination, which is the basis of personal responsibility.' Self-improvement, not State paternalism, was the key to improving morality. Men must be educated into remaining as chaste as women were supposed to be before marriage and as faithful within marriage.[29] What the Abolitionists were concerned with was the self-determination and individual moral dignity of women – the classical concerns of feminists everywhere. The double standard of morality must be replaced by a single standard of self-restraint.

Abolitionism quickly gained converts among the radical feminists. Käthe Schirmacher[30] was converted during her stay in Paris in the early 1890s; Anita Augspurg came into contact with Abolitionism while

studying law in Zürich;[31] and Minna Cauer soon came round to the
same point of view. Together they forced Bieber-Böhm to withdraw her
proposed petition on the *lex Heinze*. Then at the Frauenwohl's General
Assembly they secured her replacement on the committee by Augspurg
by 86 votes to 69. Several resignations followed, including those of
Henriette Goldschmidt and Jeaneatte Schwerin. By the end of January
1899, therefore, the Frauenwohl organisation was firmly in the hands
of the Abolitionists.[32]

THE RADICALISATION OF THE
WOMEN'S MOVEMENT, 1896-1902

Encouraged by their successes in 1896-97, the radicals launched a major
bid for power in the women's movement at the BDF General Assembly
in Hamburg in 1898. Warned by notice of the radicals' plans in Cauer's
magazine *Die Frauenbewegung*, the BDF leadership prepared for a
struggle. 'The days in Hamburg will decide', wrote Rosalie Teblée, an
influential conservative member of the BDF,[33] 'which party will hold
the rudder in future.' 'We ought', she added, referring to the 'moderate'
party, 'to hope for a majority, despite all the machinations.' The BDF
leadership proposed that the statutes, which had to be revised because
of the growth in the organisation's size, should contain a definition of
the BDF's aims tying it firmly to the traditional conception of the
function of the women's movement favoured by the General German
Women's Association.

> The Federation of German Women's Associations purposes to unite all chari-
> table women's associations and all federations of such associations, in order to
> achieve the following aims:
> 1. To strengthen and aid all women's associations in their own work through
>   communion with other associations.
> 2. To place this particular work even more successfully in the service of the
>   family and the community, in order to oppose ignorance and injustice and
>   to bring about a rise in the moral basis of life for the whole community.
> 3. To provide an opportunity for an exchange of thought, for comparisons,
>   for the consideration of exemplary institutions and for the encouragement
>   of new, independent ideas and activities.

The BDF President, Auguste Schmidt, who was also President of the General German Women's Association, summarised the aims of the BDF as increasing the opportunities of women for employment — that is, in the professions — developing the free personality of women within the home and in civic affairs, and in enlarging the extent and the activities of the BDF itself. Even Bieber-Böhm's proposals to combat prostitution, subsumed under the second point in the programme, occupied only a relatively minor place in this catalogue of aims.

The official definition of the tasks and aims of the BDF, contained in the proposed programme, was challenged at the Assembly by Cauer, Augspurg and their supporters, who proposed that the executive committee's three points be rejected in favour of the following simple but controversial definition:

> The Federation of German Women's Associations aims to unite all those women's associations which strive for the improvement of the spiritual, economic, legal and social position of women.

In addition Cauer and Augspurg wanted the BDF headquarters to be moved from Leipzig to Berlin, where they had their main sources of support[34] and where they might hope to gain control over it more rapidly than by more strictly constitutional means. They also drew up a more far-reaching plan for the reconstruction of the BDF on a more egalitarian and strictly federal basis, but they were unable to put it to the Congress because their opponents on the Frauenwohl committee, then still in a majority, rejected it. Basing her arguments on the programme proposed by the BDF leadership, Cauer asserted that the BDF's continuing desire to confine itself largely to charitable and welfare work was behind the times and irrelevant to the women's movement; its real task should be to fight for women's rights. Such criticism was not welcomed by the old guard. 'A quarrel in one's own camp is so unpleasant', complained Helene Lange in December 1898. The public, she said, was being given to understand 'through a systematic polemic in the daily papers' that the women's movement was 'senile and aimless', and that it could only be rescued by a small group of 'purposeful' reformers. Yet, she continued, reviewing various articles by Minna Cauer and her supporter Helene Stöcker, it was impossible to see what the purposes of these reformers were.[35] Lange concluded that the best thing to do if possible was to ignore the radicals.

'Moderates' such as Helene Lange had a powerful political base in the BDF General Assembly, the official policy-making body of the organisation. Under the system of voting then in operation at the General Assembly, each member association had one vote for every 200 members, up to a maximum of five. In 1900 this was amended to give even greater weight to small associations; each member association now had one vote for 30 members, two for 130, and so on up to five for 430. In order to be present in the Assembly at all, the radicals, who represented very few associations, had to resort to representing associations with which they often had only a rather tenuous connection. In the 1900 General Assembly for example, which was the last to be dominated by the old guard of the General German Women's Association, Augspurg was present as the representative of the Frauenwohl Association in Ulm, where she can hardly have been more than once or twice if at all. Moreover it was frequently the practice for those societies that could not afford to send a delegate to the Assembly to give their vote to some well-known figure. In 1894-1900 this gave a distinct advantage to the moderates. Not only were the best-known figures in the BDF generally moderates, so too were the vast majority of these poor member associations, unlike the situation in 1902-1908. So in 1900, for example, Bieber-Böhm was present at the Assembly with no less than five votes, representing a wide variety of different societies.[36] Of the old leaders, Auguste Förster and Ottilie Hoffmann,[37] had four votes each; Helene Bonfort,[38] Henriette Goldschmidt and Helene Lange each had three. Of the radicals, the Hamburg feminist Lida Gustava Heymann and the Berlin schoolteacher Maria Lischnewska each had two votes, Augspurg and Cauer one each, Hedwig Winckler (Hamburg), Mathilde Planck (Stuttgart) and Marie Raschke (Berlin) one each. Marie Stritt, who by 1898 stood somewhere between the two camps, had three votes, and Ika Freudenberg (Munich), who occupied a similar position to Stritt's, had four. Altogether there were 84 delegates with a total of 134 votes; the weight of the plural votes was clearly on the moderate side. Forty-eight towns were represented; Berlin, with 25 votes, was easily the largest, but the strong position of the General German Women's Association was underlined by the fact that the headquarters of the old women's movement, Leipzig, sent delegates with a total of ten votes, while of the more radical centres Hamburg and Frankfurt am Main had eight votes each, Munich had seven and Dresden three.[39] Even these were divided between radicals and moderates.

In 1898 the Assembly was probably even more heavily dominated by the moderates than in 1900. It is hardly surprising that one of the major planks in the radical platform from 1900 onwards was to be the replacement of this system of representation, which gave undue weight to small towns, where the moderates were usually all-powerful, by a voting machinery which would only allow unions *(Verbände)* to be represented, with a number of votes that corresponded roughly to their size; it was not, however, until 1908 that the old system was amended.[40] In 1898 the power of the moderates was reflected in the fact that the Assembly voted down the first few points in the radical programme, then resolved that it would be a waste of time even to discuss the rest. Moreover, the more narrow proposals of the radicals, to convert the BDF to Abolitionism, also failed. Bieber-Böhm's influence continued undiminished for the time being at least, and in 1900 the BDF made its position quite clear by issuing under its official auspices her petition asking the Kaiser to improve the moral education of his soldiers and, through them, his nation.[41]

Disappointed and impatient, Cauer and Augspurg returned from the Assembly convinced that it was useless to continue the struggle and that the BDF was beyond redemption. They then proceeded, perhaps rather hastily, to form a rival organisation called the Union of Progressive Women's Associations (Verband Fortschrittlicher Frauenvereine). According to Minna Cauer, there would be a 'division of labour' within the movement; the BDF would continue to devote itself to welfare work and to enlarging professional and educational opportunities for women, while their own Union would launch a vigorous and radical propaganda campaign for the enlargement of women's rights. It seemed as if the women's movement had split into two parts, the larger (the BDF) committed to supporting the status quo, the smaller (the Union of Progressive Women's Associations) committed to opposing it.[42]

The consequences of the split and the foundation of the new organisation were not, however, so far-reaching as Cauer and Augspurg at first maintained. For one thing the split was not complete. The Frauenwohl, its offshoot the Abolitionist Federation, the Commercial Union of Female Salaried Clerks, and other organisations in which Minna Cauer and her supporters were influential, all joined the Progressive Union, but they also remained full members of the BDF. The Progressive Union itself remained outside the BDF, but because of the failure of its member organisations to leave the latter it never really posed a viable alternative. In 1907 indeed it took the logical step and joined the BDF itself. The BDF was in the last instance too powerful and too prestigious a body for the radicals to be able to ignore. Even in 1898 it was beginning to identify itself with the women's movement as a whole, and once their initial disappointment at their defeat wore off, the radicals could see the advantages of remaining within the BDF and continuing the struggle to try and radicalise its programme. At the same time the creation of the Union of Progressive Women's Associations allowed them a freer hand in issuing general propaganda for women's rights than they might otherwise have had.

The radicals therefore stayed in the BDF and reappeared at subsequent General Assemblies to continue their pressure for reform. Moreover the radicals in 1898, overcome by disappointment after their victorious struggle to take over the Frauenwohl, were being too pessimistic when they drew the conclusion that the BDF was incapable of reform. The General Assembly of 1898 in fact marked the end of the dominance of the old guard of the women's movement, the leaders of the General German Women's Association, over the BDF. Many of its most influential representatives were ageing, and they now took the opportunity to retire. The most important of these changes in personnel was the resignation of the founder-President Auguste Schmidt, whose career went all the way back to 1848 and who had been a leading member of the General Association since its foundation in 1865. Of the rest of the old guard, Betty Naue resigned in May 1901, Auguste Förster in 1902, and Anna Simson and Henriette Goldschmidt retired at about the same time. The hold of the General Association over the women's movement as a whole was at last broken.[43]

Auguste Schmidt's successor as President of the BDF was the founder and leader of the Legal Protection Association for Women (Rechtsschutzverein für Frauen), Marie Stritt, who took over Schmidt's post in 1899.
the 1890s she had generally been counted among the radicals with Augspurg and Cauer. In 1895-96 she had attracted attention as the organiser and leader of the campaign against the Civil Code, and in 1896 she was voted on to the executive committee of the BDF.[44] By 1900 most of the obvious candidates, in other words the members of

the executive committee, were either too old like Auguste Förster and Henriette Goldschmidt, or too controversial like Helene Lange and Hanna Bieber-Böhm. By 1900 Stritt had gained credit among the moderates through the rapid spread of the Legal Protection Association for Women, which she had founded from the Dresden Branch of the General German Women's Association in 1896. Her continued connection with this organisation, and her refusal to go along with Augspurg and Cauer in the foundation of the Union of Progressive Women's Associations in 1899, clearly kept Stritt in good standing with the moderates. Nevertheless she had by no means abandoned her radical feminist beliefs. Her election as President of the BDF was therefore of crucial importance to the development of the women's movement, and it quickly began to pay dividends as far as the radicals were concerned. For in July 1899 Stritt paid a visit to London, and while she was there she met Josephine Butler, who succeeded immediately in converting her to her views on the prostitution problem.[45] Back in Berlin Stritt's influence soon made itself felt in favour of the radicals. As President of the BDF Stritt edited the BDF news-sheet, the *Centralblatt des Bundes Deutscher Frauenvereine,* and Bieber-Böhm was soon complaining that space was being given to Abolitionist views and not to hers.[46] Stritt's predecessor Auguste Schmidt had been a strong supporter of Bieber-Böhm,[47] but under Stritt other leading members of the BDF now began to espouse Abolitionist ideas. By 1900 Ika Freudenberg, Augspurg's successor at the head of the Munich feminists, Katharina Scheven in Dresden and more leading members of the BDF in other towns had been converted, and the Abolitionist Anna Pappritz, – perhaps more conservative than most – who ran the branch of the Abolitionist movement which Cauer and the Frauenwohl had established in Berlin in April 1899, was elected onto the BDF's executive committee.[48] Pappritz proceeded to use her position in the BDF to launch a general attack on Bieber-Böhm within the women's movement as a whole, strongly backed by the radicals.[49]

The turning-point in the radicals' fortunes proved to be the BDF General Assembly of October 1902. Under the influence of the General German Women's Association in the 1890s, the keynote of the BDF General Assembly had been unanimity. The Assembly had been conceived basically as a symbol and a demonstration of unity, a means of drawing together the disparate organisations that made up the BDF by the proclamation of a common philosophy. The radicals changed all this. They regarded the Assembly as a kind of Parliament and themselves as a sort of parliamentary opposition, and at every Assembly from 1898 up to 1908 their aggressive tactics gave rise to serious and often heated debates. This was not welcome to the moderates:

> One must simply call it childish (wrote Helene Lange in 1900) when a section of the participants in a women's meeting intended for *serious* work goes to the hall early in the morning to make sure of the left-hand seats for itself, when the debates are accompanied by shouts of 'Oho! ' and 'Hear! Hear! ', when all points of order are discussed with deadly seriousness and a slavish immitation of parliamentary forms.[50]

Nevertheless, the moderates had now to put with with these tactics.

Indeed, the General Assembly of 1902 was unusually heated. The radicals mounted their attack on two fronts. First, they criticised the report of the BDF's Morality Commission, established in 1900 alongside a series of other specialist sub-committees and dominated by Bieber-Böhm and her followers. Bieber-Böhm's report was unrepentantly conservative. It praised 'our Pastor Weber' (the Morality Association leader) and reaffirmed the doctrine of the legal prosecution of prostitutes. In an effort to prevent a debate Helene Lange supported Bieber-Böhm, but also said that the Abolitionists' ideas, though unrealistic, might be of some value in the long run and that there was no reason why the Assembly should not support both points of view. However, this was impossible. Pappritz accused Bieber-Böhm of urging local associations of the BDF to prevent the formation of Abolitionist groups in their towns. The debate that Lange tried to prevent thus took place.[51]

Against Bieber-Böhm's advice the Assembly eventually voted for the abolition of Section 361/6 of the Criminal Code, which was the legal basis of the police prosecution and regulation of prostitutes. This constituted a repudiation of Bieber-Böhm's policy of suppressing prostitution by legal prosecutions and gaol sentences. The Assembly then proceeded to vote in a new Morality Commission dominated by Abolitionists.[52] It was a signal defeat for Bieber-Böhm and a remarkable triumph for the radicals.[53]

The second issue upon which the radicals concentrated their attention at the 1902 General Assembly of the BDF was female suffrage.

The BDF had avoided making any sort of pronouncement on this issue as assiduously as had the General German Women's Association, and it was left to the radicals to start the discussion. In 1895 Lily Braun, shortly before going over to the SPD, had made a speech in favour of votes for women under the auspices of the Berlin Frauenwohl,[54] and Minna Cauer's magazine *Die Frauenbewegung* had devoted some attention to political issues, including the suffrage, which it supported since its foundation. The experience of the 1890s had convinced Cauer and the radicals that without the vote their reforming ideas could never be translated into legislative acts. 'What do we achieve with all our petitions? asked Cauer in 1901; 'little, very little. A large and more or less wasted amount of energy, time and money simply goes into filling the wastepaper bins of parliament.'[55] Female suffrage was the obvious answer. In due course, as we shall see in the next Chapter, the Frauenwohl Association went on to found (as yet another offshoot) a society devoted to fighting for votes for women; at the same time it launched a campaign within the women's movement to persuade the BDF to adopt female suffrage into its own programme.[56]

The motion to this effect, introduced by the Prussian primary school teacher Maria Lischnewska (a close associate of Cauer and Augspurg) into the 1902 General Assembly of the BDF, ran up against strong opposition from the moderates, led once more by Helene Lange. Characteristically the moderates tried to defeat the motion on a procedural point so as to avoid having to debate it. Lischewska's motion attempted to force the member unions of the BDF, as well as the main organisation, to support female suffrage. The BDF constitution, however, did not allow any intereference by the BDF in the affairs of its member unions. Lange tried to use this fact to rule out a debate on a point of order, which led to angry exchanges between her and Minna Cauer. After a long procedural debate Lange's counter-motion was defeated and a short debate was held in which Marie Stritt, Anita Augspurg and Anna Pappritz all spoke in favour of votes for women. Eventually Lischewska's motion was withdrawn in favour of another less problematical one proposed by Marie Wegner, a leading Silesian feminist who possessed strong radical sympathies. 'It is urgently desirable', read the motion, 'that the member associations advance understanding for the idea of female suffrage as far as they can, because all of the Federation's efforts will only be assured of lasting success by the granting of votes to women.' Despite the continued opposition of Lange and the leader of the Hamburg moderates, Helene Bonfort, this resolution was finally passed by a large majority.[57]

The 1902 General Assembly of the BDF thus saw a decisive breakthrough by the radicals on two major fronts; on the issue of prostitution and morality which was the dominant subject of controversy within the women's movement in the years 1898-1902, and on the issue of female suffrage which was to be the main issue for the next few years. On both these issues the radicals had imposed their views on the BDF. Moreover, the hold of the General German Women's Association on the movement had clearly been broken, and the radicals now had a number of sympathisers in the BDF leadership, the most important of them being Marie Stritt, the new BDF President. At last the German women's movement seemed to be taking on the characteristics of classical feminist movements in England and America. In the next few years the radicals set about extending and consolidating their influence. Their programme covered several other subjects that we have not mentioned here; they were pacifists where the moderates were strongly nationalistic,[58] and they wanted co-operation with the SPD where the moderates were determined to ignore the existence of the party. In a more general political sense they wanted the women's movement, as we have seen, to become an active crusading association for the gaining of full equality for women, as they understood it, in every sphere. They therefore wanted the movement to adopt more vigorous tactics than it had previously been accustomed to employ. Protest meetings, public crusades, mass petitions and lobbying, such as had been used in the campaign against the Civil Code, were now to be extended to other spheres as well. Beyond this the radicals sought a thoroughgoing reform of the entire political and social system. The moderates had refrained from commenting on general political issues; the radicals had no hesitation in doing so, and they invariably declared themselves against the pre-industrial aristocracy that ruled Germany and in favour of the creation of a complete bourgeois democracy.

In 1902, therefore, the radicals still had some way to go before they could completely convert the women's movement to support of their aims, despite the breakthrough they had achieved at the turn of the century. Meanwhile their attention was absorbed in a new crusade of their own: the Abolitionist campaign in Hamburg, a campaign that demonstrated just how far the radicals were prepared to go in their attack on the existing political system, and just how far-reaching the implications for the women's movement as a whole would be if the radicals managed to consolidate the gains they had made in 1898-1902 and move into a position of total dominance and control.

POLICE, PROSTITUTION AND POLITICAL REPRESSION IN HAMBURG, 1898-1908

The city of Hamburg, by the 1890s the second largest town in the German Empire, with a population rapidly approaching the million mark, had not up to this point played a significant role in the development of German feminism. Leipzig, Berlin, even Dresden had been more important in the women's movement up to the turn of the century. Yet from this point onwards Hamburg quickly gained an importance in the women's movement second only to that of Berlin. This was due of course in large measure to the city's booming size and prosperity. Its Protestant and cosmopolitan character also perhaps played a part; yet two other peculiarities intensified its importance as a centre in particular of radical feminism in the years 1898-1908. Hamburg, formerly an independent Hanseatic city-republic, constituted under the German Empire a separate federal State on its own, just like Prussia or Baden or Bavaria. Among other things it had its own police force and, like every other federal State, its own Law of Association. The Law of Association, like that of Baden and Württemberg, allowed women to join or form political organisations and to attend public meetings. This clearly gave the radicals much wider scope for campaigns of all sorts than they enjoyed in Berlin, Leipzig, Munich or Frankfurt, where women were not legally allowed to involve themselves publicly in political life.

The incentive for the radicals to become active in Hamburg at the turn of the century, when the State regulation of prostitution was uppermost in their minds, was provided by Hamburg's unusually strict form of regulating prostitution. All German cities except Hamburg and the small Rhineland town of Mainz employed a system technically known as *Kasernierung,* by which the police restricted prostitutes to certain areas or dwellings but dealt with them only as individuals. Hamburg and Mainz, however, regulated prostitution through the so-called method of *Bordellierung,* that is by placing the prostitutes in organised and sometimes quite large-scale brothels and controlling them through the brothel-keepers. This was clearly much nearer to the actual *running* of the vice trade than the usual system. It constituted a formal State control of the prostitution business in a way that the usual system of control did not. Moreover it was strictly speaking illegal, and to avoid prosecution under the relevant paragraph of the Criminal Code (Section 180) such as had already threatened them in the 1870s, the Hamburg police had to resort to various kinds of subterfuge.[59] In its combination of strictness and vulnerability then, the Hamburg system was doubly challenging to the Abolitionist movement; and on top of this of course came the sheer scale of the problem, unmatched anywhere else in Germany save Berlin.

The official women's movement in Hamburg was embodied in the local branch of the General German Women's Association, established in 1896 and led by two women who were 'total enemies of one another' and even more hostile to others who tried to poach on their territory, Julie Eichholz and Helene Bonfort.[60] Bonfort was the more conservative of the two, and under her influence the branch refused to acknowledge the existence of prostitution and confined itself almost exclusively to charitable work. This was an unusually conservative attitude, for two years previously in 1894 the BDF, then dominated by the Leipzig and Berlin leadership of the General Association, had fully endorsed the discussion of the prostitution problem at its meetings. Indeed, the Hamburg women's movement was not only conservative but aggressively so, as became clear when the radicals began to try and change things in the city. The radical challenge to the Hamburg General Association was led by Lida Gustava Heymann. Born on 15 March 1868 into a rich Hamburg merchant family, much of whose wealth she had inherited on the death of her father, Heymann began to engage herself in charitable work in the early 1890s, founding in quick succession a day-nursery, a cheap lunching club for single women, an organisation for actresses, a 'people's bathing establishment', a women's home and, like Minna Cauer, a society for female commercial employees.[61] In

June 1898 she was still working within the established Hamburg women's movement, but her rise to prominence had brought her into contact with Minna Cauer in Berlin and she soon espoused Abolitionist ideas. By September 1898, after she had failed to persuade the General German Women's Association in Hamburg to start an Abolitionist crusade, she was writing: 'The Committee does not work in the tendency in which I do, and I have therefore withdrawn myself more and more, and indeed have enough to do with the organisation of the commercial employees.'[62]

At the beginning of October 1898 however Heymann founded a 'Committee for the Women's Movement' which in February 1900 was refounded as the Frauenwohl Association, Hamburg branch.[63] In April 1900 the Hamburg branch of the General German Women's Association forbade its Committee members to join the new society.[64] Helene Bonfort had already devised a scheme to 'oppose all obstruction on the part of the radical associations in advance' within the BDF in March 1900. 'It is so vital to the women's movement,' she explained on another occasion, 'that the mature heads and women with a selfless character remain, otherwise our struggle against the troublemakers will be made immeasurably more difficult.'[65] The scheme, however, never succeeded in coming into operation. In 1904 there took place what the Hamburg *General-Anzeiger* called a 'palace revolution' within the General Association in Hamburg, in which Bonfort replaced Eichholz as President. Thereafter the General Association espoused the new doctrine of 'Neo-regulationism', committing itself to the maintenance of police control over prostitution.[66] In 1907, indeed, the Hamburg General German Women's Association went even further and criticised the BDF's programme for 'tastelessness and hostility to men'. They objected in particular to the demand for full legal equality between man and wife within marriage, and the legal equality of illegitimate children.[67] By then the hostility between Bonfort and Heymann had gone so far that the former accused the latter of being a secret Social Democrat. Heymann's radical Frauenwohl Association in its turn voted by 23 to 17 not to co-operate with the Association.[68] 'How differently the women in Berlin operate! ', lamented one writer, calling attention to co-operation between moderates and radicals in the capital city.[69]

It soon became clear indeed that Bonfort had some cause for alarm. From the very start it was plain that Lida Gustava Heymann and her associates, chief among them Martha Zietz, Regine Ruben, Hedwig Winckler and Charlotte Engel-Reimers, were out to arouse a public outcry against the police and force the Hamburg authorities to abandon their policy of regulation.[70] To achieve this they were both willing and able to go much further than their colleagues in Berlin. They began to hold public meetings criticising the police and the regulation of prostitution, and were soon distributing leaflets to the populace at large. 'Think of your duties to the generality! ', the people of Hamburg were urged. 'Think of your human dignity! Think of your human rights! '[71] The significance of these meetings, argued Heymann in 1901, went far beyond the narrower question of the State regulation of prostitution. 'Women have remembered their rights', she said, 'they want to be human beings, and to be a human being means to fight for our rights . . . Every day we speak out in men's assemblies, and in protest meetings we criticise men's behaviour. But they cannot accustom themselves to one thing, they cannot endure it when we women come forward as fighters for morality, because men have hitherto ruled alone and in brutal fashion in this field . . .'.[72] The rule of men was thus symbolised in the rule of the police. The reaction of the police to this kind of criticism was not slow in coming. On 9 February 1900 they forbade any discussion of the speech to be delivered against regulation at an Abolitionist meeting, thus forcing everyone to go home early.[73]

On 11 January 1901 they repeated their ban on discussion at an Abolitionist meeting. This time, however, Heymann engaged a lawyer and sent in a formal complaint.[74] This was followed by a protest meeting in Berlin on 10 February, organised by Minna Cauer, Maria Lischnewska and Else Lüders, and featuring a speech in Heymann's support by the liberal politician Hellmuth von Gerlach. The meeting was attended by a number of Social Democrats including Helma Steinbach from Hamburg, who not only supported the Abolitionists in their attack on the Hamburg Law of Association but also criticised the men of the SPD for 'old-fashioned views' on female emancipation.[75] When these actions had no effect Heymann appealed against the rejection of her complaint. This was itself in turn rejected. By the beginning of 1902 the police, unwilling to allow themselves to continue being attacked, decided to implement the ban on the public discussion of prostitution by the Abolitionists which they had agreed to in principle on the foundation of the Hamburg branch in 1899.[76]

From now on the Hamburg police refused to allow the Abolitionists to hold any meetings at all, and sent agents to supervise and harass even their closed assemblies. This ban lasted, with the exception of a brief period from the end of 1906 to the end of 1907, until the introduction of an Imperial Law of Association in May 1908 superseded the Hamburg Law and removed the legal grounds on which the ban rested.[77] It also applied to the Union of Progressive Women's Associations. The Union was unable to discuss prostitution in Hamburg at its General Assembly in the city in 1903, although Minna Cauer referred to it in terms of 'the most important women's question, the morality problem',[78]

The grounds on which the police based their action was the Hamburg Law of Association of 1893, the same that made Hamburg one of the few parts of the Empire where women could legally attend political meetings and join political clubs. Heymann, they claimed, had contravened the law by offending against public decency and endangering public order.[79] By this they meant the existence of the Hamburg system of regulating prostitution, which they considered essential to the maintenance of public order.[80] In private they described Heymann as the sworn enemy of 'the institutions of the existing social order'.[81] In the margin of an article by Heymann in which she referred to the fact that she had been away from Hamburg for some time, one police agent scribbled sarcastically, 'What a disaster for Hamburg! '[82] It was extremely rare for the police to take such strong action against a middle-class reform movement which, as we shall see, had close ties with left-wing liberalism.[83]

Nevertheless, the Hamburg police were in a very precarious legal situation. On 5 March 1900 Heymann had filed a suit with the public prosecutor against a brothel-keeper in the Schützenstrasse. When the public prosecutor refused to take any action Heymann filed a suit against him in the Bundesrat for denial of justice. The Bundesrat agreed that the Hamburg system was contrary to Section 180 and came under Article 7 of the Imperial constitution as one of the 'shortcomings that are apparent in the implementation of the Imperial Laws'. The Hamburg Senate now had to move quickly 'to avoid a further decision by the Bundesrat in the direction desired by the plaintiff', as the Senate's Justice Commission put it. If Heymann won, then the Hamburg public prosecutor would be obliged to take legal action against all the brothels in Hamburg and thus bring the system of regulation to an end. The situation, according to the Senate's ambassador in Berlin, was very serious for Hamburg. The Senate's contention that the landlords of brothels were not brothel-keepers and were therefore not subject to the provisions of Section 180, was not one that was recognised in law. By a series of complicated legal arguments, however, the Senate was able to persuade the Bundesrat first that the police only had contact with individual prostitutes. 'The police', it declared, 'refrains on principle and with intention from involving itself in the personal relationships between the landlord and his female tenants, and does not recognise the landlord as the proprietor of a house occupied by prostitutes.' Then it successfully repeated the legal arguments by which it had established that a decision of 1876, in which the Bundesrat had declared the Hamburg system illegal, was not binding on the public prosecutor. Heymann had lost her suit in a welter of legal hair-splitting.[84]

At the same time she was conducting a separate series of legal actions against the police over the ban on her meetings. Although these actions also failed[85] they served, like the suit in the Bundesrat, to bring the Abolitionist crusade before the public eye. Reaction was mixed. The moderate women's movement in Hamburg deplored the use of 'cheap slogans',[86] and Helene Bonfort declared that some of the Abolitionist meetings had been inspired by the Social Democrats – an allegation that the Social Democratic *Hamburger Echo* was quick to refute.[87] The *Deutsches Blatt* accused Heymann of 'a mania for demonstration' and seeking 'sensation at any price'. The *Hamburger Echo* launched a fierce attack on the police's 'illegal action' in banning Abolitionist meetings, and the left-liberal press was also highly critical of the police's action,[88] although it sometimes thought Heymann's language excessive and occasionally criticised the emotional nature of Abolitionist meetings. Fuel was added to the flames by the news that the Berlin police had brought Minna Cauer to trial over an Abolitionist meeting held in Berlin.[89] In March 1903 the Hamburg police ensured that the Abolitionists kept in the public eye by fining Heymann 20 marks for libel,[90] and by banning the Morality discussion of the General Assembly of the Union of Progressive Woman's Associations.[91]

Enough scandal was created, indeed, to warrant a left-wing liberal deputy, Ernst Müller-Meiningen, bringing the matter up in the Reichstag.[92] In Hamburg, he declared during a debate on 28 January 1904, prostitution had become an institution of the State. It was shameful that the police prevented the women's movement from criticising this disgraceful situation. The Hamburg Senate had received advance notice of Müller-Meiningen's speech and sent along a representative, Dr. Schäfer, to defend their policy towards the Abolitionists. Schäfer's defence, however, was not a happy one. He began by restricting his argument to proving the police had acted within the law, but the SPD repeatedly demanded he explain the grounds for their actions. Protesting that he had already been drawn on to say more than he should, Schäfer explained that he had received a complaint from a 'young theologian' who had attended an Abolitionist meeting in which:

> ... the worst sexual questions were discussed. The gentlemen observed how a growing sensual excitement became evident in these young girls of 12, 15 years of age, so that one could read it from their faces (Loud laughter).
> ... Despite her good intentions, this lady (Heymann) constitutes a far worse danger than all the thugs she has devoted herself to fighting. She does not like prostitution, nor do I, nor do the Hamburg police (laughter). If those gentlemen who demand its abolition can show us a way to achieve it, we should be very grateful to them. As long as the world has existed, prostitution has existed. (loud laughter and uproar. The President strikes his bell).

So Schäfer went on, amid increasing uproar, making one foolish statement after another.[93] The Press were critical and the Hamburg Senate was worried about the damage done to the city's reputation — not least by Schäfer's incautious reference to the Hamburg system of *Bordellierung* — 'call them brothels, it's all the same to me, the name doesn't have much significance for me'.

Müller-Meiningen returned to the attack on 5 February during the budget debate. He immediately pointed out that Schäfer had admitted the existence of police-controlled brothels in Hamburg. To applause from the left he delivered an effective condemnation of the Hamburg Law of Association by instancing in detail the inconsistency and injustice of its application to the Abolitionists. This time however, advised by the Senate, Schäfer restricted himself in reply to pointing out that the police action was designed to protect minors, and that in any case the Reichstag had no jurisdiction in the matter. This was in fact the very point that Müller-Meiningen was trying to make: his speech ended with a plea for a national Law of Association. He had to wait another four years, however, before his wish — an important plank in the left-liberals' political platform — was granted.[94] The Reichstag debate was the occasion for a furious protest meeting in Berlin, organised by Minna Cauer, which condemned both Schäfer and the 'loud laughter' that had accompanied his speech in the Reichstag. The speeches were printed as a pamphlet, which the Hamburg police attempted to suppress.[95]

Meanwhile the Abolitionists in Hamburg continued to hold meetings in Altona, a separate administrative district which was governed from Schleswig-Holstein and was subject to the Prussian Law of Association. As the Hamburg Social Democrat Emil Fischer remarked, public peace and security did not seem to be endangered when the Abolitionists met in Altona. It was, he said, shameful that the free republic of Hamburg should behave in a more reactionary manner than the Junker State of Prussia.[96] Not only did the Altona meetings denounce the Hamburg police and pass strongly-worded resolutions demanding that the ban on meetings in Hamburg be lifted, but they also created yet more sensation by taking individual sexual scandals and using them to publicise their demands. On 6 February 1905 for example, the Abolitionists held a large public meeting — known as the Blankenese Protest Meeting — to protest against the acquittal of the perpetrators of a mass rape on a young girl in the Hamburg suburb of Blankenese. The sensation aroused by the trial was used to get across to as many people as possible the message that male immorality was given its strongest encouragement by the State regulation of prostitution.[97]

These tactics were not without effect. On 15 December 1904 a report noted the public 'streaming in crowds from Hamburg to Altona' to hear an Abolitionist speech by the Berlin radical feminist Adele Schreiber on the Wiese case — another scandal like the Blankenese affair — and on 7 January 1905 the Hamburg *General-Anzeiger* reported that:[98]

> The meetings of the 'International (Abolitionist) Federation' are taking on more and more a distinct character of their own. Women flock to them from all sections of the Altona population, driven by fervent interest; the electric tramway carries wagons filled to overflowing with women from Hamburg to Altona, and the women feel themselves more and more at home and entitled to speak out at these meetings. The Federation would probably not have aroused this firm connection with the female public, which is otherwise not so strongly moved by such a burning interest for public affairs, if it had been

allowed to hold its meetings unhindered in Hamburg. The Hamburg banning has certainly given them a sensational attraction . . .

Before the clash with the police the Abolitionists had been getting on average 150 people at each of their public meetings. But their last two meetings in Hamburg, when the threat of stern police action was already in the air, drew 300 and 350 respectively, and when the Abolitionists met in Altona attendances were often over 400. Much depended on the subject to be discussed. Augspurg could only muster 250 to hear her disquisition on the Law of Association on 5 February 1903, but Heymann raised 750 for a talk on sex education and the Blankenese Protest Meeting was attended by over 900.[99] The sensation helped membership too. Between 1899 and 1901 it went up from 25 to 47, but by 1903 it stood at 76, a rise of 30 in two years. It was to be another five years before the Hamburg Abolitionists reached their peak of 113.[100] These were tiny figures of course; nevertheless in view of the extreme courage required of active Abolitionists in defying law and convention, the increase was still a remarkable one.[101]

The Hamburg Abolitionists had scored some remarkable successes indeed. They had secured a debate in the Reichstag. They had inspired articles against the Hamburg authorities in the Press. They had aroused a high degree of public interest in their cause. They had sustained that interest for a considerable period of time. Yet the Hamburg Abolitionists found it impossible to achieve a single reform of any sort in the regulation of prostitution in Hamburg, let alone the total abolition that was their declared aim.

The police and the State were too strong, the Abolitionists too weak. The Abolitionist Federation in Germany never numbered more than about a thousand people all told, but even more important than this was its lack of the financial resources necessary for a sustained public campaign. Lida Gustava Heymann's campaign in Hamburg indeed, and the lawsuits she conducted against the police, were probably paid for at least in part out of her own pocket despite the fact that the Hamburg branch, as the following table shows, was far richer than all the other Abolitionist branches put together. Taken as a whole, the sums involved were quite inadequate for the launching of a sustained national campaign. This no doubt helps explain why none was in fact launched.[102]

TABLE 1

Income and Expenditure of the Abolitionist Federation German Branch 1907-1908

Branch	INCOME				EXPENDITURE				Balance
	Subscriptions	Donations	Others	Total	Admin.	Propaganda	Others	Total	
Berlin	500	400	39	939		1055		1065	−166
Bremen	297			297	33	382		415	
Breslau	156			156				137	19
Danzig	188	20	83	291	44	72	48	164	127
Dresden	625			625	370	120	80	570	264
Düsseldorf	115	20		135	20	60	38	118	17
Elberfeld	115	10	5	130		130		130	
Frankfurt/M	319		141	490	12	499	8	519	−29
Halle/S	90			90	60	30		90	
Hamburg	650	400	747	1797		1534	261	1795	3000
Hanover	84	120		246		225		225	21
Mülhausen	255		28	255		236		236	19
Munich	174	30		232		217		217	15
Stuttgart	179	15	64	258	19	157	10	186	72
Central Organisation	304		36	340	80	235	122	437	521

Source: *Statistik der Frauenorganisationen im Deutschen Reiche* (1. Sonderheft zum Reichsarbeitsblatte, Berlin, 1909.

The Hamburg crusade was fierce and sensational partly because the hostility of the established women's movement there prevented the participation of more moderate elements, partly because the very severity of the regulation system seemed to demand more positive reforming tactics than were usual in other cities, partly because the police were harshly repressive from the start. The very isolation of the Hamburg Abolitionists made them more radical; their radicalism in turn made them yet more isolated. The Hamburg crusade was important both in itself and in the development of the women's movement. In itself it did as much as anything to bring the new radical feminism of Cauer, Augspurg and Heymann before the public eye. It cast a lurid light on the methods of the Hamburg police, and Hamburg's 'liberal' image emerged from the episode tarnished. The Hamburg police were shown by their actions as quite prepared to counter social reform with political repression. The crusade also reflected and perhaps contributed to a contrast between Hamburg and Berlin within the women's movement that was to emerge in other forms later on. Hamburg represented the radical, dynamic side of Abolitionism, Berlin the cautious and practical. The personality type of the leadership on the two cities was correspondingly different — Lida Gustava Heymann, bold, fanatical and uncompromising, in Hamburg, Anna Pappritz, cautious, thorough and flexible, in Berlin.

The Hamburg Abolitionist crusade was exceptional in its fervour, its dramatic appeal, its radical dynamism and its large-scale ambitions. It sought not merely to abolish the State regulation of prostitution in Hamburg, but by raising scandal and sensation on a national level it hoped, through parliamentary action, to abolish regulation throughout the Empire. In this, of course, it was entirely unsuccessful. In fact its importance lay above all in its radicalism. Here was a doctrine, Abolitionism, in the name of which respectable middle-class women clashed in direct and open conflict with the officers of the law. The Hamburg Abolitionist crusade made it clear that by adopting Abolitionism, the women's movement as a whole was placing itself firmly in the camp of those who opposed the existing structure of the Wilhelmine State.

NOTES

1. The prevalence of domestic service relieved middle-class housewives of most of their duties in the late 19th century. Cf. Tilly and Scott, art.cit.; Eric Richards, 'Women in the British Economy since about 1700: An Interpretation,' *History* 59/197, Oct. 1974; and F. K. Prochaska, 'Women in English Philanthropy 1790-1830', *International Review of Social History* XIX (3) 1974, 426-445.

2. This circle influenced Lily Braun (whose first husband was Georg von Gizycki), Regine Deutsch, Alice Salomon, Minna Cauer, and many other prominent feminists. Cf. Else Lüders, *Der 'linke Flügel'. Ein Blatt aus der deutschen Frauenbewegung* (Berlin, n.d.), 12-14; ABDF 2/I/4: Regine Deutsch; Hans Muthesius, *Alice Salomon, die Begründerin des sozialen Frauenberufs in Deutschland. Ihr Leben und Ihr Werk* (Koln/Berlin, 1958), 28 ff.

3. Ludwig Elm, *Zwischen Fortschritt und Reaktion. Geschichte der Parteien der liberalen Bourgeoisie in Deutschland 1893-1918* (East Berlin, 1968), 7. From this group came Gertrud Bäumer, Ika Freudenberg, and others. Cf. Gertrud Bäumer, *Lebensweg durch eine Zeitenwende* (6th ed., Tübingen, 1933), esp. 222 ff.

4. Bäumer, op. cit., 157-58.

5. For Cauer (born 1 Nov. 1841, widow of a left-liberal educationalist), see Else Lüders, *Minna Cauer, Leben und Werk. Dargestellt an Hand ihrer Tagebücher und nachgelassenen Schriften* (Gotha, 1925).

6. Dirk Stegmann, *Diu Erben Bismarcks. Parteien und Verbände in der Spätphase des Wilhelminschen Deutschlands* (Köln/Berlin, 1970), 75-80.

7. For the early history of the BDF, see Gertrud Bäumer, 'Die Geschichte des Bundes Deutscher Frauenvereine', *Jahrbuch der Frauenbewegung (JB) 1921*, and Agnes von Zahn-Harnack, *Die Frauenbewegung – Geschichte, Probleme, Ziele* (Leipzig/Berlin, 1928).

8. ABDF 5/II/1: Ottilie Hoffmann to Auguste Schmidt, 3 Oct. 1894; Helene von Forster to Auguste Schmidt, 16 Sept. 1894; Betty Naue to Auguste Schmidt, 19 Oct. 1894.

9. ABDF 5/XII/1: Auguste Schmidt to an anonymous correspondent, 27 April 1894.

10. ADLV I/2, p. 27: 'Aufruf an alle gemeinnützigen Frauenvereine Deutschlands'; 33, 'Bund Deutscher Frauenvereine.'

11. Reprinted in *JB 1921*, 18.

12. The other members were Anna Simson, Helene Lange, Auguste Förster, Anna Schepeler-Lette, Ottilie Hoffmann and Hanna Bieber-Böhm.

13. *GL* 5/5, 6 March 1895. The epithets used by the magazine were 'undemokratisch' and 'fürstenfromm'.

14. UB Rostock, NL Schirmacher: Augspur to Schirmacher, n.d. (1895). For Augspur, born 22 Sept. 1857, daughter of a liberal revolutionary of 1848, niece of a National Liberal Reichstag deputy, founder of the Association for the Advancement of the Intellectual Interests of Women *(Verein zur Vertretung der*

geistigen Interessen der Frauen) in Munich, see *Neue Deutsche Biographie* (Historischer Verein bei der Bayerischen Akademie der Wissenschaften, Berlin, 1956); Max Schwarz, *MdR*. *Biographisches Handbuch der Reichstage* (Hanover, 1965), 253; and Lida Gustava Heymann, in Zusammenarbeit mit Dr. jur. Anita Augspurg, *Erlebtes – Erschautes. Deutsche Frauen kämpfen fur Freiheit, Recht und Frieden 1850-1940* (ed. Margrit Twellmann, Meisenheim am Glan, 1972), 3-18 (hereinafter referred to as Heymann/Augspurg, *Erlebtes-Erschautes*).

15. Karl Erich Born, *Staat und Sozialpolitik seit Bismarcks Sturz* (Wiesbaden, 1957), 84-134.

16. Else Lüders, *Ein Leben des Kampfes um Recht und Freiheit. Minna Cauer zum 70 Geburtstag* (Berlin, 1911), 5-31; Lüders, *Der 'linke Flügel'*, 16-20.

17. Not to be confused with Marie-Elisabeth Lüders, who was active in politics during the Weimar Republic and represented the FDP in the Bundestag in the early years of the Federal Republic.

18. *Der Internationale Kongress fur Frauenwerke und Frauenbestrebungen in Berlin, 19 bis 26 September 1896* (Eine Sammlung der auf dem Kongress gehaltenen Vorträge und Ansprachen. Herausgegeben von der Redaktions-Kommission: Rosalie Schoenfliess, Lina Morgenstern, Minna Cauer, Jeanette Schwerin, Marie Raschke, Berlin, 1897).

19. *GL* 5/14, 18 July 1895.

20. Else Lüders, *Der 'linke Flügel'*, 23-26.

21. StA Hbg, PP. S5466/I:*HC*, 7 June 1896; *BT*, 30 June 1896, 'Das Aufgebot des Frauen-Landsturms'.

22. ABDF 5/II/1: Marianne Heidfeld to Auguste Schmidt, 15 June 1896.

23. ABDF 5/II/2: Simson to Augspurg, April 1898; von Witt to Augspurg, 26 April 1898.

24. ABDF 5/II/1: Simson to Auguste Schmidt, 27 June 1896.

25. For a general discussion, see the author's 'Prostitution, State and Society in Imperial Germany' (*Past and Present*, 70, Feb. 1976, 106-129).

26. Else Lüders, op. cit.; see also Minna Cauer, *25 Jahre Verein Frauenwohl Gross – Berlin* (Berlin, 1913).

27. Lic. L. Weber, *Lebenserinnerungen* (Hamburg, n.d.), 1-20.

28. For an excellent discussion of the lex Heinze, see R. J. Lenman, 'Art, Society and the Law in Wilhelmine Germany: the lex Heinze', *Oxford German Studies* 8, 1973), 88-113.

29. StA Hbg, PP. SA593/II: 'Was will die Internationale Abolitionistische Föderation? '

30. Hanna Krüger, *Die unbequeme Frau. Käthe Schirmacher im Kampf um die Freiheit der Frau und die Freiheit der Nation* (Berlin, 1936), 69-107.

31. Heymann/Augspurg, *Erlebtes – Erschautes*, 50; StA Hbg, PP, S5466/I: *HF*, 14 December 1897, Lüders, *Der 'linke Flügel'*, 29-30.

32. ABDF 4/4: Rundschreiben 'An die Mitglieder des Vereins "Frauenwohl" und seine Schwestervereine', Berlin, 1899, 3-15; Else Lüders, *Der 'linke Flügel'*, 34-37; StA Hbg, S5466/I: *BVZ*, 1 February 1899, giving the vote as 89:65, *BLA*, 1 Feb. 1899; *BVZ*, 3 Feb. 1899, 5 Feb. 1899, 10 Feb. 1899; *HC*, 5 Feb. 1899; Hanna Krüger op. cit., 23-96; IISG Amsterdam, NL Vollmar 3156: Bericht über die 2. Generalversammlung des Vereins fur Fraueninteressen, München. Cauer had

helped found the Women Clerical Workers' Association in 1889; her victory was supposedly gained by packing the meeting with its members (ABDF 4/4: *Rundschreiben*, cited above). Augspurg became eligible through her resignation from the Munich society (IISG Amsterdam, loc. cit).

33. ABDF, 'Frankfurter Ortsgruppe des Allgemeinen Deutschen Frauenvereins' (not indexed); Teblée to Auguste Schmidt, 8 Sept. 1898, 10 Sept. 1898.

34. StA Hbg, Senat, Cl. VII, Lit. Rf. No. 29, Vol. 41: *HC*, 3 Oct. 1898, 4 Oct. 1898, 5 Oct. 1898.

35. *DF*, 6/3 Dec. 1898, 129-134. For Stöcker, see Ch. 4 below.

36. Landwirtschaftlicher Hausfrauenverein Rastenburg, Preussischer Verein technischer Lehrerinnen Soest, Hausfrauenverein Magdeburg, Jugendschutz Berlin, Ethische Kultur Berlin.

37. For Ottilie Hoffmann, (1835-1925) the Leader of the General Women's Temperance Movement, see *Bremische Biographie 1912-1962* (hg. von der Historischen Gesellschaft zu Bremen und dem Staatsarchiv Bremen. In Verbindung mit Fritz Peters und Karl H. Schwebel bearbeitet von Wilhelm Lührs, Bremen, 1969), 240-2.

38. For Bonfort see note 60 below.

39. ABDF 16/I/1: Generalversammlung 1900 (Stenogramm, Präsenzliste.)

40. See pp. 195, 198-9, below.

41. ABDF 8/2: (1900 petition).

42. Lüders op. cit., 33-4; StA Hbg, Senat. Cl. VII, Lit. Rf. No. 29, Vol. 41: *HC*, 5 Oct. 1898.

43. ABDF 2/I/1-4 (Lebensbilder).

44. StA Hbg, PP. S5466/I: *HC*, 25 Oct. 1896. Jeannette Schwerin had been voted on to the committee at the same time, and might well have succeeded Auguste Schmidt as President but for her untimely death in 1899.

45. ABDF 5/XII/4: Bieber-Böhm to Auguste Schmidt, 18 July 1899.

46. ABDF 5/XII/4: Bieber-Böhm to Auguste Schmidt, 7 April 1900.

47. ABDF 5/XII/1: Schmidt to Stritt, 19 April 1900.

48. ABDF 5/XII/4: Bieber-Böhm to Stritt, 23 Jan. 1900; ABDF 5/XII/5: Freudenberg to Stritt, 13 April 1900, Freudenberg to Schmidt, 12 Feb. 1899.

49. HLA 16: Anna Pappritz, 'Wie ich zu meiner Arbeit kam' (MS. autobiography), 1-75.

50. *DF* 8/2, Nov. 1900, 65-7.

51. ABDF 16/I/2: Generalversammlung 1902, Stenogramm, 29-50.

52. StA Hbg, S5466/I: *NHZ*, 7 Oct. 1902.

53. Bieber-Böhm resigned from the Commission in protest, and after attempting vainly to reassert her influence, declaring that 'the Abolitionist Society is not yet identical with the Federation', she abandoned the struggle on 1 Jan. 1905, resigning from the BDF's committee. She died on 15 April 1910. See HLA 18: Protokollbuch des Berliner Zweigvereins der Internationalen (Abolitionistischen) Föderation, 27 Oct. 1902, 16 June 1903; ABDF 2/I/1: Bieber-Böhm to BDF Vorstand, Jan. 1904, 'Erwiderung auf die Erklärung der Sittlichkeits – Kommission vom Sept. 1903', 'Erklarung der Sittlichkeits-Kommission auf die Entgegnung von Frau Bieber-Böhm,' etc.; ABDF 5/XII/4: Bieber-Böhm to Alice

Salomon, 22 Dec. 1903, Pappritz to Auguste Schmidt, 28 March 1904; ABDF 2/I/2: Lebensbild von Hanna Bieber-Böhm; *DF* 17/9, June 1910, 526-9.

54. Lily von Gizycki, *Die Bürgerpflicht der Frauen* (Berlin, 1895). See the description of the event in Lily Braun, *Memoiren einer Sozialistin* (Berlin, 1908), Vol. II, 505-15.

55. *FB*, 7/24, 15 Dec. 1901, 185.

56. For a previous discussion of the female suffrage issue in Germany see Amy Hackett, 'The German Women's Movement and Suffrage, 1890-1914: A Study in National Feminism', in Robert J. Bezucha (ed.), *Modern European Social History* (Lexington, Mass., 1972).

57. ABDF 16/I/2: Generalversammlung 1902, Stenogramm, 83-107.

58. See Chapter 7.

59. Alfred Urban, *Staat und Prostitution in Hamburg vom Beginn der Reglementierung bis zur Aufhebung der Kasernierung* (Hamburg, 1927).

60. UB Hamburg, Dehmel-Archiv: Alice Bensheimer to Ida Dehmel, 23 Sept. 1906. Bonfort, like many German feminists, had been converted to feminism through contact with the women's movement in America, where she stayed in 1894-95. She was a former schoolteacher, unmarried. (ABDF 2/I/4: Helene Bonfort). See also *Die Tätigkeit des Allgemeinen Deutscher Frauenvereins Hamburg 1896-1921* (Hamburg, 1921); and *Die Tätigkeit des Allgemeinen Deutschen Frauenvereins, Ortsgruppe Hamburg, nebst Zweigvereinen, 1909-1911* (Hamburg, 1911).

61. *Wer Ist's?* (1909, 1922); *Lexicon der Frau* (Zürich, 1953), Vol. I, Col. 1398; StA Hbg, PP, S5466/I: *NHZ*, 19 July 1902.

62. ABDF 5/II/2: Hamburger Ortsgruppe des Allgemeinen Deutschen Frauenvereins to Auguste Schmidt, 1 June 1898; Lida Gustava Heymann to Auguste Schmidt, 14 Sept. 1898.

63. StA Hbg, PP, S5466/I: *HE*, 4 Feb. 1900; ibid.,/II: *HNN*, 28 March 1905.

64. StA Hbg, PP, S5466/I: *HNN*, 11 April 1900.

65. ABDF, 'Frankfurter Ortsgruppe des Allgemeinen Deutschen Frauenvereins' (not indexed, filed separately): Bonfort to Schmidt (?), 18 March 1900, n.d.

66. StA Hbg, PP, S5808/II: *GA*, 26 Dec. 1904. The reverse had occurred in 1903, when Eichholz had replaced Bonfort (UB Hbg, Dehmel-Archiv, Autographen,, Vera Tugil-Dehmel: Alice Bensheimer to Ida Dehmel, 23 Sept. 1906).

67. ABDF 5/VIII/I: Stritt and Pappritz to Gesamtvorstand, 14 April 1907.

68. StA Hbg, PP, S5466/II: *HNN*, 28 March 1905, *HF*, 28 March 1905.

69. StA Hbg, PP, S5466/I: *HNN*, 11 April 1900.

70. StA Hbg, PP, SA593/II: Versammlungsbericht 17 Oct. 1904.

71. StA Hbg, PP, SA593/I, p. 22: 'An Hamburgs Männer und Frauen! '

72. StA Hbg, PP, SA593/I, p. 162: Versammlungsbericht 13 Dec. 1901.

73. StA Hbg, PP, SA593/I, p. 15: Versammlungsbericht 10 Jan. 1901.

74. Ibid., 102-110: Grallert and Mumssen, Rechtsanwälte, to Polizeibehörde, 31 Jan. 1901.

75. Ibid., 119-121: *HE*, 3 Feb. 1901, *VW*, 12 Feb. 1901.

76. Ibid., 237-247, Versammlungsbericht, 18 April 1901.

77. StA Hbg, PP, SA593/II: Police to Heymann, 19 Feb. 1908, *NHZ*, 26 Feb. 1908, Police 'Konzept', 24 Jan. 1906. For the relaxation of the ban in 1906-07, which the Abolitionists regarded as a triumph, see *Der Abolitionist*, Vol. 6, No. 2, 1 Feb. 1907, 18.

78. StA Hbg, PP, S9000/II: *GA*, 30 Sept. 1903.

79. Stenographische Berichte über die Sitzungen der Bürgerschaft zu Hamburg 10 Oct. 1906. 33, Sitzung.

80. StA Hbg, PP, SA593/II: police notes of 15 Feb. 1904, police to Heymann, 14 Dec. 1906, Heymann to police, 22 April 1906.

81. StA Hbg, PP, S8004: Hamburg to Munich police, 3 March 1904. Cf. the accusation advanced against Gertrud Guillaume-Schack in Darmstadt in 1882, that she was 'working to undermine the existing social order' (Twellmann, *op. cit.*, Vol. II, 531).

82. StA Hbg, PP, S8004: *HC*, 15 Dec. 1901 (marginalia).

83. Though not unique. The Free-Thinkers' Association *(Freidenkerverein)* was also persecuted in this way when it discussed subjects such as contraception. Cf. StA Hbg, PP, S8897/IV: *Der Pionier*, 3 Dec. 1913.

84. StA Hbg, Senat, Cl. I, Lit. T, No. 7, Vol. 6, Fasc. 9, Inv. 6a passim; *FB*, 1 Jan. 1902, 1-2, 45.

85. StA Hbg, Senat, Cl. VII, Lit, L^b, No. 28^c, Vol. 14, Fasc. 7, passim.

86. StA Hbg, PP, S5466/I: *HC*, 24 Dec. 1901.

87. StA Hbg, PP, SA593/II: *HE*, 17 Feb. 1905.

88. StA Hbg, PP, SA593/I: *DSB*, 8 Feb. 1905, *NHZ*, 7 Feb. 1905, *HE*, 24 March 1905.

89. Ibid./I: *BT*, 10 Feb. 1903.

90. StA Hbg, PP, S8004, 61-63: police to Heymann, 30 March 1903.

91. Ibid., S5466/III: Heymann to police, 14 March 1903 et.seq.

92. See Joachim Reimann, *Ernst Müller-Meiningen Senior und der Linksliberalismus seiner Zeit* (Miscellanea Bavaria Monacensia – Neue Schriftenreihe des Stadtarchivs München, Nr. 11, Munich, 1968).

93. StA Hbg, PP, SA593/II: *DP*, 29 Jan. 1904.

94. StA Hbg, PP, SA593/II: *Weser Zeitung*, 6 Feb. 1904.

95. *Die Deutschen Frauen und die Hamburger Bordelle – Eine Abrechnung mit dem Syndikus Dr. Schäfer...* (Pössneck 1.Th., 1904); StA Hbg, PP, SA593/II: Police notes, 29 Feb. 1904.

96. StA Hbg, Senat, Cl. VII, Lit. L^b, No. 28^c, Vol. 14, Fasc. 9: 133. Sitzung der Bürgerschaft vom 10 Oct. 1906.

97. StA Hbg, PP, SA593/II: *NHZ*, 7 Feb. 1905. The meeting gave rise to slander suits against Augspurg and the editor of the *Hamburger Echo*. See ibid.; *BVZ*, 3 June 1905.

98. StA Hbg, PP, SA593/II: *GA*, 7 Jan. 1905.

99. StA Hbg, PP, SA593/I: 15, Versammlungsbericht 10 Feb. 1900, 52, Versammlungsbericht 11 Jan. 1901, 162, Versammlungsbericht 13 Dec. 1901, 216, Versammlungsbericht 3 Feb. 1902, 237, Versammlungsbericht 18 April 1902, 299, Versammlungsbericht 25 Nov. 1902; ibid/II: Versammlungsberichte 20 Feb. 1904, 17 Oct. 1904, 5 Jan. 1905, 6 Feb. 1905, 29 March 1905, 16 Nov.

1905, 22 Feb. 1906, *HF,* 28 Nov. 1906.

100. StA Hbg, PP, SA593/I, 201: II. Jahresbericht des Hamburger Zweig-vereins der Internationalen Föderation; ibid., 361 (Versammlungsbericht); Marie Wegner; *Merkbuch der Frauenbewegung* (Leipzig/Berlin, 1908).

101. For further membership figures, see   below.

102. I hope elsewhere to give an account of the equally unsuccessful though rather different Abolitionist campaigns in Baden and Frankfurt am Main. See also the author's 'Prostitution, State and Society in Imperial Germany' (*Past and Present,* 70, February 1976). The branches of the Abolitionist movement in Germany were united in 1903, and in 1906 they joined the BDF as a member union. See HLA 18: Protokollbuch des Berliner Zweigvereins der Internationalen (Abolitionistischen) Föderation, 11 December 1903; ABDF 5/IV/1: Stritt to Vorstand, 19 December 1906.

3

THE SUFFRAGE CAMPAIGN

WOMEN'S SUFFRAGE AND MORAL REFORM

While the radicals were pursuing their vigorous campaign in Hamburg against the State regulation of prostitution, they also launched another campaign of even greater significance and controversiality: the campaign for votes for women. Up to the turn of the century, the women's movement had steadily refused to join feminists in other countries in supporting female suffrage, but in 1902, as we have seen, the radicals persuaded the BDF to support the vote for women; and even before this they had begun to agitate publicly for the vote.[1] On 1 January 1902, following its usual policy, the Frauenwohl Association proceeded to found a new offshoot, the German Union for Women's Suffrage (Deutscher Verband für Frauenstimmrecht).[2] The 13 founder-members were all leading radical feminists, and most of them were closely involved in the Abolitionist campaign. They included Anita Augspurg, who became the Suffrage Union's President, Lida Gustava Heymann, the Vice-President, Minna Cauer, Käthe Schirmacher, Helene Stöcker, Charlotte Engel-Reimers and Agnes Hacker.[3] By March 1902 Marie Raschke, Martha Zietz, Regine Ruben, Hedwig Weidemann, Anna

Pappritz, Marie Stritt and Katharina Scheven had also joined.[4] Soon the Hamburg Frauenwohl also joined en bloc.[5] Meetings and General Assemblies of the Union in its early years were generally held in conjunction with those of the Union of Progressive Women's Associations. In 1903, despite misgivings by Augspurg, Cauer and Heymann, the Suffrage Union joined the BDF.[6]

There were three main reasons for the foundation of the Suffrage Union in 1902. First, the radicals were, as we have seen, becoming increasingly frustrated by their failure to secure reforms, and by 1902 were generally agreed that only the vote would enable them to achieve their aims. Secondly, stimulated by the political atmosphere at the turn of the century, they had begun to take an active interest in politics; they campaigned actively for example against the proposal of the government to increase the import duty on corn (thus raising the price of bread) in 1902, and attacked in the process the alliance of Junkers and heavy industry that lay behind the proposal.[7] The experience of the *lex Heinze* debate probably played a role as well in bringing on this process of politicisation. Finally, according to Heymann's memoirs, the fact that Germany was to be unrepresented at the first international women's suffrage congress in Washington in February 1902 persuaded Augspurg to found an organised suffrage movement in Germany; the lack of one was clearly becoming an embarrassment to the German radicals in their relations with international feminism.[8]

The headquarters of the new organisation were in Hamburg, where it was officially registered. Hamburg was chosen partly because Anita Augspurg, who seems to have been the main impulse behind the foundation, spent much of her time there, and partly because the radical feminist movement was already very active there. Above all, however, it was chosen in preference to Berlin because, although it was only the second city of the Empire and not – like Berlin – the first, the foundation would not have been legal in the capital, for the Hamburg Law of Association, like that of Baden and Württemberg but unlike that of Prussia, allowed women to take part in politics. It was only in these areas, therefore, that a female suffrage society could legally exist. Branches of the Suffrage Union were soon established in South Germany, particularly in the university towns, but they could be set up in other parts of Germany, neither in Prussia nor in Bavaria, where the Law of Association was also very strict in its exclusion of women

from political life. The Suffrage Union thus remained for the time being
confined to the classical strongholds of German liberalism — Baden,
Württemberg and the Hanseatic towns of Hamburg and Bremen.

In fact, long before the turn of the century the creation of a unified
Imperial Law of Association had been under consideration in the
Reichstag. This was eventually introduced in 1908 after being delayed
by the reluctance of the individual States to give up any of their power
to the central authority.[9] In 1902, moreover, the Prussian Law of
Association was substantially modified in its application to women. A
policeman supervising a meeting of the Agrarian League — a powerful
Junker pressure-group[10] with very strong influence in the government
— at the Circus Busch in Berlin, noticed that a number of women were
present. Not daring to dissolve the meeting, the policeman decreed that
the women could stay as long as they did not participate. This ruling
was confirmed by the Prussian Minister of the Interior, Baron von
Hammerstein, himself a leading member of the Agrarian League, who
added however that women must occupy a special 'segment' of the
assembly hall. The SPD seized upon this measure, as the law had
hitherto frequently been used as an excuse to break up SPD meetings.
From now on, women attended many SPD meetings undisturbed, as
long as part of the hall was marked off with a line of chalk or a piece of
string to denote what was inevitably referred to as 'Hammerstein's
segment'.[11] This was a sign of the growing dissatisfaction even of the
police with the Law of Association. As it became more and more
apparent that women would be admitted to political organisations in
the not very distant future, police administration of the law became
more lenient, all the more so after the founding meeting of the
International Woman Suffrage Alliance, with many delegates from
abroad, was held in Berlin in 1904.[12] Nevertheless the fact remained
that until 1908 it was illegal for women to engage actively in politics in
Prussia and many other parts of Germany. Although some suffragist[13]
groups were founded in Prussia before 1908, their activities were
severely restricted and they remained a loosely and unofficially co-
ordinated collection of local organisations until the new law came into
effect.

The centre of the Suffrage Union's activities thus remained in
Hamburg for the time being. The foundation of the new organisation
was well-publicised and attracted a good deal of attention in the Press,

where comment was not wholly unfavourable, as the *Hamburgischer Correspondent* remarked on 2 February 1902.[14] The conservative *Kreuzzeitung* declared that the suffrage movement would contribute to the growth of socialism, if it was not an agency of the Social Democratic Party anyway. But such opponents could only do the movement good, according to the liberal *Neue Hamburger Zeitung* which devoted a long leader to the subject on 2 February 1902. It linked the new foundation with a recent debate in the Reichstag and noted that a conservative deputy, von Kardorff, had claimed that if female suffrage existed, many a Social Democratic deputy would lose his seat. The *Frankfurter Zeitung* had long favoured female suffrage, but the other great liberal newspaper, the *Berliner Tageblatt,* was reluctant to lend the suffragists its support at first. It changed its mind in 1904 after the International Congress, and the anti-Semitic *Deutsches Blatt* had an explanation ready: 'The foremost law of Jewry is', it observed, referring to the paper's Jewish owner, 'always serve the idol of the day.'[15]

The *Deutsches Blatt* at least was unlikely to change its mind. It was convinced that female suffrage would lead to the destruction of femininity and the end of the family. Newspapers of this kind could be expected to oppose any extension of the suffrage at all; the dangers and uncertainties of female suffrage were thought too great for it to be worth the risk. The liberal Press, lukewarm though it may have been at first, soon came down more firmly behind the suffragists, perhaps stimulated by these attacks, and before long several papers were employing leading feminists to write occasional articles on the women's movement. Already in 1901 Minna Cauer could remark that:

> a decade ago, every woman who supported the entry of women into the Universities was 'emancipated'. . . . About five years ago, even women who called themselves friends and acquaintances of the women's movement prophesied its downfall as middle-class women called popular assemblies in which statements were made on current affairs. Today, at least in the capital city, people are immediately dissatisfied and accuse the leaders of the women's movement of forgetting their duty if they do not take a public stand on notable events.[16]

The attitude of the national papers, most of which had a regular column on the women's movement by the middle of the decade, was in her view much more enlightened than that of the provincial Press. She condemned in the same article '. . . the foolish, laughable, sometimes brutal way in which the provincial papers express themselves', and declared roundly that 'not one of these leader-writers understands anything about the basic ideas of the women's movement.' Nevertheless, the national Press at least, and in particular the liberal papers and the Social Democratic *Vorwärts,* provided a valuable service to the suffragists in making their ideas and development of their campaign generally known to the reading public. Their reports were often written by women active in the feminist movement, and the occasional leading article devoted to the movement, although often critical, was also generally – in the Social Democratic *Vorwärts* as well as the liberal *Berliner Tageblatt* – sympathetic to the suffragists.

The Press was one valuable means of publicity for the suffrage movement; leaflets were another. The Suffrage Union's first leaflet, addressed 'to the women of Germany', began by arguing that the women's movement had failed to achieve any concrete reforms and would continue to fail until the suffrage had been won.[17] That it could be won by the suffragists' own efforts was understood. Indeed, Lida Gustava Heymann claimed that the universal male suffrage in operation for the Reichstag since 1871 was not granted by Bismarck but achieved by the liberals' pressure.[18] Similar pressure on the part of the feminists, she implied, was equally destined for ultimate success. For Heymann and the other founders of the Suffrage Union, the struggle for the vote was an extension of the struggle for the dignity of the individual woman which they had been waging in their fight to abolish the State regulation of prostitution:

Only under the one-sided legislation of a man's State is it possible – as in Germany – for women to be put on a par with criminals, idiots, wards of court, bankrupts, schoolchildren and apprentices (declared a suffragist leaflet issued in 1907): A State, a people consists of men and women, and it follows that the laws under which a people lives must be made by men *and* women if the rights of women are not – as experience shows – to be perpetually curtailed.[19]

Although the human dignity of the individual woman would only be complete when she had full political equality, it did not follow for the suffragists that the struggle for the vote was being waged simply in order to give the individual woman the means of political self-expression. On the contrary, it was also being waged in order to implement a far-reaching programme of moral and social reform. The last thing the suffragists wanted was – as eventually happened – the absorption of women into the existing political system. The radical feminists were in fact, as the experience of 1898-1902 showed, highly critical of the existing political system. They hoped that it would be thoroughly regenerated by female suffrage. This regeneration was conceived by the suffragists in moral terms. In the first place, as Frieda Radel, who came to prominence in the Hamburg radical feminist movement from 1906 onwards, said, it would bring back idealism into politics which had been corrupted by the growth of economic pressure-groups.[20]

> Our politics today (she remarked) has lost those high ideals which once led our fathers to the self-confident demand and achivement of political emancipation. Our politics in the main is conducted by economic interests . . . Woman is called to reintroduce the ethical, ideal element, to give politics once more that wide vision which leads beyond the petty struggles of parties of different hues to the solution of social and cultural problems.[21]

The suffragists' long-term political aims were closely connected with the Abolitionists' programme of moral reform. 'We believe it to be our duty', explained Minna Cauer, 'to educate State and society so that a recognition of our equal rights is not only (seen as) a necessity, but also as desirable for the maintenance of order, manners and morality.'[22] Once again there was the liberal individualist accent on self-discipline and self-help. 'Women', said Martha Zietz, 'must be accustomed to self-discipline, to devotion to the generality, to an active life. Morality *(Ethik)* must form the basis of the political economy, only men of high moral standing must be called upon to make laws.'[23]

Thus the aims of the Suffrage Union included not only the abolition of State-regulated prostitution but also – after 1907 – the introduction of the local option on the licensing of bars and beer-halls. In 1908 the Union protested against the use of bars and inns as polling stations. It was not simply that, as the main suffragist periodical *Zeitschrift für Frauenstimmrecht* (Women's Suffrage Magazine), published as a supplement to the *Frauenbewegung,* remarked, '. . . it has often happened in towns and in the countryside that when men have carried out the most noble right of the citizen, namely the right to vote, they have appeared at the ballot-box not in control of their senses, tottering on their feet'.[24] The suffragists believed further that the granting of votes for women would lead to a society that would be more ordered, more self-controlled and, as they saw it, more moral in every respect.

In many ways, therefore, the suffrage movement was as much a moral crusade as a struggle for legislative reform, and transcended the merely political. In 1908 the Union claimed in a leaflet that:

> Women's suffrage spreads culture!
> *Women's Suffrage* raises the level of politics. Political life will be removed from the pub to an increasing degree and taken into the home. Excesses at election time will vanish. Only candidates of blameless character will receive support from women.
> *Women's Suffrage* demands the raising of the age of majority. In Australia the age of majority has been raised from 14 to 18 since women gained the vote.
> *Women's Suffrage* encourages peace and harmony between different peoples.
> *Women's Suffrage* effectively promotes abstinence and thus prevents the ruin of a people through alcohol.
> *Women's Suffrage* opposes the exploitation of the economically and physically weak, it takes pity on children and tormented animals, it makes laws against cruelty to animals and the exploitation of their working strength to exhaustion.[25]

In this programme of moral reform the suffragists were expressing the wider social implications of liberal individualism. Although they were hostile to the State, they were prepared to use it to legislate for equal rights and opportunities and for ordered behaviour on the part of its citizens. However they placed an equal or even greater faith in the ability of the individual to discipline himself, and constantly tried to reduce State intervention in the individual's life to a minimum.

The last paragraph in this leaflet of 1908 is perhaps the most interesting. The lower income groups ('the economically weak'), it assumes, can be put on a par with 'children and tormented animals'; society's duty is to prevent the exploitation of these groups in the sense that it should prevent 'cruelty to animals' and, it seems to imply, cruelty to the poor. But the poor, it also assumes, like helpless animals and defenceless children, will always be with us. Like the English suffragettes, Augspurg and her followers opposed the introduction of laws to prevent the employment of women in certain dangerous occupations, or to stop their exploitation in others.[26] This, they believed, was unfair discrimination against women, an unwarrantable restriction on their freedom of choice and action.

Another limitation in the female suffragist ideology lay in its sense of the realities of the political situation in which it found itself. Ultimately, the suffragists conceived their function as removing obstacles to the establishment of a meritocratic society with equal opportunities for all. That such obstacles could be removed by a few legislative strokes achieved with the aid of female suffrage, they did not doubt. Even less did they appear to doubt that their own campaign for the vote would be granted with rapid success. This naive political optimism was soon to be confounded. Nevertheless it signified a startling departure from the previous insistence of the women's movement on the need to wait for more rights until women had proved, especially by service in welfare organisations and in local administration, their ability and willingness to fulfil their duties to the State and the community.

women's rights was perhaps to be expected, in view of the growing political self-assertiveness of the Abolitionists and radicals in the years 1898-1902; yet it still marked it off sharply from the 'moderate' majority of the women's movement.

Even so, despite the fact that the Suffrage Union was less insistent than any other part of the women's movement that women should get the vote because they were fulfilling their duties to the State, this was nonetheless a constant and recurring theme in its propaganda. 'As civil servants, as teachers, as taxpayers, as social workers', declared an early suffragist leaflet,[27] 'thousands of women carry out the *duties* of citizens: they are therefore fully justified in demanding the *rights* of citizens as well.' This went further than the moderates, who did not even believe the first part of the leaflet's assertion; according to them, women still had to prove that they were fulfilling their duties as citizens. Still, it was a concession to the moderate mentality, and as time went on some radicals became unhappy about it:

> Nothing is . . . more foolish (said Minna Cauer in 1913)[28] and more indicative of immaturity or ignorance of political problems, than the perpetual repetition of the idea that the suffrage movement is an appendage of social welfare associations of women, or, as is also presented to us again and again as a new revelation, that political rights will be given to women because of their 'achievements'.

For Cauer and the other suffragists, radical aims demanded radical tactics. Because they wanted not simply to gain equal political rights but to regenerate society and reform the entire political system, they felt it was necessary to employ the tactics of a moral crusade rather than the quiet, steady pressure that had been usual in the women's movement before the turn of the century. The Suffrage Union was to be a *Kampfbund,* an organisation built on and existing for political struggle.

It was, however, a sign of their political immaturity at this stage that the suffragists did not realise the full implications of the dilemma that faced them. They wanted the vote to bring about a fundamental reform of society; yet only such a reform could in fact bring the vote in the first place. Under the existing political system, it was unlikely even that all men would win equal political rights in Prussia and the other states without a revolution. There was little sign of a growth in the influence of the Reichstag, on which the suffragists ultimately depended in the hypothetical post-female suffrage world for the implementation of all their grandiose plans of moral reform. Their tactics were in fact only appropriate to a constitutional system based on universal suffrage and the sovereignty of Parliament. In the early years of the movement, however, they were very far from realising this awkward fact, and despite their desire to reform the existing political system they began by working within it.

THE LIBERAL PHASE, 1902-1908

The struggle for the vote began in Berlin on 12 February 1902, when 1000 people attended an open meeting chaired by Anita Augspurg, President of the German Union for Women's Suffrage. Augspurg outlined three immediate aims for the suffragists: first, they must persuade those women who already possessed the suffrage to exercise it. Secondly they must support in elections those candidates who declared themselves in favour of votes for women. Thirdly they must give women a political education that would mobilise them for the struggle for the vote, and they must teach them what to do with the vote once the struggle was won.

We have seen that there were perhaps some 2000 property-owning

women in Germany entitled to vote in certain elections, usually
through a male proxy. The Suffrage Union thought it important that
these women should make the best use of their rights, if only to
demonstrate that women *could* vote; they looked up women property
owners in the tax records and sent them admonitions to vote, instruc-
tions on how to do it and even the blank form empowering the proxy.
They were not above encouraging evasion of the proxy rule. 'I know of
women in Munich', said Augspurg approvingly, 'who go to the polls
themselves in spite of the law that tells them to vote by a male proxy,
and the returning officer allows them to do so.'[29] The suffragists also
tried to extend the suffrage to women by exploiting ambiguities in the
law. Such attempts, generally based on the assertion that the word
'person' covered both sexes, invariably came to nothing. In October
1906 for example Minna Cauer tried to get herself put on the electoral
roll for the local council in Berlin-Charlottenburg on this basis. The
SPD councillors contended that what people had thought when the
laws were made was irrelevant. 'We have to take decisions according to
existing circumstances', one of them said, 'and under the latter, women
undoubtedly play a role in public life.' It was decided, however, by the
majority in the council that the assumption that the suffrage was
exclusively male was implicit in the electoral laws of 1808 and 1831.
Cauer's claim was thus rejected, as were similar claims made in the same
period by – among others – Lida Gustava Heymann, who threatened to
refuse to pay her taxes if she were denied citizenship – a threat she
does not seem to have carried out.[30] Such tactics were common to
most women's suffrage movements, and they were probably suggested
to the German suffragists by the example of suffragists in England and
America.

The last aim enunciated by Augspurg at the inaugural meeting of the
Union in February 1902, that of giving women a political education,
was vaguer and less easy to achieve. The Suffrage Union did not have its
own periodical and had to use Minna Cauer's *Die Frauenbewegung* as a
vehicle for its propaganda, thus reaching committed members of the
radical feminist movement who were likely to favour female suffrage
and have a relatively high degree of political education anyway. Some
leaflets and books were produced, but in the main the suffragists
continued the well-tried methods of the Abolitionists. Public attention
was aroused by large-scale protest meetings and public assemblies, and

an attempt was made to retain it by putting on weekly or monthly series of lectures on German politics and government. Often the speaker at the latter was a prominent figure in Hamburg liberal politics.

In the meantime, however, the suffragists began to concentrate their attention on the third problem touched on by Augspurg in her inaugural speech – the bringing to bear of suffragist influence on national politics. The Union's first action was to send a deputation to the Imperial Chancellor Bülow. Thirty-five women from various branches of the radical women's movement were led by Augspurg and were politely received by the Chancellor. They put their demands – freedom of association, equality of educational opportunity and the deletion of Section 361/6 of the Criminal Code – and were assured by the Chancellor that he was fully aware of the importance of their demands. He could promise them nothing, however. 'It should not be forgotten that I am not all-powerful', he said, hinting that he was more favourably inclined towards female emancipation than most of his colleagues.[31] Augspurg and her associates declared themselves satisfied with the way the interview had gone.[32] 'The ladies have spoken friendly words to Herr Bülow', commented the SPD newspaper *Vorwärts* ironically on 22 March, 'Herr Bülow has spoken friendly words to the ladies, and they have departed in peace and friendship. What more can one wish of an audience? ' That anything could be solved by a 'Bülow smile' the paper doubted. The suffragists, however, thought it worthwhile to try and obtain an audience with Bülow's successor Bethmann Hollweg when he came to power in 1909; but when Bethmann, a far less flexible and imaginative man than Bülow, refused to receive them, they declared their intention of refraining from trying again as the new chancellor had shown himself 'reactionary in almost every respect'.[33]

The first real opportunity for the suffragists to make themselves felt on the political scene was provided by the Reichstag election of 1903. The executive committee revealed its thinking in a circular it sent to members in August 1902, asking them to inquire of the local Reichstag deputy whether he supported the Union's programme or any part of it, 'which could lead to the support of his re-election'.[34] The question of his views on suffrage, remarked another circular, need not be decisive because its immediate realisation was not a matter of practical politics. *Vorwärts* printed this circular on 7 May under the heading 'Suffragists against the suffrage'.[35] When the election actually came, the Union in Berlin issued a manifesto urging women to prove their political maturity by helping in the campaign.[36] The trouble was that the only major political organisation to support votes for women was the SPD. With remarkable optimism the suffragists declared in a resolution adopted at their inaugural meeting in Berlin on 12 February 1902 that they 'confidently expected that this point (i.e. female suffrage) would be adopted into the programme of every party at the next Reichstag election and energetically advocated'.[37] But if liberal and other bourgeois candidates refused to declare themselves in favour of votes for women, as they generally did, the Union was powerless.

These problems were particularly acute in Hamburg, the centre of the Union's activities. The suffragists had done nothing there in 1902 except found the organisation, but with the approach of the elections Augspurg descended upon the city and held the first meeting of the local branch on 3 January 1903. After a year of complete inactivity, in which the supporters of the suffrage in Hamburg had devoted all their efforts to the Abolitionist campaign, then reaching its height, the Suffrage Union in Hamburg burst into activity. Augspurg began by warning her audience that they stood at the beginning of a long and difficult road. Then she turned to a detailed consideration of suffragist tactics in Hamburg during the forthcoming elections. Although Hamburg was firmly in SPD hands, she said, it was nevertheless the duty of all members of the Union to work for the left-wing liberal candidates even if they stood no chance of success. 'The Social Democratic deputies', she said, 'always say in their election addresses that they will support the women's cause and female suffrage, but there is little to be expected from this party for women; where it should have actively intervened in favour of female suffrage, it has totally failed.' This was perhaps not particularly convincing in a city whose Reichstag deputies included August Bebel, the man who had devoted more time and energy to supporting the women's cause than any other politician in Germany, and who was the first person to bring a motion demanding female suffrage before the Reichstag. Still, it seems to have sufficed for Augspurg's listeners, and in 1906 it was to some extent actually borne out when the SPD in Hamburg confined itself to demanding universal manhood suffrage for the City Council.[38]

As for the National Liberals, Augspurg does not even seem to have thought of trying to influence them. Not only were they clearly on the side of the government and the ruling classes in the political struggles of this period, but they also adopted consistently critical attitudes to female emancipation. Their 1887 Handbook opposed the legal equality of husband and wife in marriage, and the 1907 Handbook launched a strong attack on 'radical tendencies' within the women's movement that ignored the 'differences between the sexes intended by nature'.[39] Augspurg therefore advised her audience to work as a body for the candidate of the Liberal People's Party (Freisinnige Volkspartei) in the second Hamburg division, by raising funds, distributing leaflets and performing minor secretarial tasks.[40] There is no record of the candidate in question ever having appeared at a suffragist meeting or declared himself in favour of votes for women. But this was irrelevant: the aim of Augspurg's tactic was to get women enough influence in the party to persuade it to write female suffrage into its programme. She had already made a brief attempt at the same thing with the South German People's Party (Süddeutsche Volkspartei).[41] Hamburg was, like Baden, an area where women could join political parties, but the local branch of the Liberal People's Party had hitherto refused to admit women. On 11 April 1903 Augspurg and Heymann asked it to reverse this policy.

The motion to admit women was discussed at a crowded meeting held on 23 May. After a heated debate lasting two and a half hours, in which opponents of the motion argued that acceptance meant acceptance of female suffrage and alleged that the Social Democrats had found their women members 'very troublesome', and supporters said that if they rejected the women they would turn to another party, the motion was passed by 38 votes to 21 and women were admitted.[42] The party as a whole soon afterwards decided that women could join in all states where the Law of Association permitted it. Subsequently women were elected to the party's committee and took part in the party's congresses as delegates.[43] Although the chairman of the Hamburg meeting warned that the suffragists' achievement was not as important as the women liked to think, Augspurg and Heymann threw themselves and their followers into election work for the party with gusto. The results were disappointing. The Social Democrat was elected and the liberals did not incorporate female suffrage into their programme. Nevertheless, it was a start. In the Hamburg elections that followed at the end of the year, Martha Zietz referred to the 'useful assistance given by women at the Reichstag elections', and once more Union members were mobilised to help liberal candidates and those Citizens' Associations *(Bürgervereine)* that would permit it. Previous efforts on the part of the Union to have women admitted to the Citizens' Associations had been rejected 'amid laughter', but during the elections women were allowed to give voluntary secretarial help to some of the Associations.[44] This was again to no avail, for the Senate promptly set about revising the suffrage in Hamburg by introducing a property franchise on Prussian lines in order to ward off the threat from the SPD. The new suffrage law was passed early in 1906 amid protests, including those of the female suffragists.

By now Augspurg was a well-known public figure whose name was invoked on all sorts of occasions. At the end of 1905, for example, a Reichstag deputy from Oldenburg declared that 'we would be in a better position as regards the meat shortage if Dr. Anita Augspurg and Rosa Luxemburg stood at the cooking-pot.' Augspurg's reply was to send him a copy of the cookery book she had written and published in the early 1890s.[45] Her authority at this time seems to have been such that no objections were raised within the movement to her decision to support the Liberal People's Party, even though party-political neutrality was written into the statutes. The National Social Party in Hamburg protested that it had been admitting women as members for years, and urged the suffragists not to put their trust in people 'who sleep for five years, only to wake up four weeks before the election'.[46] The driving force in left-wing liberalism for the women's movement was indeed the National Social group. The Liberal People's Party had not made a statement on female emancipation since 1894, when it had confined itself to urging that more professions should be opened to women provided this did not entail any neglect of 'the most important female profession, that of housewife and mother.'[47] The group of National Social politicians only acquired significance when they joined the Liberal Alliance (Freisinnige Vereinigung) in 1903, carrying their enthusiasm for women's rights over into their new political home. In 1904 the 'Frankfurt Minimal Programme' of the Liberal Alliance incorporated some of their demands, and in 1908 the Alliance's party congress passed a resolution demanding full and equal political rights for women at all levels.[48]

The Liberal People's Party however was by far the largest of the left-wing liberal groups, and Augspurg was probably right if also ambitious to nail her colours to its mast. After their initial success in Hamburg however the suffragists met with a series of rebuffs from the party. In the Reichstag debate of 7 February 1906, the Liberal People's Party spokesman rejected the demand for female suffrage on the grounds that it was premature:

> We are certainly very favourably disposed towards the efforts of women to gain more rights for themselves. But to step as far as the final goal, as far as the suffrage for the German *Reichstag,* seems to me now as a leap in the dark, perhaps a *salto mortale.* Women are certainly fully the equals of men in devotion to duty, shrewdness, and also in loquacity (laughter). But, I do not yet believe we have reached the right moment. I believe that the active and passive suffrage for women should be the last stage in the structure of women's rights; but as long as the foundations of this edifice have not been firmly laid, I still have doubts as to whether we should straight away proceed to add the final touches to a structure which is still unstable.

Moreover in its 'minimal programme' — issued for the projected union of the three left-liberal parties on 10 November 1906 — the party, while recognising the need for opening more offices to women in local government and social welfare, refused to declare itself in favour of female suffrage once more. Even the National Social Union did not declare itself explicitly in favour of votes for women although some of its local associations, particularly in Baden, supported the idea.[49] They saw the suffrage as the crowning touch added to the edifice of women's rights. The suffragists however saw it as the foundation. In March 1907 Augspurg declared that 'Liberalism must include the demand for female suffrage on its programme: If it fails to do so, the women will draw the necessary conclusions.'[50] This was a clear threat to break with the left-liberals. Minna Cauer indeed, with fewer illusions than Augspurg, said as early as 1904 that she would believe the politicians' promises when they wrote female suffrage into their programme.[51] Although the Hamburg suffragists still helped the liberals in the 1906 elections for the City Council, comforting themselves with the thought that the liberals' programme was after all one of minimum demands, the united liberals of Hamburg continued to refuse to support votes for women.[52] Disillusion spread to Bavaria. The Bavarian feminists, led by Ika Freudenberg, pleaded in 1905 for a response from the Bavarian liberals.

Many of their number, they said, had joined the Social Democrats in disgust at the failure of the liberals to support their cause. This plea evoked no response.[53]

The bankruptcy of the Hamburg suffragists' policy was made quite clear in 1908, when they agreed to work for the candidate of the Liberal Alliance in Altona even though he had strongly rejected the idea of female suffrage.[54] The Berlin suffragists were more cautious, but their hopes had never been as high as those of their Hamburg colleagues. In 1908 they sent a questionnaire on female suffrage to all the Berlin Reichstag candidates except the Social Democrats who, it was assumed, would be in favour in any case. When only two candidates, Breitscheid and Witt, replied in the affirmative, the branch advised its members to support only these two or any Social Democrat.[55] This did not go unnoticed in the SPD: how long, wondered *Vorwärts* in 1908, could the suffragists go on deceiving themselves as to the true nature of the liberal parties? Perhaps the *Hamburgischer Correspondent* had been right in suspecting that Hellmuth von Gerlach and the liberals were only using the suffragists as 'party slaves' to lick stamps and write addresses on envelopes, without being prepared to make any meaningful concessions in return.[56]

For Anita Augspurg the final disillusionment came when the left-wing liberals joined with the Conservatives and the National Liberals in 1907 to form a government 'Block' in the Reichstag. Augspurg declared her hostility to this policy in the general assembly of the Prussian suffragists in 1908, comparing the Block liberals with the old liberalism of Eugen Richter: 'A few years ago, one believed that the Liberal People's Party was held back by its old leader, and one expected a powerful upsurge after its departure. But one must now give the dead Richter his due credit: the *Blockpolitik* would not have been possible in his day.' In a public meeting held under Cauer's Presidency after the Assembly was over, Augspurg declared that the Block liberals had sold their dearest principles for a mess of conservative potage. The women must now take things into their own hands. From now on, she said, feminists would put their trust in their own militancy instead of the empty promises of men. Words would at last be followed by deeds.[57]

INDEPENDENT MILITANCY,
1908-1912

The change of direction which the suffrage movement took as a result of its leaders' disillusion with left-wing liberal politics was accompanied by several other developments which make the year 1908 a turning-point in the movement's history. In 1907 Anita Augspurg and Lida Gustava Heymann left Hamburg and went to live in Munich, which now became a third centre of the female suffrage movement. The passage of the Imperial Law of Association freed the suffragists not only in Munich but also in Prussia and Saxony from legal restraints after it came into force on 15 May 1908. The Prussian suffrage organisations led by Minna Cauer formed a Prussian Union for Women's Suffrage (Preussischer Landesverein für Frauenstimmrecht). Controlled from Berlin, this now became the bastion of radicalism within the national suffragist movement. With over a quarter of the total membership of the Union, it exercised on the suffragist movement an influence from the left comparable with that exercised by Prussia on the German Empire as a whole from the right. Before 1908, however, such Prussian branches as existed had of necessity pursued an independent existence, and many of them, especially in the Rhineland, resented the sudden imposition of strong control from Berlin. This was to have unfortunate consequences for the movement later on. Meanwhile a similar re-organisation took place in other federal states, including Bavaria. The Union as a whole was at last able to constitute itself as a properly organised national political society with regional divisions corres-ponding to the federal structure of the Empire.[58]

At the same time the new centralised organisation of the Union helped Augspurg in her attempt to translate her disillusion with left-wing liberalism into practical political terms. She tried to put the Union on an independently militant basis, and turned to the suffragettes in England for inspiration. The English suffragettes had already by 1908 developed highly organised publicity and propaganda methods to draw attention to their cause. These were also used to a lesser extent by the constitutional suffragists in England. When the German Press con-sidered the possibility that suffragette methods might be exported to Germany, it thought primarily in terms of the violence that was already becoming a feature of the suffragette campaign. 'If Anita Augspurg has any say in the matter', commented the *Hamburger Fremdenblatt* in 1907, at the end of a report on suffragette disturbances outside the House of Commons in London, 'it will soon be the turn of the German Reichstag to be threatened by such storms.'[59] But violence was never contemplated by the German Suffrage Union. The methods imported were esentially peaceful, however much they might have been designed, like the Abolitionist agitation, to catch the public eye through sensationalism.

The first German suffragist leader to attend an English suffragette meeting was, predictably, Anita Augspurg, who led 30 German women in a demonstration for women's suffrage in Hyde Park on 21 June 1908.[60] She visited London again in the autumn of 1908 with Lida Gustava Heymann and again attended suffragette meetings.[61] Perhaps the first result of this was Heymann's proposal that the Union hold a self-denial week, in which members would deny themselves the usual pleasures of life and donate the money thus saved to the cause – an idea devised by the Salvation Army and subsequently taken up by the suffragette movement. This was indeed far from being the only respect in which the agitational methods of the Salvation Army served as a model for reforming crusades. When an English suffragette held a meeting in Hamburg in 1909, 'the tribune was appropriately decorated with the flower of angelic purity and innocence, with long-stemmed lilies' – so the *Hamburger Fremdenblatt.* 'The background of the tribune', continued the paper, 'and the committee table were adorned with flowers. And next to the speaker's desk the banner of the Hamburg-Altona Sisters in Struggle was defiantly planted. All this gave the impression of a Salvation Army meeting'.[62]

More significant than this, however, was the fact that the International Woman Suffrage Alliance had decided to hold its 1909 Conference in London. Although the suffragettes were not members of the Alliance, they spared no pains in winning the sympathy of the delegates with their energy and determination. Anna Pappritz was impressed by the banners, the parades and the motorcades, though she added that delegates did not consider such methods exportable. Frieda Radel concluded, 'The fact is, it is the suffragettes who have made the female suffrage question a popular one in England.' Regine Deutsch, engaged for the occasion by the *Berliner Volkszeitung,* found it all strange but imposing. 'What is known here as moderate', she wrote from London, 'would still be the summit of outrageousness in Germany.' The lavish use of suffragist colours – green, purple and white – that characterised both wings of the suffrage movement in England, the processions through the streets, the badges, the banners, the ballyhoo: all this left a deep impression upon the German delegates.[63]

English suffragette leaders had already visited Germany – Annie Kenny and Mrs. Pethick Lawrence spoke at the Suffrage Union General Assembly in 1907 – but from now on they became regular visitors. Isabel Seymour visited Germany in December 1909, surprising the Press by her gentle, harmless appearance.[64] Eleonore Tyson spoke to an unusually crowded suffragist meeting in Hamburg on 21 May 1912. Emily Wilson made a number of speaking visits in the next few years, and in 1914 Sylvia Pankhurst herself toured Germany, to be banned by the police in Dresden and Berlin.[65] From now on, many of the propaganda devices of the English suffragettes began to appear on the German scene. An observer noted at the 1909 General Assembly of the Suffrage Union in Munich, 'Everywhere you look, you see in the early morning women with green, purple and white streamers hurrying through the streets'. The Assembly Hall itself was decorated in the same colours, and on 26 September a notice appeared in the Press announcing a prize of 200 marks to be given to the winner of a competition to design a motif for the Union, for use on brooches, banners and propaganda material. In 1912 the suffragists even composed and sang suffrage songs – 'Women's Suffrage Reveille' and the 'National Anthem for Women' among them.

Most important of all, the Berlin suffragists set about planning a procession through the streets. Outraged citizens protested to the Press on hearing the news – 'Do we men really want ourselves to be completely lorded-over by women?' asked one; 'Are we still the victor race of 1870-71?' The procession was planned to coincide with the opening of the Reichstag, then postponed until the introduction of the Prussian Suffrage Reform Bill. It was projected first in carriages and then on foot. Finally it was postponed indefinitely. A similar procession to be held in conjunction with the 1909 General Assembly in Munich was also put off at the last minute.[66] It was not in fact until 1912 that a procession was actually held, again in conjunction with a General Assembly of the Suffrage Union in Munich. On the morning of 24

September 1912 the suffragists set out from Schwabing in eighteen
landaus bedecked with the suffragist colours of green, purple and white,
with banners, flowers and posters, and drove through the streets of
Munich before finishing at the Chinese Tower in the English garden.
The drive went off without incident. The police were co-operative, the
people curious or indifferent. Beery old men stopped dead in their
tracks with amazement, well-mannered gentlemen raised their hats,
children shouted 'Hurrah! ' A few passers-by made remarks such as
'These are people who haven't managed to get a husband'. A working-
class woman came up and said 'How nice it is that the rich ladies should
want to work for us now! ' She received the reply that the suffragists
were all working women who wanted to do their best to help their
poorer sisters. Adele Schreiber remarked that the event drew the
attention of many to the fight for women's suffrage, but on the whole
the procession made little impact and it was not repeated.[67]

Such a procession was harmless enough. Indeed it bore very little
resemblance to the marches and parades of the suffragettes. In
Germany street demonstrations were the favoured instrument of the
Social Democrats, and the suffragists clearly wanted to avoid identification with this sort of tactic, especially as some Social Democrats such as
Rosa Luxemburg regarded such demonstrations as rehearsals for revolution. Also, they lacked the mass support necessary for an imposing
street procession, and on the whole were well-advised to use carriages.
On one occasion, however, something resembling a Social Democratic
demonstration did take place, after a meeting of the Berlin branch on
15 February 1910 in the Arnimhallen in Kommandantenstrasse, held to
protest against the Prussian Suffrage Bill. When the meeting was over
about 400 people gathered outside the hall and marched along the
Schützenstrasse towards the Chancellery singing the Marseillaise and
shouting 'Down with Bethmann Hollweg! ' The police were alerted and
sealed off the Chancellery. The crowd then shouted slogans in favour of
universal suffrage and dispersed. A group who tried to reach the
Chancellery from another direction were similarly turned back. Some
thought the incident had only occurred because the meeting had been
held in a quarter of Berlin where 'the populace is easily roused', and at
this particular time the political atmosphere in Berlin was extremely
tense. Two days previously, on 13 February, the SPD had held nationwide demonstrations and marches; in Berlin they had proceeded in an

orderly manner but elsewhere some serious clashes with the police had taken place. The events of 13 February signalled the beginning of a great wave of street demonstrations; some of these were joined or even organised by middle-class democrats, and the female suffragist protest march of 15 February was probably one of the earliest of such processions. It owed its origin to the exceptional political climate of the early months of 1910, in which left-liberals and Social Democrats joined in condemning with passion and a deep sense of outrage the totally inadequate proposals of the government for the reform of the suffrage. In general, then, the demonstration was most uncharacteristic of the suffragists. At any rate the police were taking no chances, and after the next meeting of the Berlin suffragists, at which Minna Cauer condemned the government as 'a Junker clique' and the Berlin police chief as 'a psychopath', and recalled that the women of 1848 had fought for their freedom with their blood, the hall was surrounded by police and the audience dispersed as they came out.[68]

There was much opposition within the suffragist movement to independent militancy. The subject of non-cooperation with the liberal parties was a major topic of debate at the Union's 1911 General Assembly. Toni Breitscheid, whose husband was a prominent left-wing liberal, argued that the only way to influence political parties in favour of female suffrage was to join them. 'Just as the Catholic women today are seeking to influence the Centre Party, so conservative and liberal women must join *their* Party.' Lida Gustava Heymann argued that experience had demonstrated the futility of this course. Many suffragists disagreed with her, despite the cogency of her argument that if they all joined political parties this would weaken and damage the Suffrage Union as the main forum for their political activities. Martha Zietz and Maria Lischnewska opposed this view, but the General Assembly eventually voted by the large majority of 37 delegates to 5 against offering any official help to political parties. What individual members did was their own affair; a number of them, including Minna Cauer, joined a left-liberal splinter-group called the Democratic Alliance (Demokratische Vereinigung), which had itself broken with the main body of liberals over the *Blockpolitik*. Cauer herself opposed the policy of independent action, and many of the leading figures went ahead and joined political groups as individuals.[69]

Augspurg and Heymann's attempt to pursue a policy of militant independence, initially necessitated by the break with the left-liberals, was given a further justification by the fact that once the passage of the Law of Association in 1908 allowed women to join political parties, the Suffrage Union no longer had a monopoly in the political field as far as middle-class women were concerned. In 1910 the united left-wing liberals opened their ranks to women, in the same year the National Liberal Party began to encourage its members to enlist the support of women in the political work, and the year 1912 even saw the foundation of an 'Alliance of Conservative Women'.[70] In aligning itself more strongly than ever before with the world-wide, non-party-political struggle for women's rights, Augspurg and Heymann could thus claim that the Suffrage Union was acting in self-defence by providing a clear alternative to the existing political parties. The policy was one of defence against the centrifugal effects of the new Law of Association. It is therefore not surprising to find the two suffragist leaders issuing strong expressions of solidarity with the English suffragettes, who were involved in an increasingly violent battle with Asquith's government. In an article which throws an interesting light on the nature of their perception of English politics and society, Augspurg and Heymann declared that the reports of suffragette excesses appearing in the German newspapers were all lies. 'All these fables about attacks on human life, art treasures, animals, are barefaced lies and slanders . . . All the bombs that are supposed to have been found in well-frequented places were put there by police agents and informers . . .'[71] They issued declarations of solidarity with the imprisoned suffragettes and sent protests to Asquith about the treatment of Mrs Pankhurst and her followers on hunger strike in prison.

But the condemnation of suffragette excesses issued by the BDF probably corresponded to the views of most German suffragists,[72] even if they might object to the assertion that militancy and radicalism were foreign to the nature of woman. In declaring their solidarity with the suffragettes, Augspurg and Heymann did not have the support of most of their followers. To some it seemed that fear of the reproduction of suffragette excesses in Germany would help the suffrage movement. One Reichstag deputy from Schweinfurt remarked that 'We must grant the women's demands to some extent or we shall provoke an anger in them that can eventually lead to English conditions.' On the other hand there were those who argued that the suffragettes made things difficult for the women's movement in Germany by alienating potential supporters.[73]

In fact there was little or no evidence to support either view. As an independent political organisation the Suffrage Union made its greatest strides forward in these years. The growth in the Union's membership was overwhelmingly concentrated in the years after 1907; before then it can hardly be said to have existed as an organisation outside Hamburg, Bremen and Frankfurt. In 1908 these three were still the only branches that were financially independent and able to return figures to the Statistical Office's inquiry. It was between 1906 and 1908 that the great majority of the Union's branches were founded, and it was really only after the passage of the Law of Association in 1908 that the movement began to get off the ground as an organisation. In 1908 membership was still very small indeed, and most of the Union's branches had only just been founded.

After this, however, membership increased by leaps and bounds. Of the branches in the big cities Hamburg was the largest, rising from 196 members in 1908 to 400 in 1919, 640 in 1911, 800 in 1912 and 850 in 1913. It thus overtook Berlin, which in 1908 had 287 members, nearly 100 more than Hamburg, and in 1911 had 572, almost 70 fewer. In 1912 the Berlin organisation was split up into a number of smaller branches. The fastest-growing branch of the Union was, however, Bremen, which increased in strength from 144 in 1908, four years after its foundation, to 452 in 1912 and 646 in 1913.

No other branches existed on this scale, but other centres of the Abolitionist movement were well represented. Dresden had 92 members in 1908, rising to 132 in 1911, 187 in 1912 and 190 in 1913; Stuttgart could count on 210 members in 1913. The Union was also well represented in the Rhineland; in 1913 it had 100 members in Darmstadt, 105 in Mainz, 180 in Düsseldorf and no fewer than 200 in Cologne, where there had only been half as as many members in 1911. The radical-dominated Prussian Suffrage Union numbered 700 in 1908, rose rapidly to 1300 as it became organised, and by 1913 contributed 4200 members to the Union's total membership of 9000. By then the other provincial Unions numbered about 1000 each. The Union as a whole gained about 1000 members every year after 1911, reaching almost 10,000 on the outbreak of war in August 1914.[74]

TABLE 2

Membership of the German Union for Women's Suffrage, 1908

Branch	Year founded	Members Women	Men	Total
Prussian Union	1908	838	62	900
− Berlin	1907	254	21	275
Bunzlau	1907	12		12
Frankfurt/Main	1904	254	27	281
Liegnitz		12	2	14
Magdeburg	1908	19		19
Württemberg Union	1907	135	27	162
− Stuttgart	1906	86	16	102
Tübingen	1907	15	7	22
Ulm	1907	27	3	30
Baden Union	1907	380	35	415
− Baden-Baden	1908	17	2	19
Freiburg	1907	63	4	67
Heidelberg	1906	59	7	66
Karlsruhe	1906	26	3	29
Konstanz	1906	107	7	114
Mannheim	1906	88	12	100
Hesse Union	1907	219	31	250
− Darmstadt	1907	54	12	66
Mainz	1907	98	6	104
Bad Nauheim	1908	10	2	12
Worms	1907	57	11	68
Central German Union (Leipzig)	1906	50	25	75
Hamburg Union	1905	140	20	160
Bremen Union	1904	130	6	136
Total	1902	2242	216	2458

Source: *Statistik der Frauenorganisationen im Deutschen Reiche* (1. Sonderheft zum Reichsarbeitsblatte, Berlin 1909).

These figures are of course only approximate. If we include in the total estimate of organised female suffragists in 1914 the members of other female suffrage societies, which we shall have occasion to discuss

TABLE 3

Income and Expenditure of the German Union for Women's Suffrage
1907-1908

Branch	INCOME				EXPENDITURE				
	Subscriptions	Donations	Others	Total	Admin.	Propaganda	Others	Total	Balance
Hamburg	800			800	130	241	327	698	102
Frankfurt	1047			1047	62	497	201	760	287
Bremen	211	10	38	259	29	59	171	259	102
Central Organisation	8166	2586	432	9184	3019	3328	1944	8921	398

Source: *Statistik der Frauenorganisationen im Deutschen Reiche* (1. Sonderheft zum Reichsarbeitsblatte, Berlin, 1909). Figures in Marks.

later on, then we can safely say that the female suffrage movement
numbered 14,000 and probably more. One other female suffrage organisation had 2400 members in 1913, and if we add other suffragist
organisations to our total of the Hamburg Union branch in 1913 we
arrive at 1086 Hamburg suffragists instead of 850. Clearly the movement's strength was increasing quite rapidly in the years 1908-1914.[75]

The Union achieved its growth of support by a combination of
public meetings and regular gatherings of members once they had
joined. Supporters were attracted by public meetings at which basic
ideas about female suffrage ('Why must women concern themselves
with politics? ') were discussed, or encouraging accounts given of the
progress of the struggle for women's rights in other countries or topical
issues seized upon and their interest for women demonstrated. Attendance in Hamburg, at least during the period for which we have police
figures, generally ran between 150 and 200, falling below this only
when the subject was dull or the speaker indifferent or unfamiliar.
Rudolf Breitscheid could only muster 100 suffragists to hear him speak
on women and politics in 1908, and a lecture by Heinz Potthoff on the
Imperial Insurance scheme in March 1911 could only attract 70
listeners. 410 people went to see Eleonore Tyson the suffragette speak
in May 1912, when suffragette outrages were hitting the German
headlines and the subject obviously had sensational value, but the largest
audiences were attracted by Adele Schreiber whom newspaper reports
agree in describing as one of the most spellbinding of feminist
orators.[76] In January 1909 450 people attended her talk on 'the new
ideal woman', and no fewer than 600 attended when she spoke on
'child poverty and women's suffrage'. There was no noticeable falling-
off in support over the period, nor can one discern any seasonal
variation in attendance. Meetings were not held in the summer months.
Attendance seems to have been determined largely by speaker and
subject. It is striking, therefore, that the suffragists' public meetings were
attended in Hamburg by approximately the same size of audience as
those of the Abolitionists, but that their membership in the city was
over eight times as large.

The police were careful to note the proportion of men to women at
suffragist meetings. This too varied with speaker and subject. The
suffragist audience in Hamburg generally included between 10 percent
and 20 percent men, the percentage rising when a male politician spoke

and declining when the speaker was a woman. For a meeting in 1912 on 'inflation', a popular topic with the suffragists, 150 women turned up but only five men, yet of the 100 who attended Rudolf Breitscheid's lecture in 1908 30 were men. At Heinz Potthoff's lecture in 1911 there were only ten fewer men than women. The attendance figures for the two General Assemblies of the Suffrage Union held in Hamburg are of especial interest. 490 women and only ten men attended the first in 1903, but the second in 1912 was attended by 800 women and no fewer than 250 men.[77] Clearly the suffrage movement was making an impact upon the male community, although the German Men's League for Women's Suffrage (Deutsche Männerliga für Frauenstimmrecht) established by Hellmuth von Gerlach and Heinz Potthoff in March 1914 on the lines of similar enterprises in England and America, never really had a chance to get under way before the outbreak of the war.[78]

The fact that the female suffrage movement was growing steadily in size should not, however, be allowed to obscure the fact that in a number of ways it was running into difficulties by the end of the first decade of the 20th century. Numerically, of course, despite continual expansion, it was still very small and was in no sense a mass movement. Indeed it can hardly even be called a popular movement. Moreover, as the debate over the advantages and disadvantages of independent militancy went on unresolved, it seems to have suffered a kind of tactical paralysis. On the one hand it refused to attempt to enlist the support of political parties, in particular the left-liberals, in the way that it had done in the years 1902-1907, thus depriving itself of the only conceivable allies who could influence matters in its favour. On the other hand it stopped short of devising any viable alternative to co-operating with politicians. On the face of it the only course open to the suffragists, if they rejected the idea of enlisting help from political parties led by men, was to follow the example of the English suffragettes, if not in their violence then at least in the vigour of their propaganda. Yet even the procession through the streets proved too radical for most members of the Suffrage Union because it was an essentially SPD tactic. The increase in membership was large enough to give rise to a number of tensions and disputes within the Suffrage Union. The controversy over the alternatives of independent militancy or cooperation with political parties was really one of a number of disputes. Unlike the more serious and ultimately more disastrous quarrels that followed, it was never resolved one way or the other.

In failing to reach a decision on the issue, the suffragists got the worst of all possible worlds. Responding as so often in the course of their development to changes in the general political situation, they had broken with the left-liberals in 1907-08 as the left-liberals had moved towards an endorsement of the Wilhelmine political system by joining a parliamentary coalition — the Bülow Block — formed in order to support the government. The logic behind this break with the left-liberals was far from totally unconvincing. After all, for votes for women to become a reality, far-reaching changes would have to take place in the political system of Germany. To begin with, universal suffrage would have to be introduced in the federal States. Yet not only did the *Land* governments show no signs of giving in on this issue, they were actually engaged in moving further away from an equitable franchise in these years. In order to ward off the growing threat from the SPD, Saxony abolished its moderately liberal suffrage in 1896 and introduced the Prussian three-class system; Lübeck followed suit in 1903-04, and Hamburg introduced a four-class system in 1906.[79] In these moves the Imperial Government offered encouragement, not criticism. Under such circumstances, the only sensible course for the female suffrage movement was therefore to continue opposing the existing political system and agitating for its fundamental reform. Viewed from this angle, it was therefore right to break with the left-liberals in 1907. Indeed there is evidence that the left-liberals themselves were far from unwilling to see the perpetuation of an inequitable franchise at a local and State level, since in many cases their own survival depended on excluding from power those classes who supported the Social Democrats.[80]

Yet the break was unfortunate. It cut off the suffragists from their most natural social and political allies. In the 'liberal' phase of the suffrage movement, men such as Ernst Müller-Meiningen had provided useful support and publicity for the suffragists. Through those left-liberal deputies who took an interest in their affairs, the suffragists had gained a voice in the Reichstag and although the left-liberals were in the last analysis unlikely to give their active practical support to universal female suffrage, there still remained one chance at least that they would declare in favour of it in principle: the occasion of the eventual union of the three left-liberal parties in 1910. When this occasion arrived the suffragists had absented themselves from the scene, and it was left to others less committed than they were to put the feminist case.

Above all, however, in breaking with the left-liberals the suffragists were cutting themselves off from the social groups which provided them with their most consistent source of support. Ultimately, though, this was probably unavoidable in the long run, for the middle classes and their political representatives in the liberal parties were moving rapidly over to the support of the Wilhelmine political and social system under the impact of the growth of the SPD. In fact it was not the suffragists who abandoned the liberals but the liberals who abandoned the suffragists. In the growing atmosphere of conservatism among the middle classes after 1907-08, the radical politics of the suffrage movement appeared increasingly out of date. Under these circumstances voices were soon raised within the suffrage movement calling for the abandonment of its radical stance. This call to moderate the Suffrage Union's social and political radicalism and join the left-liberals in compromising with the State soon caused a violent controversy within the movement that ultimately led to its disintegration.

DISINTEGRATION AND FAILURE OF THE SUFFRAGE MOVEMENT, 1908-1916

The fate that overtook the Suffrage Union in the years 1908-1916 can only be understood if we realise the complications which the apparently simple and straightforward demand for 'votes for women' involved in a political system as inconsistent and contradictory as that of Wilhelmine Germany. In its original programme the Suffrage Union simply stated that it wanted 'equality of political rights for women in all fields'. Taken literally of course this meant that the Union wanted universal suffrage for the Reichstag and a property franchise for Prussia. There were also federal States with an even more inequitable suffrage than Prussia's, so that the apparently simple formula that women should have the same political rights as men thus led to startling inconsistencies in practice. In fact Augspurg and Heymann interpreted their programme from the beginning as implying universal suffrage everywhere.[81] But the impact of repeated SPD accusations that it only wanted a limited property suffrage, a *Damenwahlrecht* (Ladies' Suffrage), added to the influential arguments of Hellmuth von Gerlach and Rudolf Breitscheid and the hope that the SPD women's organisation would join forces with the Union in the campaign for female suffrage, led the union in 1907 to change its statutes at its General Assembly in Frankfurt and insert, by an almost unanimous vote, the famous Section 3 which committed it to fighting for 'universal, equal, direct and secret active and passive suffrage' for both sexes.[82]

In 1908, however, things began to change. The new Law of Association allowed women to join national political parties, and some members of the Suffrage Union joined the National Liberals, who had already begun to form women's sections of their Party in some areas. Such women soon found themselves caught in a clash of loyalties.[83] 'Now', complained Maria Lischnewska, 'they are supposed to vote on Monday in their Party meeting against the Reichstag suffrage for Prussia, and on Tuesday be bound in the Female Suffrage Union by a resolution in its favour.'[84] Most suffragists of course, if they did not repudiate party-political loyalties altogether, preferred to support the left-wing liberals, but from 1908 onwards as the Suffrage Union began to expand, many women entered the movement who, whatever their political allegiance, were extremely uneasy about the Suffrage Union's commitment to universal suffrage. Their uneasiness increased considerably as the reform of the Prussian suffrage became the central issue in German politics in 1910; and indeed, the debate within the Suffrage Union on the question of Section 3 can be seen as part of a wider debate in the country as a whole on the problem of universal suffrage, just as the debate within the BDF at the turn of the century on prostitution can be seen as part of the nationwide debate on the issues raised by the *lex Heinze*. Already in 1909, delegates at the Union's General Assembly representing the Rhineland and Westphalian provinces attempted, with no success, to delete Section 3. By the end of the year, despairing of ever persuading the Union to abandon Section 3, the Düsseldorf and Cologne branches had left the Union and founded the Women's Suffrage Union for West Germany (Frauenstimmrechtsverband für Westdeutschland). A struggle between this body and the parent association, the Prussian Union for Women's Suffrage in Berlin, followed. By March 1912 the new organisation had extended its network of branches to Koblenz, Kreuznach, Duisburg, Hamm, Münster, Hagen, Solingen and Wiesbaden. Meanwhile a similar splinter organisation had been founded in Silesia with its headquarters in Liegnitz, and in 1911 the West Germans managed to persuade some Hamburg feminists to found a North German Union. The Altona branch of the national German Suffrage Union later joined en bloc.[85]

These three regional associations then joined together to form a German Alliance for Women's Suffrage (Deutsche Vereiningung für Frauenstimmrecht) which sought women's suffrage on the same terms as men had or would in future have it:

> Where a man is measured out a portion of political influence as a representative of a certain class, a certain profession, a certain taxpaying ability or in any other way, general or particular, or simply as an individual, as a member of a people, the same should be given in the same measure and form to the women who represent the corresponding economic or social factor.[86]

The new Suffrage Alliance did not, as might have been expected, remove from the ranks of the Union all those who opposed universal suffrage. On the contrary the numbers of the 'reform party', as the group wishing to abolish Section 3 was known, continued to grow. Like their allies in the Suffrage Alliance they deployed a number of arguments to back up their case. To begin with, they argued that it was more vital than ever after the passage of the Law of Association for the suffrage movement to preserve the party-political neutrality written into its statutes. The movement's insistence on universal suffrage and its consequent alignment with the SPD, on this issue at least, was cutting off all possibility of getting new members from the political right. As for the SPD, it had shown that it did not want to co-operate with the bourgeois suffragists anyway. 'What use', asked Minna Bahnson, leader of the reform party in Bremen,[87] 'is flirting with Social Democracy, what use is the fearful avoidance of an apparent "withdrawal" from the working-class women's movement, if this movement always declares that a deep gulf divides it from all bourgeois women? '

Minna Bahnson spoke for a growing body of opinion within the Union when she said that the suffrage movement was 'too radical', and that it was time to try a policy of co-operating with the 'men's State' instead of perpetually condemning it. Section 3 carried with it the danger of a split. The Union should adopt a platform on which all its members could unite, and should take the 'purely feminist' view that sex differences were more important than class differences. The aim of the whole campaign was not to double the size of the existing political parties but to make the influence of women as such felt. This could be achieved by giving the vote to any group of them, because all women's interests were basically the same. In any case it was not practical to demand universal suffrage for women all at one go. The suffragists should be content with achieving their aims step by step.[88]

Opponents of the reform party criticised the anti-democratic implications of this view. Simply to demand the suffrage on such terms as men had it (or would in future have it) meant, as Auguste Kirchhoff, Minna Bahnson's leading opponent in Bremen,[89] pointed out '... for Prussia the three-class suffrage, for Saxony a plural suffrage, for Mecklenburg no suffrage at all ... If a reactionary wave comes along', she added, 'then these women must logically support an even worse suffrage.' The aim, she reasserted, was to secure all women the vote, not just a minority of middle-class women who would in any case suffer disadvantages under the Prussian system, because they paid less taxes than men and lost their property on marriage and the Prussian suffrage was based on tax assessment. Every woman had to decide for herself what she needed in the way of laws and institutions — a task nobody else was competent to fulfil — and these needs differed widely from class to class, from occupation to occupation. It was unthinkable, asserted the supporters of Section 3, that instead of men depriving women of their rights women themselves should do it. As for the practical arguments, it was unlikely that large numbers of conservative women would join the suffrage movement even if Section 3 were deleted. It would make life impossible for a female suffrage movement if it campaigned for the same suffrage as men, because this suffrage differed widely from federal State to federal State and all consistency was lost. Moreover, the reform party was confusing political with party-political neutrality. Any stand at all on the suffrage question could hardly be described as politically neutral. On the other hand, Section 3 was merely one point shared by the Union with a certain political party — the SPD — among many points of disagreement.[90]

Ultimately, in fact, the only really neutral point of view was that of the Augspurg-Heymann group, who combined a determination to retain

Section 3 with a refusal to work with any of the 'men's parties' *(Männerparteien)*. Indeed, for a time Augspurg and Heymann pursued a compromise line, arguing that the whole dispute was merely due to an excessive regard for the 'men's parties'. Nevertheless, there was no doubt that they intended to fight those who sought to remove the commitment to universal suffrage. On the whole indeed the leadership seemed determined to retain Section 3; pressure for change came from below and outside.[91] Nevertheless there were fatal divisions within the leadership on the question of how best to ward off the challenge from the right. At the 1911 General Assembly it sought a compromise by adding the words 'for women' to Section 3. The omission of the same demand for men was thought to put the Union on a purely feminist basis, and to assert more strongly than ever before its party-political neutrality. At the time the trend towards independence from party-political ties and towards militant self-reliance within the Union was reaching its height. The Assembly voted in favour of the resolution by 109 to 23 with twelve abstentions.[92] 'Section 3', remarked *Vorwärts*, 'was the reason why the Union had been in poor health from birth, and has finally had to undergo a critical operation in Hamburg, where it first saw the light of day. The operation . . . was successful; whether the patient will now gradually die from general weakness or burst forth into new life, must be awaited'.[93]

The alternative posed by *Vorwärts* was a false one. It was not sickness but suicide. The suffrage movement continued to tear itself apart. At the 1911 General Assembly Augspurg, Heymann, Radel and Lewison, all firm supporters of Section 3, were re-elected to the leading posts in the Union but refused to accept their election because Marie Stritt, whom they identified as an opponent of Section 3, had been elected onto the committee with them.[94] The committee therefore consisted of Marie Stritt as President, Martha Zietz, Anna Lindemann, Maria Lischnewska and Käthe Schirmacher. Not only did this introduce a strong nationalistic element onto the committee with Lischnewska, Schirmacher and Zietz, but it also weakened the power base of the democratic faction for Lischnewska and Schirmacher favoured a restricted suffrage and Stritt was prepared to compromise.[95] 'Now', wrote Schirmacher, 'there will really be a fight against Social Democracy.'[96] At this stage Anita Augspurg, who still retained great influence within the Union as its founder-President, and kept her post as

President of the Bavarian Federal Union, made another suicidal error. She should have realised that any compromise on the principle of Section 3 would be anathema to the Prussian Suffrage Union and its leader Minna Cauer, who was a member of the Democratic Alliance and closely involved in the suffrage struggle in Prussia. Like the Hamburg branch, and perhaps even more so, they were locked in a battle with the Women's Suffrage Alliance for the support of women in their catchment area. At this stage they were still striving to retain control of those branches in the Rhineland that had not already gone over to the Alliance. Any weakening of the principle of Section 3 would threaten their very foundations.

However, at the meeting of the Suffrage Union's advisory board[97] in Weimar in December 1912, Augspurg proposed to recommend the next General Assembly to amend Section 3 to demand only 'equal suffrage for all women'. This dropped the requirement to campaign for universal suffrage and was vague enough to be capable of the most varied interpretations. The board voted in favour by 16 to 11. In itself the decision had no effect: it would still have to be put to the next General Assembly and passed by the usual two-thirds majority required for the amendment of the Statutes. But the Berlin radicals regarded the decision as a fatal step on the road to a limited suffrage demand. Minna Cauer resigned and was followed by many others, including Toni Breitscheid, Else Lüders, Meta Hammerschlag in Frankfurt am Main and Johanna Elberskirchen in Bonn. The upheaval in the Prussian Suffrage Union was completed by the accession to the Presidency of Regine Deutsch, who had voted with the majority at Weimar, assisted by Alma Dzialoszynski, Adele Schreiber — a convert from universal suffrage — and Maria Lischnewska. Schreiber and Lischnewska had ensured, against Cauer's wishes, that the meeting at which all these decisions were taken was a closed one.

With Cauer and her supporters out of the Union it could only be a matter of time before the other radicals followed. At the General Assembly at Eisenach in 1913 the reform party mustered a sizeable vote — though not the necessary two-thirds majority — for a proposal to form a loose federation of female suffrage societies and leave the framing of the Statutes to the constituent unions. They nevertheless failed once more to amend Section 3. A proposal to remove the demand for the vote from the Statutes altogether — a somewhat desperate expedient for resolving the controversy – was defeated by 123 votes to 68; the reform party's motion was also defeated by 130 votes to 52, and the Prussian suffragists' compromise formula by 102 votes to 73. Section 3 therefore remained unamended. The executive committee also narrowly lost a vote to alter Section 9 of the Statutes so that amendments to the Statutes would require a simple instead of a two-thirds majority. Despite these failures of the reform party Augspurg and Heymann resigned from the Union, giving as their reason the fact that Stritt was re-elected President although she had supported the reform party's proposals. They were followed out of the Union by several hundred members and by two whole federal unions, the Hamburg under Frieda Radel and the Bavarian under Augspurg.[98] Thus the founders of the German Union for Women's Suffrage abandoned their creation little more than ten years after its birth.

The radicals in Berlin, Hamburg and Munich now joined together in a third female suffrage society, the German Women's Suffrage League (Deutscher Frauenstimmrechtsbund), led by Augspurg, Heymann and Cauer. This had originally been founded immediately after the Weimar board meeting in 1912 by Johanna Elberskirchen as the Imperial Association for Women's Suffrage (Reichsverein für Frauenstimmrecht) with branches in Bonn and Berlin.[99] Cauer had opposed its original foundation and hesitated for two years before joining, but once she took the plunge the League rapidly gained in strength.[100] August Kirchhoff set up a branch in Bremen, and other branches – newly established or won over from the Union – soon existed in Nuremburg, Würzburg, Bamberg, Aschaffenburg, Baden-Baden, Bergedorf, Darmstadt, Frankfurt am Main, Konstanz and Lahr. The centre of support for the League was in Hamburg, where the branch numbered 850 and could still claim 500 members in 1917. It was controlled however from Munich, where Augspurg and Heymann insisted on rigid adherence to universal suffrage and the original moral reform concepts that had motivated the suffrage movement in its early years.

Neither the League nor its competitors had recovered from the struggle by the outbreak of war however. It was not long before the Union set up a reconstituted branch in Hamburg, under the patronage of Martha Zietz and led by Hedwig Weidemann. On the eve of the war there were thus three rival female suffrage societies in the city, presided over respectively by Ida Dehmel, Hedwig Weidemann and Frieda Radel.

This situation was repeated in other parts of the country as the struggle descended to a local level. In November 1913 Luise Kesselbach, the leader of the Association for the Interests of Women in Munich, expressed her concern at:

> . . . the latest events in the Suffrage Union under Augspurg and Heymann, who have now freed the Bavarian Association from the German and have exclusive control over the suffrage movement in Bavaria. A few groups, Nuremburg, and Bamberg, and a number of members here, oppose this, and it is our duty to help them. I would very much like to speak with you (she wrote to Gertrud Bäumer) and ask your advice in this matter too. I think it would be best if we could lead these groups privately to the German Alliance, bceause the circumstances of the German Union after the Eisenach meeting give the impression of being untenable.

But on 17 December Martha Zietz travelled down to Munich and reconstituted the branch of the Union in the city. The same process was repeated in May 1914 in Baden. In Nuremberg, to take a final example of a process that was continuing in various forms all over Germany in the winter of 1913 and spring of 1914, the local branch voted by 50 to 28 to leave the Union on 14 January 1914. On 20 Feburary the minority seceded and founded a new branch loyal to the Union; this soon had 50 members itself. All in all, although things were becoming clearer by the summer of 1914, the major part of the energies of all suffragists seems to have been taken up in internecine struggles from 1912 onwards.[101]

At the same time various schemes were being proposed to heal the wounds caused by these struggles. Augspurg and Heymann called for a Cartell of Women's Suffrage Societies on 1 June 1914, and put forward a draft constitution on 15 July. It was to be an organisational expedient for demonstrations, petitions and representation in the International Woman Suffrage Alliance. On 25 May 1915 representatives of the three suffrage societies met and approved the draft constitution, with a few minor amendments. This however was rejected by the Alliance, whose leadership was on the point of persuading the Union to abandon Section 3 altogether, which the Augspurg/Heymann plan did not envisage. The merging of the Union and the Alliance had already been proposed by Eisenach in 1913 and again early in 1914 by Maria Lischnewska, Minna Bahnson, Emma Nägeli and Eleonore Drenkhahn from Hamburg, and unofficial negotiations began soon after. Augspurg and Heymann's support of the peace movement in the First World War, while it led to the defection of many of their former supporters,helped the Union and the Alliance to make up their minds to join forces without the League. After a preliminary conference on 25 May 1915 the two societies voted in principle to unite at a meeting held on 12 November. A commission was elected to arrange the details and on 18 March 1916 the Suffrage Union voted by 98 to 10 to join, finally dropping Section 3 and opting for limited suffrage. The Göttingen, Halle, Breslau and Kattowitz branches — which had supported the Cartell plan — and the Silesian Union left the Suffrage Union. The first three joined the League. The Silesians remained an independent regional association on the left, much as the original Silesian Suffrage Union had been on the right from 1908 to 1911. Meanwhile the united society, called the German Imperial Union for Women's Suffrage (Deutscher Reichsverband für Frauenstimmrecht) was led by Marie Stritt. The executive committee included Ida Dehmel, Li Fischer-Eckert and Illa Uth from the Alliance, and Rosa Kempf, Luise Koch, Alma Dzialoszynski and Emma Nägeli from the Union.[102] Though the Union had a majority, its style and ideology had through successive secessions become almost indistinguishable from that of the Alliance.[103]

The suffragists tried to console themselves with the thought that the same process of fragmentation had occurred in women's suffrage movements elsewhere, and that it was a sign of vigour and commitment rather than lassitude and indifference.[104] Yet the Union's executive committee had been forced to admit in 1913 that 'the positive work of the Union had been seriously limited and handicapped in the last years through the continual struggles over the Statutes and through other polemics.'[105] The fact was that the suffrage movement, which began with such high hopes in 1902, was in total disarray on the eve of the First World War. The measures of realignment which occurred thereafter only brought to a logical conclusion the development that had begun soon after the passage of the Law of Association in 1908 — the reduction of the supporters of universal suffrage and feminist militancy to a small and impotent fringe. In 1914 the Union had perhaps 9000, the Alliance 3000 and the League about 2000 members.[106] United, the Union and the Alliance could safely afford to ignore the League.

Moreover, despite a decade or more of pressure, the suffragists of all varieties had achieved no concrete reforms. Their influence on left-wing

liberalism, the political force with which they were most closely associated, declined in these years. Within the women's movement the
direct agitation of the suffragists was increasingly rejected in favour of
what Helene Lange termed the 'indirect way', through work in political
parties and local government. The opportunities offered by the union
of the left-wing liberal parties in 1910 were not grasped by the Suffrage
Union, which made no effort to influence the liberals to incorporate
votes for women into their new programme. Tactical paralysis and
internal dissension were the two chief characteristics of the female
suffrage movement in Germany in the last years of peace; the sanguine
hopes of its founders had not been fulfilled, and in many ways indeed
the situation was less promising than it had been even at the start of the
movement's activities in 1902.

NOTES

1. StA Hbg, PP, S5466/II: Versammlungsbericht, 24 Jan. 1900; ibid.,
SA593/II: *HE,* 28 Feb. 1900.
2. From 1902 to 1904 *Deutscher Verein für Frauenstimmrecht.*
3. StA Hbg, PP, S9001/IV: Augspurg to police, 1 Jan. 1902.
4. Ibid., S9000/I: *BLA;* 21 Mar. 1902; ABDF 5/II/4; 194: Stritt to Augspurg, 4 Mar. 1902.
5. StA Hbg, PP, S5466/II: *HN,* 15 Nov. 1903.
6. UB Rostock, NL Schirmacher: Schirmacher to Schleker, 6 March 1903.
7. StA Hbg, PP, S9001/I: *HE,* 12 May 1903.
8. Heymann/Augspurg, *Erlebtes-Erschautes,* 97.
9. E. R. Huber, *Deutsche Verfassungsgeschichte Seit 1789, Vol. 4: Struktur
und Krisen des Kaiserreichs* (Stuttgart, 1968).
10. Hans-Jürgen Puhle, *Agrarische Interessenpolitik und preussischer Kon-
servatismus im Wilhelminischen Reich (1893-1914)* (Hannover, 1967), for the
standard account of the Agrarian League.
11. StA Hbg, PP, S5466/I: *DP,* 27 Feb. 1902. Before this, SPD women often
evaded the regulations. 'In those days', recalled Klara Weyl later, 'we women were
not allowed to go to meetings, and we used to wear a man's overcoat and put on a
man's hat and disappear into the crowd . . .' (FES/ASD Bonn, NL Gerda Weyl 19:
Lebenserinnerungen von Klara Weyl, MS.).

12. DZA Potsdam, Reichskanzlei, 2266, Bl. 44-60. The IWSA was a break-away from the International Council of Women and its foundation was opposed by the BDF. (Else Lüders, *Minna Cauer. Leben und Werk.* (Gotha, 1925), 163.)

13. In this study, the word 'suffragette' is reserved for those who used violence in pursuit of the aim of female suffrage.

14. StA Hbg, PP, S9001/II: *HC,* 2 Feb. 1902. The impression given by Heymann/Augspurg, *Erlebtes-Erschautes* 98, of the reception of the Union's foundation in the Press, is less than fair.

15. StA Hbg, PP, S9001/II: *HC,* 2 Feb. 1902, *HNN* 11 Feb. 1902, *DSB* 22 June 1904, *NHZ* 2 Feb. 1902; *GL* 5/5, 20 March 1895, 43, 7/7, 29 Sept. 1897, 160.

16. Minna Cauer, 'Nachklänge', *FB* 7/21, 1 Nov. 1901, 161.

17. StA Hbg, PP, S9001/IV: 'An Deutschlands Frauen! ' (Flugblatt).

18. Ibid./II: *HE,* 27 Sept. 1907.

19. StA Hbg, PP, S9001/IV: Lida Gustava Heymann, *Gleiches Recht, Frauenstimmrecht!* (Munich, 1907).

20. Ibid./II: *NHZ,* 13 Dec. 1906.

21. Ibid./I: Frieda Radel, *Warum fordern wir das Frauenstimmrecht?* (2nd ed., Gautzsch bei Leipzig, 1910).

22. StA Hbg, S9001/I: *HF,* 4 Oct. 1905.

23. StA Hbg, PP, S9001/I: *GA,* 3 Oct. 1903.

24. *ZFS,* Vol. 2, No. 4, 1 April 1908, 18.

25. StA Hbg, PP, S9001/I: Flugblatt: 'Warum fordern wir das Frauenstimm-recht? '

26. Remme, op. cit., 114-15.

27. StA Hbg, PP, S9001/IV: 'An Deutschlands Frauen! ' (Flugblatt).

28. Minna Cauer, 'Entwicklungen', *FB,* 19/1, 1 Jan. 1913, 2.

29. *Report of the Second and Third Conferences of the International Woman Suffrage Alliance* (Copenhagen, 1906), 79.

30. StA Hbg, PP, S9001/II: *VW,* 5 Oct. 1906, 14 Oct. 1906, *HC,* 3 July 1907, *BT,* 17 Sept. 1907; ibid., S8004: *HE,* 12 Oct. 1902; *Report of the Fourth Conference of the International Woman Suffrage Alliance* (Amsterdam, 1908), 99. According to Käthe Schirmacher, Heymann managed to avoid paying taxes by never living in one place more than six months at a time. (UB Rostock, NL Schirmacher. Schirmacher to Schleker, 20 March 1910).

31. StA Hbg, PP, S9001/II: *DP,* 20 March 1902.

32. Minna Cauer, 'Ein Schritt vorwärts', *FB,* 8/7, 1 April 1902, 49.

33. StA Hbg, PP, S9001/II: *VW,* 22 March 1902, 25 May 1910; DZA Potsdam, Reichskanzlei, 2266, Bl. 10-19: Augspurg to Bülow, 4 March 1902 and 16 March 1902, Bülow to Augspurg, 14 March 1902; ibid., Bl. 96-100: Augspurg to Bethmann Hollweg, 4 and 21 Nov. 1909, Bethmann Hollweg to Augspurg, 17 Nov. 1909.

34. StA Hbg, PP, S9001/II: *Kölnische Zeitung,* 10 Oct. 1902.

35. StA Hbg, PP, S9001/II: *VW,* 17 May 1903.

36. Ibid.: *HC,* 26 April 1903.

37. StA Hbg, PP, S8004: *BLA,* 13 Feb. 1902.

38. *Stenographische Berichte über die Sitzungen der Bürgerschaft zu Hamburg im Jahre 1906*, 113.

39. Agnes von Zahn-Harnack, op. cit., 287.

40. StA Hbg, PP, S9001/I: *HE*, 6 Jan. 1903, *NHZ*, 28 April 1903.

41. StA Hbg, PP, S9001/I: *GA*, 3 Oct. 1903.

42. Ibid./I: *HC*, 23 May 1903, *HF*, 11 April 1903, 24 May 1903, *NHZ*, 23 May 1903.

43. *JB 1912*, 120 f.

44. StA Hbg, PP, S9001/II: *NHZ*, 3 Dec. 1903.

45. StA Hbg, PP, S14139: *HE*, 5 Dec. 1905.

46. StA Hbg, PP, S9001/II: *HF*, 12 May 1903.

47. Helene Lange, 'Reaktion im Liberalismus', *DF*, Vol. 17, No. 5, Feb. 1910, 290-292.

48. *JB 1912*, 120 ff.

49. Agnes von Zahn-Harnack, op. cit., 288-9.

50. StA Hbg, PP, S9001/II: *VW*, 28 March 1907.

51. StA Hbg, PP, S9001/II: *BT*, 8 Oct. 1904: ibid./I: *VW*, 6 Oct. 1905.

52. Ibid./II: *HF*, 3 Jan. 1907.

53. *DF*, 12/5, Feb. 1905, 307.

54. StA Hbg, PP, S9001/II: *NHZ*, 3 March 1908.

55. Ibid.: *BVZ*, 2 May 1908. The Suffrage Union in Bremen also refused to help the liberal candidate in 1906 because he did not declare himself in favour of female suffrage. See *Deutscher Verband für Frauenstimmrecht. Dritter Arbeitsbericht* (Munich, 1907).

56. StA Hbg, PP, S9001/II: *VW*, 16 Dec. 1908, *HC*, 1 Oct. 1908, *HC*, 3 Aug. 1902. The liberals, with a relatively small membership in comparison with the number of people who voted for them, stood in particular need of such assistance.

57. StA Hbg, PP, S9001/II: *BT*, 11 Dec. 1908, *BVZ*, 13 Oct. 1908. Although the *Reichsvereinsgesetz* of 1908 gave freedom of assembly to women, Augspurg and Heymann opposed it because it discriminated against national minorities in Germany by stipulating that German was the language to be used in public assemblies. It was this that seems finally to have decided Augspurg and Heymann to oppose the Block. In 1907, the Suffrage Union still saw nothing unusual in supporting Block liberals at the elections. Cf. *Deutscher Verband für Frauenstimmrecht. Dritter Arbeitsbericht* (Munich, 1907).

58. Previous reorganisations had taken place in 1904 and 1907 to keep pace with the growth of the society. See *Report of the Fourth Conference of the International Woman Suffrage Alliance* (Amsterdam, 1908), 100-101.

59. StA Hbg, PP, S9001/II: *HC*, 16 Feb. 1907, quoting *HF*.

60. StA Hbg, PP, S14139: *GA*, 23 June 1908; *ZFS* 2/7, 28, 1 July 1908, 'Der grosse Zug der Suffragettes in London'.

61. StA Hbg, PP, S8004: *HE*, 27 June 1908: *ZFS* 2/8, 1 Aug. 1908, 31, 'Suffragettes', von Lida Gustava Heymann.

62. StA Hbg, PP, S9001/I: *HF*, 19 Dec. 1909.

63. StA Hbg, PP, S9001/II: *HF*, 18 Oct. 1908, *HC*, 6 May 1909, *BT*, 14 May 1909, *BVZ*, 5 May 1909.

64. Ibid./I: *HNN,* 19 Dec. 1909.

65. Ibid./II: *NAZ,* 20 Sept. 1907, 28 April 1909, *BVZ,* 24 April 1914; ibid./I: Versammlungsbericht, 20 May 1912.

66. StA Hbg, PP, S9001/II: *HF,* 26 Sept. 1909, 30 Sept. 1909, *HC,* 30 Oct. 1909, *HN,* 16 Aug. 1909, 19 Aug. 1909, *BVZ,* 29 Sept. 1909, *BT,* 24 Oct. 1909, 27 Oct. 1909; *ZFS,* 3/9, 1 Sept. 1909, 39; *FS,* 1/7, Oct. 1912, 156.

67. StA Hbg, PP, S9001/II: *BT,* 26 Sept. 1912; *FS,* 1/7, Oct. 1912, 140-142.

68. StA Hbg, PP, S9001/II: *HE,* 18 Feb. 1910, *FZ,* 16 Feb. 1910, *BVZ,* 23 March 1910, *BLA,* 16 April 1910; Dieter Groh, *Negative Integration und revolutionärer Attentismus. Die deutsche Sozialdemokratie am Vorabend des Ersten Weltkrieges* (Berlin/Frankfurt, 1973), 140-2.

69. StA Hbg, PP, S9000/I: *HF,* 7 Oct. 1911, 12 Oct. 1911; *HE,* 2 Nov. 1911: UB Rostock, NL Schirmacher: Marie Horuschuck to Schirmacher, 21 Jan. 1912.

70. Agnes von Zahn-Harnack, op. cit., 287-303.

71. *FS,* 2/2, May 1913, 64-5.

72. See p. 186 below.

73. ABDF, 4/1: Marie Meyer to Gertrud Bäumer, 26 April 1913.

74. *JB 1912-14;* StA Hbg, PP, S9001/I: *HF,* 8 Oct. 1911.

75. Cf. the membership of the American National Association of Woman Suffrage Associations; 13, 150 in 1893; 12,000 in 1905; 45,501 in 1907; 75,000 in 1910; 100,000 in 1915. (Aileen S. Kraditor, *The Ideas of the Woman Suffrage Movement 1896-1920* (Columbia, 1965), 7.)

76. StA Hbg, PP, S14459: *GA,* 3 Aug. 1906.

77. StA Hbg, PP, S9001/I: Versammlungsberichte, 2 Oct. 1903, 6 Dec. 1907, 6 March 1908, 23 Jan. 1909, 6 March 1909, 1 Oct. 1909, 22 April 1910, 19 Jan. 1911, 9 March 1911, 16 March 1911, 26 April 1911, 17 Nov. 1911, 17 April 1912, 27 April 1912, 20 May 1912, 6 Oct. 1912, 22 Oct. 1912, 18 Nov. 1912, 25 Nov. 1912, 20 Oct. 1913.

78. StA Hbg, PP, S19031, passim; *FS,* 1/7, Oct. 1912, 144-149: 'Ein Männerliga für Frauenstimmrecht in Deutschland? Ja natürlich! ! '; ibid., 1/8, 171; ibid., 2/11, Feb. 1914, 240-2; *SB,* 1/April 1914, 15.

79. See Carl E. Schorske, *German Social Democracy 1905-1917. The Development of The Great Schism.* (New York, 1955), 45-49.

80. James J. Sheehan, 'Liberalism and the City in Nineteenth-Century Germany', *Past and Present,* No. 51 (May, 1971), 116-132.

81. Käthe Schirmacher was ousted from the executive committee in 1903 because she did *not* support universal suffrage. See Hanna Krüger, op. cit., 116-118.

82. StA Hbg, PP, S9001/I: *GA,* 8 Oct. 1911.

83. StA Hbg, PP, S9000/I: *VW,* 11 Oct. 1911, for a discussion of this problem. The clash of loyalties was felt even in the case of Conservative women such as Paula Müller. See pp. 195-201, below.

84. Maria Lischnewska, *Die deutsche Frauenstimmrechtsbewegung zwischen Krieg und Frieden* (Berlin, 1915), 15-16, 25.

85. *FS,* 1/7, Oct. 1912, 158; StA Hbg, PP, S9001/II: *BT,* 24 Oct. 1909;

HLA 50; Jahresbericht des Frauenstimmrechtsverbandes für Westdeutschland 1912; *FS*, 1/12, March 1923, 277.

86. For the North German Section of the Alliance, see StA Hbg, PP, SA1767, passim. See also *Grundlagen des Stimmrechts* (Frauenstimmrechtsverband für Westdeutschland, Solingen, 1911), 1-12; Adelheid Steinmann, 'Die Forderung politischer Neutralität in der Frauenbewegung', *DF*, 17/11, Aug. 1910, 641-648; StA Hbg, PP, S9001/II: *HC*, 27 Oct. 1911.

87. For Minna Bahnson (1866-1947), see *Bremische Biographie 1912-1962* (hg. von der Historischen Gesellschaft zu Bremen und dem Staatsarchiv Bremen. In Verbindung mit Fritz Peters und Karl H. Schwebel bearbeitet von Wilhelm Lührs); 22-24.

88. For the reform party's arguments, see Minna Bahnson, *Ist es wünschenswert, dass der §3 aus den Satzungen des Deutschen Verbandes für Frauenstimmrecht gestrichen wird?* (Bremen, 1912): Maria Lischnewska, op. cit., 29; Steinmann, art. cit.

89. For Auguste Kirchhoff (1867-1940), the wife of a leading Bremen politician and, usually, a lapsed Catholic, see *Bremische Biographie* (op. cit.), no. 254.

90. Auguste Kirchhoff, *Warum muss der Deutsche Verband fur Frauenstimmrecht sich zum allgemeinen, gleichen, geheimen und direkten Wahlrecht bekennen?* (Bremen, 1912); Maria Lischnewska, op. cit., 33; *ZFS* 3/10, 1 Oct. 1909, 41-2; *DF* 17/11, Aug. 1910, 648-655; *FS* 1/7, Nov. 1912, 159-161; Toni Breitscheid, *Die Notwendigkeit der Forderung des allgemeinen, gleichen, geheimen Wahlrechts* (Berlin, 1909).

91. Though Käthe Schirmacher, who remained prominent in the Union until 1913, opposed universal suffrage, and Martha Zietz voted against Adelheid von Welczeck's attempt to get the BDF to support universal suffrage in 1910. (UB Rostock, NL Schirmacher: Schirmacher to Schleker, 11 Oct. 1910; cutting of *Rostocker Anzeiger*, 13 Sept. 1907).

92. Or, according to another source, by 95-47. The division of votes at the Congress was: Prussia 59, Baden 18, Bavaria 15, Württemberg 8, Hessen 8, Hamburg 7, Saxony 7, Bremen 6, Mecklenburg 6, Thuringia 4, Alsace-Lorraine 2, Oldenburg 1, Lübeck 1. See StA Hbg, PP, S9000/I: *HF*, 7 Oct. 1911.

93. Ibid.: *VW*, 11 Oct. 1911.

94. Augspurg and Heymann later admitted that this step was ill-advised. See *Erlebtes-Erschautes*, 109.

95. *ZFS*, Vol. 5, No. 11, 1 Nov. 1911, 42; StA Hbg, PP, S9001/II: *NHZ* , 9 Nov. 1911.

96. UB Rostock, NL Schirmacher: Schirmacher to Schleker, 11 Feb. 1912. Schirmacher, increasingly in conflict with the internationalism of the Union and its continued nominal adherence to universal suffrage, resigned in 1913. See Hanna Krüger, op. cit., 125.

97. Set up in 1909, consisting of the executive committee and the Presidents of the federal Unions (StA Hbg, PP, S9001/II: *BT*, 25 Sept. 1912, 27 May 1912; *BVZ*, 6 Dec. 1910).

98. StA Hbg, PP, S9001/II: *VW*, 12 Oct. 1912, 10 Nov. 1912, 15 Nov. 1912,

26 Nov. 1912, *HC,* 18 Oct. 1912, *BVZ,* 20 Oct. 1912; Else Lüders, 'Zur Entwicklung der deutschen Stimmrechtsbewegung', *FB,* 19/20, 15 Oct. 1913, 155-157; Minna Cauer, 'Erklärung', *FB,* 18/22, 15 Nov. 1912, 174; *FS,* 2/9, Dec. 1913, 206; Maria Lischnewska, op. cit., 34; Auguste Kirchhoff, *Zur Entwicklung der Frauenstimmrechtsbewegung* (Bremen, 1916), 9.

99. Elberskirchen's *Reichsverein* must not be confused with the later *Reichsverband,* founded in 1916 (see below), as it is, unfortunately, by Margrit Twellman, in a footnote on 108 of Augspurg/Heymann, op. cit.

100. The exact connection between Elberskirchen's *Reichsverein* and the *Frauenstimmrechtsbund* is not entirely clear.

101. Minna Cauer, 'Frauenstimmrecht und Demokratie', *ZFS,* 7/10, 15 May 1913; *FS,* 1/12, March 1913, 267; 2/1, April 1913, 24-25, on the *Reichsverein;* StA Hbg, PP, S19925, passim, for the League. For events at a local level, see *FS,* Vol. 2, No. 10, Jan. 1914, 234; ABDF 5/XVI/1; Kesselbach to Bäumer (Munich): *FS,* 2/11, Feb. 1914, 250; *SB,* 1/1, April 1914, 10 (Nuremberg); ibid., 1/3, June 1914, 44-5 (Baden); *FS,* 2/10, Jan. 1914, 230 (Hamburg).

102. *ZFS,* 8/9, 1 May 1914, 29-30, 8/11, 1 June 1914, 35-6, 8/14, 15 July 1914, 43, 9/12, 15 July 1915, 23, 10/7, 1 April 1916, 13; *SB,* Aug. 1914, 75-77, April 1916, 1-10; StA Hbg, PP, S9001/IV: *VW,* 16 Nov. 1915, 21 March 1916; *FS,* 2/9, Dec. 1913, 203-6; ABDF 5/XVI/3: Bäumer to Dehmel, 11 July 1915.

103. *ZFS,* 10/14, 15 July 1916, 29 (article by Hellmuth von Gerlach, criticising the new organization's 'undemocratic' and 'authoritarian' nature).

104. *FS,* 1/10, Jan. 1913, 205-6, 'Erklärung'.

105. Ibid., 2/9, Dec. 1913, 265, 'Erklärung des Vorstandes'.

106. Cf. for the Alliance UB Rostock, NL Schirmacher: Schirmacher to Schleker, 24 March 1911, where Schirmacher reckons the Alliance to have 1500 members in West Germany and 800 in Silesia.

4

THE NEW MORALITY

ORIGINS OF THE NEW MORALITY

In taking the story of the female suffrage movement up to the middle of the First World War, we have pursued one strand in the development of the women's movement almost to its end, and we must now go back to the turn of the century to pick up the other threads of the story where we left them. From 1898 to 1902, debate within the women's movement centred on the moral issues raised by the radical feminist supporters of the abolition of State-regulated prostitution; in the first two or three years after the foundation of the Suffrage Union it was the political question that aroused most controversy. From 1905 to 1910, however, attention and discussion shifted back to moral issues, and once again it was the Abolitionists who were at the centre of the controversy. We have seen that Abolitionism was morally repressive in its outlook and held that prostitution and sexual deviance resulted in large measure from men's inability to discipline their sexual instincts.[1] Gradually, however, some Abolitionists began to question the validity of this outlook and the assumptions that lay behind it, and they developed by 1905 a new and radically libertarian set of ideas about sexual morality. In effect, they began to preach a gospel of free love, and to argue that the prostitution problem and other connected social evils could be solved not by moral repression but by moral libertarianism.

The key figure in the development of what came to be known as the New Morality was a leading member of the Berlin Abolitionist movement, Helene Stöcker.[2] Born in Elberfeld in 1869, the eldest of eight children, she rebelled against the narrow Calvinism of her parents, who belonged to a strict religious community that had rejected the Calvinist-Lutheran Church Union of 1814. By the mid-1890s she had broken free from her family, and had trained as a school-teacher. As with many leading feminists, this was, however, merely as a means to an end; Stöcker saw this training, probably correctly, as the only way to reach University entrance standard. For three years, beginning in 1896, she studied in Berlin and worked as a research assistant to the philosopher Wilhelm Dilthey. Here she also met Minna Cauer and became active in the radical wing of the women's education movement, the Verein Frauenbildung-Frauenstudium. By the end of the 1890s, therefore, she was already an active member of the radical women's movement.[3] Besides being a member of the educational society, she belonged to Minna Cauer's Commercial Association for Women Salaried Employees in the mid-1890s,[4] and worked in the Abolitionist movement and the Berlin Frauenwohl; she joined the executive committee of the latter in 1902.[5] She was also a delegate at the Federation of German Women's Associations' General Assembly in 1898.[6] She contributed regularly to Minna Cauer's magazine *Die Frauenbewegung,* as well as to other contemporary magazines, notably Maximilian Harden's *Die Zukunft.* She edited a short-lived magazine which she tried to use as a vehicle for disseminating her own individual views on female emancipation until she was ousted by more conservative colleagues,[7] and she also helped found the Suffrage Union in 1902.[8] From 1900 Stöcker studied for a doctorate in Bern, researching part of the time in Munich, where she came into contact with the feminist leader Ika Freudenberg and the radical literary and intellectual circle centred on the novelist Ricarda Huch. Here, among others, she met feminists such as Marie Baum and Frieda Duensing. By 1901 she had finished her dissertation, on 18th century Germany Literary Life, and returned to Berlin which she now made her headquarters.[9]

The dominant intellectual influence in Helene Stöcker's life, already plainly visible in her first article, published in 1893, was Friedrich Nietzsche.[10] Not surprisingly she was careful to refute the prevalent — and not wholly unjustified — belief that Nietzsche was hostile to female emancipation and regarded women as inferior beings. Nietzsche, she wrote, had taught women to be spiritually independent. True, there was little in his works explicitly about female emancipation, apart from a chance aside praising 'the noble and liberally-minded women who aim at the improvement of their sex'.[11] His message to women was of a much more general, much more profound kind; it was that women should live and experience life to the full, and no longer be content with the narrow existence which bourgeois custom laid down for them. Stöcker's unexpected interpretation of Nietzsche's message, which is generally thought to have been concerned with will and power and is often considered to have been an influence in the spread of fascist ideology in Germany, was striking evidence that many people in fact understood Nietzsche to be propagating a romantic form of liberal individualism, teaching the conquest of the self and the development of the creative powers of the individual.[12] At any rate, this is how Helene Stöcker interpreted Nietzsche. She argued that until the mid-1890s the women's movement had confined its attentions to increasing opportunities for women to engage in higher education and the professions. No-one, however, expected that *married* women would either demand or exploit these enlarged opportunities when they came.

Stöcker's early articles were therefore devoted to urging middle-class women to follow Nietzsche's philosophy and live life to the full by marrying, having children *and* entering higher education and the professions. She rejected the implicit division of womankind into a minority of intellectual, unemotional spinsters and a majority of un-educated, emotional mothers. Instead, she urged a 'higher synthesis', the all-round woman who would break free from this kind of constricting convention. The radicalism of these ideas should not be over-emphasised. Helene Stöcker's active role in the radical feminist movement in the years 1898-1902 shows that her colleagues found them unexceptionable enough. At the same time these ideas also seem to have been well in accordance with the thought of Nietzsche. In 1897, for example, Stöcker wrote a satire entitled *Die Männer-Bewegung,* in which she imagined men forming a movement to emancipate women. The point was to show that female emancipation was in men's own interest. In this satire, she declared that:

> The strict discipline which has been imposed on woman for centuries in sexual
> matters had bred in her a sense of purity, a reluctance to surrender herself
> fully, or even to any degree whatsoever: anything else would signify for her
> the destruction of her innermost personal integrity ... This virtue dis-
> tinguished women from men like a cultural difference for a few thousand
> years – and the only men who are able to share it and enjoy it to the full, are
> those who possess a similar sense of purity themselves. It would be slanderous
> to doubt that men, who are notoriously 'superior' to women, could not
> achieve this sense of purity ... 'The achievement of power is costly', says
> Nietzsche, 'power stultifies'. Ah, it does not only stultify, it also brutalizes –
> and for this reason, it is necessary above all for the upbringing of men to be
> improved.[13]

Stöcker was thus fully in agreement with the Abolitionists, to whom,
indeed, as we have seen, she belonged from their foundation, when she
made this demand that men exercise more sexual self-control out of
respect for women's feelings.

However, it is perhaps significant that already here Stöcker was
asserting that distaste for and lack of enjoyment of sex had been
culturally imbued in women by society; the Abolititionists believed
that the inability to enjoy sex was innate in women, that it was part of
their nature. The latent clash of opinion here became explicit some
time after the turn of the century, when Stöcker's views began to
change because of an unhappy love-affair with a married man.[14] It was,
she wrote later, a 'purely aesthetic love'.[15] Nevertheless, Stöcker's
love-affair influenced her intellectual convictions in two ways. First, it
led her to concern herself with the institution of marriage. Up to 1900
her attitude to marriage, apart from her concurrence in the general
feminist condemnation of the relevant provisions in the Civil Code, had
been basically uncritical. Now, however, she began to see the institution
itself as a constriction on women's freedom to live life to the full. 'The
women's movement', declared Stöcker at the General Assembly of the
Union of Progressive Women's Associations in September 1903, 'has
ignored all problems of love, marriage and motherhood for decades. But
today it is recognised that emancipation from economic subjection also
involves emancipation from sexual subjection.'[16] Marriage in a
patriarchal society, she said, had as its inevitable consequences the
growth of prostitution on the one hand and the stigmatisation of the

illegitimate child on the other. It further condemned the unmarried
mother to the status of a moral inferior. Stöcker wanted the abolition
of patriarchal attitudes and the laws framed and carried out in a
patriarchal spirit. 'Only thus can we succeed in emancipating women
from their sexual subjection, in replacing brutal despotism by the
consciousness of responsibility, prostitution by love.' Among these
'patriarchal' laws, Stöcker undoubtedly included the divorce laws laid
down in the Civil Code, but her speech went further than demanding
legislative change — it also demanded a change in the values that lay
behind marriage. She now regarded sexual love as the basis of marriage.
The Abolitionists, however, tended to place the emphasis on much
more impersonal values — in particular the desire to have children and
raise a family. Although they too wanted a marriage of equals they did
not — unlike Stöcker — consider sexual love as a proper basis for such a
partnership. Mutual respect was what they demanded.

Where Stöcker differed most sharply from her Abolitionist colleagues after her love-affair was, however, in her growing tendency to
reject the belief that women were naturally chaste. Once again she
called on Nietzsche as a witness for her views. Women's chief debt to
him was now, in Stöcker's revised views, that he taught them to reject
the old conventions of sexual morality as well as the old restriction of
their role in life. 'Above all', she wrote in 1901, 'we must be grateful to
him for replacing the old life-denying ascetic morality of the Church
Fathers, who saw in sexual love something sinful and in women something lowly and impure, with his proved, life-affirming morality, which
frees human beings from its guilty conscience and sanctifies their
love.'[17] This argument was a direct contradiction of the fundamental
moral repressiveness of the Abolititionists; and stage by stage Stöcker
now began to draw the consequences of this contradiction. If — Stöcker
argued in the Berlin Abolitionist branch in 1903 — women who were
driven to prostitution were often unmarried mothers, to whom such
stigma attached that they were subsequently unable to support themselves by any honest employment, one way to save them from this fate
would be to increase the availability of contraceptives and hence
remove the problem at its root. This of course implied a degree of
sexual permissiveness that would not find favour with Stöcker's
Abolititionist colleagues. Anna Pappritz rejected Stöcker's view and
said that it represented the 'man's point of view'; worse still, it would

encourage promiscuity and extra-marital sexuality. The Abolitionists had hitherto believed that men should be educated to be as chaste as they expected the women they married to be. Stöcker, supported in the meeting by Maria Lischnewska, was denying that this was possible and accepting the consequences.[18] The difference of opinion soon widened into a full-scale controversy. Pappritz was supported by a majority of the Berlin Abolitionists, including Minna Cauer, who had previously quarrelled with Adele Schreiber on the same issue. Adele Schreiber, for her part, supported Stöcker.

Stöcker and her supporters could not hope to impose their views on the Berlin Abolitionist movement as a whole. The organisation was by now too firmly in the hands of Pappritz to allow that to happen. But they did enjoy the sympathy of a number of other leading figures in the movement, among them the social worker Frieda Duensing, the revisionist Social Democrat Henriette Fürth and the eminent venereologists Max Flesch and Alfred Blaschko. Stage by stage they broke loose. In October 1903 Stöcker's relations with the Berlin Abolitionist leadership became very cool, and after a violent quarrel with Pappritz on 29 October she ceased to play an active role in the movement, much as Augspurg, Cauer and their associates were also doing for different reasons.[19] For a time, however, she remained within the Abolitionist movement, at least nominally. The problem that faced the Stöcker group was really to find an appropriate vehicle for their ideas. Their disengagement from the Abolitionists was far from sudden and they do not seem to have been able to decide for some time what to do. However, towards the end of 1904 an ideal opportunity presented itself to the Abolitionist rebels in the creation of a new and radical society for the improvement of the condition and status of unmarried mothers, the League for the Protection of Motherhood and Sexual Reform (Bund für Mutterschutz und Sexualreform).

The League for Mutterschutz, soon to become notorious, was founded in Leipzig on 12 November 1904. The founder, Ruth Bré, an unsuccessful and impecunious poetess,[20] had already written and published a number of books arguing for the end of the 'capitalist rule of man' and the restoration of a matriarchate. She was influenced by Social Darwinism and by the ideas of the Swedish social reformer and writer Ellen Key, several of whose books on love and motherhood were published in German translation during this period.[21] The League's first manifesto declared that it would found 'mother-colonies' in the countryside, where unmarried mothers and their children would live supported by State pensions and light agricultural work. The ultimate aim was 'the improvement of the state of the nation through the breeding of the healthy', and with this in mind only 'healthy' mothers would be allowed to participate in the scheme. Pointing to the high incidence of child mortality, sickness and criminality among the illegitimate, Bré argued that her scheme, if extended to a large proportion of the 180,000 children born illegitimately in Germany every year, could bring about a dramatic change for the better in the nation's 'racial health', and hence by implication in its military effectiveness.[22]

Ruth Bré's rural Utopia, with its Social Darwinist and racialist overtones and its anti-urban philosophy, was very similar to the many *völkisch* Utopias being mooted by groups on the extreme right at this time.[23] Although it differed from most of them in its feminist emphasis, it shared with them a common impracticality. The first mother-colony was supposed to have opened in a village near Erfurt on 1 April 1905, but it never seems to have come into existence. Bré's League seemed to be yet another eccentric and impractical society operating on the fringe of politics and doomed to failure from the very beginning. It was at this point that Walter Borgius intervened. Borgius was General Secretary of the Trade Treaty Union (Handelsvertragsverein), an association of left-wing liberals, Hanseatic merchants, bankers and leading representatives of the chemical, engineering and electrical industries, founded in 1900 to fight the proposed erection of a tariff wall urged by heavy industry and agrarian interests.[24] Borgius had already expressed the desire to found an Association for the Reform of the Whole of Sexual Life (Verein zur Reform des gesamten Sexuallebens), but abandoned this scheme on hearing of the foundation of the League and wrote to Ruth Bré instead, offering to set up a branch in Berlin.

Bré, unsuspectingly enough, agreed, and Borgius set about his task with energy and determination. Soon a whole host of prominent people had been persuaded to pledge their support. There were politicians such as Hugo Boettger, a Social Democratic member of the Reichstag who later joined the National Liberals, Friedrich Naumann, the National Social Leader, Heinz Potthoff, another leading member of the Trade Treaty Union, left-liberal member of the Reichstag and enthusiast for women's suffrage, and Anton Erkelenz, the liberal trade union leader;

there were professors and *Kathedersozialisten,* including Max Weber and Werner Sombart; there were doctors and professors of medicine – mostly specialists in dermatology and the venereal diseases – including Iwan Bloch, author of a vast tome on prostitution, the sexologist Max Marcuse and the Berlin Professor of Medicine Ernst Kromayer. Later on the League won the support of the revisionist Social Democratic Reichstag deputies Heinrich Braun and Eduard David. The psychologists Auguste Forel and Sigmund Freud were attached to sister Leagues in Switzerland and Austria;[25] but the League does not appear to have been influenced by their ideas, though Helene Stöcker, like other disciples of Nietzsche, did join the Psychoanalytical Society founded in Berlin in 1910.[26]

Among those feminists who agreed to support the League were Lily Braun, Minna Cauer, Hedwig Dohm, Frieda Duensing, Agnes Hacker,[27] Auguste Kirchhoff, Meta Hammerschlag, Margarete Selenka, Adele Schreiber and Helene Stöcker. The breakaway Abolitionists grouped around Stöcker quickly became dominant in the Berlin branch, aided initially by the sexologist Max Marcuse and by Borgius himself, and they now proceeded to take over the League as a whole. Ruth Bré was persuaded to resign the Presidency on the grounds that the movement could be led most effectively from Berlin. Her Utopian ideas and her plans for homes in the countryside, as well as the most marked features of her Social Darwinism, were dropped, and the new League concentrated on welfare and homes for unmarried mothers in the cities.

These changes appeared to Bré as a perversion of her original intentions in founding the League, and she complained bitterly about the programme of charitable work issued by the Berlin League:

> Instead of providing mothers and their children with a modest standard of life on a small country estate, instead of preparing a *home* for them, a home that the father or husband cannot or will not provide – instead of this, they are to be put in 'homes' with an *institutional* character, within city walls. – Instead of breeding human beings who are capable of work, they are bothering with the *inferior* once more.

Bitterly disappointed, Ruth Bré resigned all her offices in the League,[28] accusing Borgius and his associates of unfair tactics at the founding meeting in Berlin. She attempted to continue her efforts in a re-named '*First* German League for *Mutterschutz*' but her organisational talents were minimal, and the new League was no more successful than the proposed 'mother-colony' near Erfurt. From now on, the destinies of the Mutterschutz movement were to be controlled by Helene Stöcker and the former Abolitionists who had followed her in her rebellion against Pappritz's moral repressiveness.

PROPAGANDA AND PRACTICE, 1905-1908

With the departure of Ruth Bré, the Mutterschutz League was able to concentrate on the task of organising itself and putting its plans into effect. Helene Stöcker who, unlike Borgius, was both willing and able to put all of her considerable energies into work for the League, was elected President, and Max Marcuse Secretary. A periodical with the title of *Mutterschutz* was established, an office was opened in Berlin where Marcuse dispensed free advice to unmarried mothers, and members of the League sallied forth into the provinces to raise support. By 1907 these efforts were beginning to bear fruit. Branches had been founded in Hamburg, Breslau, Mannheim, Berlin, Dresden and Frankfurt am Main, and these were beginning to involve themselves in constructive work, though the Berlin group had to postpone indefinitely the erection of a home for unmarried mothers because of lack of funds.[29]

A number of pamphlets had also been published and several petitions distributed, including one to all town councils in Germany demanding that municipal welfare be extended to unmarried mothers[30] — most of the authorities did not even bother to reply, let alone take the demand seriously — and one to all Ministries of Education in the various federal States asking for the introduction of sex education in State schools.[31] This second petition already bears the characteristic stamp of the League's ideology. It was useless, it argued, to fight the spread of prostitution, venereal disease, sex crimes, pornography and sexual hypocrisy by police measures and repression: the evil must be attacked at its roots, in the mind of the people. Many parents were beyond help, but at least their children could be taught the basic facts of life, as a measure of self-defence if nothing else, and given a positive attitude towards sex, instead of regarding it as something vulgar and immoral.

In January 1906, after a dispute with Stöcker, Marcuse resigned as Secretary, ostensibly for financial reasons.[32] His post was taken over by Lily Braun. She proved a most unsatisfactory Secretary, however, as she declared that she had no time to do any work, and she was eventually succeeded by Adele Schreiber. In the meantime, the Secretary's tasks, from giving advice to unmarried mothers to preparing for the General Assembly, were taken over by Stöcker. These developments left Stöcker in a position of great strength within the League. She was President and Acting Secretary and controlled the movement's periodical as well as running its day-to-day business. It was largely because of this that the League did not develop into what Ruth Bré had feared it would become, a charitable organisation with nothing but a modern outlook to distinguish it from others working in the same field. Stöcker believed firmly in the value of propaganda, and from now on the League's central organisation in Berlin concentrated its efforts on ideological rather than practical measures to improve the status of the unmarried mother.

At the beginning of 1908 Stöcker proposed that the League draw up a detailed programme of its intentions, in order to avoid public misunderstanding about its work. She was opposed on the executive committee by the economist Werner Sombart, who said that all propaganda, verbal and written, in all fields, was completely hopeless. 'There are in general two kinds of people,' he said, 'those who believe in solutions and those who do not. I stand on the ground of the latter . . . One cannot propagate ideas.' Sombart's colleagues did not share this gloomy view. Borgius declared that such views would prohibit any sort of activity in the field of social reform. Propaganda had proved effective in the past. 'How can we help', he asked, 'if we do not cause State and society to cease their brutality? We must throw slogans into the masses.' The general view was summed up by Adele Schreiber, who argued that effective practical work for the improvement of the status of the unmarried mother depended on the alteration of prevailing moral values. 'A large part of those in need is only in need because of the prejudices that make parents, friends and relations turn away from them.' It was up to the League to destroy these prejudices.[33]

Against the advice of Sombart, who soon withdrew from active participation, the League now proceeded to formulate its theoretical principles. Arguing that the existence of large numbers of unmarried mothers proved 'that the existing institution of marriage is no longer in a position to encompass the entire sexual life of the nation', it rejected the 'traditional clerical-ascetic moral teaching, which condemns extra-marital sexual intercourse', and propounded the 'modern, individualist, scientific moral teaching', which it called the New Morality *(Die Neue Ethik)*. Sexual activity was a 'natural and self-evident right', and its moral content could only be judged from the motives that lay behind it.[34] As Heinrich Meyer, a writer of novels on prehistoric themes and one of the League's founders in 1904, put it, 'If physical union is the expression of spiritual communion and true love, then it is moral.'[35] What was immoral was not only marriage without love but also any form of promiscuity or mere hedonism. Ernst Kromayer declared that 'sexual intercourse is a natural thing, like eating or drinking', but he also insisted that 'monogamy, legalised or not, temporary or per-manent, is . . . the only valid form of sexual union.'[36]

Nevertheless, by insisting that marriage, legal or not, was a free contract between equals, based on sexual love, the League was not only arguing, as Kromayer put it in the same speech, merely for 'the liberation of human society from an unnatural and harmful sexual morality' but also taking a stand for 'the liberation of woman'. This part of the League's philosophy was summed up by Stöcker in a speech she delivered in reply to criticisms made at the Union of Progressive Women's Associations' General Assembly in 1905. She denied that she wanted to destroy the institution of marriage. On the contrary, she and her supporters believed in a higher form of marriage, of which the present institution was merely a shadow. She wanted to help men out of their thoughtless tyranny to a better insight and more genuine values. Marriage, she thought, would in no way be threatened if woman developed into a free personality within its bounds. Stöcker was ex-tending the arguments of the radical feminists into the field of marriage and sexuality. 'One sex should never dispose over the other to so great an extent as it does in our society, in its social life, its legislation, and in its sexual and love-life.'[37]

While the central organisation of the League in Berlin set about propagating this new ideology, it was left to the branches to con-centrate on the practical side of the League's programme. This division of labour was quite deliberate. As Helene Stöcker, writing from Berlin, put it:[38]

> All of us here, subscribing as we do to the reform of sexual morality, have been quite clear that *purely practical work would encounter fewer difficulties in public than theoretical* work. *Nevertheless,* we have regarded this theoretical work as far more essential, because every individual piece of work would be no more than a drop in the ocean as far as the great general need is concerned. We believe *the combination of practical welfare work with general propaganda to be particularly effective* so as to give the most different kinds of people the opportunity to work for the great cause in *their* own way. We are equally clear that the *branches* in their *provinces* would in the first place take up *practical* work, and that propaganda and persuasion must remain more the concern of the big *principal cities.*

The question of the relationship between practical welfare work and propaganda, however, was not to be settled as easily as this. In every branch of the League there were two or more less well-defined parties, one favouring welfare, the other propaganda. The difference of emphasis, which repeated on a small scale the split between moderates and radicals within the women's movement as a whole, was to recur with varying intensity throughout the League's history.

In the Stuttgart branch of the League, for example, only a small minority was thought to believe that 'the New Morality is the essence of *Mutterschutz*',[39] and the branch was forced to alter its statutes to accommodate the League's ideological tenets before it was admitted to full rights within the organisation.[40] In Frankfurt am Main the League was apparently in danger of being taken over by members of the Jewish Women's League, who had a conservative concept of social welfare; Ines Wetzel, who tried to run the branch on the lines of the Berlin one, with a strong emphasis on propaganda for the New Morality, complained that Clementine Kramer, the general secretary of the Jewish Women's League, was conspiring to oust her. 'She is fomenting the Jewish elements, who are in the majority and under her control, Frau Fürth is indebted to her for business reasons, she is winning over (Max) Flesch with flattery, in short, it could soon be the case that the whole struggle goes against me.'[41] At one stage indeed it was feared that all the South German branches would break away in a group.[42] Alice Bensheimer was also reported to be trying to take over the Mannheim branch.[43] Hanover's Mutterschutz League, founded in 1907, did not establish any connection with the Berlin organisation but attached itself to the local Frauenwohl instead.[44] Nor was the League able to found a branch in Munich at all: 'nothing can be done in Munich as far as *Mutterschutz* is concerned', remarked Adele Schreiber in 1909, 'as long as Frau Schön-fliess, who really possesses great influence in the Press, has the matter under her control.'[45] The kind of practical work carried out by the League's branches is best exemplified by the successful activity of the Mannheim branch. The City council provided it with free rooms to give advice to unmarried mothers, and the branch dealt with 193 women in 1907-09. It was able to direct most of them to maternity homes, provided 69 of them with material support and helped 18 of them to start legal proceedings for alimony. It also held a number of meetings, at which mainly practical subjects were discussed, petitioned maternity homes to admit the unmarried on the same basis as the married, and asked factory owners with women in their labour force to start maternity insurance schemes. The branch was, however, unable to found its own maternity home because of lack of funds.

Other branches were often slower to get off the ground. Hamburg, for example, led by the free-thinking 'Pastor' Kiessling and the radical suffragist Frieda Radel, complained in 1908 that:

> The two years that have passed since the constitution of the Hamburg branch had to be almost entirely given over to more or less fruitless organisational work. The executive committee changed its composition several times, because it turned out to be endlessly difficult to find the representatives of a unified purpose for all the ideas contained in the concept of *Mutterschutz*. We are very conscious that these internal struggles have placed a great strain on the confidence of members who have wanted to see practical results and had to be continually put off to a later date.

Nevertheless although a number of members had left, the total member-ship of the branch had steadily grown and at the end of 1907 stood at over 380. Clearly the practical side of the League's activities was attracting a lot of support. It was carried out on a modest scale, because the financial resources of the League were never very substantial. However the Frankfurt branch opened its own maternity home in 1907, followed by the Stuttgart branch in 1909. Several other branches opened homes in 1910-11. Their work differed from previous efforts of a similar nature by its refusal to indulge in moral condemnation of the unmarried mother, by its attempt to provide her with employment and legal aid and by its insistence on keeping mother and child together.[46]

The League, as the following table shows, differed from other feminist organisations in two important respects. First, it contained an unusually large number of men, nearly a third of the total. In one branch indeed, Breslau, men actually predominated. The membership also included a number of revisionist Social Democrats. Many of the men were doubtless physicians, dermatologists and venereologists, or social reformers of an advanced type who would prefer the League to social welfare organisations based on Christian morality. Secondly, it is clear that the League depended to an unusually large extent on donations, and the fact that these were almost always made in support of its practical aims was vital. In fact, in this respect it was, as the Statistical Office's figures show, akin to associations on the right wing with definite practical aims, such as the German Colonial Women's League or the German-evangelical Women's League, which also depended to a great extent on donations to support their practical purposes. Unlike the financial backing for these conservative societies, however, the Mutterschutz League's money clearly came from liberal circles, and the figures do indicate that the League's practical aims at least enjoyed considerable support here.

Many liberals, however, found the League's radical ideology distasteful. 'I have advised Frau Stöcker', wrote Anton Erkelenz in April 1905, just as Stöcker's influence in the League was becoming paramount, 'to pursue her Nietzscheanism *outside* the League'.[47] The liberal *Neue Hamburger Zeitung* described the *Mutterschutz* ideology as a 'totally inextricable knot' consisting of 'radical egalitarianism, eccentric fantasy, that reminds one of the French Utopians, of St. Simon and Fourier, and a wild desire, that sometimes seems like a cry for sexual self-indulgence.'[48] The liberal Hamburg *General-Anzeiger* forewarned the League of the inadvisability of advocating free love. 'Economic considerations alone', it said, 'should suffice to demonstrate that when people abandon themselves to the indulgence of their sexual appetites, it is the woman who pays the price.' It thought that the radical views of the leadership in Berlin were hindering effective practical work and alienating many potential supporters, and it advised a more narrow concentration on the concrete problems of helping the unmarried mother.[49] Even the *Frankfurter Zeitung* condemned the League's policies.[50]

TABLE 4

Membership and Income of the Bund für Mutterschutz 1908

Branch	MEMBERSHIP			INCOME		
	Women	Men	Total	Subscriptions	Donations	Total
Berlin	388	217	605	2000		2000
Breslau	124	175	299	1518	25	1543
Dresden	123	50	173			
Frankfurt/M	350	76	426	2912	5580	8492
Hamburg	277	141	418	1000	8000	9000
Königsberg	75	5	80	235		235
Leipzig	94	53	147	750	400	1150
Liegnitz	46	6	52	361		361
Mannheim	108	57	165	686	505	1191
Posen	34	13	47	150		150
Central Organisation	2424	1302	3726	956		956

The membership figures in the bottom row represent the total branch and unattached individual membership of the League. The figures are for January 1908.

Source: *Statistik der Frauenorganisationen im Deutschen Reiche* (1. Sonderheft zum Reichsarbeitsblatte, 1909).

Although its reception among liberals was mixed, the New Morality, not least because its main aim was the liberation of women, found a much wider support within the women's movement as a whole. Indeed the part it played in the development of the women's movement was crucial, and it is to this that we now turn.

THE NEW MORALITY AND THE WOMEN'S MOVEMENT, 1905-1914

The New Morality, as we have seen, began as a splinter-group from the Abolitionist movement. The leaders of this movement were in no way satisfied with the secession of Stöcker and her supporters; on the contrary the foundation of the Mutterschutz League spurred them to fresh attacks. Since the triumph of Abolitionist ideas within the women's movement in 1902, Pappritz had gradually broken with the radicals and moved to the right. By 1908 indeed she had long since abandoned the progressive wing of the women's movement. In 1904 Pappritz felt obliged to resign her seat on the Frauenwohl committee in order to remain in the inner counsels of the BDF since relations between the two organisations were rather strained. Minna Cauer promptly accused Pappritz of 'defection' and 'betrayal' of the radical women's movement. She saw Pappritz's resignation as part of a concerted plot by the BDF leadership to undermine the entire radical movement. Although Pappritz considered herself a radical as late as 1909, she was already urging the BDF to take a hard line against Cauer in March 1904, and she moved close to the German-evangelical Women's League, one of the most conservative of all women's organisations. She had also criticised the sensational methods of the Hamburg Abolitionists, only to be accused in her turn by Lida Gustava Heymann of neglecting propaganda in favour of practical work. Relations between Pappritz and the radicals were so bad by 1907 that the Agitation Commission of the Progressive Women's Union, led by Cauer, Augspurg, Adele Schreiber and Helene Stöcker, tried to call a conference on prostitution for April 1908 without even referring to the Abolitionist organisation or to its leaders Anna Pappritz and Katharina Scheven.[51]

Anna Pappritz and the Abolitionist movement continued to stress the sexually repressive aspects of their ideology, and it was they who led the attack on the New Morality within the women's movement.[52] Their objections to the New Morality were shared by many of the moderates. According to Helene Lange for example, the New Morality had nothing to do with feminism at all – 'the women's movement', she said, 'cannot count women who advocate it among its own.'[53] Yet the New Morality, in the years immediately after the League's foundation, seemed to be carrying all before it in the women's movement. In 1904 Minna Cauer came round from her previously hostile position to full support of Stöcker's views.[54] Else Lüders was not slow in following her lead. Cauer's successor as President of the Union of Progressive Women's Associations, Meta Hammerschlag, was also active in the Mutterschutz movement, as were a number of prominent radical suffragists including Frieda Radel, Auguste Kirchhoff, Regine Deutsch, Adele Schreiber and Maria Lischnewska. Anita Augspurg and Lida Gustava Heymann were also enthusiastic supporters of the New Morality.[55]

From 1904 until 1908 the women's movement became increasingly polarised over the issues raised by the Mutterschutz movement. Protest meetings were held, articles, books and pamphlets for or against circulated with growing frequency. As support for the League and its ideas grew, so the vehemence and determination of the opposition increased. Just as Abolitionism had been the key issue in the women's movement at the turn of the century, so 'Sexual reform' became the key issue in the middle of the 1900s. In both cases the underlying ideological dispute was the same. In both cases the radicals were drawing the consequences of their liberal individualism and applying them to personal life. The Mutterschutz theorists simply took this process one large and very decisive step further than the Abolitionists. The implications of this process of intellectual development were not simply to be found in theoretical writings on the New Morality. They seemed indeed even more radical when they were incorporated into the League's proposals for legislative reform. As far as the Civil Code was concerned, the New Moralists wanted the legal equality of man and wife within marriage and also in their legal relations to the children of the marriage. They wanted easier divorce. They wanted the legal recognition of 'free marriages' to the extent that police interference – not unusual in such cases — would not take place, and that the children of such 'free marriages' should be subject to the same legal conditions with regard to their parents' power over them, and given the same legal rights as the children of legal marriages.[56]

Moreover, the League's views on sexual morality, and its concern for improving the condition of unmarried mothers, led it to reject the traditional belief that the function of marriage was to produce children and thus secure the continuity of the race and the preservation of the State:

> Woman has often been reduced — callously, if unconsciously — to the level of a childbearing machine (remarked Stöcker in 1908), her children regarded as the property of the State while still in the womb. But in reality, unfortunately for her, woman is not a thing, she also has a head and a heart. Motherhood ... should no longer be forced on women by threats of imprisonment, but consciously and responsibly *chosen* ... clarity and truth, planned and conscious decision must take the place of blind chance.

This was in the first place an encouragement to people to use contraceptives.[57] Stöcker and the League were convinced supporters of 'Neo-Malthusianism' as it was known. 'I am convinced', wrote Stöcker to Henriette Fürth,[58] 'that Neo-Malthusianism is not only morally permissible, but morally *necessary* ... I see in Neo-Malthusianism one of the most effective means of solving the woman question, and indeed the social question in its entirety.' The League arranged lectures on contraception for working-class women,[59] and propagandised in a more general way for the use of contraceptives. When a proposal came up in the Reichstag to ban their sale and advertisement altogether, the League launched a vigorous campaign against it.

When she mentioned motherhood being forced on women by threats of imprisonment, Stöcker was referring to Section 218 of the Criminal Code which stipulated that a pregnant woman who deliberately aborted her child was to be imprisoned for a period of between six months and five years. It was on this subject that the League made its influence most strongly felt within the women's movement. The BDF had established a Legal Commission to prepare a set of proposals which would be put to the Government as representing the women's point of view on the reform of the Criminal Code being prepared in these years. When this Legal Commission came to consider Section 218, a sharp divergence of opinion soon emerged among its members. The key factor was the presence in the Commission of Marie Stritt, the President of the BDF, who was an active member of the League and sat on its Council. Her radicalism in this respect may have been in part due to her long experience in the Dresden Legal Protection Association for Women (Rechtsschutzverein für Frauen), which gave legal advice to women and girls in trouble. Julie Eichholz, also a member of the Cómmission and the leader of the Hamburg Legal Protection Association, was of the same opinion as Stritt.[60]

Stritt was the mainstay of the party within the Commission that pressed for the complete deletion of Section 218. In the course of the long debates within the Commission on the subject, Stritt wrote on one occasion:[61]

> ... S218. I can only repeat emphatically once more, what I have already said on previous occasions in favour of deletion. If we women do not take a stand for our own responsibility for ourselves here, in the most female of all tasks in life, in that of 'giving life', if we do not take a stand here against our being regarded merely as the involuntary producers of cannon-fodder – then in my opinion we do not deserve to be regarded as anything else! That as far as the principle of the matter is concerned. As regards the practice, experience and observation of daily life shows that this penal clause is simply laughable.

Stritt, supported on the Commission by one of her lieutenants from Dresden and by Julie Eichholz, convinced the Commission's legal experts – Camilla Jellinek, wife of the liberal Heidelberg jurist Georg Jellinek, and Anna Schulz, a law student also in Heidelberg and a member of the Committee of the Union of Progressive Women's Associations[62] – of the desirability of deleting the paragraph. It was Jellinek who, in a remarkable speech, presented the Commission's demand to the BDF General Assembly in 1908.[63]

> If anybody had told me two years ago, (she began) as I learned for the first time of the demand of some members of the Commission that this paragraph be deleted – that is, that the action punishable under this paragraph should be made exempt from punishment – if anybody had told me that it would fall to my lot to represent this demand to the General Assembly of the Federation of German Women's Associations, I would have laughed heartily at such an idea.

Yet, she continued, she had been gradually persuaded over the past two years that the paragraph should be entirely abolished. She pointed out that the legalisation of abortion was neither without legal precedent nor a danger to the race since, if legalisation increased the frequency of abortion, nevertheless infant mortality and illegitimate births, both the origin of many social evils, would decline. Moreover, legalisation probably would not increase the frequency of abortion, since illegal abortion was already practised on a very wide scale. She denied both that the embryo was a legal person, with its own rights, and that any third party — for example, the father — had any rights over it. To punish abortion, she concluded, was an unwarrantable intrusion into the right of a woman to dispose over her own body. This was the most fundamental of legal rights and she demanded its recognition 'in the name of the right to self-determination, in the name of the free personality of woman! '

Jellinek and the Commission did their best to meet all possible objections to their proposals. To begin with, they proposed to retain Section 219, which made it illegal to assist in the performance of an abortion. In Jellinek's view, abortion could be performed without assistance in the early stages of pregnancy but not later on. In effect, then, the proposals only covered the first few weeks of pregnancy.[64] To the argument that the legalisation of abortion would free sex-life from all responsibility, Jellinek replied that this was already the case as far as men — who did not have to bear the consequences of their actions — were concerned, that Section 218 was no deterrent to them and that it was foolish to expect that one could educate them into responsibility. To objections that abortion was immoral and should therefore be punishable by law, she replied that:

> if we punished everything that was morally deplorable, the world would be one huge prison. It cannot lie within the competence of the modern State to forbid actions simply on the grounds that they are morally inferior, for its competence is limited by the necessity of preserving the freedom of the individual over his own body, irrespective of how that disposition is to be morally judged in individual cases.

That Jellinek's arguments were couched in such defensive terms was a sign that heavy opposition to the proposal was expected by the Commission. Indeed the idea of making abortion legal only if it was unassisted was already a last-minute compromise, reached in the Commission despite the protests of Marie Stritt.[65] Originally the Commission had intended to abolish this paragraph too, but had withdrawn the proposal in order to blunt the onslaught of the conservatives. Yet the Commission received powerful support at the Congress. It is striking that many of the women who spoke in favour of the deletion of Section 218 at the Assembly were married, and that those who spoke for its retention were with one exception unmarried. Even more important than this was the fact that the majority of those who supported Jellinek were prominent in the League for Mutterschutz. Helene Stöcker herself spoke only briefly, saying that Jellinek had already expressed her views better than she could. Meta Hammerschlag made an emotional speech 'as a mother', Else Lüders declared that the Berlin Frauenwohl supported the deletion of the paragraph, and Marie Wegner also backed the Commission. Although she did not speak, Anita Augspurg too was an enthusiastic supporter of the campaign to delete Section 218, and the Hamburg Suffrage Union backed her in this.[66]

However, the most powerful speech in favour of the Legal Commission's recommendations was delivered by Adele Schreiber. She brought to the question a social insight that most speakers entirely lacked, and which was to lead her into the Social Democratic party after the war. One of the most frequent arguments for the retention of Section 218 was that women had recourse to abortion because their desire for a comfortable and pleasurable life led them to avoid the responsibility of bearing children. A deterrent was therefore thought necessary for such morally irresponsible people. But, said Schreiber:

> ... those women who reject motherhood out of lust for pleasure and comfort are almost never punished. They do not belong to the 400 women who are sent to prison every year (under this paragraph), because we are dealing here with a class law, because propertied women are in a position to prevent this happening to them ... The victims are victims of our social order ...

As the debate wore on, however, it became clear that the majority of the Assembly would probably vote against the Commission's report. 'It would be a sad page in the history of the women's movement', said Jellinek in her closing speech, 'if the General Assembly of its main organisation refused today to take an important step forward on the road to the emancipation of women.' Nevertheless, she was pessimistic about the outcome of the debate. 'Section 218 will be deleted one day', she concluded, 'even if you vote to retain it today.' In fact the vote was close. Many delegates supported the Commission's proposals, but they were in a minority. The Assembly voted to reject the Report and retain Section 218 in an amended form. The decision was in every way a momentous one. The actual rejection of a Commission's report was in itself almost unprecedented, and caused bitter resentment among the Commission's supporters. Marie Stritt made a speech from the chair regretting the destruction of her hopes, and said that 'what has not come to pass today, will happen another time'. A group of radicals led by Adele Schreiber, Helene Stöcker, Meta Hammerschlag, Frieda Radel, Hanns Dorn, Martha Schnee, Käthe Schirmacher, Adelheid von Welczeck and Else Lüders — in other words, by the Mutterschutz League — issued a statement regretting the Assembly's decision, but it was final and never to be reversed. Section 218 remained on the statute book throughout all the political vicissitudes of subsequent decades, to become a major political issue once more after the accession of the SPD/FDP coalition to power in 1969. Never again however did the bourgeois women's movement come as near to declaring itself in favour of total deletion of the paragraph as it did in 1908.[67]

The decision provoked an immediate crisis in the ranks of the Mutterschutz League. Those who thought that the League's propaganda aims should be played down and more attention given to its practical work seized the opportunity offered by the BDF's decisive rejection of the League's ideas. Led by Adele Schreiber, they demanded that most of the funds of the League be devoted to the establishment of maternity homes. Stöcker strongly resisted this attack as an attempt to supplant her as President (which it was not) and a bid to water down the radicalism of the League in order to make it more palatable to the general public (which, ultimately, it was). Soon the League's energies were entirely absorbed in this internal struggle in a way all too reminiscent of what was happening in the Suffrage Union in these same years. Faces were slapped at committee meetings; branches, then whole sections, broke away from the League in protest; leading figures in the women's movement, including Marie Stritt, Minna Cauer and Lily Braun, spent many sleepless nights sitting on arbitration committees that failed to arbitrate; a whole series of the League's most prominent supporters resigned, including Werner Sombart, Anton Erkelenz, Friedrich Naumann, Alfred Blaschko, Iwan Bloch, Lily Braun, Auguste Forel, Ernst Kromayer, Max Flesch, Henriette Fürth, Maria Lischnewska, Regine Deutsch, Adele Schreiber and Frieda Radel.

Schreiber also set up a new society called the German Society for the Rights of Mothers and Children (Deutsche Gesellschaft für Mutter – und Kindesrecht), and Radel and Kiessling took the Hamburg branch out of the League without affiliating it to any other national organisation.

The rump of the League remained effectively under Stöcker's control. She retained the support of those who had continued to have faith in her integrity – including Eduard and Gertrud David, Auguste Kirchhoff, Max Rosenthal and Ines Wetzel. Those who were left, however, were few. Moreover, between 1910 and 1914 the ruin of the League was completed by a series of disastrous scandals. In the middle of the quarrel Schreiber had discovered that Stöcker was living secretly in a 'free marriage' with one of her main supporters Dr Bruno Springer. Stöcker in her turn attempted to prove that Schreiber had also been sleeping with one or more of her supporters on the League's committee. The seven lawsuits that resulted from these accusations brought the whole affair out into the open and kept it there for four years, during which time the German public was treated to the unsavoury spectacle of the leading members of the Mutterschutz League accusing each other in court and in print of sexual promiscuity. This was not only extremely damaging to the League; it also made it clear that the League's leaders had not been able to free themselves from the conventional sexual morality which they spent so much of their time in denouncing. This above all else made it impossible any longer to take the League seriously.[68]

The achievement of the Mutterschutz League then, like that of the suffragist movement, was minimal. It had a few practical results to show for its efforts, in the form of a small number of maternity homes catering for unmarried mothers, but on the whole its propaganda for the idea of free love had done more harm than good. It had had no effect on public opinion save to arouse a great deal of public hostility to German feminism, though it was wilfully misinterpreted by anti-feminists into something much more radical than it really was; and, as we shall see, it provided the opportunity for the conservative forces within the feminist movement to rally and eventually to reverse the trend to the left that had been dominant within the movement since the late 1890s. Yet all this should not be allowed to obscure the true significance of the Mutterschutz League. We have seen that for a time at least the Female Suffrage Union, pushed to the left by the logic of the German political situation was, in its support for universal suffrage and in its political stance on other issues, more radical than women's suffrage organisations in other countries, including Britain and America. The New Moralists also represented something more radical than the feminism of the Anglo-Saxon world. They extended the feminist demand for individual self-determination to the personal sphere. They rejected the sexually repressive aspects of liberal individualism. They attacked the code of sexual respectability laid down by bourgeois society. For a time at least they attempted to ally liberalism, Social Darwinism and Nietzscheanism into a new social ideology that would preserve the most libertarian and individualist elements in all three creeds and translate them into the practical demand that the individual woman should be allowed to dispose over her own body without interference from the State.

The demands of the Mutterschutz League for the availability of and dissemination of knowledge about contraceptive methods, for the legalisation of abortion, for the recognition of 'free marriages', for State financial support of unmarried mothers, and all the more general demands that lay behind the League's official legislative programme — that women should be equal to men in their freedom to determine and enjoy their personal life — these demands outraged respectable society in Wilhelmine Germany. In many ways they were more akin to the demands of the Women's Liberation Movement of the 1960s and 1970s than to those of the feminism of pre-1914 days. In its heyday in the brief period from 1905 to 1910, the Mutterschutz League represented an aspect of feminism that was not to be found in other countries. What Helene Stöcker was saying and doing in her campaign was not of course unique; Victoria Woodhull and Annie Besant, Margaret Sanger and Marie Stopes campaigned for similar aims. What *was* unique was the fact that Stöcker's programme enjoyed the broad support of the radical feminist movement. The exponents of free love and of contraception were generally ostracised by the feminist movement in England and America; even Josephine Butler had been treated by them with obloquy and distrust.[69] Helene Stöcker and the movement she led were by contrast *part* of the feminist movement in Germany. Meetings of the Mutterschutz League were reported regularly in the radical feminist press; radical feminists spoke out in favour of Stöcker's ideas; leading members of the Mutterschutz League such as Adele Schreiber, August Kirchhoff and Frieda Radel held important posts in the female suffrage movement without any difficulty. When the crisis in the League was reaching its height, the two most senior figures in the German women's movement, Marie Stritt, the President of the BDF, and Minna Cauer, the spiritual leader of the radicals, were concerned enough to spend many fruitless hours trying to persuade the parties involved to come to a settlement.[70] In this respect then the feminist movement in Germany was, at its most radical point, more advanced than any other feminist movement. Not everyone was happy with this situation however; and there were many more moderate feminists who were determined to put an end to the situation in which the ideals of the Mutterschutz League threatened to become the ideals of the feminist movement as a whole. These people triumphed at the BDF General Assembly of 1908; and their triumph gave the signal for a general onslaught on radical feminism as a whole.

NOTES

1. For discussion of the ideology of sexual repression in the 19th century see Peter T. Cominos, 'Late Victorian Sexual Respectability and the Social System', *International Review of Social History,* 1963; and Carl N. Degler, 'What Ought to Be and What Was: Women's Sexuality in the Nineteenth Century', *American Historical Review,* 79/5, Dec. 1974.

2. Helene Stöcker was prominent in the bourgeois pacifist movement in the Weimar Republic, and a number of short biographical sketches exist. They are all extremely inaccurate, however, particularly on Stöcker's career before 1914 (e.g., Istvan Déak, *Weimar Germany's Left-Wing Intellectuals. A Political History of the Weltbühne and its circle.* (Berkeley/Los Angeles, 1968), 270-1). The following account is based largely on Stöcker's manuscript autobiography, preserved in the Helene Stöcker papers, Swarthmore College Peace Collection (hereinafter SCPC), Swarthmore, Pennsylvania, and on the Adele Schreiber Nachlass in the Bundesarchiv, Koblenz.

3. SCPC Swarthmore, NL Helene Stöcker, 1/2: Selbstbiographie (B), 2/1-6, 3/26-28.

4. ABDF 4/4: 'Rundschreiben an die Mitglieder des Vereins "Frauenwohl" und seine Schwestervereine', (Berlin, 1899), 3-15; Else Lüders, *Der 'linke Flügel'*, 34-37.

5. HLA 16: Pappritz Tagebuch (MS), January 1902.

6. StA Hbg, Cl. VII, Lit. Rf. No. 29, Vol. 41; *HC*, 4 Oct. 1898.

7. SCPC Swarthmore, NL Helene Stöcker, 1/2: Selbstbiographie (B), 9/8-9.

8. StA Hbg, PP, S9000/II: *BLA*, 21 March 1902.

9. SCPC Swarthmore, NL Helene Stöcker 1/2: Selbstbiographie (B), 6/3, 7/5-8, 10-11a, 15, 17-18; 9/1-2. Most biographies refer to her as the first woman Ph.D. in Germany; she herself, however, more plausibly, attributed this distinction to Käthe Schirmacher (ibid. 12/3).

10. 'Frauengedanken', in Helene Stöcker, *Die Liebe und die Frauen* (2nd ed., Berlin, 1908), 24-29.

11. 'Nietzsches Frauenfeindschaft', in ibid., 21-80.

12. See R. J. Hollingdale, *Nietzsche* (London, 1974) for this interpretation.

13. op. cit., 47. For Nietzsche's views, see Rudolph Binion, *Frau Lou. Nietzsche's Wayward Disciple* (Princeton, 1968), 211 and n.. Stöcker's enthusiasm for Nietzsche brought her within the social circle of his disciples, who included such notorious literary apologists (and practitioners) of free love as Lou Andreas-Salomé. Cf. Binion, op. cit., 210n., 220, 309, 312, 320-1, 323, 447, 487-8.

14. HLA 17: Stöcker to Pappritz, 13 Feb. 1900, 22 Feb. 1900.

15. SCPC Swarthmore, NL Helene Stöcker, 1/2: Selbstbiographie (B), 4-5 passim. The man concerned 'Dr A. T.' was a *Lektor* at Glasgow University, and Stöcker pursued him there in 1899, returning to Germany early in 1900 after finding he had become embittered because his wife had recently died. He was forced to leave by demonstrations of students and sailors against his criticisms of Britain's conduct of the Boer War. The affair is described in Stöcker's novel *Liebe* (Berlin, 1922).

16. StA Hbg, PP, S9000/I: *GA*, 30 Sept. 1903. Cf. SCPC Swarthmore, NL Helene Stöcker, 1/2: Selbstbiographie (B), 12a/3-7.

17. 'Nietzsches Frauenfeindschaft', in Helene Stöcker, *Die Liebe und die Frauen* (2nd ed., Berlin, 1908), 80.

18. HLA 16: A. Pappritz, 'Wie ich zu meiner Arbeit kam', 154-159; *FB*, 15 April 1904, 58-59.

19. HLA 17: Stöcker to Pappritz, 22 Oct. 1903, 30 Oct. 1903, 21 Oct. 1903, 3 Nov. 1903.

20. BA Koblenz, NL Schreiber, Pak. 25: cutting of *Neue Zeitung* (Strassburg), 7 Jan. 1912 (obituary of Ruth Bré). Citations from this uncatalogued *Nachlass* are made with the number of the *Paket* followed by the number of the letter (B1-B367) or minute (P1-P183), where available. The numbers are marked in blue crayon. The material is in reverse chronological order in *Pakete* 1-3, mostly in carbon copy form.

21. Ellen Key was also in contact with Georg von Vollmar, the Bavarian revisionist Social Democrat, whose papers contain a quantity of her letters.

22. BA Koblenz, NL Schreiber, 3: 'Ruth Bré und der Bund fur Mutterschutz'.

23. George L. Mosse, *The Crisis of German Ideology* (London, 1966), 108-125.

24. Dirk Stegmann, *Die Erben Bismarcks. Parteien und Verbände in der Spätphase des Wilhelminischen Deutschlands* (Köln/Berlin, 1970), 75-80.

25. BA Koblenz, NL Schreiber, 3: 'Ruth Bré und der Bund fur Mutterschutz'. Freud donated 20 Kronen to the Austrian League on its foundation and joined it at the same time. Cf. BA Koblenz, NL Schreiber, 3: Jahresbericht 1907 des Österreichischen Bundes fur Mutterschutz.

26. Peter Gay, *Weimar Culture. The Outsider as Insider* (London, 1969), 35; Rudolph Binion, *Frau Lou* (op. cit.), 447.

27. Agnes Hacker was one of the earliest women physicians in Germany, and was personal physician to the leading radical feminists. She died in 1909.

28. BA Koblenz, NL Schreiber, 3: Ruth Bré, 'Der erste deutsche Bund fur Mutterschutz', in *Die Neue Heilkunst,* Sonderdruck aus No. 9 vom 8. Nov. 1905. Cf. ibid.: Protokoll der 1. konstituierenden Ausschusssitzung am 5. Jan. 1905. In subsequent accounts of the foundation of the League, Stöcker asserted that she herself had founded it in January 1905. Stöcker's account however, as the documents in the Schreiber *Nachlass* indicate, was misleading. In her autobiography, Stöcker portrayed Bré as an interloper who was 'ein wenig "crazy" wie die Engländer sagen'; her account confirms that she first tried to persuade the Abolitionists to adopt her ideas. (SCPC Swarthmore, NL Helene Stöcker, 1/2: Selbstbiographie (B), 12a passim.

29. BA Koblenz, NL Schreiber, 3: Protokoll der Ausschusssitzung 23 Oct. 1906. For the foundation of the Frankfurt branch, see IISG Amsterdam, Collection Henriette Fürth: Stöcker to Fürth, 30 Dec. 1904, 15 Feb. 1905, 21 March 1905, 21 March 1905 et seq.

30. BA Koblenz, NL Schreiber, 3, P44: Praktische Kommission, 16 Sept. 1908.

31. BA Koblenz, NL Schreiber, 1: Petitionen und Veröffentlichungen.

32. For the complicated quarrels that led to Marcuse's resignation, see ibid., 3, P2: 'Stöcker-Marcuse 1906' (Rundschreiben von Helene Stöcker); 1: Marcuse-Angelegenheit; 3, P166: Fall Marcuse 1907, 1: 'An die Mitglieder des Bundes fur Mutterschutz' (Berlin, Dec. 1907). Marcuse captured the League's Journal *Mutterschutz* and renamed it *Sexual-Probleme.* The change of title is indicative of the clash of views that led to Marcuse's departure from the League.

33. BA Koblenz, NL Schreiber, 3, P18: Sitzung des Vorstandes, Jan. 1908. Sombart's pessimism, reflected in his growing disillusion with Social Democracy, probably indicated an attitude towards social reform that owed more and more to a peculiar kind of economic determinism. See Werner Krause, *Werner Sombarts Weg von Kathedersozialismus zum Faschismus* (East Berlin, 1962), and Chapter II of Herman Lebovics, *Social Conservatism and the Middle Classes in Germany, 1914-1933* (Princeton, 1969).

34. BA Koblenz, NL Schreiber, 3, P28a: Flugblattentwurf, 'Zur Aufklärung! '

35. Heinrich Meyer, *Das Christentum und die Neue Ethik* (Berlin, n.d.).

36. BA Koblenz, NL Schreiber, 1: Thesen zum Referat des Herrn Professor Kromayer. Hamburg, 1909.

37. StA Hbg, PP, S9000/I: *HF*, 4 Oct. 1905.

38. IISG Amsterdam, Collection Henriette Fürth: Stöcker to Fürth, 12 Oct. 1905.

39. BA Koblenz, NL Schreiber, 2, B3a: Renetta Brandt to Stöcker, 27 Oct. 1908.

40. ibid., 2, B19: Renetta Brandt to Schreiber, 7 Nov. 1908; 3: P60, P62.

41. ibid., 2 B25: Wetzel to Schreiber, 20 Nov. 1908.

42. ibid., 2, B17: Borgius to Schreiber, n.d. (Nov. 1908).

43. ibid., 2, B1: Stöcker to Schreiber, 27 March 1907.

44. ibid., 3: Geschäftsbericht der Ortsgruppe Hamburg 1907-1908.

45. ibid., 2, B28b: Schreiber to Stöcker, 28 Jan. 1909.

46. ibid., 1: Geschäftsberichte der Ortsgruppen. See also Max Rosenthal, *Zur Geschichte des Bundes für Mutterschutz* (Breslau, 1912).

47. BA Koblenz, NL Schreiber, 5: Erkelenz to Bré, 22 April 1905.

48. StA Hbg, PP, S9000/I: *NHZ*, 5 Oct. 1905.

49. ibid.: *GA*, 17 April 1909.

50. StA Hbg, PP, S8326: *HC*, 6 Aug. 1905. For the League's practical welfare work, see also Max Marcuse, *Aus unseren bisherigen Erfahrungen und Erfolgen. Rückblick auf das 1. Jahr des Bundes für Mutterschutz – Jahresbericht des Vorsitzenden* (Frankfurt am Main, 1906); Maria Lischnewska, *Unser Praktischer Mutterschutz. Bericht, erst. auf der 1. Generalversammlung des Bundes für Mutterschutz* (Berlin, 1907).

51. ABDF 5/XII/7: Pappritz to Stritt, 12 March 1904; HLA 17: Hedwig Winckler to Pappritz, 13 Feb. 1901, Cauer to Pappritz, 29 June 1904, Pappritz to *Frauenwohl* Vorstand, Berlin, 23 June 1904, Paula Müller to Pappritz, 5 July 1907; ABDF 5/IV/1: Stritt to Vorstand, 18 Dec. 1907, 4 April 1908; HLA 16: Anna Pappritz, 'Wie ich zu meiner Abeit kam' (MS. autobiography), 72.

52. cf. IISG Amsterdam. Collection Henriette Fürth: Stöcker to Fürth, 12 Oct. 1905.

53. Helene Lange, 'Moderne Streitfragen in der Frauenbewegung', *DF* Vol. 13, No. 2, 75.

54. HLA 16: Anna Pappritz, 'Wie ich zu meiner Arbeit kam', 159-60. There may well have been a connection between this change of mind and Cauer's quarrel with Pappritz which occurred at the same time.

55. StA Hbg, PP, S9000/I: *HC*, 8 Oct. 1905; ibid., S9001/II: *HN*, 21 May 1905. Lida Gustava Heymann, in *FB*, 13/12, 15 June 1907, 92; StA Hbg, PP, SA593/II: *NHZ*, 21 March 1905, *HNN*, 22 March 1905; StA Hbg, PP, S9001/II: *HF*, 18 Oct. 1908.

56. *FB*, 13/3, 1 Feb. 1907, 20-21, 'Die Tagung des Bundes für Mutterschutz'.

57. BA Koblenz, NL Schreiber, 1: Referat über den Vortrag von Helene Stöcker am 27 Nov. 1908.

58. IISG Amsterdam, Collection Henriette Fürth: Stöcker to Fürth, 20 Oct. 1905.

59. BA Koblenz, NL Schreiber, 3; P49: Vorstand der Ortsgruppe Berlin, 1 Nov. 1908.

60. ABDF 2/III/4: Eichholz to Bensheimer, 9 Jan. 1907.

61. ABDF 2/III/3: Stritt to Bensheimer, 12 July 1906.

62. *FB*, Vol. 13, No. 20, 15 Oct. 1907, 156, footnote.

63. The following account of the Assembly is taken from ABDF 16/I/5: Breslauer Generalversammlung 1908, Stenogramm, pp. 14-20, 365-468.

64. i.e. the proposals approximated to the so-called '*Fristenlösung*' which would legalise abortion carried out in the first three months of pregnancy.

65. ABDF 2/III/4, Stritt to Bensheimer, 28 Sept. 1908.

66. StA Hbg, PP, S14139: 'Auszüge aus Versammlungsberichten über die Schriftstellerin Dr. jur. Anita Augspurg', 26 Nov. 1906; ibid., S9000/I: *HF*, 18 Oct. 1908.

67. ABDF 16/I/5: Breslauer Generalversammlung 1906, Stenogramm, 14-20, 365-468. For the key factor in the voting, the intervention of the German-evangelical Women's League, see below.

68. For a full account of this affair, with extensive documentation from the Schreiber *Nachlass*, see R. J. Evans, 'The Women's Movement in Germany' (Oxford D.Phil. thesis, 1972), Chapter 4. See also Regine Deutsch, Francis Sklarek (eds.), *Zur Krise im Bund für Mutterschutz* (Berlin, 1910); Helene Stöcker, *Krisenmache. Eine Abfertigung* (The Hague, 1910). I hope to write at length about the break-up of the Mutterschutz League on another occasion.

69. See William H. O'Neill, *The Woman Movement. Feminism in the United States and England* (London, 1969), 25-29, 36-38.

70. BA Koblenz, NL Schreiber, 2: B150, Cauer to Schreiber, 6 Dec. 1909; ibid., 1: B281, Cauer to Schreiber, 9 April 1910 et seq.; ibid., 3: P182, General-versammlung Halle (1910).

5

THE RADICAL COLLAPSE

A PALACE REVOLUTION:
THE REMOVAL OF MARIE STRITT
1906-1910

We have seen in the last two chapters how the two most radical of the feminist organisations, the Suffrage Union and the Bund für Mutterschutz, collapsed and disintegrated in the years 1908-1914. It is now time to turn to the more general context of these events. The collapse of the Suffrage Union and the New Morality movement was in fact part of a general process in which the women's movement as a whole, after becoming steadily more radical from 1898 onwards, began in 1908 to move rapidly to the right, away from the liberal individualism that had been its most marked feature in the first half of the 1900s. It affected in the first instance the largest and most important of German feminist organisations, the BDF. With 150,000 women[1] united behind its strongly feminist programme in 1908, the BDF could stand comparison with many of the most influential organisations in the land, at least in terms of numbers. The left-wing liberals for example, united in 1910, could only muster 133,000 members.[2] This growth in numbers and comprehensiveness meant that the BDF was on the way to becoming what in 1908 it was already beginning to claim to be: identical with the women's movement itself.

In 1906 the BDF finally adopted the definition of its aims suggested by the radicals before the turn of the century and rejected in the General Assembly of 1898: it was now officially committed to the 'improvement of the female sex in economic, legal and spiritual matters', although it still insisted that it also aimed at 'the improvement of the community'.[3] In 1907 it went further and produced a document entitled 'Principles and Demands of the Women's Movement'. This was a set of demands to which members and member associations were expected, though not required, to subscribe. In many ways it was a liberal, even a radical document, incorporating many of the ideas advanced by the radical feminists which the BDF had rejected in 1899. The conservative Hamburg Branch of the General German Women's Association indeed, led by Helene Bonfort, took very strong exception to its markedly feminist character.[4] The document was divided into four main parts. The first, dealing with the need to reform the Civil Code, demanded full equality for women within marriage; a wife was to have equal power over all decisions affecting herself, the family and the children, and full control over her own property. If she had no earnings or possessions, the husband was obliged to make over a portion of his own income for her personal use. In its section on 'marriage and the family', the programme went on to include the whole range of reforms advocated by the Abolitionists, including the ending of State regulated prostitution and the double standard, the education of men to 'moral self-control' and the responsibility of the father for the support of his illegitimate child and its mother.

The programme's section on education began with the demand that children of both sexes must be treated as equals from the very beginning. Boys, it declared, must be taught at home to regard their sisters as having equal rights in every respect. Daughters must be given an equal chance of a good education and must be brought up to be independent and capable of supporting themselves. Girls whose formal education ended when they left the *Volksschule* must be provided with an obligatory period of further education to give them skills necessary for the proper fulfilment of the tasks they must later undertake in marriage and employment. Those girls who wanted to pursue their formal education further must be admitted to all higher boys' schools — that is, the BDF demanded the implementation of full co-education since, as its programme pointed out, 'higher school education for girls is at the moment little suited to educate them to intellectual independence and to an understanding of the economic and social life of our time'.

As far as employment was concerned, the BDF demanded equal pay for women, the ending of all restrictions on female employment save where such employment was felt by women themselves to be unsuitable, the right to be promoted to higher positions and participation in all representative bodies connected with their profession or post. Married women employees were to have proper insurance schemes and protection in the event of childbirth. The most advanced of all the four sections in the BDF's programme was undoubtedly that dealing with 'public life'. It included in the first place all the demands of the moderates – principally the admission of women with equal rights to responsible administrative positions in various organs of the social and welfare services, from women's prisons to the education authorities, and the admission of women to juries and the legal profession. It also went on to demand full rights of assembly and association, and active and passive suffrage at all levels up to and including the Reichstag. The programme concluded by affirming that full political rights for women were necessary in order to secure their rights in other fields.[5]

This was an impressive and far-reaching programme. Clearly the BDF had come a long way since the days when, in the late 1890s, it had merely aimed to bring together women's welfare and charity associations to facilitate co-operation and discussion. The sections in the programme dealing with political rights and moral reform indicate how successful the radicals had been in persuading the women's movement as a whole to adopt their demands, but two reservations must be made about the effectiveness of this programme. First, although all the member associations of the BDF of course subscribed to the policies laid down in the programme, few of them pursued them actively. As the BDF grew larger, so it came to unite more and more groups of women whose aims can only be described as feminist in the vaguest sense of the word. Societies such as the German-Colonial Women's League (Deutsch-Kolonialer Frauenbund), dedicated to the preservation of the purity of the white race in the German colonies through the export of white women from the mother country, founded in 1907 and numbering some 12,000 members by 1911,[6] or the German Association against the Misuse of Alcoholic Drinks (Deutscher Verein gegen den Missbrauch geistiger Getränke), founded in 1883 and numbering 37,600 (mostly men) in 1911 — had little interest in actively campaigning for female suffrage or the abolition of State-regulated prostitution, despite the fact that both groups as members of the BDF subscribed at least nominally to both these aims. The pace was set by the radicals: the BDF leadership followed at a slower rate and the bulk of member societies lagged far behind. 'It can indeed be said', wrote the author of the official history of the BDF in later years, 'that the Federation as a whole was well in advance of a large part of its members in its demands.'[7]

Secondly, it was really up to the leadership of the BDF to decide which of its aims it would pursue most actively; and here the emphasis was in the first place on fulfilling the more 'moderate' part of the programme. The petitions sent by the BDF to the Reichstag and to the various legislative assemblies at a more local level dealt in the main with local suffrage *(Kommunalwahlrecht)* and the admission of women to offices in local administration and welfare; only the Suffrage Union campaigned actively for more far-reaching reforms. In other fields the BDF was even less actively radical, and tended to leave campaign work to the relevant member association, although on occasion, particularly in the spheres of education, admission to posts in local government and welfare and moral reform, the BDF was prepared to lend its authority to petitions and campaigns organised by member associations.

Nevertheless, the steady radical pressure exerted on the BDF since the end of the 1890s not only continued on all fronts in the early years of the new century, but was also extended to include a further area of moral and social reform not mentioned in the programme of 1907: the reforms of relations between the sexes urged by Helene Stöcker and the advocates of the 'New Morality'. As we saw in the last chapter, the years 1905-1908 saw a campaign waged by the supporters of the 'New Morality' to gain influence on the BDF, culminating in the attempt in 1908 to commit the BDF to the complete abolition of Section 218 of the Criminal Code and the full legislation of abortion. This attempt was ultimately defeated at the BDF General Assembly in 1908. We have seen how this was a turning-point in the history of the Mutterschutz League; more important, however, was the fact that it also constituted a turning-point in the history of the BDF.

The defeat of the proposal to abolish Section 218 was in fact the first step in a concerted campaign, organised by a combination of remnants of the old moderates and a new group of determined conservatives whose ideas were profoundly hostile to the liberal individualism of the radicals, aimed at reversing the trend towards radical feminism within the BDF and eliminating the influence of all those within the BDF who supported it. The reasons for the organisation of this campaign were many, although it was first galvanised into action by the prospect of the BDF supporting legalised abortion; the chief victim of the campaign was to be Marie Stritt, President of the Federation of German Women's Associations.

We have seen that Stritt was an active opponent of Section 218, and was instrumental in persuading the BDF Legal Commission to urge its abolition. She was also on the Council of the Mutterschutz League. Although it was not officially part of the BDF, the League was nevertheless represented in the BDF through most of its leading figures, who were active in other member societies. It was the Mutterschutz League that led the drive within the BDF for advanced policies on sexual freedom. It was Stritt who provided the major support for it within the BDF hierarchy. Although her relations with the radicals were not always entirely cordial,[8] it was nevertheless in some measure due to her influence that the radicals' position within the BDF grew more powerful in the years from 1900 to 1908. It was partly because of Stritt's advocacy that the BDF incorporated the demand for female suffrage into its programme in 1902; that it voted for a resolution condemning the activities of the Black Hundreds in Russia in 1906; that Helene Stöcker could speak unhindered at the 1907 General Assembly on 'The New Marriage'; and that the Legal Commission voted to legalise abortion in 1908. With Stritt at the head of the BDF, the radicals could feel there was a chance of ultimate victory.[9]

In October 1907 the Union of Progressive Women's Associations, founded in 1899 by Minna Cauer and Anita Augspurg as a radical alternative to the BDF, then still entirely dominated by the old moderates, voted in favour of a resolution moved by Maria Lischnewska and Käthe Schirmacher to join the BDF, now that the latter organisation had largely lost its conservative character. The motion was supported by Minna Cauer, who felt however that she was too closely identified with the policy of staying outside the BDF to be effective within it, and she resigned as President when the vote was passed. A compromise motion proposed by Adele Schreiber by which Cauer, together with Augspurg and Heymann, who also resigned because they were opposed to the policy of joining the BDF, formed an 'agitation commission' to steer the Union from behind the scenes, was also passed.[10] But this was never very active, for now the leading radicals became more and more exclusively absorbed in the suffrage campaign. Under Cauer's successor, Meta Hammerschlag, reported Käthe Schirmacher in 1910, 'everything is vegetating'.[11] The Union of Progressive Women's Associations had lost its driving force and its real leadership, and it fell gradually into obscurity. Its development in 1909-1910 was also marked by a series of quarrels that further impaired its effectiveness, and it is scarcely surprising that Käthe Schirmacher concluded that it could not be long before the Union's final dissolution.[12]

In 1907, however, these developments still lay in the future; and the decision of the Progressives to join the BDF seemed yet another step in the general spread of radical influence within the women's movement. With Stritt in charge, the BDF seemed about to capitulate to the radicals all along the line. Already in 1906, indeed, a first attempt had been made to oust her by those who disagreed with her support of the radicals. The opposition, led by Anna Pappritz, had objected to her refusal to allow the BDF's own magazine, the *Centralblatt,* to review a conservatively inclined book on marriage by Marianne Weber, wife of the sociologist Max Weber and a leading figure in the moderate women's movement in Baden.[13] In Hamburg Helene Bonfort and the moderates wanted to replace Stritt with Weber herself, in order to 'rescue the Federation',[14] or in other words to defeat the radicals. Stritt disliked quarrels and intrigues of this sort, and in August she declared her intention of resigning at the General Assembly in October.[15] She had already threatened to resign once before;[16] and now it looked as if she would really go after all. In September 1906, just before the Assembly, Alice Bensheimer told Ida Dehmel, wife of the poet Richard Dehmel and a personal friend of Bensheimer's, that in the manoeuvres behind the scenes preparatory to the election of Stritt's successor, Anna Pappritz had secured 19 votes, Helene von Forster 9, and Helene Lange 8. Moreover, Lange intended to refuse the candidature, while many people were busy persuading Stritt to change her mind. Stritt had already in fact been promised 7 votes, and Bensheimer added: 'I am *convinced* that Stritt will be elected, because Eichholz, Wegner and Bennewiz (the latter President of a member Union) all support her and they all have so many votes at their command, and the latest is that the radicals are also voting for her. Only Lida Gustava among them has actually answered and she wrote in her noble honesty: "Stritt is still the most suitable person to represent the Federation in its relations with the outside world".'[17] On this occasion the radicals and their allies did persuade Stritt to stay, and she was duly voted in for another term of office despite the opposition of Pappritz and Bonfort. The radicals heaved a sigh of relief. 'We need the woman', declared Käthe Schirmacher soon afterwards.[18]

From 1907 onwards, however, the moderates gathered their forces once more, their determination fortified by the decision of the Union of Progressive Women's Associations to enter the BDF. They persuaded the German-evangelical Women's League, a powerful conservative body, to enter the BDF against Stritt's will.[19] and with its help they outvoted Stritt on the subject of abortion at the 1908 General Assembly. They now proceeded to try and get the BDF to launch a general campaign against Stöcker and her ideas. Marie Stritt, of course, was on the council of the Mutterschutz League as well as being a firm supporter of its policies. Constantly outvoted on the executive committee of the BDF on these questions, she found the conflict of loyalties between her position in the BDF and in the Mutterschutz League ever more severe. In 1909 Pappritz and the conservatives, having succeeded in defeating Stritt's attempt to swing the BDF behind the abolition of Section 218, tried to remove Stritt from her position as editor of the *Centralblatt,* where she exercised her control over articles and publications in a way that Alice Salomon found 'one-sidedly radical'.[20] They raised the question of Stritt's refusal to review Marianne Weber's book in 1906 once more, and the dispute quickly took on the character of a personal quarrel between Stritt and Pappritz, both of whom sent in their resignations in the course of the controversy only to withdraw them at a later stage.[21] The affair ended with all parties dissatisfied. The conservatives had failed to dislodge Stritt's hold over the *Centralblatt.* 'Frau Stritt is a very difficult character', one of them remarked, 'far more cunning and adroit than we imagined . . .'[22] Stritt herself declared 'my strength is at an end', and decided she could not go on much longer.[23] The continued strain of resisting the mounting opposition within the committee was clearly getting her down. Already when Käthe Schirmacher visited her in January 1909, she found her 'very nice, but all the same, she is not her old self'.[24]

The next attack by Pappritz and the conservatives was finally successful. The Mutterschutz League applied to join the BDF in 1909 and the BDF's executive committee was not long in deciding that the application should be rejected. The decision was taken against the advice of Stritt in August 1909, but the conservative members of the committee wanted to accompany this with a statement making clear the BDF's abhorrence of *Mutterschutz* principles. On 11 March 1910 the committee resolved by 11 votes to 10, Stritt abstaining, to print this statement in the *Centralblatt*. Stritt thereupon pointed out that this was not normal practice. It was a specially vindictive measure towards the League. As a member of the League's Council she must interpret the whole affair as a vote of no confidence in herself. She could no longer remain President of the BDF. Pappritz declared that 'for years it has been a well-known fact that two different world-views have been opposing each other in this matter.' Despite some half-hearted efforts to reach a compromise, Stritt finalised her decision on 13 March and resigned.

The departure of Stritt was of the utmost importance for the future of the BDF. Whoever replaced her was not likely to be tolerant towards the radicals if Anna Pappritz had a say in the appointment. It was Pappritz who conducted the search for a successor to Stritt, while the BDF's business was carried on for the time being by one of the senior members of the executive committee, Helene von Forster, and the BDF's Statutes were altered to oblige every President to resign after four years in office as a safeguard against any individual becoming as independent as Stritt again. Pappritz's first candidate, Katharina Scheven, whose views were identical with hers in almost every respect, despite considerable pressure declared her reluctance to take over the Presidency, since she was too heavily committed to the Abolitionist movement. She agreed however to step in if no-one else could be found.[25] At this stage Martha Zietz proposed Helene Lange's personal secretary and assistant, Gertrud Bäumer. The proposal was supported by the conservative-evangelical women's organisations of Westphalia.[26] As a consistent and committed opponent of the New Morality, Bäumer was quite acceptable to Pappritz and she was duly elected. Adelheid von Welczeck, long-standing treasurer of the Suffrage Union, remarked that Stritt had always favoured the radicals. Bäumer's succession to her post filled her and the other radicals with anxiety for the future.[27] The anxiety was fully justified.

GERTRUD BÄUMER AND THE MOVE TO THE RIGHT, 1901-1914

Gertrud Bäumer, who was to be President of the BDF for the next nine years, from 1910 until 1919,[28] and to be the guiding spirit behind its destinies for many more, was 36 years old when she took up office. Like most German feminist leaders she had begun as a schoolteacher. Unlike many of them, however, she also had strong religious convictions. She came from a family of evangelical priests, her father was a theologian as well as a teacher, and her family had many connections with evangelical-social circles and was strongly influenced by the social criticism of Adolf Stöcker, though she found his populist demagogy distasteful. These were the influences that had led her to the women's movement. After six years as a teacher, in which she was active in various women's teachers' associations, she went to Berlin in 1898 to study at the University, although at this time full matriculation was not allowed. There she met Helene Lange through the General German Women Teachers' Association, and began to help her out with various tasks; in 1899 she became her full-time secretary, and in 1900 was elected to the BDF's committee at the early age of 26.

Gertrud Bäumer was undoubtedly a woman of considerable ability. She had an instinctive grasp of political tactics. She could often be eloquent and persuasive. She was energetic and untiring in the pursuit of the goals she set herself. More important than these abilities, however, was the ideology in whose service they were exercised. It was an ideology that bore many resemblances to the ideas developed by the liberal politician Friedrich Naumann in these years. Naumann had himself begun as an evangelical priest. He had come into politics through Adolf Stöcker's Christian socialism, to which he reacted in much the same way as did Gertrud Bäumer. His ideology rejected liberal individualism in favour of *völkisch* collectivism, rejected pacifism in favour of nationalism, rejected laissez-faire in favour of social interventionism. In 1910 it triumphed within German liberalism as the left-liberal splinter groups united under its banner; in the same year it triumphed within German feminism with the change in leadership and the departure of Marie Stritt. Gertrud Bäumer was the Friedrich Naumann of the women's movement. In later years, when she tried to explain her ideas about female emancipation, it was Naumann's terminology that she employed. The women's movement had to be national, in the sense of supporting an aggressively imperialist foreign policy, and it had to be social, in the sense of devoting itself to reducing social tension and class conflict through social reform and organised welfare work. It had to serve 'what Naumann called the "conversion of the masses into a people" *(Volkwerdung der Masse).*' These were very different ideas from those that had inspired the liberal individualism of the radical feminists. It seemed only logical that from the end of 1912 Bäumer took over the responsibility of editing the non-political part of Naumann's magazine *Die Hilfe,* and became his literary collaborator as well as his political colleague.[29]

Bäumer put forward her ideas most clearly in an article in *Die Frau* in 1905, in which she set out to answer the question, 'what does the "older" and the "newer" party within the women's movement mean? ' Conceived as a reply to the constant barrage of propaganda from Minna Cauer on this point, the article reversed the radicals' terminology and argued that it was in fact Cauer and her associates who were behind the times. According to Bäumer they represented the 'old formulas of the 18th century', 'the spirit of the oldest sort of liberalism', which demanded for women no more and no less than equal rights, and as much freedom to develop their personality and run their life in the way they chose as men had. This, Bäumer declared, was a superficial and outdated concept of feminism. The new ideal proposed by Bäumer was 'something endlessly finer and deeper'. 'We have learned to accept that the importance of what woman can do, the real values she gives to the whole society, lie in her female nature, in what she is and what she gives to society as woman,' she said. 'It is possible', she went on, 'indeed certain, that woman, who is different from man, occupies in many ways a different sphere of life and work, and one must simply leave it to her to seek out this sphere.' Removing the hindrances to this process was what Bäumer called female emancipation:

> For (she went on), the ultimate aim is not formal equality, but the equally living, equally full and rich influence of all female values on our culture, a richer flow of specifically female forces into the total of the world's activities. The original aim (of the women's movement) was to prove through achievements that we had a claim to rights. Our aim now however is only to demand such rights insofar, and in such a form, as they really can release (female) forces and bring about (female) achievements.

Translated into practical terms, this meant that since as far as women were concerned motherhood and marriage were 'specifically female', a strengthening of this aspect of women's life could now be regarded as an act of female emancipation. 'If she (woman) limits herself to house and family', declared Bäumer, 'she is under certain circumstances acting in this way more in accordance with the ideals of the women's movement than if she goes into any male profession'.[30]

This doctrine, repeated on innumerable occasions[31] and with innumerable variations after 1905, and still more after 1910, was far more subtle than the old doctrine of the moderates that the women's movement should consider the needs of society as a whole as much as, or even more than, the needs and demands of women in particular. Its outstanding merit was that it covered every conceivable form of activity under the umbrella of 'female emancipation', and was thus completely neutral and uncontroversial. It was indeed subjected to very little criticism, either within the women's movement or without. It was popular with the moderates, and in many respects indeed was little more than an ingenious reformulation of some of their main ideas. Moreover, the doctrine enabled at a stroke any group of women, whatever its purpose — be it only a knitting circle — to claim that it was part of the women's movement because it was working for female emancipation. It thus allowed the BDF, despite its bewildering heterogeneity, to consider itself a united whole working for a single purpose.

On the other hand, the doctrine was a powerful weapon in the hands of those — principally Bäumer — who knew how to use it. To exclude a society from the BDF, all that was necessary was to declare that it did not represent the 'specifically female spirit'. Since motherhood was seen as the essence of femininity, every society — and especially the

League for Mutterschutz — whose aims could be construed as denying women or allowing women to deny themselves the opportunity to fulfil themselves as mothers, and thus denying women the opportunity to express their 'femaleness', could be rejected as being specifically directed against female emancipation. Female sexuality, argued Bäumer, was different from male sexuality; it was directed towards the personal fulfilment of the soul rather than to mere sensual enjoyment. It found its fulfilment firstly in 'a deep alive Germanic racial instinct, (namely) the urge to faithfulness', and secondly in the fact that 'the desire to have children is natural to a woman of healthy character'. The New Morality, in Bäumer's view, committed the same error in its theory of sexuality as the radical suffragists committed in their theory of women's rights: the assumption that men and women were essentially the same.

The original purpose of the machinations that had led to her election had been to allow the Abolitionists freedom to use the weight of the BDF in the campaign against the New Morality. The Abolitionists now moved to claim their due:

> I want (wrote Katharina Scheven to Gertrud Bäumer on 10 February 1911) an evening to be devoted at the next General Assembly to the morality question, which has not been dealt with in the Federation for years. It seems to me to be in the interests of the whole women's movement that a programmatic lecture be devoted by us to this question, because Stöcker's views are much discussed in Berlin at the moment, and are likely to mislead the general public as to our demands on the subject of sexuality.[32]

The BDF thus mounted a large campaign from 1911-14 against the New Morality. When the BDF mounted a large-scale exhibition in Berlin in 1912, under the title of 'Woman at Home and at Work', it refused all offers of help from the Mutterschutz League, and even banned the League's publications from the bookstalls at the exhibition.[33] The BDF also carefully refused to allow any discussion after a speech given at the 1914 General Assembly on the declining birth-rate because, as Bäumer explained, 'we would get a terrible argument about Neo-Malthusianism, and because the most radical speakers always make the most spectacle in such debates, it would tend to give the outside world the impression that we were all of their opinion'.[34] Bäumer now insisted that the Legal Commission which had proposed the legalisation of abortion in

1908 was entirely unrepresentative of the BDF as a whole. The BDF, she insisted,[35] firmly supported the view that abortion should be a criminal offence punishable by imprisonment, because from the moment of conception a foetus was a living creature with a right to live, because legal sanctions were 'a necessary and salutary barrier against the brutalisation and degeneration of natural motherly feelings', and because the outlawing of abortion stimulated 'a sense of moral responsibility in sexual matters' which was 'the best way of raising the general level of morality in the country at large.' 'No-one,' she concluded, 'can appeal to the Federation if they represent lax views on the question of termination of pregnancy.' In July 1914, indeed, the conservative line had gained such ascendancy that Bäumer could claim with confidence that the anti-Section 218 lobby within the Federation had almost completely disappeared.[36]

Between 1908 and 1914, therefore, the BDF took a sharp turn to the right. A determined group of senior members, led by Anna Pappritz, first of all stopped the BDF from supporting Helene Stöcker's doctrines of sexual emancipation, then drove the supporters of these doctrines out of their positions of power. The chief victim was Marie Stritt, the BDF's President, whose presence in the leadership was a guarantee of radical influence. Stritt was replaced by Gertrud Bäumer in 1910, and under Bäumer the BDF moved even more rapidly to the right than it had been doing since 1908. We have seen that Bäumer propounded a doctrine of female emancipation that differed radically from the liberal individualism that was the basis of women's movements elsewhere and had inspired the radicals and profoundly influenced even the moderates in the German women's movement from the turn of the century. Combined with the disintegration of the two most radical feminist societies, the Suffrage Union and the Mutterschutz League, these developments ensured that after 1908 the German women's movement became in many respects conservative rather than progressive.

To present this development as a clash between radicals and moderates in which the moderates, their ideas updated by Bäumer's theories, were victorious, would, however, be too simple. In our examination of the disintegration of the suffrage movement, we have seen how ideas hostile to liberal individualism came to dominate all but a tiny section of the movement in the years 1911 to 1916. These ideas were primarily political — acceptance of a limited property franchise,

corporate view of democracy, belief in *Interessenpolitik*. There was
however a more profound sense in which the women's movement as a
whole, including even radical societies such as the Mutterschutz League,
underwent a conservative revolution in these years. We have argued that
its whole way of thinking ceased, in a general sense, to be dominated
and influenced by liberal individualism; what replaced this as the
dominant ideological background of the movement was a body of ideas
that has generally been regarded by historians as exclusive to *völkisch*
intellectuals and petty and eccentric groups on the far right: Social
Darwinism.

SOCIAL DARWINISM AND THE WOMEN'S MOVEMENT, 1908-1914

We have seen that the 1908 BDF General Assembly was a turning-point
in the development of the women's movement in Germany. Its most
significant feature was the rejection of the radicals' attempt to commit
the BDF to the legalisation of abortion. During the Assembly, many
opponents of the legalisation of abortion employed ideas derived from
Social Darwinism or, more precisely, 'racial hygiene'. History, according
to Social Darwinists, consisted in a struggle between nations for the
survival of the fittest. Individuals were the product of heredity and not
environment. They had a duty to subordinate themselves to the require-
ments of racial or national survival. The ultimate test of a nation's
capacity to survive was to be seen in the quantity and quality of its
population; and it was thus with population policy *(Bevölkerungs-
politik)* that the rapidly growing number of Social Darwinists within
the women's movement were in the first place concerned.[37]
    From this point of view the legalisation of abortion could be seen as
a threat to the race, and it is significant that the official reply of the
BDF executive committee, approved by the committee against the
wishes of Marie Stritt, to the proposal to legalise abortion at the 1908
General Assembly, was couched in Social Darwinist terms.[38] The
committee's spokesman, Marie Baum, declared that the legalisation of
abortion would lead to a drop in the birth-rate large enough to overtake

the current fall in the death-rate. The population of Germany would therefore cease to grow. Moreover, since only the laziest and stupidest unmarried pregnant women would fail to avail themselves of the opportunity offered by the deletion of Section 218, the 'racial level' of illegitimate children would suffer a drastic dècline, as the 'superior' women would no longer be forced to give birth. The legalisation of abortion would make the State 'an accomplice to the deadening of our racial conscience'.

These arguments were put most clearly and most crudely by none other than Maria Lischnewska. In order for Germany to win the struggle for world supremacy, she said, 'we need people to defend our achievements against the vast hordes of our enemies . . . we need people to populate the colonies we have, and the colonies we still have to conquer . . .'. The nation's 'will to live' was expressed in its birth-rate. In France, where, according to Lischnewska, abortion was accepted as something quite normal, the birth-rate had long sunk far beneath the death-rate. The French were a 'dying, sinking people'. The same, she argued, was true of the USA, where the white population also had continual recourse to abortion, and where as a consequence 'within a few decades, the negroes, with their strongly increasing population and fertility will have the power of deciding the affairs of the USA in their hands'. 'The future of the nation', asserted Lischnewska 'lies in the will of the woman to motherhood'. Section 218 must therefore remain, to encourage this.

However, she added, it must be amended to permit abortion under certain circumstances. 'I believe', she said, 'that our people is going totally to ruin because of the mass of completely degenerate elements that are brought into the world.' Abortion was therefore to be allowed in cases where the embryo was likely to be 'inferior', that is, where the mother or father was idiotic, alcoholic, syphilitic, crippled, epileptic or tubercular. In order to reach a decision in individual cases, an official government commission or commissions were to be established. Lischnewska had not held these views for very long,[39] but in putting them forward she was carrying on a strand in *Mutterschutz* thinking that came originally from Ruth Bré herself. This strand of thought was now moving from the eccentric Utopian fringe that Bré represented into the main arena of feminist politics. According to this view, extra-marital or pre-marital sexuality was to be approved not merely because it made people happier, but also because it produced more children for the continuance of the race. Whether or not children were born in wedlock was, from the point of view of the Social Darwinists, immaterial, all the more so since the numbers of people who remained unmarried were increasing all the time.

Indeed, all the *Mutterschutz* enthusiasts believed to some extent in some form of racial hygiene, though few of them went as far as Lischnewska whose strong nationalism also distinguished her from the bulk of the leading radical feminists and gave her Social Darwinist views a strongly authoritarian tint. In the original programme of Ruth Bré, it was emphasised that only healthy mothers were to benefit from the League's activities. Lily Braun had objected to this, 'because the word "healthy" is capable of the most arbitrary interpretation'.[40] The word was duly removed from the programme, but this did not mean that the League had abandoned such ideas altogether. Helene Stöcker believed that contraception should be applied 'in the interests of the race',[41] and at a meeting of the League's Council on 15 May 1905 attended by – among others – Adele Schreiber, Helene Stöcker, Gertrud Israel, Agnes Hacker, Iwan Bloch, Walter Borgius and Max Marcuse, it was agreed that the word 'healthy' had only been removed from the programme for practical reasons. Women and children suffering from infectious and constitutional diseases, 'especially syphilis and tuberculosis', were not to be allowed to benefit from the League's maternity home schemes.[42] Moreover the League insisted later that everybody should be subjected to a medical examination before marrying, to discover whether they had hereditary ailments of any kind. 'However', the League added in an important rider, 'these certificates of health should, even if they give evidence of a bad state of health, never lead to a ban on marrying'.[43]

The emphasis which members of the League placed upon 'racial hygiene' differed from person to person, however, and the strong element of liberal individualism still present in the League at this stage ensured that all the other speakers in the 1908 debate who belonged to the League condemned the views put forward by Lischnewska. The arguments advanced by Hanns Dorn, a leading member of the Mutterschutz League, were perhaps the most level-headed. He pointed out that the birth-rate of all industrialised nations had been in decline for decades. Germany, he said, had an exceptionally high death-rate which could be expected to decline sharply over the next decade. Contrary to Lischnewska's views, abortion was strictly punished in France. In any case abortion had very little effect on the birth-rate when all other things were taken into consideration. It was, rather, contraception that played the major role. Section 218 had made no contribution to the growth of a 'racial conscience' in Germany, as Marie Baum had asserted, even if such a thing could be said to exist. The idea that an encouragement of population growth was either practicable or necessary, or could contribute anything to foreign policy, Dorn dismissed as fantastic Utopianism. The proposal that a commission should decide on the legality of abortion in individual cases he attacked, in common with many other speakers, as an unwarrantable intrusion into the personal affairs of the woman concerned.

As we have seen, however, arguments such as these were not sufficient to persuade the majority of delegates at the BDF's 1908 assembly to approve of the Mutterschutz League's ideas. After the Assembly had voted to retain Section 218, it proceeded to vote in favour of Lischnewska's plan which, in lieu of anything better, was acceptable to the majority of the *Mutterschutz* supporters even if the reasoning that lay behind it was not. Abortion was still to be punishable by a prison sentence, but it was to be a lesser one than the five years laid down by the existing law. Abortion was to be legal where pregnancy was dangerous for the life and health of the mother, caused by rape, or likely to result in the birth of a mentally or physically handicapped child. A commission of experts would judge each case on its own merits.[44]

The BDF thus decided for a solution on the lines of the Social Darwinists' proposals. The decision was powerful ammunition for the nationalist-Social Darwinist right wing of the Mutterschutz League, led by Borgius and Lischnewska. They now proceeded to secure a reversal of the League's previous wholesale rejection of the Section 218 in favour of Lischnewska's 'racial-biological' proposals. At the League's Hamburg General Assembly in 1908, Borgius argued that the legalisation of abortion would cause a drop in the birth-rate which 'in view of the threat to our high German culture from the growth of Slavdom', would be highly undesirable.[45] In a compromise vote, the League declared in favour of a maximum penalty of a 'few months' instead of five years, and freedom from prosecution altogether in cases where pregnancy was 'likely to be accompanied by serious disadvantages for mother and child, for example, when the pregnancy is caused by rape, or when one of the parents is tubercular, syphilitic, insane, alcoholic etc.' In order to determine whether these 'disadvantages' were serious enough to warrant abortion, the League proposed the establishment of a standing committee of experts. Should they decide in the affirmative, the abortion was to be carried out at the expense of the State.[46]

This represented in large measure the programme that Lischnewska had put to the BDF earlier in the same year. The victory therefore went on this point to the most decided group of the Social Darwinists. Yet the League remained in many ways a very radical movement. Under Stöcker's leadership it continued to preach and, as we have seen, to practise free love and 'free marriage', it continued to propagandise for the equality of unmarried mothers and the alteration of public views on sexual morality that it considered necessary to achieve this end. It did not cease to preach the New Morality. It persisted in doubting the value of the family as an institution, and in supporting women's right to sexual independence. From this point of view it was still regarded by conservatives as a revolutionary organisation. Moreover, it continued to propagandise for the use of contraceptives and launched a campaign against proposals made in the Reichstag in 1913 — proposals which the BDF to a large extent supported — to outlaw their sale and advertisement. Furthermore, on certain points, above all in her militarism, Lischnewska remained relatively isolated within the League. Many members in fact became pacifists during and after the war. For most members 'racial hygiene' was a means to a more ordered, progressive and humane society, and not a means of providing generals with cannon fodder.[47]

Nevertheless, despite the increasing confusion of ideas and policies that accompanied the League's disintegration from 1908 to 1914, we may discern a steady decline of liberal feminist ideas and a steady growth in Social Darwinist and racialist ideas of one kind and another. This was present to an even more marked degree in the Abolitionist movement, in which Stöcker had first tried to launch her ideas. The Abolitionists, whom Pappritz and Katharina Scheven had led since the early 1900s had come a long way since those heady days of crusading against the State in the name of the dignity of the individual. By the outbreak of the war in 1914, Abolitionist ideology had undergone important changes. Liberal individualism had given way to Social Darwinism. Concern for the dignity of the individual woman had been replaced by concern for the future of the race. Suspicion of the State had yielded to a readiness to see in it the highest expression of the unity of the people and a corresponding willingness to employ its organs to achieve political ends which the early Abolitionists would have tried to realise through moral suasion.

This change in emphasis was partly made possible through the withdrawal of many of the early Abolitionists into the suffrage movement. After 1902 people such as Minna Cauer and Anita Augspurg, Lida Gustava Heymann and Martha Zietz devoted more and more of their time to agitation for the vote. A further group of the early Abolitionists, chief among them Helene Stöcker, Maria Lischnewska, Adele Schreiber, Auguste Kirchhoff, Meta Hammerschlag and Frieda Radel, abandoned Abolitionism after 1905 and thereafter owed their allegiance to the Mutterschutz League. Nevertheless, in themselves these personal changes do not explain the victory of Social Darwinism within the movement.

A major influence was the availability from 1905 onwards of statistics on venereal disease as the German Society for the Suppression of Venereal Disease (Deutsche Gesellschaft zur Bekämpfung der Geschlechtskrankheiten), founded in 1902, began to publish the results of its investigations. The revelation that venereal disease was more widespread than had previously been thought the case, whether in fact it was true or not, had a profound effect upon the Abolitionists. They soon came to the conclusion that prostitution was at the root of these developments, but this conclusion then led to a modification of the Abolitionists' original liberal individualist premises. Already at a meeting of the Berlin Abolitionists in March 1905, Agnes Bluhm could propose, with the approval of a number of members, that no-one should be allowed to marry unless they could produce a medical certificate proving they were free from venereal disease. On 29 November 1905 she demanded that this condition be extended to the 'constitutionally insane'.[48] At that date these views were by no means generally accepted within the movement; but after 1908, when the main protagonist of the liberal individualist view, Lida Gustava Heymann, went to live in Munich and withdrew from the main centres of activity in Berlin and Hamburg, they rapidly gained national acceptance. In 1912 Heymann resigned from the Abolitionist movement and her post in Hamburg was taken over by Hedwig Weidemann. Weidemann's first speech as leader of the Hamburg Abolitionists was remarkable for the total absence of any reference to the insult done by regulation to the individual dignity of woman. It concentrated instead on the role of the brothel as a centre of the white slave trade, sexual perversions and 'general immorality'.[49] Already in 1908 the Abolitionists' General Assembly had demanded that the State punish everyone who indulged in sexual intercourse knowing that he had a venereal disease with up to two years in prison.[50] In 1912 they issued a pamphlet describing their aims in general terms. Gone were the rousing calls for all-out war on men and their State, and the fervent assertions of the individual dignity and independence of woman, no matter how low her status or how despised her occupation. Instead, all we find is a monotonous insistence on the connection between regulated prostitution and the spread of venereal diseases.[51]

The rise of the Mutterschutz movement had led the Abolitionists to insist more than ever before on the need to preserve the institutions of marriage and the family. At the turn of the century this insistence had simply been part of a more general emphasis on the need for stricter standards of sexual morality, and it had been coupled with a demand that marriage be a partnership of equals. It was now made for quite different reasons. Venereal disease, sexual promiscuity, the use of contraceptives and the attacks of the New Morality upon marriage all led to the weakening of the race and the decline of the birth-rate. Pappritz herself had modified her views on these questions. From believing that the individual should discipline herself, she had come to demand that she be disciplined by the State. Pappritz later traced the history of the changing ideology of the Abolitionist movement in her 'Introduction to the Study of the Prostitution Question',[52] published after the war. In explaining the differences between the German and the 'English-French' wings of the International Abolitionist Federation, she wrote that

> While the foreigners concentrated principally on the purely *negative* Abolitionist aim, and many of them even wanted to limit themselves completely to this objective, there emerged among the Germans more and more the attempt to construct a positive programme alongside the negative one, in the conviction that the German government and the Reichstag would only consent to

the removal of Regulation when other measures designed to combat immorality and protect the health of the people *(Volksgesundheit)* were put in their place. The German Abolitionists found little understanding for their efforts among their foreign comradess, . . . (But) the German Abolitionists have never allowed themselves to be led astray by this difference of opinion. They have enlarged their *positive programme* more year after year, and put it across with ever greater energy.

As Pappritz's account suggests, these differences of view between the German Abolitionists and their English and French counterparts emerged only gradually over the years from 1903 onwards. Already in 1906 the Hamburg Abolitionists were strongly criticised by the International Federation for their comparative tolerance of State control over prostitution.[53]

Yet this change of ideological standpoint towards the acceptance of the popular reliance on the State for social reform was not accompanied by any corresponding change in the Abolitionists' fortunes. The following table shows their strength in 1908.

TABLE 5

Membership of the Abolitionist Federation German Branch, 1908

| Branch | Founded | Membership | | Total |
		Women	Men	
Berlin	1899	130	20	150
Bremen	1902	73	18	91
Breslau	1904	46	2	48
Danzig	1904	57	1	58
Dresden	1901	104	14	118
Düsseldorf	1903	38		38
Elberfeld	1902	30	4	34
Frankfurt/M	1905	84	6	90
Halle/S	1902	24	6	30
Hamburg	1899	102	13	115
Hanover	1906	16	6	22
Mülhausen	1904	55	32	87
Munich	1901		4	4
Stuttgart	1905	50	8	58
Total		810	134	944

Source: *Statistik der Frauenorganisationen im Deutschen Reiche* (1. Sonderheft zum Reichsarbeitsblatt, Berlin, 1909).

All the foundations had taken place between 1899 and 1906; the Suffrage Union, by contrast, saw most of its branches founded in 1906-1908. Doubtless the concentration on the suffrage issue within the radical movement was attracting support away from the Abolitionist organisation. Moreover, as the BDF itself was by now actively campaigning for Abolitionist aims, there seemed less and less justification for a separate society. After 1912 the Abolitionist movement's membership, never large, began to decline steadily. From 1912 to 1914 the Berlin branch's membership sank from 200 to 180. Between 1908 and 1914 Hamburg fell from 113 to 90, Bremen from 100 to 83. Dresden reached a peak of 120 in 1912 and then fell to 110 by 1914. Stuttgart fell from 66 to 57 and Wiesbaden from 80 to 72 in the same period. There were exceptions – a series of scandals in Frankfurt pushed up membership there from 60 to 75 between 1908 and 1914, and the presence of Augspurg and Heymann in Munich may have helped to increase membership there from 65 to 75 over the same period. In general, however, the Abolitionists lost support steadily after 1912, and they also had to close down one branch for lack of support in every year from 1911 onwards until the outbreak of war.[54] It may be that the frustration of total failure in reforming the institution of State regulation was to blame. Also, as Lida Gustava Heymann put it, 'the more the interest of women turns to the political issue of female suffrage, the more on the whole the participation in subordinate fields declines'.[55] As the participation in the Abolitionist movement declined, so it turned to Social Darwinism.

These ideas were by no means confined to those whose main sphere of interest was population policy or prostitution reform, and they did not simply find their expression when these problems were discussed. Female suffrage propaganda now began to include the claim that female suffrage would 'raise the strength and prolong the life of the race' and that it was being demanded, among other things, 'in the interests of racial hygiene'.[56] In 1913 Martha Zietz published a long article in the Suffrage Union's journal *Frauenstimmrecht!* about an illiterate, mentally subnormal dwarf from a cripples' home who had the right to vote simply because he was a man. If women were in the Reichstag, she asserted, this kind of thing would not be allowed.[57] In 1911 Else Lüders endorsed Hermann Popert's view that racial hygiene would only receive its due in the legislature when women's suffrage had been realised.[58]

What this might mean in practice Lüders demonstrated in an article – one of an increasing number on such subjects that appeared in the suffragist Press in these years – on 'Racial and Legal Questions in the Colonies', published in the *Zeitschrift für Frauenstimmrecht* in 1912. She asserted after the fashion of Gertrud Bäumer that 'women, because of their feminine nature, must come to a different view of things than men', particularly as the bearers of the next generation. From this she went on to argue that they were bound to support the proposal, shortly to be debated in the Reichstag, that racially mixed marriages be made illegal. Quoting Wilhelm Solf, the Colonial Secretary, and Paul Rohrbach, she declared that 'half-castes' were 'mostly inferior'. The dangers of a 'bastard population' in the colonies must be avoided. Ignoring the Social Democrats' argument that all races were equal, she concentrated on their other objection to the proposal, namely that such a measure was an unwarrantable intrusion into the right of the individual to govern his own personal life. She declared that 'the rights of the individual have to experience a limitation when the higher rights of the generality come into consideration'.[59] That Else Lüders, with the approval of Cauer, could make such statements, shows how far the radicals had come since the turn of the century.

In the same year, Adele Schreiber put forward for the first time another demand that gained in popularity among radical feminists in these years: that 'drinkers' be sterilised.[60] In support of her demand she cited the case of 'the notorious family O., whose genealogical tree revealed that the descendants of one alcoholic consisted of 839 people, of whom 181 were prostitutes, 76 hardened criminals, including 7 murderers, 64 inmates of work-houses and 142 beggars'. She demanded that alcoholics undergo 'a minor, harmless operation' that would make it impossible for them to have children. 'If this suggestion means a strong interference in the freedom of the individual', she added, 'nevertheless it is justified.' Among conservatives too, who had once been the Abolitionists' bitterest enemies, concern about prostitution as a source of social disorder was giving way to a more urgent preoccupation with prostitution as a danger to the strength and purity of the race. From this point of view State regulation was a disastrous policy, and the view that it should be eliminated as a major source for the spread of venereal disease gained ground in conservative circles in these years. Within the women's movement, the German-evangelical Women's League had come round to an Abolitionist point of view by 1912 at the latest.[61] If we take into account the growth of Social Darwinist influence in the Mutterschutz League, and the victory of Social Darwinist views in the BDF in 1908, it seems that almost all branches of the women's movement were strongly influenced by this ideology in the last years of peace. At the turn of the century, liberal individualism had been the most lively, influential ideology within the women's movement. Now it was Social Darwinism.

Social Darwinism had of course its progressive aspects. The desire to improve the quality of the race could – and did – lead to a concern for social reform, especially in matters of welfare, housing and hygiene. In the early years of the Mutterschutz movement it clearly provided support for the movement's radical ideas about marriage, contraception and abortion. Social Darwinism involved a concern for social reform, for improving the nation's standards of health, for lowering Germany's notoriously high rate of infant mortality and for bringing about better living conditions for the population. However, these had been the concern of the women's movement since the first days of Abolitionism, when these and similar measures had been seen as a means of eliminating the evil of prostitution.[62] The advent of Social Darwinism did not remove them, but it brought with it a number of new features which, taken together, far outweighed these positive aspects.

First and foremost it brought with it an overwhelming concern, quite new in the women's movement, with the birth-rate. Here, particularly in versions such as that of Lischnewska, quantity counted for at least as much as quality. The desire to increase Germany's capacity to survive in the international Darwinian struggle by increasing her population led to a growing emphasis within the women's movement on the importance of women's role as mothers. It gave a new twist to the old 'moderate' emphasis on the importance of marriage. In the 19th century feminists such as Auguste Schmidt and Helene Lange had stressed the sanctity of marriage for social and moral reasons. Now the importance of marriage was seen in the production of children – if possible, lots of children, all of them healthy and strong. By stating that women's most important function was to give birth to large families of children, this ideology was denying the basic tenet of feminism, that women should have equal opportunities with men in all spheres of life, and it was devaluing all the efforts of the feminist movement to open up careers for women and encourage them to commit themselves to public and professional life.

Secondly, the variety of Social Darwinism that took root in the German women's movement in the years 1908-1914 contained a strong element of authoritarianism. The proposals of the Social Darwinists that alcoholics be compulsorily sterilised, that racially mixed marriages be made illegal, that the mentally subnormal and the illiterate be disfranchised, that every young couple intending marriage be subjected to a compulsory medical examination, and, if found to be 'constitutionally insane' or suffering from inheritable ailments, be forcibly prevented from carrying out their intention, that a committee of 'experts' have the power to decide whether a woman was entitled to have a legal abortion or not, that anyone who indulged in sexual intercourse knowing that he was a carrier of venereal disease be imprisoned for two years — all these proposals constituted an unprecedented interference by the State in the private life of its citizens, an interference that might without too much exaggeration be described as totalitarian.[63]

It was on this point that much of the debate on Social Darwinist issues within the women's movement took place. Those who advanced these proposals clearly realized the curtailment of individual rights which they involved. That they were prepared to accept this curtailment 'in the interests of the generality' was a sign that the concern with the rights and liberties of the individual that had been the original impulse behind the radicalisation of the women's movement in the years 1898-1902 was becoming less important with every year that passed after the turning-point reached by the movement in 1908. Taken with the disintegration of the suffragist movement and the Mutterschutz League, the various developments surveyed in this chapter form a major turning-point in the history of German feminism. They mark the collapse of radicalism within the women's movement. Within the space of a few years, essentially from 1908 to 1912, the whole direction in which the women's movement had been going since 1898 was reversed. From a position of growing influence and importance within the movement, liberal individualists such as Minna Cauer, Anita Augspurg, Lida Gustava Heymann, Helene Stöcker and their followers were suddenly reduced to a small minority group, deserted by many of their followers and ignored or attacked by the rest of the movement. The character and nature of the German women's movement was set in a mould which held firm with only minor alterations for the next 25 years. The alignment of the movement with the opponents of the existing political system, the espousal of radical doctrines of social reform, the adoption of a liberal individualist ideology, the proclamation of a vigorous campaign for female equality in all spheres of life – all those features which characterised the German women's movement in the years immediately after the turn of the century – proved in the event to be ephemeral.

This rightward turn in the policies of the feminist movement did not escape the attention of *Die Gleichheit,* the SPD women's magazine, which always took a keen interest in the affairs of its bourgeois rival. Already in 1910, after the BDF's General Assembly at Heidelberg, the magazine noted the change that had taken place since 1908:

> In the German feminist movement, (it commented) . . . internal changes are taking place. It is adopting a policy of uniting the majority of active feminists of various persuasions in a centrist policy which more than ever isolates the extreme left without losing contact with the extreme right. It is easy to see that these changes are symptomatic of the process of change which is taking place in the German bourgeoisie as a whole.

The political expression of this process of change, continued *Die Gleichheit,* was to be found in the realignment of the bourgeois liberal parties, in which liberals of the classical sort, from Theodor Barth to Minna Cauer, were being pushed onto one side by the leaders of the neo-liberal Progressive Party, an organisation that in most respects was far to the right of the liberalism of Eugen Richter and his followers.[64] The diagnosis was an accurate one;[65] and it is to these more general political features of the rightward turn of the women's movement that we must now direct our attention.

NOTES

1. See pp. 193-4, below.
2. Ludwig Elm, *Zwischen Fortschritt und Reaktion. Geschichte der Parteien der Liberalen Bourgeoisie in Deutschland, 1893-1918* (Berlin, 1968), 212. It was well-known that the liberal parties had a low membership in comparison with their electoral support.
3. ABDF 1/A 2: Satzungen (1906).
4. See p. 55, above.
5. *Centralblatt des Bundes deutscher Frauenvereine,* Vol. 9, No. 7, 1 July 1907, 49-51.
6. See Richard V. Pierard, 'The Transportation of White Women to German Southwest Africa, 1898-1914', *Race,* Vol. XII, No. 13, Jan. 1971.
7. Gertrud Bäumer, 'Die Geschichte des Bundes Deutscher Frauenvereine', *JB,, 1921,* 25. For the *Deutscher Verein gegen den Missbrauch geistiger Getranke,* see *JB, 1913.*
8. e.g. ABDF 4/4: Cauer to Stritt, 27 April 1904, Augspurg to Stritt, 5 Nov. 1904.
9. StA Hbg, PP, S5466/II: *HF,* 7 Oct. 1906, *NAZ,* 20 Sept. 1907.
10. StA Hbg, PP, S9000/I: *HE,* 2 Oct. 1907, *VW,* 4 Oct. 1907; *FB,* 13/20, 15 Oct. 1907, 155-7.
11. UB Rostock, NL Schirmacher: Schirmacher to Schleker, 13 March 1910. In February 1908 the Union had 1500 members and a balance of 13 Marks (ibid., 7 Feb. 1908). From 1907 too, Cauer had to bear the costs of producing *Die Frauenbewegung* herself (Else Lüders, *Minna Cauer. Leben und Werk,* (Gotha, 1925), 129-131.)
12. Kruger, op. cit., 122-4.
13. HLA 16: Pappritz Tagebuch, 5/7 Jan. 1906. Marianne Weber (b. 2 Aug. 1870. d. 14 March 1954) was BDF President 1919-23. For an excellent discussion of the political views of Max Weber, which were undoubtedly shared in most respects by his wife, and were certainly well to the right of Marie Stritt's type of liberalism, see Wolfgang J. Mommsen, *Max Weber und die deutsche Politik 1890-1920* (Tübingen, 1959).
14. *Des Lebens wie der Liebe Band. Briefe von Gertrud Bäumer* (ed. Emmy Beckmann, Tübingen, 1956), 17: Bäumer to Marianne Weber 4 April 1906.
15. StA Hbg, PP, S5466/II: *HC,* 25 Aug. 1906, 26 Aug. 1906, 27 Aug. 1906, 2 Sept. 1906.
16. ABDF 16/II/1: Protokoll der Vorstandssitzung, 29 Feb. 1904.
17. UB Hbg, Dehmel-Archiv: Bensheimer to Ida Dehmel, 23 Sept. 1906.
18. UB Rostock, NL Schirmacher: Schirmacher to Schleker, 25 Nov. 1907. See also Else Lüders, *Minna Cauer. Leben und Werk* (Gotha, 1925) 137.
19. See below pp. 195-6.
20. ABDF 2/I/1: Salomon to Alice Bensheimer, 7 April 1909.
21. ABDF 2/I/1: Stritt to executive committee, 21 Aug. 1906, Pappritz to

executive committee, 7 March 1909, Bensheimer to Pappritz, 7 March 1909, 'Sitzung des engeren Vorstandes 7.3.1909' (Abschrift), Bensheimer to Salomon, n.d., Salomon to Bensheimer, 9 March 1909, et. seq. This file is marked on the cover with the words 'not to be shown to outsiders'.

22. Ibid.: Bensheimer to Salomon, n.d.

23. Ibid.: Stritt to executive committee, 15 April 1909.

24. UB Rostock, NL Schirmacher: Schirmacher to Schleker, 21 Jan. 1909.

25. ABDF 16/II/1: Protokoll der Sitzung des Gesamtvorstandes 11 March 1910, 13 March 1910; ibid. 5/XIII/4: Bensheimer to Stritt, 18 Aug. 1909, 11 Sept. 1909, Bensheimer to von Forster, 11 Sept. 1909.

26. ADEFB, A14b: Martha Dönhoff to Bundesvereine (Rheinisch-Westfälischer Frauenbund), July 1910.

27. *FB* 16/20, 15 Oct. 1910, 162; BA Koblenz, Kleine Erwerbungen 258-1, 76-78: Bäumer to Marianne Weber, 24 Jan. 1911.

28. She was due to retire at the end of 1914; this was prevented by the outbreak of the war, so that the new clause only became operative in 1919.

29. Gertrud Bäumer, *Lebensweg durch eine Zeitenwende* (Tübingen, 6th ed., 1933), pp. 1-253; S. T. Robson, *Left-wing Liberalism in Germany, 1900-1918,* (unpubl. Oxford D.Phil. thesis, 1966), *passim.* For two views of Naumann, see Gertrud Theodor, *Friedrich Naumann oder der Prophet des Profits* (East Berlin, 1957), and Theodor Heuss, *Friedrich Naumann. Der Mann, das Werk, die Zeit* (2nd ed., Stuttgart/Tübingen, 1949).

30. Gertrud Bäumer, 'Was bedeutet in der deutschen Frauenbewegung "jüngere" and "ältere" Richtung? ', *DF,* 12/6, March 1905, 321-9.

31. StA Hbg, PP, S8326: *HN,* 1 July 1906; ibid., S5808/I: *HG,* 15 Sept. 1907, for two early examples.

32. ABDF 5/XII/6: Scheven to Bäumer, 10 Feb. 1911.

33. Ingeborg Richarz-Simons, *Zum 100. Geburtstag von Dr. phil. Helene Stöcker* (Typescript, Munich 1969, ABDF Bibliothek).

34. ABDF 5/XVI/2: Bäumer to Agnes Bluhm, 4 April 1914.

35. ABDF 5/XV/1: Bäumer to Professor von Thorn, n.d. (1910/11).

36. ABDF 5/XVI/2: Bäumer to Max von Gruber, 13 July 1914.

37. See Hans-Günter Zmarzlik, 'Social Darwinism in Germany, seen as a Historical Problem', in Hajo Holborn (ed.), *Republic to Reich. The Making of the Nazi Revolution* (New York, 1972), and Hans-Ulrich Wehler, 'Sozialdarwinismus im expandierenden Industriestaat', in I. Geiss and B. -J. Wendt (eds.), *Deutschland in der Weltpolitik des 19. und 20. Jahrhunderts. Festschrift für Fritz Fischer* (Düsseldorf, 1943), 133-142.

38. For the following account of the debate, see the verbatim report in ABDF 16/I/5: Breslauer Generalversammlung 1908, Stenogramm, 365-468.

39. Cf. the complete absence of Social Darwinist overtones in her discussion of 'the reform of marriage' in 1905, StA Hbg, PP, S9000/II: *HF,* 4 Oct. 1905.

40. BA Koblenz, NL Schreiber, 1: Protokoll der Ausschusssitzung, 26 Feb. 1905.

41. IISG Amsterdam, Collection Henriette Fürth: Stöcker to Fürth, 20 Oct. 1905.

42. BA Koblenz, NL Schreiber, 1: Protokoll der Ausschusssitzung, 15 May 1905.

43. *FB,* 13/3, 1 Feb. 1907, 20-21, 'Die Tagung des Bundes für Mutterschutz'.

44. Verbatim report of the debate in ABDF 16/I/5: Breslauer General-versammlung 1908, Stenogramm, 365-468.

45. BA Koblenz, NL Schreiber, 1: Bericht für die Zeitungen über den Vortrag von Helene Stöcker.

46. Ibid.; Resolution über §218.

47. For a further discussion of Stöcker's Social Darwinism, see Daniel Gasman, *The Scientific Origins of National Socialism. Ernst Haeckel and the German Monist League* (London, 1971), esp. xxxi, n.34. Gasman's account, though a valuable conective to earlier works, is in general disappointingly one-sided.

48. HLA 18: Protokollbuch des Berliner Zweigvereins der Internationalen (Abolitionistischen) Föderation, 2 March 1905, 29 Nov. 1905.

49. StA Hbg, PP, SA593/II: Versammlungsbericht, 21 Jan. 1913.

50. *FB,* 14/9, 1 May 1908, 70, 'Deutscher Zweig der I.A. Föderation'.

51. StA Hbg, PP, SA593/II: Flugblatt 'Internationale Abolitionistische Föderation: Zweck' (n.d. (1912)).

52. Anna Pappritz, *Einführung in das Studium der Prostitutionsfrage* (Berlin, 1926), 226.

53. 'Die Internationale Föderation und der Hamburg-Altonaer Zweigverein', *Der Abolitionist,* 5/11, 1 Dec. 1906, pp. 105-108.

54. *JB 1912, 1913:* Wegner, op. cit.

55. StA Hbg, PP, SA593/II: *HF,* 21 April 1910.

56. StA Hbg, PP, S9001/1: Flugblatt: 'Warum fordern wir das Frauenstimm-recht? '; Versammlungsbericht, 22 Oct. 1912, speech of Heymann.

57. *FS* 2/5, Aug. 1913, 93-4.

58. Else Lüders, 'Volksgesundheit und Frauenfrage', *FB,* 17/14, 15 July 1911, 110.

59. *ZFS,* 6/7, 1 Aug. 1912.

60. BA Koblenz, NL Schreiber, 25: *Das Kleine Journal,* 5 Aug. 1912.

61. StA Hbg, PP, SA593/II: 'Deutsche Frauen! ' (Flugblatt des Deutsch-Evangelischen Frauenbundes).

62. See p. 271, below

63. For a similar advance of Social Darwinist ideas in the American Women's Movement in 1910-14, connected with the feminists' hostility to immigrant labour, see Grimes, op. cit., 107.

64. *GL,* 21/2, 24 Oct. 1910, 21.

65. Cf. Ludwig Elm, op. cit., and Konstanze Wegner, *Theodor Barth und die Freisirunge Vereingung. Studien zur Geschichte des Linksliberalismus in Wilhelminischen Deutschland (1893-1910)* (Tübingen, 1968).

6

THE ANTI-FEMINISTS

THE ANTI-LEAGUE AND ITS
ALLIES, 1912-1914

At the same time as the women's movement in Germany was under-
going internal changes that led it away from radical feminism, it was
also experiencing new external pressures which operated in the same
direction. Opposition to female emancipation had always been exceptionally strong in Germany. From 1898 to 1908, however, it seemed
as if this opposition was rapidly weakening. In the Reichstag, the
deputies were at least beginning to pay lip-service to the ideals of
female emancipation. In the Press, interest in and sympathy for the
feminists' demands was on the increase. Opposition to women entering
the universities and the medical profession had been overcome and
women students and doctors were by 1908 a novelty no longer. No-one
seemed to give serious thought any more to the idea that women should
be excluded from industry. As the women's movement became more
radical, public opinion became less hostile.

In 1912, however, this situation suddenly seemed to change, with
the establishment of a League for the Prevention of the Emancipation
of Women (Bund zur Bekämpfung der Frauenemanzipation). Published

in June 1912, the manifesto of the Anti-League (as it came to be known) was signed by a group of people most of whom, as the Social Democratic Press remarked, shared the distinction of being completely unknown. There were twelve professors, a handful of admirals and generals, a number of pillars of the cultural establishment and a few local politicians and professional men. They even included the Academy Director and official painter Anton von Werner, of whom the *Hamburger Echo* wrote that 'as an artist, he already counts among the living dead'. The best-known supporters of the Anti-League, however, consisted of a mixture of pan-German militarists and racial theorists. They included General August Keim, organiser of the Navy League; General von Voss, who led nationalistic celebrations in Berlin on the 100th anniversary of the defeat of the first Napoleon; Dietrich Schäfer, Professor of History at Berlin and a leading member of the Pan-German League; Ludwig Schemann, a member of the Richard Wagner circle and populariser of the French racial theorist Gobineau in Germany, also a member of the Pan-German League; Philipp Stauff, a disciple of Guido von Liszt and author of a book purporting to show that the German race possessed a secret runic language preserved in the wooden beams of old houses; Professor L. Kuhlenbeck, who introduced many important racialist ideas into the Pan-German League through his friend Heinrich Class, its director; and Dr. Schmidt-Gibichenfels, editor of the Social Darwinist *Political-Anthropological Review*.[1]

Thirteen of the Anti-League's leading members came from Berlin. Two other important centres of the movement were Kiel, a reservoir of pan-German support and home of the Anti-League's most active publicist, Professor Ludwig Langemann; and Weimar, where the movement's President, Professor Sigismund, lived.[2] The idea of an antifeminist society was borrowed from England and America, and the Anti-League kept in contact with its English opposite number. It invited the leader of the English Anti-Suffragette Society, Lady Griselda Cheape, to speak in Berlin in January 1914. However, the Anti-League, despits its fondness for using foreign antifeminist material and propaganda, was also a product of very specific German political and social circumstances. As Minna Cauer remarked, it was 'a sign of the times, in which Reaction is trying to raise its head as strongly as it can'.

The Anti-League directed its hostility primarily against the bourgeois women's movement, rather than against female emancipation in general. Its arguments were based on the belief that Germany was subject to growing hostility and danger from forces inside the country and without. Internal divisions must be healed so that the nation could oppose these forces united. The women's movement was creating fresh divisions by rousing women against men. It was destroying the family, the basis of society, by encouraging married women to take jobs, by supporting unmarried mothers and by urging women in general to be more independent. It was endangering Germany's military potential by discouraging marriage. It was outraging nature by campaigning for the systematic equalisation of the sexes and by inciting women to do things they were unsuited for. It was international in spirit and unpatriotic. It was led by its most radical members, for whom the moderates were no more than a front. It had no sense of responsibility to nation and society. In view of the dangers it posed, all efforts to gain female suffrage and thus bring feminism into power must be resisted. Married women should not be allowed to take jobs, co-education should be banned and women students, if they were exceptionally gifted, should be given their own universities, where their subjects would be restricted to those suited to the female nature.[3]

The women's movement was in something of a dilemma over the antifeminists. Was it to dismiss them as crackpots and run the risk of losing the argument by default, or was it to take them seriously and thus perhaps give them an importance they might not deserve? The feminist movement chose the latter course, perhaps wisely in view of the influential social and political positions held by many of the Anti-League's members. It reaffirmed in general terms its support of the institution of marriage and its patriotism, and it criticised as wholly unrealistic the practical proposals such as the removal of women – or at least married women – from the labour market.[4] More radical feminists were not slow to organise counter-moves to the rise of the Anti-League. They attended the Anti-League's meetings en masse and created scenes. At a meeting in Charlottenburg in March 1913, for example,[5] the speaker had to leave the podium amid uproar and a section of the audience, led by Minna Cauer, walked out after he had called the leaders of the women's movement 'men-women', 'degenerate' and 'perverse'. Scenes such as this did much to make the Anti-League a laughing stock, which of course was the intention. Gertrud Bäumer even concluded that the creation of an antifeminist league would help the women's movement by persuading the liberal parties of the need for closer co-operation with the women's movement in the face of a common enemy.[6]

In fact it did not. Bäumer admitted privately that 'we suddenly feel that men and women are completely without sympathy for our efforts'.[7] Indeed, who could blame her, when the pan-German foreign policy columnist of the extreme right-wing *Deutsche Tageszeitung*, Count Reventlow,[8] could explain his opposition to the women's movement at the Anti-League's first congress by saying that:

> Women want to rule and we don't want to let them . . . . The German Empire (he continued)[9] was created with blood and iron. That was man's work! (Interjection: 'No, not alone!) If women helped, it was not women of the sort of the new women's movement, but women of the Spartan and old German kind, who stood behind their men in battle and fired them on to kill as many enemies as possible. (Fervent applause.)

This kind of propaganda was continually issued in pamphlets, assemblies, letters to the Press and in the Anti-League's own periodical. During the war it was backed by petitions to those authorities and legislatures who seemed about to give in to the women's demands.[10] The Anti-League however never had more than a handful of members, most of whom were apparently senior teachers anxious to stop female competition. It was interesting as a symptom but ineffective as a body. So hard up was it for support that it had to leave much of its local propaganda, the organisation of many of its meetings and the provision of stewards and bouncers to another organisation altogether – the German-national Commercial Employees' Union (Deutschnationaler Handlungsgehilfenverband, or DHV), a white-collar union formed on a nationalistic, patriotic and anti-Semitic basis, whose main preoccupation was the struggle against social and economic proletarianisation.[11] 'One of the many causes of the progressive worsening in the situation of clerks', it declared in 1894, 'is, as has already been said many times, a phenomenon that has been occurring on the largest scale in recent years, the invasion of female elements into the profession'.

Women, the DHV argued, were mostly untrained, kept their jobs only until marriage, and did not need to support themselves or a family. They were used as cheap temporary labour, put trained male employees out of a job and forced wages down. To give them proper training would be even worse, however, as it would enable them to compete for the best jobs, and here too their frequent absenteeism, illnesses and — if married — pregnancies would combine with their tendency to take short-term employment and again force wages down. When these arguments were challenged the union fell back on cruder propaganda. Combining sexual innuendo and anti-Semitism in a way that was to become familiar in similar propaganda after the war, it suggested that female employees were being exploited sexually as well as economically by unscrupulous, usually Jewish employers. The DHV's periodical was continually bringing individual cases to the notice of its readers. Describing a protest meeting called by an employee of the firm N. L. Nathan in Essen, for example, it reported that 'the speaker depicted in drastic fashion the way in which Nathan tried to approach the female employees he fancied', and concluded: 'there is scarcely another profession so full of dangers for female honour as commerce.'[12]

The DHV was an extremist organisation, but it was far from being on the margin of politics, as were other unions of the same sort — for example, the Union for the Limitation of Female Employment in the Commercial Profession, founded in Hamburg in April 1905 and wound up the following June after failing to recruit more than 11 members.[13] With well over 100,000 members, the DHV represented a large and growing body of lower-middle-class opinion. By 1903, however, it had almost given up the struggle against female employment in the face of irresistible economic forces, and members could complain that the Union's views on the female labour question were not what they used to be and that the question was being neglected.[14] In the years immediately before the outbreak of war the DHV began to switch its anti-feminist campaign onto a broader front, and to launch a general attack on the women's movement itself which it had previously hardly mentioned in its propaganda. Its first full-scale critique of the women's movement came out in 1913 in the form of notes for lectures to be delivered by its speakers and agitators. Once more it was the women's movement that was singled out for attack. The author, Werner Heinemann, considered that the Law of Association of 1908 had shifted the balance within the movement from the moderates to the radicals. Any idea that divisions of opinion within the movement disproved this was dismissed by Heinemann: 'they march divided', he said, 'to strike united'. The moderates had the task of winning over unsuspecting members of the upper classes. When the stratagem succeeded the mask would be dropped and all would unite in the struggle for the vote. If this demand were granted, the SPD, as the only party to support it, would be the principal beneficiary. Armed with the suffrage the feminists would erect a matriarchy under which their entire programme would be ruthlessly implemented. Male professions would be flooded with women, pacifism would spread everywhere, abortion would be available on demand. 'In this moment the existence of our people would be as good as ended.'

For Heinemann and the DHV, feminism was part of a Jewish world conspiracy aimed at overthrowing the nation-State in general and Germany in particular. 'We meet Jewry everywhere in the women's movement,' he wrote. 'The women's movement, the peace movement, Social Democracy and Jewry, these four are intimately related to one another, they are international and work in an anti-national spirit.'[15] In this belief the DHV was not alone. The historian Dr. Peter Pulzer has indeed pointed out that 'most anti-Semites were anti-feminist and most anti-feminists were, if not actively anti-Semite, at least strongly nationalist when this was coming to mean almost the same thing.'[16] This was certainly true of the Anti-League. Ludwig Langemann once declared, for example, that 'the modern women's movement is, like Social Democracy, an international, foreign body in our national life. Both movements', he went on, 'are, considering the great participation of the Jewish element, international in origin and fight with equal fanaticism against all fundamentals of the people's life.'[17] Other active antifeminists were generally also anti-Semitic, and the anti-Semitic *Deutsch-Soziale Blätter*[18] said of the women's movement that 'in this field it is of course Jews who are the real leaders, as anyone who has concerned himself with female emancipation over a long period knows. This movement provides a possibility of subverting German ideals and destroying the heart and soul of the German woman — hence the remarkable zeal of the Jewesses in this connection.'[19]

Yet it would be wrong to conclude from this that 'the identification of the feminist movement with Jewesses was no doubt inspired by the fact that most of the leading female advocates (outside the Social Democratic Party at least) were Jewish.'[20] Dr. Peter Pulzer, who makes this claim, lists three names — Anita Augspurg, Lida Gustava Heymann and Regine Deutsch. They can of course hardly be described as *the* leaders of the women's movement, prominent though they were. It was often asserted by the Anti-Semitic Press that they were Jewish. The *Deutsch-soziale Blätter* declared in 1905 that 'the reforms of the ladies Augspurg, Heymann, Deutsch, Lischnewska and Lewysohn . . . have — which is easily explicable — damned little to do with *Germandom*', The same paper 'accused' Augspurg and Heymann of being Jewish again in 1907. But there is no evidence that either Augspurg, who came from a family of evangelical pastors, or Heymann, whose family were upper-class Hamburg merchants, or Lischnewska, daughter of a Prussian army officer, was Jewish. It was typical of the methods of the anti-Semitic Press that it also accused Minna Cauer, whose father was an evangelical minister, of being in reality Jewish and having altered her name from 'Krakauer'.[21]

When the Jewish Press came to consider the part played by Jewish women in the women's movement, it could only think of Alice Salomon, Alice Bensheimer, Adele Schreiber and Lina Morgenstern.[22] Most names advanced by the *völkisch* antifeminists to support their case were of women who were either not Jewish or not seriously involved in the women's movement. The majority of feminist leaders came to the women's movement through evangelical social welfare. Jewish women, like Catholic women, had their own organisation, the Jewish Women's League (Jüdischer Frauenbund), which like the other confessional organisations was mainly confined to welfare work and social administration, and adopted a very conservative line on all major questions of female emancipation.[23] Of course, there is no doubt that there were Jewish women among the rank and file of the women's movement, as one would expect from organizations drawing their support from the educated middle classes; but there is no evidence that they were either particularly numerous or very dominant.

In its claim that the women's movement was part of an international Jewish conspiracy that supposedly threatened to undermine the popular morality and national integrity of the German Empire, the Anti-League with its ally the DHV was thus indulging in the politics of fantasy. The same could be said of all the other charges it brought against the feminists. It accused them of plotting to destroy the family, when in fact they were becoming increasingly vociferous in its defence. It accused them of working to reduce the birth-rate, when in fact they were rapidly becoming obsessed with the problem of increasing it. It accused them of dividing the nation when they were laying more stress than ever before on the need to unite it. It accused them of pacifism when they were beginning to espouse the creed of aggressive nationalism. It accused them of campaigning for the systematic equalisation of the sexes when they were to an ever greater extent emphasising the differences between them. It accused them of being dominated by the radicals when the threat of that domination had long since been overcome. In almost every respect the Anti-League and its allies believed in the exact opposite of the truth. Absurd though their views were, however, they were no lunatic fringe. On the contrary, they represented a new and increasingly powerful movement among the ruling classes – the movement of the 'national opposition'. As such they represented vaguer and more widespread feelings than they themselves articulated. Only by looking at the more general context of antifeminism, therefore, can we discover the reasons for its sudden appearance.

THE RISE OF ANTIFEMINISM

The Anti-League and the DHV directed the attack against the women's movement itself; for them, feminism meant the body of ideas they imagined the women's movement to be supporting. For most antifeminists, however, feminism meant something much more diffuse and vague. It meant the negation of the values they were concerned to assert; pacifism instead of militarism, rights instead of duties, individualism instead of collectivism, social criticism instead of social solidarity, reform instead of reaction. Some writers were quite conscious of these two types of antifeminism, though in fact of course the first was only a more specific expression of the second. Hans Blüher, the historian of the youth movement, for example, called the wider and vaguer set of beliefs 'spiritual antifeminism' as opposed to the mere 'bourgeois antifeminism' of the Anti-League which represented part of the old bourgeois morality he hoped the youth movement would overthrow. Blüher thought that the nature of men and women was totally different, their relationship one of ruler and ruled, master and serf. It was from this standpoint that he criticised the Anti-League. The Anti-League admitted that gifted girls should be given educational opportunities. Blüher did not believe that girls *could* be gifted. The Anti-League defended the institution of marriage against the propagandists of free love. Blüher considered marriage an institution designed to fit the needs of women, and he rejected 'spurious bourgeois values', advocating polygamy as more suited to male needs.[24]

Blüher's theories owed much to a large book called *Sex and Character*, published in 1904 by Otto Weininger, a young and mentally unstable Austrian who committed suicide at the age of 23. Weininger had contrasted the 'feminine-motherly' with the 'masculine-creative' and translated this cosmic dichotomy into racial terms by arguing that Jews were 'feminine' – materialistic, shallow and inferior – and Aryans were 'masculine'. Weininger's book was huge, turgid and absurd, but it went through 11 editions by 1909 and its influence was widespread.[25] It probably had an effect on Colonel Max Bauer, a close associate of Erich Ludendorff, the soldier who came to dominate the military conduct of Germany in the First World War. Bauer thought it worth devoting several hundred – mercifully unpublished – pages to a rambling and incoherent 'Critique of the Women's Movement' in these years. Like his chief Bauer believed in the necessity of war. 'The idea of war', he wrote, 'is the mightiest impulse of cultural work and morality.' War was the supreme manifestation of male creative powers, which he equated with male sexuality. He therefore condemned all restraints upon 'this male urge, which in fact rules the world', including sexual abstinence before marriage, contraception and even severe penalties for rape. 'The polygamous instinct of man', he declared, 'cannot be suppressed.' He therefore defended prostitution. 'Marriage', he wrote, 'in itself is dispensable.' It was an unfair bargain in which the wife provided sexual satisfaction in return for money to squander on frivolities, and then demanded that the husband remain faithful, which was against his nature, since male sexuality was active and creative, female sexuality receptive and passive.

Bauer summed up woman's qualities as 'materialism' and contrasted them with man's 'idealism'. The military virtues of toughness, aggressiveness, group loyalty and individual enterprise were, he believed, sinking in a morass of 'female' egotism, hedonism, pacifism and humanitarianism.[26] This more general view was shared by most *völkisch* publicists and groups on the extreme right, and was common enough even before the emergence of what Blüher called 'bourgeois' anti-feminism. The Hammer Bund, for example, frequently printed anti-feminist articles of this sort in its journal *Hammer*. One such article by Justizrat Schnauss of Leipzig declared that:

> Feminism is a sign and at the same time a cause of the decline of a people. It destroys manly feelings and capabilities, it ruins women for motherhood, it dilutes, weakens and finally exterminates the people. Because feminism is a sign of its decay, the people itself can hardly succeed in fighting it . . . Prince Bülow is the leading personality in Prussia and the Empire, (but) his policies contain an element that if not feminism itself, is at least closely related to it. Only a statesman who does not pursue a policy of compromise or opportunism, but ruthlessly and single-mindedly follows the aim of securing the future of his people − a second Bismarck − only such a statesman could rescue our people from the morass of degeneration.[27]

For the antifeminists, whether they chose to organise themselves in the Anti-League or to co-operate with the Commercial Employees' Union, or to act as independent publicists, or in groups not specifically committed to fighting the women's movement, feminism was part of a global process of degeneration, finding its other major expressions in the industrialisation that transformed Germany after 1890 and in the liberalism against which all *völkisch* writers directed their main hostility.

It is no coincidence that moves to found an antifeminist movement began very soon after the Reichstag elections of January 1912. The elections saw a major victory by the SPD, which now became the largest single party in the Reichstag. This event caused a profound crisis of confidence in the ranks of the ruling classes. It seemed that more and more of the German people were committing themselves to the doctrine of the total overthrow of the existing social and political order. The months following the election thus witnessed renewed efforts on the part of the ruling classes to divert the attention of the masses from the need for social reform by attempting to pursue an aggressively nationalistic foreign policy.[28] A spate of new societies and organisations appeared,[29] all designed to rally the propertied classes to the defence of existing political system and instil in the masses a sense of loyalty to the Kaiser and commitment to the national community.

Viewed from this angle, the establishment of the Anti-League was part of an attempt to impress upon the German people the need to reassert traditional Prussian military 'masculinity' in the face of growing signs of national weakness and 'femininity'.

As well as this, however, the attention of the 'cultural pessimists' was drawn to the women's movement by the publication in 1912 of a report sponsored by the Prussian Ministry of the Interior entitled 'The Decline of the Birth-Rate in Germany'.[30] Historians of course have frequently noted the fact that Germany had a more rapid population growth than that of many other European countries, in particular France, whose population had almost ceased to grow by the turn of the century. This is often cited as a ground for German's growing assertiveness in world politics.[31] German Imperialism was not, however, based on self-confidence but on a far more complex set of emotions, ideas and developments. When we examine more closely the debate on population growth in Germany we find, beginning in 1912, a *crisis* of confidence in the capacity of the German population to continue growing. According to the official statistics, the rate of live births per thousand of the population had in fact been steadily sinking for nearly 40 years[32] – from 41.82 in 1872/76 to 33.20 in 1907/11, reaching 29.48 in the year 1911. This had been more than compensated for by the decline in the death-rate and by the virtual cessation of net emigration. In 1872/76 the excess of live births over deaths per thousand was 12.58, and this had increased to 14.39 in 1902/06. Thereafter, however – and this was the source of anxiety, as it became apparent that this was no passing phenomenon but a long-term trend – it had declined to 13.62 in the year 1910 and 11.33 in the year 1911. 'If the decline continues at the pace of the last ten years', commented Agnes Bluhm in January 1913, 'we shall be in the situation of France even sooner than unpopular pessimists saw themselves compelled to believe a short while ago.'

From 1912 well into the war, when the situation was further worsened by mass slaughter on the battlefield, books, pamphlets and articles appeared in floods on the subject, societies were set up to consider ways of fighting the decline, conferences were held, speeches delivered, dire warnings issued, drastic remedies advised. Many believed a further examination of the official statistics to reveal an even gloomier picture. The number of marriages per thousand of the population, for instance, had been declining since 1900, as had the size of the average family. These developments were to be seen at their most startling in the big cities. From 1876/80 to 1901/05 live births per thousand in Berlin had gone down from 40.2 to 25.0. Meanwhile, as a government commission reported on 25 February 1909, venereal disease was reaching a comparable extent to that of tuberculosis and alcoholism as a corrupting influence on the development of the race.[33]

The publication of the report, and its statement that the women's movement bore part of the responsibility for the decline, either by encouraging women to take jobs which removed them from their function as childbearers, or by persuading them to lead an independent existence outside the family, or by spreading ideas about free love, contraception and abortion, and leading them to neglect their duty to produce children, was a major stimulus to the growth of antifeminism. As we have seen, much of the Antis' propaganda insisted on the dangers of feminism for the birth-rate. In emphasising this point, the antifeminists led the women's movement to reiterate even more strongly than before its belief that it was not doing anything to dissuade women from marrying and having children. In the same way, the antifeminists' concentration on the horrors of the English suffragette campaign led the German feminists to issue a public condemnation of suffragette violence 'as a defence against our opponents'.[34] The BDF set up a special Commission on Population Policy to discuss the birth-rate. In 1913 it decided that 'Population Policy' must be the subject of its next Congress, especially because the women's movement was being widely held responsible for the decline of the birth-rate.[35] The Congress was held in 1915, when slaughter on the battlefield made the problem seem more urgent than ever.

The effect of the rise of antifeminism was thus to reinforce the rightward drift of the women's movement. The relationship between feminism and antifeminism was therefore more complex than the simple appearance of mutual animosity might lead the casual observer to suppose. For the antifeminists, feminism was a symbol of the modern values they rejected. Their concept of feminism bore little relation to the reality. Yet because they then identified their concept of feminism with the women's movement, and accused it of trying to subvert society and morality, the women's movement was led to ward off these attacks by identifying itself ever more closely with the very values the antifeminists accused it of wanting to subvert. The discrepancy between the antifeminists' accusations and the feminists' real doctrines thus became ever wider. In reality, the feminists were step by step coming to support the ideas of their opponents. This was an indication of the very weak position in which the women's movement found itself in the politics and society of Wilhelmine Germany, its lack of self-confidence, and its inability to assert itself in the face of indifference and hostility. It was also, however, a result of the general shift of the movement away from liberal individualism that occurred in these years, and for which, as we have seen, many other factors besides the rise of antifeminism were responsible. In the final years of peace, liberals as well as conservatives were moving to the right.

WOMEN'S SUFFRAGE AND PARTY POLITICS, 1908-1914

From the late 1890s onwards politicians, as we have seen, were in general far more sympathetic to the demands of the moderate feminists than they had previously been. By 1908 these demands had in large measure been granted. There was little or no sympathy for more radical demands such as female suffrage among those politicians who had supported the entry of women into the universities and the medical profession. The Free Conservatives, favourably inclined though individual members may have been, were in general as hostile as the Conservatives — antifeminists to a man — on this issue. The Catholic Centre continued to oppose female emancipation in every form. The National Liberals made a few concessions in theory, none in practice. Of the bourgeois parties, only the left-wing liberals seemed to entertain the possibility of supporting votes for women.

Here, however, the situation was complicated by the fact that the German Union for Women's Suffrage had repudiated co-operation with the left wing liberal parties after 1907. Naturally enough, in view of the hostile statements of the Union's leaders, Anita Augspurg and Lida Gustava Heymann, leading liberals in their turn began to hold themselves increasingly aloof from the Augspurg-Heymann wing of the suffrage movement; Naumann and Müller-Meiningen refused, for example, to speak for Frieda Radel's radical suffragist society, loyal to Augspurg and Heymann, in 1914.[36] In their turn, the leading suffragists tended after 1908 to ignore the left-liberal parties or to join the Democratic Alliance (Demokratische Vereinigung), a small left-liberal splinter group founded on the basis of the liberal individualism that the major parties were now deserting in 1908. Its leader was Theodor Barth, and among its most prominent members were Minna Cauer, Regine Deutsch, Toni Breitscheid and Adele Schreiber. The Democratic Alliance did actually include female suffrage in its programme, but it had little influence on national politics and held aloof from the union of the left-liberal groups in 1910.[37]

It is not surprising then that the initiative for female suffrage within the left-wing liberal movement was now taken up by people who either had nothing to do with the suffrage movement, such as Gertrud Bäumer, or who belonged to its right wing and acted in any case in an independent capacity, such as Martha Zietz and Maria Lischnewska. In 1910 after some years of debate and discussion, the three left-wing liberal parties united to form a new political party, the Progressive People's Party (Fortschrittliche Volkspartei). As the three groups which formed the new party tried to hammer out a common political programme, the question naturally arose of whether or not to include votes for women. The strongest pressure for female suffrage to be included in the programme of the Progressives came from the Liberal Alliance (Freisinnige Vereinigung), which in 1907 had taken up many of the demands of the women's movement including active and passive female suffrage. Martha Zietz, the Hamburg suffragist, and Gertrud Bäumer both belonged to this party. At a meeting of the executive committee of the Liberal Alliance held on 8 and 9 January 1910 to discuss the programme of the new united party, Bäumer proposed that women should be included in every section of the programme that demanded more rights of any kind for any group of people. Thus to the words 'the party demands the full participation of all citizens' in Section 3 was to be added the phrase 'of both sexes'. To the clauses demanding more democracy in law, economic life, education and local government were to be added phrases ensuring that this would include women as well as men. To make sure that there were no misunderstandings, a short sentence was to be inserted demanding the 'fundamental recognition of the equal political rights of women in Empire, State and local community'.[38] Bäumer's motion was accepted against one dissenting vote.

During the negotiations between the three left-wing liberal parties on union, the Liberal Alliance's point of view was supported by members of the largest of the three liberal groups, the Liberal People's Party (Freisinnige Volkspartei), in particular by Ernst Müller-Meiningen. However the objections of the third group, the South German People's Party (Süddeutsche Volkspartei) under Conrad Haussmann and Friedrich Payer, proved an insurmountable stumbling-block. Haussmann had already declared in October 1906 that he opposed female suffrage on principle. Most men and women did not want it, he said, and to grant it would in no way enrich the political life of the nation because the suffragists themselves were only interested in a tiny and specialised area of politics. The *Stuttgarter Beobachter*, chief organ of the South German liberals, thought that most party members agreed with Haussmann.[39]

Müller-Meiningen considered that Friedrich Payer was to blame for the ultimate rejection of the Bäumer proposals. Most liberals were obviously not prepared to upset Haussmann and Payer. There were also formal difficulties. The South Germans had been the first to hold a Party Congress to discuss the fusion and had declared themselves in favour, on the condition that only minor alterations were to be made to the original provisional programme. Before they could accept the Bäumer proposals they would have to hold a fresh Party Congress, and this would entail a delay in the fusion as well as offering its opponents within the South German party another chance to rally their support. The risk was too great for the other parties to accept. The final programme of the new Progressive People's Party (Fortschrittliche Volkspartei) did at least go further than the old Liberal People's Party had done, in demanding that women be granted active and passive suffrage in the commercial courts and State insurance bodies. Taken as a whole, however, it constituted a concession on the part of the Liberal Alliance to the South Germans. The delegates of the Alliance's last Party Congress reaffirmed that they would continue to work for the political equality of women as individuals.[40]

The women within the Progressive Party aimed from the very beginning at a reversal of this decision. On 4 October 1910, sixty leading women members of the Party attended a conference in Frankfurt called by a working committee under the leadership of Zietz and Bäumer. It discussed how the liberal women were to be organised. A scheme for a separate semi-independent 'Liberal Women's League (Bund Liberaler Frauen) devised by Maria Lischnewska was rejected. Bäumer's suggestion of a women's section closely integrated with the Party was adopted in its stead. The conference also resolved to press for the inclusion of female suffrage in the Party programme.[41] On 21 November 1910 these decisions were discussed by the Party's central committee at the instigation of Bäumer, who had been elected to it on its formation. She promised that the women would all join the local party organisations as ordinary members. Her proposals were accepted, but members took the opportunity to remind the women that they must toe the party line if they wanted the party's support. One member said:

> If the women want to join the party organisation of the Progressive Party, that is to be thoroughly welcomed, but they must consider that the content of their statutes stands in contradiction to the programme of the Progressive Party in the matter of female suffrage. The danger arises of a State within a State. They must first make a declaration that all deputies, including those who are not in favour of female suffrage and indeed the party as a whole, are supported by the women.

Other members, including Georg Gothein, argued that the demand for female suffrage was in no way a contradiction of the party's programme, since the paragraph on women's rights would be extended later anyway.[42] Friedrich Voss even attempted to secure for Martha Zietz a seat on the central committee as President of the Women's organisation. This was perhaps not entirely out of ideological conviction, however, for he married her not long afterwards.[43]

The women of the Progressive Party made one more serious attempt to get the party to support female suffrage. This was at the Party Congress in Mannheim in 1912. There were more motions tabled on women's rights at this conference than on any other topic, and the question had first place on the agenda. A meeting held on 12 September 1912 between the women's representatives and the Party leaders failed to avoid an open clash at the Congress.[44] Of the 13 motions tabled by party branches, all but a very few were in favour of amending the party programme. The two most important motions were those of the central committee, calling for the retention of the existing party statute because of the differences of opinion within the party on the subject, but reaffirming the right of party members to campaign for female suffrage as individuals, and a counter-motion proposed by Martha Zietz and seconded by – among others – Gertrud Bäumer, Helene Lange, Helene von Forster, Bertha Wendt, Carl Petersen, Ludwig Quidde and Curt Platen, which declared that the granting of equal political rights to women was inevitable and urged party members 'to support the women in their struggle for their political rights up to full civic equality'. This motion was eventually passed with an amendment tabled by Müller-Meiningen adding the words 'according to the opinion of a broad section of the party' after the statement that the gaining of equal political rights was inevitable.[45]

This defeat of the party leadership seemed at first sight to have opened the way for the women to press home their case and convert the promise into reality by getting female suffrage inserted into the party's programme. Martha Zietz reckoned it was highly probable that 'the last remnants of opposition will soon disappear'.[46] The Mannheim resolution was indeed generally recognised as an advance on the position adopted by the party in 1910, and the supporters of female suffrage might legitimately have expected final victory at the next Party Congress. Looked at from another angle, however, the resolution was a step backwards for the women. In 1910 they had been unanimous in demanding that the party incorporate female suffrage into the party programme, just as the Liberal Alliance had done in its acceptance of Bäumer's proposals in 1910 and in its resolution of 1907, and the Democratic Alliance had done ever since its foundation in 1908. In 1912, however, all the women asked was that the party support female suffrage by urging its members to back the women's own struggle for political equalty, not to enter the struggle itself or to commit itself to female suffrage as a party.

The women also failed to secure a really strong position for themselves in the party organisation. In the broadest sense they met as the 'women of the Progressive Party', with some 70 agents at a local level and a plan – never realised – for a conference of liberal women in conjunction with the Party's own biennial Congress, on the lines of the SPD Women's Conferences. A more centralised body was the 'Working

Committee of the Women of the Progressive Party', which met on a regular basis. Most of its members were leading figures in the BDF.[47] Finally there was the Liberal Women's Party (Liberale Frauenpartei), sometimes known as the Association of Liberal Women of Greater Berlin, formed in January 1907 by Maria Lischnewska. Maintained against strong opposition from the suffragists, it was nationalistic, pressing for a bigger battle fleet and more colonial railways; anti-clerical, opposing the repeal of the Anti-Jesuit Law; and, at the begin-ning, radically feminist, urging the abolition of the State regulation of prostitution and voting at various times to 'carry on the struggle' for women's suffrage. Yet it was significant that by 1913 its propaganda entirely lacked any direct demand for female suffrage.[48]

None of these organisations had any official standing within the party. Because the Progressive women were divided into these groups they did not concentrate their efforts. Because Bäumer's scheme had been accepted in 1910 and women joined the party as individuals and ordinary members they never again after 1910 had sufficient repre-sentation in the party's decision-making bodies. The party's local organ-isations naturally tended to elect men with political rights to con-ferences and committees. Naumann wanted the women to have an official, permanent representative on the central committee – Gertrud Bäumer – just as he wanted the liberal trade unions to have a repre-sentative – Anton Erkelenz – but he was overruled on this point.[49] Martha Zietz found herself in 1912, and Maria Lischnewska on sub-sequent occasions, without the right to attend the Party Congress, and they had to request admittance as guests. Such requests were not always granted.[50] As a result of this organisational weakness the women were unable to make any headway within the Progressive Party by the outbreak of war.[51]

If the BDF leadership was unsuccessful in its attempts to commit the Progressive Party to supporting votes for women, however, it could be least console itself with the knowledge that the membership of the BDF was increasing by leaps and bounds in the last years of peace. Its growth in size indeed was one feature that called the attention of conservatives and reactionaries to the movement. It seemed to be gaining in influence and importance; hence the need to stop it before it was too late. By 1914 the strength of the movement seemed truly impressive. The BDF was beginning to claim that it represented German women in a way that no other organisation could. It was, so the title of its annual publication the 'Yearbook of the Women's Movement' implied, the embodiment of the entire feminist movement. It even began to claim that it spoke with the voice of German women as a whole.

Subject to close examination, these claims were in fact much less impressive than they appeared at first sight. True, by 1912 the BDF was accustomed to say that it spoke for 'half a million German women',[52] and it pointed to the membership statistics published in its Yearbook as evidence for this statement. As the Yearbook reveals, however, the BDF was subdivided into national organisations with local and regional branches, into unions uniting all member associations in a particular region, and into confessional, specialist and professional associations. Many women's societies belonged to more than one of these organisations. As the figure of 500,000 was arrived at simply by adding together the total membership of all these various subdivisions of the Federation, such societies appeared more than once in the final reckoning. In the yearbook for 1913 for instance the Association of Prussian Primary School Teachers (Landesverein preussischer Volksschullehrerinnen) appeared on its own and also as part of the General German Women Teachers' Association (Allgemeiner Deutscher Lehrerinnenverein), thus contributing to the BDF 9200 members instead of 4600.

Moreover, a list of 'directly affiliated associations' was appended to the main list of member societies and also added to the membership total. In the Yearbook for 1913[53] no fewer than 225 of these associations had already been counted at least once in the main list. Altogether in the whole membership list 265 societies were counted twice, 72 three times and four even appeared four times over. Separating these out gives a total of about 315,000 for the BDF, counted by people and not by membership cards. This must, however, be further reduced because many constituent societies contained large numbers of men. The German Association against the Misuse of Alcoholic Drinks (Deutscher Verein gegen den Missbrauch geistiger Getränke) provided the Federation with 40,000 members, but only 5000 of these were women. This consideration reduces the likely total of women who belonged to the BDF in 1912 to about 280,000 at the most.

As we have seen, however, many women belonged to more than one organisation. Membership in the three radical feminist societies in Hamburg, for example (the Abolitionist Federation, the Frauenwohl and the Suffrage Union), was more or less identical between 1902 and 1908, and the same can be said of Berlin and most other major cities as far as the Suffrage Union and other radical groups were concerned. Nearly all women prominent in the women's movement belonged to two or more different societies. Taking this into account it is probable that the BDF represented a total of not more than 200,000 women in 1912, and had not exceeded 250,000 by the outbreak of war. This is considerably less than the figure of 351,870 given by Alice Bensheimer in January 1912, or the estimate of 300,000 made by Gertrud Bäumer in July 1911, but it does fit in with the figure of 150,000 worked out by the counting of heads and not membership cards by Marie Wegner in 1908, and the figure of 200,000 advanced by the BDF itself at Heidelberg in 1910. Both these figures, however, included large numbers of men organised in societies such as the temperance organisations. Two years after Wegner, in 1910, Julie Eichholz put the number of *women* in the BDF at a mere 120,000.[54]

Furthermore, when the BDF issued petititions and declarations it naturally gave the impression that it spoke on behalf of all its member associations. However, many of these — such as the temperance societies — were not primarily interested in the emancipation of women, and many more did not subscribe even to the modest concept of emancipation advanced by the BDF leadership. Nevertheless, despite all this, the BDF gave the impression of a rapidly-growing, powerful and strongly supported body whose claim to represent the women of Germany and put their views in the questions that affected them, however feeble it may have been in reality, could certainly not be bettered by any other organisation. As the BDF grew in size, so the government began to find it convenient to consult it in order to obtain 'the women's point of view' on questions in which it thought women had a special interest. As Gertrud Bäumer remarked in 1913, 'the State has come nearer to women, has become more alive and more comprehensible to them'.[55] The beginnings of this process, which was immensely accelerated by the war, were already visible in the last years of peace, particularly at a local level, where the BDF's member associations were beginning to co-operate closely with the authorities in welfare and education.

This gradual integration with the political system, as the women's movement grew larger, naturally speeded up the process whereby German feminism ceased to be opposed to the existing structure of politics and society, as it had been at the turn of the century, and became steadily more cautious, conservative and conventional in its ideas. As it grew, moreover, the BDF recruited its membership to a large extent from the more conservative elements of the middle classes. The most important accession to the BDF from this direction was the German-evangelical Women's League (Deutsch-evangelischer Frauen-bund), which had been founded in June 1899 under the aegis of Pastor Weber, the leader of the Morality Associations.[56] It was initially intended to arouse women to oppose the advance of radical feminism by the classic methods of the evangelical social movement: its first manifesto declared that its aim was to stop the class war and the sex war which radical feminism preached by 'seeking to establish personal relations' between evangelical women and 'the People'.[57] It opposed most of the aims of the feminist movement, especially female suffrage. In 1905, however, it sent observers to the BDF General Assembly,[58] and it was soon considering whether to join the BDF itself. The question became urgent in 1908, when it was learned that the radicals were now so influential in the BDF that the reorganisation they had been urging for many years was likely to be voted into effect at the next General Assembly. This would reorganise the BDF into a federation consisting exclusively of *Verbände,* that is, national or regional unions each uniting a number of branches in a certain field (e.g. female suffrage) or a certain area. Individual branches would no longer be able to join by themselves. No member union joining after 1 October 1908 would have more than 10 votes at the General Assembly. Unions joining before that date would retain their present number of votes. Paula Müller, the leader of the German-evangelical Women's League, thus urged that the League should join the BDF before 1 October since this would probably be its last opportunity to make its influence felt within the BDF. If it joined now, she said, it would have over 50 votes. Müller went on to remark that in this case, 'we would, together with the moderate party, far outweigh the radical and progressive elements; indeed, we would have a great majority over them'.[59] For their part, the radicals were quite clear as to the threat which this move posed for the liberalism of the BDF.[60] Marie Stritt herself was opposed to Müller's plan. Müller thought that Stritt 'now relies more on the radicals ... out of personal animosity towards Helene Lange'.[61] Nevertheless the Evan-gelical League's executive committee voted by 9 votes to 6, with one abstention, to join; the branches supported the move by 61 to 44; and a special eleventh-hour General Assembly held on 25-26 September endorsed the decision.[62] The Evangelicals thus succeeded in joining the BDF with nearly 50 votes.

It was quite clear that these votes would be used in the first place to defeat the radicals, and in particular the New Morality; the German-evangelical Women's League, indeed, regarded this as one of its major tasks. The New Morality, it declared, was 'dangerous in principle and hostile to Christianity in intent'.[63] Moreover, there is no doubt that the votes of the Evangelicals were a major influence, perhaps indeed a decisive influence, in turning the tide against radicalism at the 1908 BDF General Assembly. They even managed to block at least part of the radicals' scheme to reorganise the BDF, so that member associations and branches were still able to join individually.[64] Problems soon arose, however, because the Evangelicals did not fully support the BDF programme of 1907, particularly in its demand for female suffrage. Although Marie Stritt had pointed out that the programme was in general binding on member unions, particularly in the question of female suffrage,[65] the BDF executive committee had nevertheless come to an arrangement with the Evangelical League in 1908 whereby the League agreed to remain neutral on the subject and abstain from all votes on it in the BDF. This meant that the League was not expected to support any propaganda the BDF issued in favour of votes for women, and in return for this concession would not do anything to oppose it either.[66]

In the first two or three years of the League's membership this arrangement seemed to work reasonably well. Things changed, however, when in 1911 Paula Müller, together with some of her Evangelical colleagues, founded an Alliance of Conservative Women (Vereinigung konservativer Frauen). From early on in the history of the German-evangelical Women's League, the connection between the organisation and the Conservative Party had been obvious; now it was made explicit.[67] The foundation was embarrassing to the Conservatives, who did not quite know how to react to a group of women simultaneously outraging their beliefs by engaging in politics and flattering their vanity by engaging in politics on their side.[68] The Conservative Party welcomed the support of Müller and her colleagues, but declared firmly that:

It rejects however the numerous attempts now being made to bring about the political equality of the female sex, and every kind of so-called female emancipation, as incompatible with the real interests of true womanhood and the natural tasks of human society.

The most it was prepared to tolerate, declared the party, was an encouragement by the Alliance of Conservative Women of an enlargement of women's activities in social welfare work and to a certain extent in education and the professions as well. It insisted:

that the Alliance emphatically rejects female suffrage and all endeavours that are in the last analysis aimed at leading up to female suffrage, and that, while refraining from actual political activities, it seeks its end in the propagation of conservative ideas in the home, society and the people.[69]

There was thus powerful pressure from the Conservative Party for Paula Müller and the German-evangelical Women's League to abandon the neutral position they had agreed to adopt towards female suffrage on joining the BDF. It was also reinforced by pressure from the Anti-League, many of whose members were themselves active in Conservative politics. As soon as it was founded in June 1912, indeed, the Anti-League mounted a vigorous campaign to try and persuade the German-evangelical Women's League to withdraw from the BDF, arguing that its 'hands were tied' while it remained.[70] A certain Pastor Werner in Frankfurt even formed a so-called 'Christian-national Group against the Emancipation of Women' (Christlich-nationale Gruppe gegen die Frauenemanzipation), which conducted a vigorous public campaign to wean the German-evangelical Women's League away from the BDF and was supported by right-wing newspapers such as the *Reichsbote*.[71]

Under the combined pressure of the Conservatives and the Anti's, Paula Müller came out in open opposition to female suffrage in August 1912. In an article in the Evangelicals' own magazine, the *Evangelische Frauenzeitung*, Müller declared that female suffrage would help the SPD and the Catholics and lead inevitably to universal suffrage.[72] On 20 September she went further and threatened to boycott the BDF's next General Assembly if things did not change.[73] These actions clearly contravened the agreement under which the League had joined the BDF, and could not be allowed to pass unchallenged. Yet the claim of the BDF to stand above party interests and represent all German

women made it vital to keep the conservative women within the fold
and so avoid too close an identification with the Progressive Party. The
formation of the Anti-League in the summer of 1912 and the agitation
that accompanied it in the right-wing Press made it imperative for the
BDF itself that the most obviously conservative and respectable of its
member associations — an organisation which indeed, as Helene Lange
pointed out, held roughly the same views as the Anti-League — shuld
not leave at this particular juncture.[74] The moment was, as Bäumer
remarked on 10 September, 'especially unfavourable for a break with
the Evangelicals'.[75]

Urged on by Bäumer, the BDF repeated with greater force an
assertion originally made when the League's entry into the BDF had
first been mooted in 1907 and then subsequently denied by Stritt[76] —
that the BDF programme of 1907 was nothing more than a set of
proposals with which member unions were free to agree or disagree as
they pleased.[77] It also declared that the agreement of 1908 had only
pledged the Evangelicals to neutrality *within* the BDF; outside it they
were free to say what they liked. Bäumer added that if this were
recognised, many members and a large proportion of the local branches
of the Evangelical Women's League would declare themselves in favour
of female suffrage — what kind of female suffrage she did not say. She
went on to point out that 'in the last analysis, in our Federation of
500,000 members, the German-evangelical Women's League only plays
a small role, which cannot alter our course'.[78] An agreement was
worked out at a joint conference of the two executive committees at
Gotha on 3 October 1912 and finalised in December.[79]

Yet Bäumer's arguments were disingenuous. The German-evangelical
Women's League was not numerically strong, although its size was
roughly comparable with that of the Suffrage Union. In 1908 it had
9,000 members. However, its unimpeachable respectability and its connections with the ruling classes made it doubly valuable. Within the
BDF it wielded nearly 50 votes because all its member associations and
branches and joined separately, and its presence at General Assemblies
was especially useful in keeping the radicals at bay. The Suffrage Union,
by contrast, joined as one society and had only one vote. This was a
matter of principle for the suffragists, who campaigned throughout the
years 1898-1908 to alter the BDF constitution so that only large
organisations such as the Suffrage Union would be represented. As

Alice Bensheimer pointed out, the suffragists were quite at liberty to increase their voting strength by allowing their branches to join separately. However, when the Union actually began to make plans to add another 24 votes to its representation by doing this, Bensheimer was the first to object.[80] Moreover, though Bäumer thought that individual branches and members of the German-evangelical Women's League might support female suffrage, the leadership, supported by a majority of the League, was firmly opposed to it and was quite able to keep its constituent branches in line.

The League's decision to stay in the BDF was strongly criticised by the political Right.[81] Yet the results of the affair weakened the ties of the BDF – both in reality and in the public eye – with liberalism, and strengthened the influence of the conservatives even further. If Bäumer argued, as she sometimes did, that the inclusion of female suffrage in the BDF programme proved that the women's movement supported female suffrage, opponents could now point to the German-evangelical Women's League and refute her claim. Their argument can only have been strengthened when in 1913, against strong opposition from the radical feminists, the German Women's League (Deutscher Frauenbund), founded in February 1909 as the women's section of the right-wing Imperial League against Social Democracy (Reichsverband gegen die Sozialdemokratie), joined the BDF as a full member society.[82] The League claimed to have dissolved its connection with the anti-SPD organisation, and the BDF insisted it confirm this before it be allowed to join. Nevertheless, opinion in the BDF leadership was in any case favourable; Alice Salomon felt it would help avoid too great an emphasis on the 'liberal element' and encourage conservative women to join the BDF.[83] At Stritt pointed out, Bäumer had regarded the BDF programme as binding on member associations in questions of sexual morality and abortion law reform, but did not regard it as binding in the question of votes for women. In fact Bäumer was clearly bending the rules so as to make concessions to the conservatives that she denied to the radicals.[84]

The results were soon apparent. Not only did Müller and her associates denounce female suffrage as a matter of principle, they also attacked the BDF programme on a number of other points. The BDF made concession after concession, but there was a limit beyond which even Bäumer could not go. That limit seemed to have been reached in

1914 when the *Evangelische Frauenzeitung* printed a highly favourable review of Adolf Bartels' book *The German Degeneration (Der Deutsche Verfall)* which called for the regeneration of Germany through the banishment of a 'judaized liberalism' which Bartels imagined was corrupting the nation. The fact that Bartels was a prominent member of the Anti-League was the least of Bäumer's objections:

> I myself (she wrote to Paula Müller) belong to this 'judaized liberalism' and I want to say something about the word 'judaize'. I know that neither the race itself nor the individual person as such is meant by this word, but a certain dangerous subversive frame of mind. Neither this frame of mind however, nor Jewry itself, is such a power within liberalism as is alleged by its opponents. For those Jews namely, who have such an irresponsible frame of mind, have either long been Social Democrats (Liebknecht) or apply themselves to those circles where social success is to be found, namely to the right wing.[85]

In attacking Muller's view, Baumer, it is important to realise, was not attacking Anti-Semitism or refuting the Anti-Semites' negative view of the Jewish character; she was merely denying that liberalism was influenced by Jews. Nor was she consistent in the long run even in this attitude. In 1927 Bäumer threatened to leave the Reichstag and resign from the German Democratic Party because the Party's deputies had 'subordinated themselves to the agitation of the Jewish-liberal circles of Berlin' in opposing stiffer moral censorship of books and plays.[86] Moreover, in naming Karl Liebknecht as her example of an 'irresponsible' Jew, Bäumer was unconsciously providing evidence for her 'subjective' interpretation of the word 'judaize', for there is no evidence that either Liebknecht or any of his forefathers was Jewish. Paula Müller herself, of course, was far less equivocal in her attitude to Antisemitism. In reply to Bäumer's letter and to a protest from Alice Bensheimer — herself Jewish — Müller spoke up in defence of the review. 'We can have no doubt', she wrote to Bensheimer, 'that this (Antisemitism) is the point of view of broad circles of people . . . You know the esteem in which I hold you personally and many excellent people of your creed . . . but you must also appreciate that I can do nothing further in this matter.'[87]

As a long-term solution, the compromise between the BDF and the German-evangelical Women's League was clearly unsatisfactory. The final break was, however, delayed by the outbreak of war. Meanwhile, Bäumer did her best to accommodate her uneasy allies. On their instigation she agreed to publish a declaration condemning in the name of the BDF all those who wanted to legalise abortion and abolish Section 218.[88] As this indicated, its efforts to keep the Evangelicals within the fold were in the last analysis yet another contributing factor to the BDF's abandonment of social and political radicalism. As the SPD women's magazine *Die Gleichheit* observed in 1910, 'bourgeois feminism is on the march towards the right'.[89] This rightward march of the German women's movement was to continue into the First World War.

NOTES

1. StA Hbg, PP, S18848: *HN*, 8 June 1912, *HC*, 12 June 1912, *HE*, 8 June 1912; ABDF 4/2: cutting of *BLA*, 18 June 1912; George L. Mosse, *The Crisis of German Ideology* (London, 1966) 74 (Stauff), 90-92 (Schemann), 222-3 (Kuhlenbeck); Dirk Stegmann, *Die Erben Bismarcks* (Köln/Berlin, 1970), 289, 302, 428, 476 (Schmidt-Gibichenfels). See Stegmann, op. cit., for Schäfer also.

2. According to Minna Cauer, Sigismund's mother-in-law was the President of the Weimar branch of the Women's Suffrage Union (ADEFB, A14c: *Vossiche Zeitung,* 10 Oct. 1908). Doubtless this played a role in his conversion to antifeminism.

3. StA Hbg, PP, S18848: *BNN*, 6 Jan. 1914, *BLA*, 15 June 1912; Ludwig Langermann, Helene Hummel, *Frauenstimmrecht und Frauenemanzipation* (Berlin, 1916).

4. ABDF 4/2: Erklärung des Bundes Deutscher Frauenvereine zur Organisation der Gegner.

5. StA Hbg, PP, S18848: *NHZ*, 15 March 1913.

6. StA Hbg, PP, S18848: *NHZ*, 11 June 1912.

7. ABDF 4/2: Bäumer to Else Lens, 11 July 1912.

8. Cf. H. Boog, *Graf Ernst zu Reventlow, 1869-1943* (Phil.Diss., Heidelberg, 1965).

9. StA Hbg, PP, S18848: *BVZ*, 5 Jan. 1912.

10. Examples may be found in GStA München, MA92765 (29 Oct. 1915); StA Hbg, PP, S9001/IV: *BVZ*, 1 April 1916; etc.

11. See Iris Hamel, *Völkischer Verband und nationale Gewerkschaft. Der Deutschnationale Handlungsgehilfenverband 1893-1933* (Frankfurt am Main, 1967). For the background, see Jürgen Kocka, *Unternehmensverwaltung und Angestelltenschaft am Beispiel Siemens 1847-1914. Zum Verhältnis von Kapitalismus und Bürokratie in der deutschen Industrialisierung* (Stuttgart, 1969).

12. *Mitteilungen des Deutschnationalen Handlungsgehilfenverbandes,* No. 4, 1 Dec. 1894; *Deutsche Handelswacht,* No. 20, 15 Oct. 1906, 390.

13. StA Hbg, PP, V858, passim.

14. *Schriften des Deutschnationalen Handlungsgehilfenverbandes,* Vol. 15: *Verbandstag 1903,* 4.

15. Werner Heinemann, *Die radikale Frauenbewegung als nationale Gefahr!* (Hamburg, 1913), 15-16, 28, 12.

16. P. J. G. Pulzer, *The Rise of Political Anti-Semitism in Germany and Austria* (New York/London, 1964), 221-222.

17. Quoted in Pulzer, loc. cit.

18. Formerly known as the *Deutsches Blatt.*

19. StA Hbg, PP, S18848: *DSB,* 15 June 1912.

20. Pulzer, loc. cit.

21. StA Hbg, PP, S9000/I: *DSB,* 7 Oct. 1905; ibid., S7484: *DSB,* 9 Oct. 1907; ibid., S7484: *DP,* 16 June 1904. Cauer, of course, was her *married* name. Her maiden name was Schelle.

22. StA Hbg, PP, S7484: *Israelitisches Familienblatt,* 17 May 1906.

23. StA Hbg, PP, SA1023, passim.

24. Hans Blüher, *Der bürgerliche und der geistige Antifeminismus* (3rd ed., n.d., c.1920), *Frauenbewegung und Antifeminismus* (Lauenburg a.E., 1921); Mosse, op. cit., 176-7, 212-4.

25. Mosse, op. cit., 215-216. See also Viola Klein, *The Feminine Character. History of an Ideology* (London, 1946), for a discussion of Weininger's ideas.

26. BA Koblenz, NL Bauer, No. 1c, 120; No. 1d, 20, 92, 95-7, 102, 155, 160, 174, 177-81, 191, 65-67.

27. DZA Potsdam, Reichskanzlei, 2266: copy of Justizrat Schnauss, 'Die Gefahren der Frauenbewegung', *Hammer,* No. 158, 15 Jan. 1909. The word *Feminismus* in German was generally reserved for the abstract qualities Schnauss was describing. The English 'feminism' had no equivalent in German: the nearest were '*Frauenrechtlerin*' ('feminist'), '*Frauenrechtelei*' ('feminism', but with a strongly pejorative flavour), and '*Frauenbewegung*' ('women's movement').

28. See Fritz Fischer, *Krieg der Illusionen* (Düsseldorf, 1969).

29. cf. Dirk Stegmann, *Die Erben Bismarcks* (op. cit.). For a brief summary of these developments, see V. R. Berghahn, *Germany and the Approach of War in 1914* (London, 1973), Ch. 8-9.

30. *Der Geburtenrückgang in Deutschland. Seine Bewertung und Bekämpfung* (im Auftrage S. Exzellenz der Herrn Ministers der Innern, hg. von der Medizinal-Abteilung des Ministeriums, Berlin, 1912). See also Fritz Stern, *The Politics of Cultural Despair* (Berkeley/Los Angeles, 1961).

31. Cf. Fischer, op. cit., 18.

32. See John E. Knodel, *The Decline of Fertility in Germany, 1871-1939* (Princeton, 1974).

33. Henriette Fürth, 'Der Geburtenrückgang und die Frauen', *FB*, 19/6, 15 March 1913, 42; Agnes Blühm, 'Der Geburtenrückgang in Deutschland', *DF*, 20/4, Jan. 1913, 221-234. For the wider context of this debate, see Ulrich Linse, 'Arbeiterschaft und Geburtenentwicklung im Deutschen Kaisserreich von 1871', *Archiv für Sozialgeschichte*, 1972, 205-272. The article's reliance on printed sources leads it into error in its treatment of the BDF.

34. ABDF 16/II/2: Gesamtvorstandssitzung, 8 March 1913.

35. ABDF 16/II/2, Gesamtvorstandssitzung, 7 March 1913. For an examination of the possible connection between feminism and declining birth-rates in an English context, see J. A. and Olive Banks, *Feminism and Family Planning in Victorian England* (Liverpool, 1964).

36. DZA Potsdam, Fortschrittliche Volkspartei, No. 54, 8-10; Frieda Radel to Weimer, 9 March 1914.

37. Ludwig Elm, *Zwischen Fortschritt und Reaktion. Geschichte der Parteien der liberalen Bourgeoisie in Deutschland. 1893-1918.* (East Berlin, 1968), 234. The Prussian Union for Women's Suffrage joined en bloc on its foundation in 1908. See Maria Lischnewska, *Die deutsche Frauenstimmrechtsbewegung zwischen Krieg und Frieden* (Berlin, 1915), 15-16.

38. DZA Potsdam, NL Naumann, No. 59, 247-251: Protokoll der Vorstandssitzung des Wahlvereins der Liberalen am 8. und 9. Januar 1910.

39. StA Hbg, PP, S9001/II: *HF*, 10 Oct. 1906.

40. Gertrud Bäumer, 'Die fortschrittliche Volkspartei und die Frauen', *DF*, 17/7, April 1910, 385-9; StA Hbg, PP, S9001/II: *BT*, 6 March 1910, *BVZ*, March 1910; DZA Potsdam, NL Naumann, No. 59, 98; Entwurf eines Einigungsprogramms (marginalia); 100 (First Draft), 230, Protokoll des 5. Delegiertentages des Wahlvereins der Liberalen, Sonnabend den 5. März 1910. It is characteristic of the neglect into which the subject has fallen that the standard work by Walter Gagel, *Die Wahlrechtsfrage in der Geschichte der deutschen liberalen Parteien 1848-1918* (Düsseldorf, 1958), makes no mention of female suffrage.

41. StA Hbg, PP, S9000/I: *BT*, 13 May 1910, *FZ*, 6 Oct. 1910

42. DZA Potsdam, Fortschrittliche Volkspartei, No. 37, 203-6: Zentralausschuss Protokoll, 21 Nov. 1910.

43. UB Rostock, NL Schirmacher: Schirmacher to Schleker, 26 March 1911. After her marriage, Martha Zietz took the name of Martha Voss-Zietz; to avoid confusion, however, she is referred to below as Martha Zietz.

44. Ludwig Elm, op. cit., 214-5.

45. DZA Potsdam, Fortschrittliche, Volkspartei, No. 20: II. Parteitag vom. 4.-7. Oct. 1912, 54, 72, 76, 78, 81, 122-123.

46. *FS*, 1/8, Nov. 1912, 165-7, 'Die Frauenfrage auf dem Parteitag der Fortschrittlichen Volkspartei'.

47. HLA 57: Satzungsentwurf Bäumer; *DF*, 19/5, Feb. 1912, 268-275. Members included Gertrud Bäumer, Agnes Bluhm, Elly Heuss-Knapp, Maria Lischnewska, Anna Plothow, Alice Salomon and Martha Zietz among its founders, and later on Elisabeth Altmann-Gottheiner, Marie Baum, Alice Bensheimer, Eleonore Drenkhahn, Helene von Forster, Ika Freudenberg, Margarethe Friedenthal, Agnes Gosche, Ottilie Hoffman, Helene Lange, Anna Pappritz, Marianne Weber, Hedwig

Weidemann, Bertha Wendt, Käthe Windscheid and others. See HLA 57, 'An die liberalen Frauen! ' (Sept. 1912).

48. HLA 57: Programm der Liberalen Frauenpartei, *FZ*, 4 Oct. 1910; DZA Potsdam, Fortschrittliche Volkspartei, No. 54, 7-14: Liberale Frauenpartei; StA Hbg, PP, S9001/II: *BT*, 9 March 1907; ibid., SA593/II: *GA*, 22 March 1907; Elm, op. cit., 214; UB Rostock, NL Schirmacher: Schirmacher to Schleker, 29 March 1907.

49. DZA Potsdam, Fortschrittliche Volkspartei, No. 36/1: Geschäftsführende Ausschuss Protokoll, 4 Nov. 1912.

50. ibid., 128: Protokoll 28 March 1912; ibid., No. 26, 65-7: Lischnewska and Ledermann to Preussentagausschuss, 3 March 1913.

51. Cf. DZA Potsdam, Fortschrittliche Volkspartei 21: Parteitag Eisenach 1914 (motions for a Party Congress which was not held owing to the outbreak of the war).

52. ABDF 5/XV/2: Bäumer to *Reichsbote*, 11 July 1912; StA Hbg, PP, S5466/II: *HC*, 6 June 1912.

53. This gives membership figures for 1912.

54. *JB 1912-1914;* Wegner, op. cit., ABDF 4/2: *Schleswiger Nachrichten*, 2 Jan. 1914; Sta Hbg, PP, S5466/II: *NHZ*, 11 Oct. 1910; ibid., S9168: *Hamburger Frauenzeitung*, 7 Sept. 1910.

55. Gertrud Bäumer, 'Frauenbewegung und Nationalbewusstsein', *DF*, 20/7, April 1913, 387-394. See also *JB 1913, 1914.*

56. StA Hbg, PP, S5466/I: *HC*, 2 Aug. 1903.

57. ADEFB, B1: 'Der Deutsch-evangelische Frauenbund' (Flugblatt 1899).

58. StA Hbg, PP, S5466/I: *HE*, 18 June 1905.

59. ADEFB, B1: Müller to Ortsgruppen, 19 August 1908.

60. StA Hbg, PP, S5466/I: *HF*, 18 Oct. 1908, *LVZ* 23 Dec. 1908.

61. ADEFB, B1: Müller to Vorstand, 3 Sept. 1908.

62. ibid., Müller to Ortsgruppen, 19 Aug. 1908.

63. ADEFB, B1: 'Der DEFB vertritt der Neuen Ethik gegenüber folgende Grundsätze' (n.d.). Cf. Paula Müller, *Die 'Neue Ethik' und ihre Gefahr* (Berlin, 1908).

64. Cf. the Constitution printed in *JB 1912, 1913, 1914.*

65. ADEFB, A14c: Stritt to Müller, 19 Aug. 1908.

66. ABDF 5/IV/5: Bäumer to Vorstand, 10 Sept. 1912, 21 Oct. 1912; ABDF 5/XV/2: Bäumer to Müller, 26 Aug. 1912.

67. For connections with the Conservative Party, see, e.g., ADEFB, B1: A. von Bennigsen; Ausführungen Paula Müllers über die Stellung des DEFB zur Politik. Vorstandssitzung 5 Feb. 1913. Adelheid von Bennigsen came from a National Liberal background.

68. Cf. the similar attitude of Heinrich Class, leader of the Pan-German League, to Käthe Schirmacher's activities on behalf of Pan-German aims in the Prussian part of Poland. (UB Rostock, NL Schirmacher: Class to Schirmacher, 29 Dec. 1911).

69. Zahn-Harnack, op. cit., 298-301.

70. ABDF 5/IV/5: Bäumer to Vorstand, 20 Oct. 1912.

71. ADEFB, B1: DEFB Vorstand to *Reichsbote,* Aug. 1912; 'Zur Lage des DEFB'.

72. ABDF 3/4: *Evangelische Frauenzeitung,* 15 Aug. 1912.

73. ABDF 5/IV/5: Bäumer to Vorstand, 20 Oct. 1912.

74. *DF* 20/7, April 1913, 434-6; ABDF 5/IV/5: Bäumer to Vorstand, 10 Sept. 1912, 21 Oct. 1912; ABDF 5/XV/2: Bäumer to Müller, 26 Aug. 1912.

75. ABDF 5/IV/5: Bäumer to Vorstand, 10 Sept. 1912.

76. ABDF 16/II/1: Sitzung des Gesamtvorstandes, 14 May 1907; ADEFB A14c: Stritt to Müller, 19 Aug. 1908.

77. ABDF 5/IV/5: Bäumer to Vorstand, 5 Sept. 1912, 21 Oct. 1912.

78. ibid., Bäumer to Vorstand, 21 Oct. 1912.

79. ABDF 3/4: Müller to Bäumer, 20 Sept. 1912; ABDF 5/IV/5: Resolution des Ausschusses des Deutsch-Evangelischen Frauenbundes, 13 Dec. 1912; *Evangelische Frauenzeitung* 13/6, 15 Dec. 1912.

80. ABDF 5/XIII/4: Bensheimer to Stritt, 6 Nov. 1908, Bensheimer to Bäumer, 8 Feb. 1911. The plan was thwarted by the break-up of the Suffrage Union.

81. StA Hbg, PP, S8326: *BNN,* 12 Oct. 1912, 7 Dec. 1912, 4 Jan. 1913; 3 Nov. 1912, 10 Dec. 1912.

82. StA Hbg, PP, S3502/II: *VW,* 16 May 1909, *HN,* 7 April 1909; ibid.; S5466/II: *VW,* 15 Dec. 1911; Minna Cauer, 'Wohin die Fahrt? ', *FB,* 19/9, 1 May 1913, 67-69. Cf. Stegmann, op. cit., 42-50.

83. ABDF 16/II/2, Gesamtvorstandssitzung, 7 March 1913, 8 March 1913.

84. ABDF 4/1: Stritt to Bäumer, 26 Aug. 1912.

85. ABDF 3/4: Bäumer to Gräfin v.d. Gröben, n.d. (March 1914).

86. BA Koblenz, NL Koch-Weser, No. 36, 57, 59, 67-9, 71-5, 135.

87. ABDF 3/4: Müller to Bensheimer, 18 March 1914.

88. ABDF 4/2: Gröben to Bäumer, 20 Dec. 1913, Bäumer to Müller 27 June 1914.

89. *GL* 21/2, 24 Oct. 1910, 23.

7

THE UNFINISHED REVOLUTION

THE WOMEN'S MOVEMENT AND THE
FIRST WORLD WAR, 1914-1918

The outbreak of the First World War in August 1914 gave the BDF leadership a chance to put into action a scheme which had frequently been the subject of debate within the women's movement in the years before 1914: the 'Women's Year of Service' (Weibliches Dienstjahr). This scheme, proposed by a number of feminists and in particular by Helene Lange, envisaged that young women should be subject to one year's compulsory service to the community. The purpose of this was partly to educate women in the techniques of social work, and partly to prove beyond all doubt the value of the services that women rendered to the nation – the essential prerequisite, in the view of 'moderates' such as Lange, for any successful request for the extension of women's rights. Above all however it was meant to forestall what was, in the militaristic society of Wilhelmine Germany, one of the most frequently reiterated objections to female equality and votes for women: the idea that men possessed the suffrage because they performed military service in the defence of the nation, and the consequent objection that, since women were not subject to military service, they were not entitled to ask for equal rights. In addition, as Käthe Schirmacher wrote, the purpose of the Women's Year of Service was to educate women in the 'German virtues . . . devotion to duty, commitment to the matter in hand, willing obedience to the needs of the whole people. These are social virtues, which must now be made familiar and acceptable to women, who have hitherto been brought up to be individualistic.'[1]

Now, on the outbreak of the First World War, Gertrud Bäumer grasped the chance to put this scheme, suitably modified, into effect. Already, on 31 July, the BDF had set up a 'National Women's Service' (Nationaler Frauendienst) in close co-operation with the Ministry of the Interior in Berlin,[2] who advised local authorities to help this organisation at a local level.[3] Here and there frictions arose,[4] but on the whole the scheme worked well and the National Women's Service did a lot of work in looking after the families of men who were at the front, in directing women to jobs made vacant by mobilisation and in maintaining the supply of foodstuffs. The work was organised at a local level. The BDF quickly secured the co-operation of other women's organisations, including those that were not members of the BDF itself. The feminists busied themselves with setting up soup kitchens and improvised hospital wards, looking after the orphans and the homeless and knitting long woollen socks for the soldiers at the front. Almost the entire energies of the women's movement from August 1914 to Easter 1917 were taken up with the organisation and execution of this kind of work. Feminist activity as such was abandoned altogether during this period.

Through the National Women's Service the women's movement was constantly in contact with the government at all levels; it was consulted on matters of social welfare, and co-operated in the organisation of female labour. In November 1916 indeed Marie-Elisabeth Lüders, a younger member of the BDF leadership – not to be confused with Else Lüders, Minna Cauer's secretary – was put in charge of a department of the War Office to deal with female labour.[5] The new relationship of the women's movement to the State was summed up by Gertrud Bäumer:

Women have been recruited to help run various departments of government, such as the Military Office, the Food and Clothing departments etc. To some extent, this constitutes the achievement of the demands of liberalism with reference to the position of our women in government. Women are to come into contact with the State and with legislation; the civic consciousness of women is to be awakened, trained and educated . . . Women . . . will still bring their talents and interests to bear in the interests of the Fatherland even in times of peace; that is the desire of many women, that has been said from the women's point of view. Now it is also being said from the point of view of the State itself.[6]

Naturally enough the BDF hoped that support of the war effort would bring the women's movement much-desired concessions when the war was over. The supply of a proof of loyalty to the Fatherland would, it was thought, be rewarded after the war with an enlargement of women's rights, perhaps also by the granting of female suffrage.[7]

The loyalty of the BDF to the German government and its aims was expressed not only in deeds but also in words. Indeed from its very foundation, first of all under the influence of the General Association, then under the control of Gertrud Bäumer, the BDF had consistently pursued a strongly nationalistic line in its statements on foreign policy. In 1899 and 1907, for example, it had refused to join in worldwide 'women's demonstrations for peace' organised by middle-class women's organisations in other countries. In 1899 it gave the following reasons for its refusal:

We do not want Germany to disarm, as long as the world bristles with weapons around us. We do not want any lessening of our position in the world or the renunciation of any advantage that we could gain in peaceful competition. We do not want Germany to face other nations weaker by even the smallest fragment of her resources if she should be compelled, despite her love of peace, to defend her national integrity in any war that might be forced upon her.

The influence of the General German Women's Association, which strongly supported Tirpitz's naval expansion programme, can clearly be discerned in this statement. Indeed the General Association itself even issued a special declaration urging women to support Tirpitz's plans, quoting a poem by its founder Louise Otto-Peters declaring that 'the German axe should fashion *German ships*' to rule the Ocean 'from the Sea of Adria to the Sound'.[8]

In questions of war and peace, as in so many others, Marie Stritt occupied a position somewhere between the radicals and the moderates. In 1902 she opposed the radicals' suggestion of annual women's demonstrations for peace. Her reasons, however, were practical rather than theoretical. 'I am quite certain', she said, 'that such demonstrations would only be a pathetic failure in the present warlike atmosphere which also, unfortunately, has strongly affected our women, and instilled in them an absurd kind of patriotism . . . In this matter, which is so important to me, I feel very strongly the powerlessness of the individual person'.[9] After the war she wrote that the 'war psychosis' which had gripped the masses in 1914 had profoundly shocked and saddened her.[10] The attitude of Gertrud Bäumer to questions of war and peace was very different. Here again, as in other respects, her accession to the Presidency of the BDF in 1910 signified the triumph of more conservative policies. Shortly after assuming the Presidency of the BDF she made a speech to the Progressive Party Women's Conference in 1910 at which she outlined her ideas on war and peace:[11]

> Once (she said) liberalism was the declared enemy of all military demands . . . This tactic is now outmoded. However, as far as liberalism is concerned, military power is in no sense simply a brilliant setting for the display of dynastic ambition, but simply a necessity of national self-preservation. People now accuse liberalism – and the women's movement – of diverting the *Volk* from its national tasks – nowadays it is called its *völkisch* individuality – and of supporting cosmopolitan aims and international policies instead. We must insist that, on the contrary, the importance of our national character is not underestimated either by liberalism or by the women's movement. In fact, it is to be expected that with the strengthening of liberalism and the greater participation of women in national life, the national consciousness will develop even further . . .

With views such as this dominant in the BDF, it is not surprising that a dissatisfied member could complain, even before Bäumer took up the Presidency, that although 'the women's movement in all countries . . . is becoming more and more interested in the idea of international understanding . . . unfortunately . . . this is not the case to the same extent in the German women's movement as it is in other countries'.[12] Following upon Bäumer's statement came the BDF's decision to organize a large-scale exhibition on the subject of 'Woman at Home and at Work'. Gertrud Bäumer wrote on a later occasion that:

> The unity of the Congress of 1912 took on of its own accord a strongly national character. Women felt their national identity *(Volkstum)* above the variations of party, class and belief, and they sensed the meaning of their movement as the fulfilment of a national task, the task of increasing the

achievements of German women from the resources of their own nature, and of making these achievements a meaningful contribution to the welfare of the whole people.[13]

The BDF also showed a marked reluctance to co-operate with the International Council of Women in the immediate pre-war years as it tried to work out a common policy on peace.[14]

These nationalistic attitudes were further developed during the First World War with the active encouragement of the government which naturally wished to give the outside world the impression that the German people, including women, were united behind the government's policies. During the war, the BDF issued statements condemning Wilson's Peace Note of 1917, the Armistice Terms, the Treaty of Versailles and the League of Nations. On 22 October 1918, for example, it issued a declaration 'to give voice to the feelings of millions of women' in rejecting the proposed peace terms.[15]

> We can have no confidence in a League of Nations that is founded on the trampling-down of German honour. We cannot believe in a programme that supports the rights of nations when it simultaneously includes the surrender of German people and old sites of German culture to foreign States . . . The German women believe it to be a demand of national self-respect and a duty to the dead who have died of their own free will for the honour of the Fatherland, that the German people does not submit to measures that have the character of a 'punishment'. Before the German people accepts conditions that deny the memory of its dead and attach everlasting disgrace to its name, the women of Germany will also be prepared to use their strength in a defensive struggle to the last.

It is not surprising that after one of these statements had been issued, Hindenburg sent a personal telegram of thanks to Gertrud Bäumer saying 'We German men bow down our heads before the German women in reverence'.[16]

This development of more nationalistic attitudes in the last years of peace, and then in the years of the First World War, can also be followed in a number of individual feminists. Martha Zietz, who had strongly condemned Tirpitz's naval expansion programme in 1903, left the Progressive Party in 1917 and joined the Fatherland Party (Vaterlandspartei) a Pan-German, proto-fascist mass movement led by men such as Admiral von Tirpitz, the creator of the German navy, and

Wolfgang Kapp, who was to lead an attempted anti-democratic coup in 1920.[17] The views of the Fatherland Party on feminism and the 'woman question' were, like its other political views, similar to and in some respects even more extreme than those of the Anti-League and the DHV. Indeed it is not unlikely that there was a considerable overlap in the membership of the two organisations; and at least one man, Professor Dietrich Schäfer, sat on both committees. A women's section was formed in 1918.[18] Despite her membership of the Fatherland Party, however, Martha Zietz continued to play a role in the BDF, though no longer in the suffrage movement. During the war she became President of the Union of German Housewives' Associations (Verband deutscher Hausfrauenverein). The Housewives' Associations had been founded in various German towns before the war primarily as a means by which middle-class housewives could find a ready supply of 'reliable' domestic servants, untainted by Social Democracy and unlikely to complain about pay or conditions. The major effort of these Associations before the war was put into the establishment of employment agencies *(Stellenvermittlungen)* for domestic servants, which acted as an indirect means of combating the spread of Social Democracy. They thus formed a kind of housewives' version of the industrial employers' federations. During the war, however, the Housewives' Unions were joined in a national Union, largely at the insistence of the BDF, and their main function was to help housewives adjust to wartime economic conditions by co-operating with the government in distributing information and advice about household management. Given this semi-official status they expanded rapidly and soon became one of the largest member unions of the BDF.[19]

The Housewives' Union was not as overtly political as the German Women's League, with its origins in the Imperial League Against Social Democracy, or the German-evangelical Women's League, with its close ties to the Conservative Party. Yet there could be no doubt that the origins of the Housewives' Union lay in strongly right-wing sentiments; and during the First World War the close ties of the Union with government agencies, and even more the connections of its leadership with the Fatherland Party, brought out the right-wing character of the Union far more clearly than before. Moreover, unlike the German-evangelical Women's League, the Housewives' Union was not fundamentally opposed to female suffrage. That this was so was to a great extent due to the influence of Martha Zietz; and her paradoxical political behaviour caused the leadership of the BDF some anxiety:

> On the one hand, (complained Alice Bensheimer)[20] she supports female suffrage, on the other the Fatherland Party. There are committee members of the Housewives' Union who are afraid that if Frau Zietz is compelled because of this to resign the Presidency, the Housewives' Union will fall into the hands of a Leadership that will take it out of the Federation.

For the duration of the war, however, the Housewives' Union remained within the BDF, though it maintained its right-wing links. Zietz was followed into the Fatherland Party by Eleonore Drenkhahn, a moderate Hamburg suffragist who was completing a similar political somersault to that executed by Zietz; Drenkhahn had said at a meeting of the German Peace Society in 1906, referring to the Russian revolution, that 'War and revolution are man's politics and the consequences of the political system of men', a sentiment that she completely repudiated ten years later.[21] A third feminist who pursued this remarkable course from left to right was Käthe Schirmacher, who at the turn of the century had believed that 'women are the born allies of all international efforts for peace'.[22] Born in Danzig, she became an enthusiast for the Germanisation of the Prussian part of Poland after a speaking tour of Poland early in the first decade of the 20th century, and in 1905 she made a speech on the *Ostmarkenpolitik* at the Suffrage Union's General Assembly. After remarking that she had evidently obtained all her material from the German-nationalist *Ostmarkenverein, Vorwärts* wondered:[23]

> What Fräulein Dr. Schirmacher still wants in the radical wing of the German women's movement, what she should still be doing there, is incomprehensible to us. In contrast to Fräulein Lischnewska, in whose head at times radical ideas freely accumulate side by side with far more reactionary ones, Schirmacher is thoroughly and consistently reactionary in all her views and statements. Just as two years ago she only claimed the suffrage for women of property and education, in other words, a naked class suffrage, so she declared her unreserved allegiance yesterday to an exceptional policy against the Poles that has been condemned on all sides as wrong.

Already by 1903, as the article suggested, Schirmacher had declared herself against universal suffrage. After 1913 she played very little part in the women's movement, devoting most of her energies to supporting the efforts of right-wing pressure-groups to Germanise the Prussian part of Poland. In the National Assembly of 1919 she was a deputy for the German-national People's Party,[24] (Deutschnationale Volkspartei or DNVP), successor organisation to the old Conservative party. She died in 1930.

These three individual examples were unusually extreme; yet there can be no doubt that the German women's movement as a whole became more nationalistic during the First World War, nor — what may not at first sight seem quite so obvious — that this growth of nationalist sentiment began at least four years before the war broke out. The course followed by Zietz, Drenkhahn and Schirmacher was followed by many other lesser figures at the same time. Increasing nationalism did not mean increasing conservatism in all spheres of politics, however, and we shall see later on in this Chapter that it was actually accompanied by a new boldness in demanding reforms such as the vote for women. Nor was this growth in nationalism experienced in all sections in the movement. A small but significant minority of feminists firmly repudiated it; and it is to this group that we must now turn our attention.

FEMINISM AND THE PEACE MOVEMENT

The women who had introduced the ideas of classical liberal individualist feminism into the German women's movement, and seemed for a time to be carrying all before them until 1908, were by 1914 once more a small and beleaguered faction. If they had already been pushed to the fringes of the movement, the war was to remove them from its confines altogether. The issue over which they were finally expelled from the movement was the main issue of the day, that of war or peace. Yet though it was only made immediate by the fact of war itself, it had occupied an important place in the thinking of the radicals long before 1914. Anita Augspurg and Lida Gustava Heymann, the leaders of the only remaining radical suffrage society, the 2000-strong Women's Suffrage League, had for many years been passionate advocates of international understanding. Unaffected by the nationalistic campaigns of the Navy League, they had as early as 1899 led the unsuccessful campaign for German participation in a world-wide women's demonstration for peace. Throughout their political careers they had persistently upheld pacifist ideals, not least because of their awareness of the role of militarism in German society and its effect on attitudes towards female emancipation. In a speech delivered in Berlin on 7 December 1908, for example, Augspurg attacked 'barracks-drill' and 'school-drill' as influencing young men's character in an undesirable way.[25] As a body, however, the radicals did not campaign actively for peace for some years. In 1907 indeed, the chairman of the German Peace Society's Eisenach branch complained that the radical feminists never concerned themselves with the peace question and that most of them misunderstood the issues at stake.[26] It was only after 1911, as the atmosphere in the German public became more and more aggressively nationalistic,[27] that articles urging women to campaign against warmongering became more and more frequent in the radicals' periodicals and that more speeches began to be devoted to the subject by radical suffragist leaders.

Unlike the moderates, who had always been reluctant about joining in international organisations, the radicals took an active part in the foundation and organisation of the International Woman Suffrage Alliance, established in Berlin in 1904. Anita Augspurg was the First Vice-President, and Käthe Schirmacher the First Assistant Secretary. The Committee of the International Alliance in its early years consisted of two Americans, two Englishwomen, a Dutch representative and Schirmacher and Augspurg. At the biennial congresses of the Alliance Augspurg frequently took the chair, proposed motions and, with Minna Cauer, Frieda Radel, Lida Gustava Heymann, Adelheid von Welczeck, Adele Schreiber, Anna Lindemann, Else Lüders and Käthe Schirmacher took a prominent part in the debates and discussions. To contemporary suffragists in other lands the German suffrage movement must indeed have seemed vigorous and dynamic, its leaders familiar and decisive figures.[28] In 1909, however, Augspurg and Heymann withdrew from participation because they felt that the International Alliance had 'let itself be carried along in the wake of the warlike character of male politics, and was governed by the petty fear that a stand for pacifism might damage the prospects for female suffrage'.[29]

The record of Helene Stöcker and the Mutterschutz League was similar to that of the radical suffragists. It is easy to see an element of pacifism implicit in the New Morality as it was developed by Stöcker

and her followers after the turn of the century. The emphasis that
Stöcker placed on the need to release Nietzschean forces of love and
understanding between individuals led on naturally to a similar interpretation of relations between States. Stöcker took a prominent part in
the pacifist movement as an individual, and was a leading figure in the
New Fatherland League (Bund Neues Vaterland), perhaps the most
active of the German pacifist groups during the war. However, the
Mutterschutz League as a whole was really in too bad a way in 1914 to
take on a significant role in the peace movement; and the Social
Darwinist right had gained sufficient influence within its ranks to
ensure that many, if not most, members supported the war effort. It
was the Suffrage League (Frauenstimmrechtsbund) that provided the
strongest links between feminism and pacifism during the war.[30] Indeed a list of the most prominent women pacifists reads almost like a
roll-call of its leading members: it includes Anita Augspurg, Lida
Gustava Heymann, Minna Cauer, Else Lüders and Helene Stöcker – five
out of the 13 founder-members of the first Suffrage Union in 1902;
August Kirchhoff and Rita Bardenheuer, leaders of the Suffrage League
in Bremen; Frida Perlen and Mathilde Planck, the League's representatives in Stuttgart; Helene Lewison, who ran the Frankfurt branch; Ida
Jens, Henriette Holländer, Christine Thies, Wilhelmine Harder and
Gertrud Baer, who between them controlled the powerful Hamburg
branch after the resignation of Frieda Radel; Marie Wegner, the foremost radical suffragist in Breslau; Helene Schiess, President of the
Konstanz branch; Konstanze Hallgarten, Secretary of the Bavarian
Suffrage Union; Alma Dzialoszynski in Berlin; Selma Reichenbach;
Margarete Selenka, a friend of Augspurg's and, like several others in the
list, a member of the Mutterschutz League, and many more.[31]

The outbreak of war caused a great deal of confusion within the
Women's Suffrage League. In a number of branches meetings were held
at the beginning of August 1914 in which 'the war was described as
what it is, mankind's greatest crime'. Some branches raised protests
against the invasion of Belgium and the atrocities alleged to have been
committed there. Not surprisingly, a large number of resignations from
the League followed. In many places it was preserved only through the
social work it undertook – mostly involving the use of international
contacts to give news of internees to relatives, sending supplies to
prisoners of war and the like.[32] 'Had this not been the case', remarked

Heymann after the war, 'many of the branches could not have kept even 10 percent of their members.'[33]

Some branches had little to do with pacifism. The city authorities in Nuremberg reported on 3 March 1916 after inspecting the membership lists of the local branch that 'nothing is known of any kind of activity of the members of the group in question in the peace movement, and there seems to be no occasion for taking any action in the matter'.[34] But the Hamburg branch, which with 500 members still in 1917 numbered a quarter of the League's total membership, got into trouble at times, especially after its leader Frieda Radel, a supporter of the war effort, resigned on 9 September 1914.[35] The League's Congress, planned to take place on 15-16 April 1916 in Frankfurt am Main, was at first banned and could only be held after protracted negotiations with the authorities. A meeting of the League in Breslau, where the leader of both the Suffrage and the New Morality movements in Bremen, Auguste Kirchhoff, spoke[36] at the invitation of Marie Wegner on 'Pacifism and the Women's Suffrage Movement', was broken up by the police. The League's periodical, the *Zeitschrift für Frauenstimm-recht,* was subject to heavy censorship, and several pacifist articles were not allowed into print or were strongly cut by the censor.[37]

Virtually no organisations of any kind in Germany opposed the war in 1914-15, and the pacifism of the Suffrage League soon brought down the wrath of the military authorities upon the radical women's movement.[38] Many antifeminists believed that radical feminists were in any case fundamentally pacifist. As a speaker at the First Congress of the German League for the Prevention of the Emancipation of Women in 1912 put it, 'our modern women would let their international *apparat* come into play in the event of a war – just like the Social Democrats – and try to end the war as quickly as possible'.[39] The leading Anti-League publicist, Ludwig Langemann, frequently asserted that the women's movement was 'international in character'.[40] These beliefs were evidently shared by the military authorities. When the Bavarian War Ministry came to issue a secret report to the peace movement at the end of 1915, it devoted no less than a third of it to the role of women in the movement. 'It would be a mistake', the report declared, 'if the supreme military authorities, charged as they are in this war with maintaining the defence of the land and public security, decided to treat the women's movement as a matter of secondary importance.'[41] Indeed the authorities regarded all feminist activity during the war with extreme suspicion. The Prussian War Ministry thought that the women's movement was being infiltrated by pacifist ideas.[42] The Bavarian War Ministry declared that 'the cessation of all feminist activity during the war, irrespective of what side it comes from, is a prerequisite of public security.' It was a controversial issue whose discussion would divert attention from other more pressing matters. The war demanded 'a *Burgfriede* between the sexes' as well as between political parties. 'It is only too well-known', wrote the Ministry, 'that the patriotically-minded part of the women's movement is very easily liable to lose those whom it has won over to the cause to the left-wing internationalist group of feminists, over whose activities it has no control.'

This applied above all to the female suffrage societies. 'The feminist (female suffrage) movement', said the Bavarian War Ministry, 'is connected with the pacifist movement in the closest way.'[43] The Berlin police, too, noted the presence of 'well-known leading campaigners for women's suffrage' at a pacifist meeting in September 1916.[44] Not all female suffragist groups were suspect; the Munich branch of the German Alliance for Women's Suffrage, for example, was considered quite respectable. But the Suffrage League aroused the gravest suspicions in the mind of the authorities, particularly in Munich, by far the strongest and most radical centre of pacifism within the League. Pacifist themes were regularly discussed at meetings of the League, and as a result, the branch was banned from holding any public or private meetings from March 1916 onwards.

All this was due largely to the presence of Anita Augspurg and Lida Gustava Heymann in the city. They and their supporters believed in the inseparability of pacifism and feminism. 'Women who sincerely fight for pacifism', Heymann told the Munich branch of the German Peace Society, 'must also work for female suffrage.' When female suffrage was granted, women's naturally peaceful instincts would come into play, she believed, and war would be banished from the face of the earth.[45] The outbreak of war, they argued, made the task of getting votes for women more urgent than ever, not less urgent as the other suffragist organisations thought. 'Men steer the fate of all countries', they wrote in October 1914; the result was plain for all to see. 'The whole globe is piled with weapons, Europe has become a slaughterhouse. Under men, murder is being committed on a scale more vast and more gruesome than the world has ever known.' Men's political system *(Männerpolitik)* had clearly failed. The war was their creation alone – a 'men's war' fought between 'men's States'. Women, denied participation in political life, were absolved from any responsibility for the disaster. It was up to them to repair the damage, for 'true humanity knows no hatred of nation against nation, no genocide, and women stand closer to true humanity than men.' It was for this reason, they wrote on another occasion, that 'the political emancipation of women is more than a formal measure, it means a fundamental change in the nature of the State.' Not surprisingly the Bavarian War Ministry said that 'the female suffrage that they demand is for them a means of achieving not the equality of women, but their superiority'.[46]

At the very beginning of war some radical suffragists had tried to secure their pacifist aims through individual action. On 3 August 1914 Frida Perlen and Mathilde Planck, the Suffrage League's leaders in Stuttgart, had telegraphed the Kaiser asking him to stop the war. Two days previously, Lida Gustava Heymann had gone in person to the Bavarian War Ministry and managed to secure an interview with the Minister, whom she requested to telegraph the Tsar to the same effect. When it became clear that these attempts had failed, and when the radical pacifist women came to believe that the charitable work they had been doing within the Suffrage League was indirectly supporting the war and therefore ceased to do it, they began to organise themsevles on an independent basis. Some of them met at Amsterdam at a brief gathering of pacifist women in February 1915, arranged via the League's international connections. Twenty-eight managed, despite interference from the authorities, to get to the larger congress that was arranged at this meeting for April the same year. This congress, held at the Hague, marks the real beginning of the feminist/pacifist movement in Germany.[48]

The Hague Congress was attended by 224 English women led by Chrystal Macmillan, 49 American women led by Jane Addams, 1700 women from Holland, and a number of others from Austria-Hungary, Brazil, Italy, Norway, Poland, Russia and Sweden. Augspurg led the German delegates and took a leading part in the proceedings. She proposed that all secret treaties be declared invalid. Other motions framed by various delegates included the settling of international

conflicts by a court of arbitration, concerted international action
against individual nations resorting to arms, democratic control of
foreign policy, by women as well as men of course — the congress
naturally also passed a motion demanding votes for women — no
further annexations without the consent of those to be annexed, and
the creation of a League of Nations. The questions of war guilt and
atrocities were excluded from the discussions.

After the Congress was over, delegates of the women went to ask the
governments of Europe for peace. They were received with courtesy
but non-cooperation. The BDF condemned the Congress and took
action to try to stop its members attending. Originally its leader,
Gertrud Bäumer, had intended to pass over the conference in silence;
reports in the Press, however, forced her hand. The BDF executive
committee issued a confidential notice to member associations branding
participation in the conference as 'incompatible with the patriotic
character and the national duty of the German women's movement . . . (and) with any responsible position and work within the
Federation of German Women's Associations'.[49] The authorities also
prevented some women from going. The pacifists' efforts to arrange a
second Congress came to nothing, and attempts to get international
co-operation in other ways were equally futile. The most tangible
results of the Congress were on a national level, where it had resolved to
set up national committees for peace. When Augspurg and her associates returned from the Hague they at once put this into effect and
founded a German Women's Committee for a Lasting Peace (Deutscher
Frauenausschuss für einen dauernden Frieden).[50]

The Committee was a loosely organised group with no written
constitution. It relied on donations instead of subscriptions and possessed no official membership lists. This was to make it more difficult
for the authorities to dissolve it, and the tactic was successful. The
authorities made a number of attempts to persuade the Committee to
constitute itself in a conventional way but never succeeded, and the
organisation remained active until the end of the war.[51] Indeed, by the
autumn of 1918 it was said to be making very good progress in the
smaller towns.[52] It drew most of its members from the Suffrage League
and worked by discussion in small groups. Some of these groups were
indeed so small as to be almost without significance — in Stuttgart, for
instance, an official observed that 'the Württemberg Women's Com-

mittee (for a Lasting Peace) has consisted up to now of nothing more than the political ambitions of Mesdames Perlen and Planck and two more world-stormers.'[53] Nevertheless, it was strong enough in Hamburg and Munich at least to cause serious concern to the authorities, more than anything else by its attempts to print and distribute anti-war propaganda.

The language of this propaganda was certainly alarming and extravagant. One of the Committee's leaflets began with the statement:

> Millions of women's hearts blaze up in wild grief . . . Cannot the earth reeking with human blood, the flayed bodies and souls of millions of your husbands, betrothed, sons, the horrors that oppress your own sex . . . — cannot all this inspire you to burning protest? . . . The wheel of time is running with blood: you must seek to grasp it.

The leaflet was reprinted in *Die Frauenbewegung,* but after this the military censors made quite sure that such material could not be printed in Germany. Attempts by the Committee to have this policy reversed — including letters to the Chancellor — predictably came to nothing. Instead of distributing the pamphlets they could not print, the Committee sent thousands of anti-war letters through the post to potential sympathisers, whereupon the authorities placed the members' correspondence under surveillance. In July 1915 the Committee sent a petition to Bethmann Hollweg suggesting Germany give up her annexations on condition she get her colonies back, and in December 1917 it wrote privately to Bethmann Hollweg demanding no annexations or reparations from the defeated countries on the Eastern front.[54]

The authorities were generally worried that pacifist activity would damage morale in Germany and give comfort to the enemy. More specifically, however, they were concerned that the anti-war propaganda of the radical feminists would influence a class of women who had long been seen as the mainstay of the women's movement: women teachers. The Committee protested vigorously against militarism in schools, and there was a danger that schoolmistresses might try to influence their pupils in this sense. Even more serious was the possibility that country schoolmistresses, who enjoyed high social status and great influence in rural society, would espouse the pacifist cause. As the Bavarian War Ministry put it, citing the case of a schoolmistress in the village of Gräfendorf who had been found distributing pacifist literature obtained from Munich:

Even if this was only an isolated incident, and evidence for a misuse of the
school for the purpose of agitation is lacking, nevertheless, in view of the
position that teachers enjoy in small towns and villages as a result of their
higher standard of education, it is obvious that the defence of the land would
be jeopardised by the spread of an unpatriotic peace movement, mistaken in
both its timing and its aims, to the female members of the teaching profession.
A collapse of will on the part of the women working in rural areas could place
our economic staying-power during the war in question, because the greater
part of the control of the rural economy rests at the moment in their hands.

With this in mind, the educational authorities in Bavaria warned schoolmistresses not to meddle with pacifism, and banned an article in *Die
katholische Lehrerin* calling for an 'education for peace' to be given in
the schools. These measures were accompanied by the gradual repression of the pacifist movement itself. On 23 November 1915 Lida
Gustava Heymann was banned from making public speeches. On 6
March 1916 the Suffrage League in Munich was closed down and
Augspurg, Heymann and Selenka forbidden to indulge in any form of
public agitation or to correspond with or visit other countries. The
Munich authorities had already noted that the local branch of the
Suffrage League had a much higher proportion of non-German, and —
what was almost as bad — non-Bavarian members than the Alliance (12
percent non-German and a further 25 percent non-Bavarian), and they
now proceeded to make use of this fact to rid themselves of unwelcome
strangers. On 11 February 1917 Heymann was officially expelled from
Bavaria.[55] For the rest of the war, according to her memoirs, she lived
as before at Anita Augspurg's home in the Isartal and continued
working illegally, successfully concealing her presence from the
Bavarian authorities.[56] These measures were not revoked until 28
October 1918 and were, apart from the expulsion order, extended to
the rest of Germany. Frida Perlen's peace campaign had already been
suppressed in Stuttgart on 20 October 1915. Marie Wegner had been
subjected to harrassment and house-searches by the Breslau police from
early 1916. In April 1917 Heymann herself was banned from public
activities in Hamburg. In what must surely have been a last act of
personal spite, the Hamburg police stopped her from speaking as late as
7 November 1918.[57]

These measures of repression carefully stopped short of anything —
outright arrest or imprisonment for example — that might turn the
pacifists into martyrs or lay the German authorities open to criticism

from their enemies abroad for the harshness of their reaction to internal opposition. However, when contrasted with the close co-operation that existed between the Government and the bulk of the women's movement – the BDF – at the same time, they demonstrated quite clearly how wide now was the gulf that separated the radical minority of the feminists from the conservative majority. The irony was, as we shall see, that neither the co-operation of the BDF nor the radicalism of the pacifists in fact did anything to bring the ultimate goals of the women's movement any nearer.

THE RENEWAL OF THE WOMEN'S SUFFRAGE, CAMPAIGN, 1917-18

In 1917 and 1918, as the pressure of the long war on the structure of German politics and society grew ever greater, political life in Germany began to revive. By 1917 the government clearly felt it was necessary to grant limited reforms in order to maintain national morale, as well as to meet Allied criticism. In his 'Easter Message' to the German people in 1917, Kaiser Wilhelm II promised to allow the greater participation of his subjects in government and political life. In particular, this was interpreted as a call to the federal states, especially Prussia, to liberalise their franchise. Soon, prodded by the Social Democrats, the State legislatures got down to discussing the extension of the suffrage. The Kaiser had said nothing about giving the vote to women, however, and in the circumstances the women's movement was neither willing nor able to avoid putting in a demand that women be included in this process of liberalisation. The two remaining female suffrage organisations, Marie Stritt's German Imperial Union for Women's Suffrage and the more radical and much smaller German Women's Suffrage League led by Anita Augspurg and Lida Gustava Heymann, held what must have been practically their first real political meetings on the subject of female suffrage since the outbreak of war, and formulated their demands. By the Summer of 1917 these had already been submitted to the various legislatures and to the constitutional committee of the Reichstag[58] in the form of petitions for votes for women. The women's petitions were debated in the constitutional committee of the Reichstag in June 1917, and in the Prussian Diet in December the same year. The Conservatives and Catholic Centre declared their opposition to female suffrage on principle, and the National Liberals and Progressives said that while they were in sympathy with the women's demands, the time had not yet come for them to be put into effect. Only the socialist parties were in favour. In this respect, therefore, nothing had changed since pre-war years. The Prussian Diet, when discussing the communal suffrage for women in January 1918, refused even to grant this modest demand, although it was supported by the confessional as well as the political women's organisations.[59]

To the women's movement, however, the omens in 1917 seemed more propitious. A major campaign for the vote was now launched by the BDF, whose contacts with the political parties – particularly the Progressives – were far better than the suffragists'. The fact that both in the Suffrage Union and in the BDF there now seemed no question but that female suffrage, if introduced, would be universal suffrage, indicated a certain shift to the left on the part of the women's movement and its supporters, at least as far as their own political rights were concerned.[60] Early evidence of this was given at the Progressive Party's Congress in 1917. Among the motions put forward were four in favour of various kinds of female suffrage. The Berlin women's branch – the 'Liberal Women's Party' – cautiously only asked for the communal suffrage for women. The party branches in Aachen and Stettin went further and demanded respectively female suffrage in Prussia and at all levels. The initiative was seized, however, by the Working Committee of the Progressive Party; this body, dominated from the beginning by the BDF, was now led by Margarethe Bernhardt, who had been connected with the BDF for some years and remained in close contact with Gertrud Bäumer throughout the new campaign. On 7 June 1917 it wrote to the executive committee of the Prussian Party organisation insisting that it was the duty of liberalism to demand equal political rights for women at all levels of politics. At the instigation of the Aachen Branch the Congress decided on 10 June to appoint a commission on women's rights. The commission met four times and resolved on 11 June 1918 to recommend full and equal political rights for women.

Before the commission's resolution could be adopted by the party as a whole, however, a number of objections had to be overcome. The Prussian section of the party was reluctant to force a decision on the national party by making a public declaration in favour of votes for women. Furthermore, the party leaders were anxious not to jeopardise the campaign for the reform of the Prussian suffrage by demanding too much. The Progressive women therefore put their case to the Party's Central Committee on 6 October 1917. Margarethe Bernhardt argued that women deserved the vote because of their achievements in the war and needed it to play their part in the peacetime reconstruction of Germany. Members did agree that 'it is neither good nor useful for the party to keep putting off the Woman Question to some future date', but the most telling argument was again that 'the women would do good not to endanger the small reform now in prospect by more far-reaching demands to Parliament'. Further pressure was put on the Party leadership by Gertrud Bäumer, who advised the Prussian Women's Rights Commission in its later stages and moved the Party some way towards demanding at least the communal suffrage for women.[61] Moreover at a local level things were moving in the Progressive Party too. In 1917 the Hamburg Progressives, led by Carl Petersen, declared unanimously in favour of female suffrage to the Hamburg City Council.[62] Nevertheless, in the party as a whole, the opposition, led by Conrad Haussmann, remained strong, and by mid-1918 the cause of female suffrage had not progressed significantly further towards acceptance by the national Progressive Party than it had at its foundation in 1912. Local and regional Progressive organisations were beginning to support female suffrage while the national party, despite the pressure of its women members, declined to follow suit.

The renewed agitation for votes for women, and the BDF's memorandum on women's rights in the new political system promised by the Kaiser's Easter message of 1917,[63] – a memorandum that demanded female suffrage – were bound to lead to renewed friction between the BDF and the German-evangelical Women's League. The League had already threatened to leave the BDF in 1912 because it opposed the BDF's stand on female suffrage. Even before matters reached crisis-point at a national level, branches of the League were faced with the problem locally. In April 1917 the Hamburg branch of the German-evangelical Women's League refused to support the petition of the Hamburg City Union of Women's Associations, to which it belonged, for female suffrage in the City Council elections. At the same time it wanted to stay in the Union.[64] On a national level, however, there was a stronger sentiment in favour of leaving the BDF. On 15 November 1917 Paula Müller, the Evangelicals' President, condemned the BDF's support of female suffrage and even more, its co-operation with the SPD women in raising the demand, and urged the Evangelicals to leave the BDF as soon as possible.[65] Already, on 7 November, the Evangelical League's executive committee had decided to leave; a personal interview with Bäumer and Lange in December only strengthened this resolution.[66]

On 6 February 1918 Müller attended a meeting of the BDF executive committee to put her case. The BDF memorandum, she alleged, made female suffrage the sine qua non of all further reforms. The memorandum had met with strong criticism from all Evangelicals and left-wing National Liberals. Some 70 branches of the German-evangelical Women's League had threatened to split if it did not leave the BDF — a disingenuous argument since it was the Evangelical League's committee that persuaded the branches to leave and not the other way around.[67] Müller implied that the Evangelicals might stay if the BDF dropped the demand for female suffrage. However, it was no longer possible for the BDF to do this. Gertrud Bäumer protested that the memorandum did not adopt the position that Müller implied. Alice Bensheimer added that the BDF would lose all credibility if it merely became a forum for the exchange of opinions and ceased to make policy decisions. Müller declared however that 'the Federation should only make policy decisions in matters of great importance'. Was female suffrage not such a matter? It was important enough in one respect — Müller could not be prevailed upon to change her mind.[68] On 14 March 1918 the Evangelicals held a General Assembly and voted to leave the BDF immediately (by 1310 votes to 82 with 49 abstentions) because of the 'growing predominance of radicalism within the BDF'.[69] Despite the argument that it would at least prevent those branches of the Evangelical League which opposed the suffrage from opposing all the other demands of the BDF if the two societies parted on a reasonably amicable basis, the general result of the break was to drive the League even further to the right. Alice Bensheimer was soon complaining to Gertrud Bäumer that the Evangelical Women's League was recruiting many people who had been unwilling to join while it had remained tied to the BDF — 'people whose ideas are the opposite of freedom and self-determination'. By August, indeed, it was conducting what Bens-heimer called 'a huge propaganda campaign' in Berlin, partly directed against the BDF itself.[70]

For its part the BDF could afford to let the Evangelicals go, now that, as a result of its organisation of the National Women's Service, it no longer felt the need to prove its loyalty and respectability to the conservative social forces that stood behind the Evangelicals. The event had virtually no repercussions outside the women's movement. It was unlikely that the retention of the Evangelicals within the BDF would have made any difference to the hostility to female suffrage still felt by all political parties right of the Progressives. Female suffrage became a reality in other countries in the course of the war: Denmark and Iceland gave women the vote in 1915; Norway had already granted it in 1913 and Finland as early as 1907; Holland conceded the passive suffrage in 1917; the Russian Revolution of 1917 also brought women the vote; Hungary, Sweden and finally Britain also seemed by the beginning of 1918 ready to introduce female suffrage.[71] There was no sign, however, that Germany would follow suit. There was no sign that the experience of the war did anything to improve the political position of women in Germany. It was only when the Wilhelmine political system was overthrown by revolution that things began to change.

WOMEN AND THE REVOLUTION, 1918-19

On 29 September 1918 Germany's warlords Field-Marshal Hindenburg and General Ludendorff realised at last after the failure of their Spring offensive and the defection of Germany's ally Bulgaria, that the war was lost. American troops were pouring into Europe to reinforce the Allies; Germany was exhausted. It was time to sue for peace. Only a democratic or at least a parliamentary Germany would be acceptable as a negotiating partner with the Allies, however, and at Ludendorff's instigation a new Imperial Government was put into office under Prince Max of Baden to conclude peace and guide Germany towards constitutionalism. The government's majority in the Reichstag was run by the

Joint Parliamentary Committee of the Catholic Centre, the Progressives and the SPD, and to it belonged in effect the power of deciding whether the new government's scheme to democratise the constitution would succeed or fail.

Prince Max's reforms laid stress on the introduction of universal suffrage in the states, particularly Prussia. Plans were rapidly drafted: they were signed by the Emperor on 28 October 1918. As Otto Landsberg, an SPD member of the committee, pointed out on 5 November, no mention was made of votes for women.[72] In this respect at least, the constitution of 28 October was not fully democratic. It soon became clear, however, that this reform was not enough. On 28 October the sailors of the North Sea Fleet refused the order to set sail in an attempt to go down fighting against the British. By 5 November the sailors had taken over Kiel and were demanding the abdication of all the German monarchs and (among other things) the introduction of female suffrage.[73] By 7 November the movement had spread to most cities in Germany, and workers' and soldiers' councils were being established everywhere to supersede the old authorities. The revolution had broken out. It was a spontaneous mass movement which the government entirely lacked the power to oppose. Further measures were clearly needed if the revolutionary masses were to be placated, and the Joint Parliamentary Committee set about devising a further set of reforms. But it was unable to decide on whether or not to include votes for women. In the session of 7 November, Landsberg, the SPD representative, demanded the inclusion of female suffrage; Gustav Stresemann, the National Liberal representative, objected.[74] Later in the day, the Committee arranged consultations with representatives of the three parties in the Prussian Chamber of Deputies, and the introduction of female suffrage at all levels was agreed upon.[75] When the Committee's representatives reported this decision, however, not only Stresemann but also Conrad Haussmann (of the Progressives) objected, and the meeting broke up without any decision having been reached.[76]

Meanwhile the revolution continued on its course. At the next meeting of the committee on 8 November, Eduard David reported that 'things have already gone even further than our proposals in Bavaria, Saxony and Hesse, and in Hesse there is also a majority in favour of female suffrage'.[77] He urged its acceptance by the committee as a means of 'calming' the revolutionary masses. However, the Catholic

Centre representative, Savigny, suggested that in order that a quick decision be reached, the SPD should drop its insistence on female suffrage. The National Liberals, too, refused to agree on the inclusion of votes for women in the deal. Haussmann's suggestion that a referendum be held on female suffrage, in which both men and women would vote, was not taken up. At one stage Landsberg did in fact suggest that the female suffrage be left to an amendment to be brought in later on the floor of the Reichstag, while David tried to persuade the Centre Party that they would gain most from giving women the vote. Had the situation not been so desperate, it seems then that the SPD would have been prepared to put off the decision for women's suffrage and leave it to be decided upon by a Reichstag that might have voted it down. Late in the evening of 8 November, however, under the pressure of events, the Centre and the National Liberals, who had already consented to a free vote on the issue, changed their minds and finally agreed the inclusion of female suffrage in the new programme.[78] It was really only under the pressure of the revolution that the Joint Parliamentary Committee agreed to introduce female suffrage; the same pressure, however, now made the committee redundant. In an atmosphere of mounting revolutionary chaos, the Kaiser was forced to abdicate, and Prince Max handed over the government to the SPD and USP (Unabhängige Sozial-demokratische Partei Deutschlands or Independent Social Democratic Party of Germany), a radical breakaway party which was gathering within its ranks most of those Social Democrats who opposed the SPD leadership over the war. The new government, or Council of People's Delegates, rested on the revolutionary authority of the workers' and soldiers' councils, not on the old constitution which disappeared in the revolutionary turmoil, and its programme announced on 12 November — like that resolved upon by the Joint Parliamentary Committee four days previously — included female suffrage.[79]

After this, there was no going back. Despite the misgivings of Hugo Preuss, the architect of the new republican constitution,[80] women were given the vote for the constituent National Assembly, which confirmed the decision of 12 November 1918. In the Weimar Republic all women over the age of 21 had the vote. Those on the left and in the USP who wanted to delay the calling of the National Assembly or to elect it from the ranks of the all-male workers' and soldiers' Councils, failed to get their way.[81] They were defeated, however, by a Social Democratic government whose fear of the extreme left led it to take into alliance the old institutions of the Empire — the army, civil service, judiciary, police and nobility — which the left wished to destroy. The Weimar Republic was thus founded on the basis of the old Imperial institutions.[82] It was merely one of the ironies of the revolution that this gave women their political rights sooner than a council-based system could have done. More predictable was the fact that the survival of the institutional basis of the Empire would make it very difficult for women to gain equal rights in other spheres, despite their possession of the vote.

NOTES

1. See the interesting critique of this idea in StA Hamburg, PP, S8897/IV: *VW*, 7 July 1912, where it is pointed out that the scheme, if put into effect, would be entirely inappropriate for working-class girls and would probably harm their families by depriving them of the daughters' earnings for a year. It would also spread the *Kasernengeist* among women as well as men. Cf. UB Rostock, NL Schirmacher, Vortrag, 22 Feb. 1915.

2. ABDF 5/VIII/2: Bäumer circular, 31 July, 1914.

3. HStA Hannover, Hann. 122a, XXXIV, No. 348: Ministerium des Innern to Oberpräsident, 1 Aug. 1914.

4. BA Koblenz, NL Gothein, Vol. 14, 297-299, for examples.

5. ABDF 5/VIII/3: Bäumer/Bensheimer circular, 28 Nov. 1916; Ursula von Gersdorff, *Frauen im Kriegsdienst* (Beiträge zur Militär- und Kriegsgeschichte, hrsg. vom Militärgeschichtlichen Förschungsamt, Vol. 11, Stuttgart, 1969), 15-37; Gerlad D. Feldman, *Army, Industry and Labor in Germany, 1914-1918* (Princeton, 1966).

6. *JB 1916*.

7. Many people predicted this kind of reform. The revisionist SPD deputy Eduard David, for example, told Helene Stöcker on 30 August 1914 that the war would bring about universal suffrage in Prussia at the very least. (SCPC Swarthmore, NL Helene Stöcker 3: Kriegstagebuch, 5).

8. StA Hbg, Senat, Cl. VII, Lit. R, No. 166, Vol. 35: *HF*, 14 May 1899; ABDF 4/3: Selenka to Stritt, 6 July 1901, et. seq.; *Centralblatt des Bundes Deutscher Frauenvereine*, 15 May 1899; ABDF, 'Frankfurter Ortsgruppe des

Allgemeinen Deutschen Frauenvereins' (not indexed, filed separately), 'An die deutschen Frauen! ' For a description of the peace demonstration, see *FB*, 15 Aug. 1901, 122-4.

9. Quoted in Remme, op. cit., 24.

10. BA Koblenz, NL Camilla Jellinek, Pak. 1: Stritt to Lady Aberdeen (1927), *(Aberdeen – Festschrift)*.

11. HLA 57: *HC*, 7 Oct. 1910.

12. ABDF 4/3: Berendsohn to Stritt, 21 Nov. 1909.

13. *JB 1921*, 38.

14. ABDF 5/XVI/2: Bäumer to Mrs. Cadbury, 21 July 1914. See also Remme, op. cit., 37-40.

15. StA Hbg, PP, S5466/III: *HF*, 22 Oct. 1918. See also ABDF 5/VIII/5, 'Kundgebung des Bundes Deutscher Frauenvereine gegen die Wilson-Note'. These statements were issued at the request of the government: see ABDF 5/VIII/5: Bäumer/Bensheimer circular, 30 Oct. 1918.

16. ABDF 5/VIII/3: Hindenburg to Bäumer, 27 Sept. 1917.

17. StA Hbg, PP, S9001/I: *HE*, 12 May 1903.

18. Stegmann, op. cit., 497-519; Schäfer was a disciple of the strongly antifeminist historian Heinrich von Treitschke.

19. *JB 1916*, 9.

20. ABDF 5/XIII/4: Bensheimer to Bäumer, 21 Jan. 1918.

21. ABDF 5/XIII/4: Bensheimer to Bäumer, 3 Aug. 1918; StA Hbg, PP, S4930/II: *NHZ*, 22 Dec. 1906. Eleonore Drenkhahn was the sister of the Bremen moderate suffragist Minna Bahnson.

22. StA Hbg, Senat, C1. VII, Lit. R^f, No. 29, Vol. 41: *HC*, 5 Oct. 1898.

23. StA Hbg, PP, S9001/1: *VW*, 7 Oct. 1905; for the *Ostmarkenpolitik*, see Martin Broszat, *Zweihundert Jahre deutsche Polenpolitik* (2nd ed., Frankfurt am Main, 1972), 152-172.

24. Krüger, op. cit., 147-157.

25. StA Hbg, PP, S9001/II: *BT*, 11 Dec. 1908.

26. *FB*, 13/10, 15 May 1907, 74.

27. For this change in public opinion, see Klaus Wernecke, *Der Wille zur Weltgeltung. Aussenpolitik und Öffentlichkeit im Kaiserreich am Vorabend des Ersten Weltkrieges* (Düsseldorf, 1970).

28. *Report of the Second and Third Conferences of the International Woman Suffrage Alliance* (Copenhagen, 1906), 1, 6, 21, 39, 79-80. *Report of the Fourth Conference . . .* (Amsterdam, 1908), 5, 8, 21-2, 30, 37-8, 40, 77, 98-100; *Report of the Fifth Conference . . .* (London, 1909), 5, 17, 20, 28, 35, 39, 44-48, 57, 99-102.

29. Irmgard Remme, op. cit., 50-63. Minna Cauer's attitude towards the Alliance was rather less hostile than Augspurg and Heymann's. For a detailed but rather one-sided account of these quarrels, see Hanna Krüger, op. cit., 120-122. For the background to the pacifist movement in the First World War, see Richard Barkeley, *Die deutsche Friedensbewegung (1870 bis 1933)* (Hamburg, 1948).

30. For the pro-war attitudes of the Suffrage Union, see *SB* 3/6-7, Oct. 1914, 82, 87, 125.

31. For lists of women pacifists see: StA Hbg, Senat-Kriegsakten AII P47, No. 5815: Report of 20 Aug. 1918; HStA Stuttgart, NL Haussmann, No. 52: leaflet 'Zentralstelle für Völkerrecht', August 1916; AStA München, M Inn 66132: Abdruck des Monatsberichtes des Internationalen Frauenausschusses für einen dauernden Frieden, 1 Dec. 1915, 'Übersicht über die Friedensbewegung' No. 101948; *ZFS,* 21/4, 15 Feb. 1915, 16. For the Suffrage League see StA Hbg, PP, S19925: passim; and (Lida Gustava Heymann), *Völkerversöhnende Frauenarbeit während des Weltkrieges* (Munich, 1920), 14. For Marie Wegner see DZA Potsdam, Reichskanzlei, No. 2266, 152: Wegner to Bethmann Hollweg; ABDF 5/IV/2, *passim;* ABDF 5/XIII/4: Bensheimer to Stritt, 7 Aug. 1909; ABDF 5/XV/1: Bäumer to Meyer, 10 Jan. 1911, Bäumer to Stritt, 10 Jan. 1911, Bäumer to Wegner, 11 Jan. 1911; ABDF 5/XV/2: Bäumer to Bensheimer, 8 July 1912. For Selenka see ABDF 5/II/2: Selenka to Schmidt (c. 1900). For Cauer, who supported the war at first but was a pacifist by the end of February 1915, see ABDF 4/4: Lüders to Bäumer, 10 Oct. 1914, Bäumer to Lüders, 12 Oct. 1914; ABDF 5/XIII/4: Bensheimer to Bäumer, 1 May 1915; Else Lüders, *Minna Cauer* (1925), 173-206. For Hallgarten, *FS* 2/3, June 1913, 70.

32. GStA München, Ges. Bern, Kriegsakten 8, for an example of this work.

33. (Lida Gustava Heymann), *Völkerversöhnende Frauenarbeit während des Weltkrieges* (Munich, 1920).

34. AStA München, M Inn 66132: Nuremburg city authorities to Kriegsmin., 3 March 1916.

35. StA Hbg, Amtsgericht-Vereinsregister, B1953-52.

36. DZA Potsdam, Reichsamt des Innern, No. 12295, 251-2: An den deutschen Reichstag! Anlage – die Handhabung des Gesetzes über den Belagerungszustand gegenüber den deutschen Pazifisten.

37. Else Lüders, op. cit., 178, 190.

38. For a recent survey of the general background, see James D. Shand, 'Doves among the Eagles: German Pacifists and their Government during World War I', *Journal of Contemporary History,* 10/1, Jan. 1975.

39. StA Hbg, PP, S18848: *BVZ,* 5 Jan. 1912. The speaker was Count Reventlow.

40. See p. 180, above.

41. AStA München, M Inn 66132, No. 101948, 'Übersicht über die Friedensbewegung'.

42. HStA Hannover, Hann. 122a XXXIV, No. 365, Vol. 1, 19.

43. AStA München, M Inn 66132, No. 101948, 'Übersicht über die Friedensbewegung'.

44. DZA Potsdam, Reichsamt des Innern, 12295: Versammlungsbericht.

45. AStA München, M Inn 66132, No. 101948, 'Übersicht über die Friedensbewegung'.

46. *Völkerversöhnende Frauenarbeit . . .* 14-15; AStA München, M. Inn No. 66132: Versammlungsbericht, 12 Nov. 1915, 'Übersicht . . .'.

47. Frida Perlen was a member of the Suffrage League; b. Ludwigsburg 4 April 1870, married 1889, d. 21 Dec. 1933; she came from a Jewish background (information from Stadtarchiv Stuttgart). For her attitude to the BDF's stance on

the war, see her exchange of letters with Bäumer in ABDF 5/XVI/2.

48. StA Hbg, PP, S7484: *VW*, 1, 2, 11, 17, 20 and 27 May 1915, *HC*, 29 April 1915, *FZ*, 15 March 1915, *HE*, 4 May 1915; *ZFS*, 7 March 1915, 5: 'Bericht über die Vorbereitung für einen internationalen Frauenkongress'.

49. ABDF 16/II/2: Gesamtvorstandssitzung, 14 April 1915.

50. For the Conference and the organisation it founded, see Gertrude Bussey and Margaret Tims, *Women's International League for Peace and Freedom 1915-1965: a record of fifty years' work* (London, 1965).

51. *Völkerversöhnende Frauenarbeit . . .* (loc. cit.).

52. StA Hbg, Senat – Kriegsakten, A II P. 47, No. 5815: Report of 20 August 1918.

53. Stuttgart, Stellv. GK XIII. AK, Bund 93, No. 54, p. 16. See also StA Ludwigsburg F201 Bü 653 112, Verzeichnis der Vorstandsmitglieder 22 March 1918.

54. AStA München, M Inn No. 66132: 'Übersicht . . .', Anlage 7; DZA Potsdam, Reichskanzlei No. 2266, 156-7: Augspurg et al., to Bethmann Hollweg, Dec. 1917; *FB*, 21/4, 15 Feb. 1915, 14: 'Frauen Europas, wann erschallt Euer Ruf?'

55. AStA München, M Inn 66132.

56. Heymann/Augspurg, *Erlebtes-Erschautes* 142-145.

57. StA Hbg, PP, S8004: police to Ida Jens, 7 Nov. 1918; DZA Potsdam, Reichsamt des Innern, No. 12295: Wegner to Bethmann Hollweg, 14 July 1916. For the general background to these measures, see W. Deist (ed.), *Militär und Innenpolitik im Weltkrieg 1914-1918* (Quellen zur Geschichte des Parlamentarismus und der politischen Parteien, 2. Reihe, Bd. 1, 2 Vols., Düsseldorf, 1970). For positive efforts to get women to support the war, see AStA Stuttgart, M 1/4, Nr. 1727, 8, 19; ibid., Stellv. Gk XIII. Ak, Bund 99.

58. HStA Stuttgart, NL Haussmann, 30, for copies of the petitions.

59. Frieda Ledermann, *Zur Geschichte der Frauenstimmrechtsbewegung* (Berlin, 1918), 45-8.

60. Cf. Jürgen Kocka, *Klassengesellschaft im Krieg. Deutsche Sozialgeschichte 1914-1918* (Göttingen, 1973), Ch. on 'Linksrutsch der Angestellten'.

61. DZA Potsdam, Fortschrittliche Volkspartei, No. 26/1, 5, 7, 12, 14, 20, No. 49, 3-7, No. 22, 35-6, 49, 52, No. 37, 16-19, No. 50, 49, No. 54, Arbeitsausschuss der Frauen to Geschäftsführender Ausschuss, 10 Nov. 1918 and reply, 16 Nov. 1918.

62. *Stenographische Berichte über die Sitzungen der Bürgerschaft zu Hamburg in Jahre 1917*, 216.

63. Bund Deutscher Frauenvereine. *Die Stellung der Frau in der politisch-sozialen Neugestaltung Deutschlands* (1917).

64. ADEFB, Q1: Ortsgruppe Hamburg to Vorstand, 4 May 1917. See also *Stenographische Berichte über die Sitzungen der Bürgerschaft zu Hamburg in Jahre 1917*, 192, 214 ff (6 June 1917, 27 June 1917). The City Union was a local organisation of the BDF.

65. ADEFB, A14e: Müller to Ortsgruppen-Vorstände, 15 Nov. 1917.

66. ADEFB, A14e: Vorstandssitzung 7 Nov. 1917; Gröben to Müller, 16 Dec. 1917; Müller to Bäumer, 3 Dec. 1917.

67. ADEFB, A14e: Gröben to Bäumer, 10 May 1918.

68. ABDF 16/II/4: Sitzung des engeren Vorstandes, 16 Feb. 1918.

69. ADEFB, A14d: Austritt aus dem BDF; Gründe, weshalb Einige für Lösung sind.

70. ABDF 5/XIII/4: Bensheimer to Bäumer, 8 Feb. 1918, 2 April 1918, 3 Aug. 1918.

71. For a corrective to traditional views of the connection between the First World War and the granting of female suffrage in Great Britain, see Martin D. Pugh, 'Politicians and the Women's Vote, 1914-1918', *History*, 59/197, Oct. 1974, 358-374.

72. *Die Regierung des Prinzen Max von Baden,* bearbeitet von Erich Matthias und Rudolf Morsey. (Quellen zur Geschichte des Parlamentarismus und der politischen Parteien, 1. Reihe, Bd.2, Düsseldorf, 1961), 515-6.

73. *Die Regierung des Prinzen Max von Baden,* (op. cit.), 537. For the general background, see F. L. Carsten, *Revolution in Central Europe 1918-1919* (London, 1972).

74. *Die Regierung des Prinzen Max von Baden* (op. cit.), 571-2.

75. Ibid., 573.

76. Conrad Haussmann, *Schlaglichter. Reichstagsbriefe und Aufzeichungen* (ed. U. Zeller, Frankfurt am Main, 1924), 266.

77. *Die Regierung des Prinzen Max von Baden,* (op. cit.), 593.

78. Ibid., 598-9, 602, 606-9. The documents dealing with the final agreement have unfortunately not been found.

79. *Die Regierung der Volksbeaufragten 1918/19,* eingeleitet von Erich Matthias, bearbeitet von Susanne Miller unter Mitwirkung von Heinrich Potthoff. (Quellen zur Geschichte des Parlamentarismus und der politischen Parteien, 1.Reihe, Bd.3, Düsseldorf, 1969), 38.

80. Ibid., 221.

81. Ibid., 179-193; for women and the Councils, see further F. L. Carsten, *Revolution in Central Europe 1918-19* (London, 1972), 133, n.17; Gundula Bölke *Die Wandlung der Frauenemanzipationstheorie von Marx bis zur Rätebewegung* (Berlin, n.d. c.1970), 56 ff.; Toni Sender, *Die Frauen und das Rätesystem* (Berlin, 1919), 20, 22; Peter Oertzen, *Betriebsräte in der Novemberrevolution* (Düsseldorf, 1963), 43, 277. The Councils themselves took an active part in dismissing women workers. Cf. FES/ASD Bonn, NL Emil Barth, I/97, II/269. For the situation in Bavaria, where Kurt Eisner is said to have proclaimed female suffrage on 8 November 1918 and arranged for Anita Augspurg to be a member of the 'revolutionary central workers' council' set up immediately after this, as 'representative of the women's movement', see Heymann/Augspurg, *Erlebtes-Erschautes,* 160-1, 166.

82. Reinhard Rürup, 'Problems of the German Revolution 1918-19', *Journal of Contemporary History,* 1968.

8

THE BITTER END

THE FAILURE OF THE WOMEN'S MOVEMENT IN THE WEIMAR REPUBLIC, 1919-1932

The first act of the BDF after the end of the war and the foundation of the Weimar Republic was to consolidate the victory of nationalism within its ranks by replacing the radical 'guidelines' of 1907[1] with a new programme that breathed a strongly *völkisch,* nationalistic spirit. The programme was clearly drawn up under the guidance of Gertrud Bäumer. It began by asserting that the BDF 'unites German women of every party and creed, in order to express their national identity . . . The special civil tasks of women lie . . . in the maintenance of German unity, in the promotion of internal peace, and in the conquest of social, confessional and political antagonisms through a spirit of self-sacrifice, a sense of civic duty and a strong, unified national consciousness . . .' The aim of the BDF, it concluded, was 'to gather women in a spirit of unified constructive work (and) with a faith in the strength of our people to rise again . . .' This programme, which remained in force until 1933, committed the BDF to 'the conquest of social, confessional and political antagonisms'. Women indeed, it said, were specially called to fulfil this task. They would inspire German men to abandon their political struggles through the example of 'the spirit of self-sacrifice'.[2] Translated into practical terms, this meant that German women would continue to be encouraged to engage with little hope of adequate recompense in various kinds of communal social and welfare work, just as the suggestion that internal political and social differences could be forgotten if Germans managed to build up a 'strong, unified national consciousness' meant in practice a reassertion of the nationalism which the BDF had espoused under Bäumer and during the First World War. It was in pursuit of these nationalistic ideals that shortly after the war the BDF, invited by the International Council of Women to participate in its first post-war Assembly, declined the invitation as 'incompatible with our dignity'. This led to the resignation of the moderate, Alice Salomon, from the executive committee of the BDF. Salomon was the Secretary of the International Council; she refused to abandon the responsibilities of this position, which involved playing an important part in the preparations for the Assembly. The BDF executive Committee apparently thought that she should do so.[3] Later on in the Weimar Republic, the BDF did rejoin the International Council, but it never ceased to oppose the provisions of the Treaty of Versailles, and on occasion launched vigorous protest actions against the policies of the Entente Powers. It mounted demagogic attacks on their 'refusal' to disarm, which it denounced on the rather specious grounds that Germany herself was already disarmed and without the means of defence.[4]

As the BDF's attitude to the problem of increasing the birth-rate had indicated for some years, the 'selfless dedication to the whole people' stressed in the programme of 1919 meant in the first place, as far as women were concerned, fulfilling their duty to the State by getting married and having as many children as possible. The programme laid far greater stress than its predecessors on the importance of the family, both from a female and a national point of view. 'The family, as the highest and most intimate form of lifelong human community, is destined to be the most important milieu for the cultivation of all forces of spiritual life', declared the new programme. 'The purity of family life is thus the basic condition of social health and national fitness.' The extent to which the women's movement had by now moved away from the concept of feminism as a struggle for equal rights and the modification of traditional roles was also reflected in the parts of the new programme which dealt with the problem of female employment. 'Women', it said, 'must be in a position to develop their abilities freely, and to invest their aptitudes in the organism of professional life *according to their nature and qualities.*'[5] Women were not to compete with men on equal terms in the same professions. On the contrary, 'the competition of the sexes must be overcome through an appropriate social division of labour, within which men and women assume tasks appropriate to their nature.'[6]

All these various aims can be summed up in the idea of the organic national community, the so-called *Volksgemeinschaft,*[7] the idea that German women and men were united by racial ties stronger than any ideological divisions, and that the aim of politics should be to strengthen these ties and eliminate the divisive influences of party conflicts. These views indicated that, far from welcoming the advent of the Weimar Republic, the BDF, in common with most other middle-class organisations, had little understanding of the parliamentary system and rejected party politics as divisive and unpatriotic. The BDF never came to terms with the political realities of the Weimar Republic. The role which it played was thus a very limited one. Basically, as Gertrud Bäumer argued, the aim of the BDF was to unite women of all parties in exerting a 'motherly' influence over society.[8] In accordance with this view the BDF was sometimes referred to as the embodiment of 'organised motherliness' *(organisierte Mütterlichkeit).* The BDF's most persistent efforts in this sense were directed towards combating sexual libertarianism, pornography, abortion, venereal diseases, advertisements for contraceptives and the double standard of sexual morality. It campaigned for representation on film and other censorship bodies, and regarded as its greatest single triumph the enactment of a law in 1927 making all forms of brothels or regulated prostitution illegal, and establishing draconian penalties for people who knowingly spread venereal infections.[9] The BDF's obsession with what it regarded as the moral laxity of Weimar culture, besides diverting its attention from more pressing and important problems,[10] was also part of a more general hostility to the Weimar system. Agnes von Zahn-Harnack, President of the BDF from 1931 to 1933, made this clear in her standard book on the women's movement, published in 1928. Implausible though it may seem, she appeared to look back nostalgically to the days of the Wilhelmine Empire. After giving a brief account of the BDF's fight against the New Morality and its rejection of the

Mutterschutz movement before the war, she went on to complain that the New Morality, despite the collapse of the Mutterschutz movement, had taken hold of the young and was creating 'a serious sexual crisis'. 'The sexual crisis', she continued, 'is inseparable from the disintegration of our whole way of life after the war. State, Society and Family have been affected by this disintegration, and today, after nearly ten years, neither the form of the State, nor the form of Society, nor that of the Family, has been soundly reconstructed.'[11]

There was never any real chance under the Weimar Republic that the BDF's conservative orientation could be changed, its hostility to the Republic mitigated or its approach made more effective. To start with, the radicals, as we saw in Chapter 7, had been expelled from the BDF because of their pacifism during the First World War. While the BDF continued to be strongly nationalistic, the radical leaders, Anita Augspurg, Lida Gustava Heymann and Helene Stöcker, continued to campaign for pacifist and feminist causes outside the BDF, in their own organisations and through their own propaganda machinery.[12] They remained a tiny faction without any influence, while the BDF continued to grow steadily in size, swelled by the influx of new organisations. The growth of the BDF, and the considerable changes in its internal structure, which took place at the same time, constituted the second factor militating against a revival of radicalism within the movement. The old bastions of radicalism, the suffrage societies, wound up their activities after the achievement of their aims,[13] and there was a general decline in the strength of those member associations which actively promoted specific measures of legislative reform, the so-called *Fachverbände*. The Abolitionist Federation was unable to stop the decline in its fortunes that had already begun before the war. In 1919 it had 900 members organised in 14 branches; by 1931 its numbers had sunk to 355, and 9 out of its 14 branches had ceased to exist. Membership in Berlin had fallen from 240 to 45. Other *Fachverbände*, too, declined in numbers. Membership of the women's temperance societies fell from 5515 in 1919 to 4152 in 1931. The educational pressure group 'Women's Education – Women's Study' (Frauenbildung-Frauenstudum), once the leading radical feminist society under Hedwig Kettler in the early 1890s, fell from 4028 members in 1919 to 893 in 1931. Only nationalist and *völkisch Fachverbände* actually increased their membership in the Weimar Republic. The Union for German

Women's Culture (Verband Frauenkultur), which aimed to develop a specifically 'German' type of clothing for German women and thus free them from the tyranny of Paris fashions, increased in numbers from 5000 in 1919 to 8000 in 1931. The German-colonial Women's League, (Deutsch-Kolonialer Frauenbund), founded in order to send white women from Germany to Germany's overseas colonies in order to prevent racially mixed marriages and thus secure the dominance of the 'master race', rose in numbers from 18,000 in 1919 to 20,000 in 1931, despite the fact that its original aims had been nullified by the mandating of Germany's colonies to the League of Nations in 1919. Insofar as the *Fachverbände* did remain a force in the BDF therefore, it was force on the right and not on the left as it had been in the years 1898-1908.

The regional unions, whose rise after 1908 had done much to help the BDF's move to the right, continued to expand, though more slowly, during the Weimar Republic. Some, of course, particularly those affected by territorial losses, declined in number. Others remained static, while a few grew very rapidly indeed. Perhaps the most remarkable increase in the membership of a regional union occurred in the Free City of Danzig, transferred to League of Nations suzerainty in 1919 but regarded as part of Germany by most nationalist organisations including the BDF. It had reached a total of 8275 members by 1927, then leapt to a total of 28,330 by 1931. There can be little doubt that the weight of membership *within* the regional unions shifted in the same way as the weight of membership in the BDF as a whole during the 1920s, since the regional unions were merely groups of member societies of the BDF organised on a provincial level, and thus duplicated its structure on a smaller scale.

The really rapidly expanding member unions of the BDF in the 1920s were, however, the economic pressure groups. The older professional groups, it is true, remained static; the Teachers' Union did not grow at all, for example, but the society devoted to representing the interests of the women postal workers grew from 21,617 to 35,492, and the commercial salaried employees' organisation from 65,495 to 100,492. There were many entirely new professional and white-collar associations, from a women doctors' union with 898 members to unions of social workers (4500), female local government employees (15,876), kindergarten teachers (5300), lawyers (100), university lecturers (40) and so on. Numerically however the weight was shifting very much to the newer white-collar associations, though the leadership of the BDF remained in the hands of the professional, highly educated women of the *Bildungsbürgertum*. In addition to the white-collar associations, the Housewives' Union also underwent a rapid expansion during the Weimar Republic. In 1919 the major housewives' organisation, the Imperial Union of German Housewives' Associations (Reichsverband der deutschen Hausfrauenverein), led by Martha Zietz, already numbered 100,000. There were in fact two separate organisations, the 'urban' housewives who retained the old name, and a union of 'rural' housewives, the Union of Rural Housewives' Associations (Verband Landwirtschaftlicher Hausfrauenvereine), numbering perhaps 90,000.[14] Taken together, the growth of the white-collar unions and the housewives' organisations represented a major change in the balance of membership within the BDF, vastly increasing the strength of economic pressure-groups within the Federation.

These changes were reinforced by amendments to the BDF Constitution of 1912 passed in the General Assembly at Hamburg in 1919, Mannheim in 1924 and Königsberg in 1929. The effects of these amendments on the Constitution were twofold. First, they greatly increased the power of the central leadership over the member unions. We have seen that among other things, in order to accommodate right-wing associations such as the German-evangelical Women's League, the BDF under the influence of Gertrud Bäumer, insisted before the war that the radical programme of 1907 was not binding on member unions. No such liberties were taken with the more conservative programme of 1919. All member unions of all kinds were required to 'represent the principles' of the BDF. Provincial unions were now defined (1919) as 'executive organs', and the new programme was declared binding on all members. Second, they greatly increased the power of nationally organised economic pressure-groups in the decision-making bodies of the BDF. In 1924 the previous twofold division of member unions into provincial unions and *Fachverbände*, in force since 1908, was replaced by a threefold division in which professional associations were added to the other two existing categories. Among 'professional unions' the BDF included the Housewives' Unions, insisting that housewifery was as much a profession as teaching or being a secretary or typist. This change was accompanied by amendments increasing the representation of national associations, as opposed to provincial unions, in the General Assembly.

According to the provisions of the 1919 Constitution each union, whether provincial or national, was represented in the General Assembly with 5 votes. In addition there was one vote for each of its member associations that joined separately from the central union to which it belonged. This latter provision was retained, but in 1924 each national or provincial union with more than 15 member associations acquired 15 votes, and with more than 100 member associations 20 votes. In 1929 this was further amended to give even more representation to the large national unions. National unions with up to 1000 members were given 5 votes at the General Assembly, with up to 2,000 members 8 votes, and so on up to unions with over 128,000 members which had no less than 57 votes at the General Assembly — in addition, it must be remembered, to one vote for every member association or branch joining separately if it had less than 3000 members, or 2 votes if it had more than 3000 members. This last provision, unlike the first, also applied to provincial unions, but each provincial union itself had a maximum of only 20 votes at the General Assembly. Thus by 1929 a national member union of the BDF with, say, 150,000 members, organised in 250 local branches of about 600 members each, would wield over 300 votes at the General Assembly.

There is no doubt which organisations benefited most from these provisions. By 1931 all the largest nationally organised member unions of the BDF were economic pressure-groups of one kind and another. The largest was the 'urban' Housewives' Union with 200,000 members. Second was the liberal white collar association, the Women's Groups of the Trade Union League of Salaried Employees (Frauengruppen des Gewerkschaftsbundes der Angestellten) with 100,492 members. Like the Housewives' Unions it had only appeared on the scene since the end of the First World War, though it owed its origin to the associations founded by Minna Cauer and Lida Gustava Heymann before the turn of the century.[15] The third largest member organisation of the BDF was the 'rural' Housewives' Union, numbering (probably) about 90,000. No other organisation was anything near as large as these, though as we have seen there were some other fair-sized economic pressure-groups such as the Women Postal Workers' Union (35,492 members in 1931) in the BDF. Giving extra representation to large national member associations thus meant in the first place giving extra representation to these organised economic interest groups. By 1931 they possessed enough representation to dominate the official policy-making organ of the BDF, the General Assembly, and to exert an extremely strong influence in the BDF's various committees.

These changes in structure, which were accompanied by corresponding structural changes in the General Committee (Gesamtvorstand), meant that the BDF now represented three kinds of organised economic interest. First, it represented the professional associations, the relatively small groups such as women doctors, teachers, lawyers, etc., who continued to dominate the BDF leadership as they had done before the war. Secondly it represented much larger organisations of white-collar workers such as the salaried employees and post office workers. Finally it represented the consumer interests of housewives who, with the white-collar unions, dominated the BDF General Assembly by sheer weight of numbers. This was a very different situation from the pre-war years, when the strongest and most influential member unions of the BDF had been associations aimed at social welfare or social reform. It meant that the focus of attention of the BDF's constituent groups moved away from rights and towards interests, even though the rights had not been granted and the interests could sometimes be in conflict with one another, especially in times of economic difficulty. However, the changes in the balance of forces within the BDF after 1918 also had important political effects. The decline of liberal feminism and the growth in numbers and influence of right-wing organisations such as the German-colonial Women's League, reinforced the trend to the right that had begun within the BDF in 1908. Even more important than this, however, was the fact that middle-class economic interest groups of the kind that were now coming to dominate the BDF were generally on the right of the political spectrum. The Housewives' Unions in particular were close to the German-national People's Party (Deutschnationale Volkspartei or DNVP), the radical right-wing successors of the old conservatives, implacable opponents of democracy and fervent supporters of an aggressively nationalistic foreign policy. The change in structure of the BDF was thus followed by a change in political composition.

Before the war the BDF had been entirely dominated by members of the Progressive Party, whose successor in the Weimar Republic, the

German Democratic Party (Deutsche Demokratische Partei or DDP) was one of the few middle-class parties to support the Weimar Constitution. Now, however, the political composition of the BDF leadership became more varied. Members of the German People's Party (Deutsche Volkspartei or DVP) successor to the old National Liberals, and the DNVP, now gained a foothold in the BDF leadership. This reflected both the shift to the right that had taken place since the days when the leadership owed its allegiance to the Progressive Party, and the changes that occurred in the structure of the movement during the 1920s, particularly in the growth of DNVP-oriented societies such as the Housewives' Unions and the German-colonial Women's League. In this respect, at least in the early years of the Weimar Republic, when a number of pre-war leaders still played an important role in the BDF, the movement's members were further to the right than the movement's leaders, just as they had been before the war. Many leading women members of the DNVP indeed had abandoned contact with the BDF altogether. Käthe Schirmacher was a deputy in the National Assembly for the DNVP and Paula Müller sat for the same party in the Reichstag, but both had severed their contacts with the BDF; Martha Zietz, who was active on the party's behalf in the local politics of Schleswig-Holstein, was also to do so in 1926. Zietz and Schirmacher seem to have belonged to the party's extreme anti-Semitic wing.[16] But by the mid-1920s the right was beginning to penetrate the ranks of the BDF leadership. Emma Ender, a leading member of the conservative Hamburg branch of the General Association before the war, and from 1924 to 1931 President of the BDF itself, represented the DVP (successor to the National Liberal Party) in the Hamburg City Council.[17] Before the war a leader of the BDF who belonged to the National Liberals would have been unthinkable.

Gertrud Bäumer resigned the Presidency of the BDF in 1919 in favour of Marianne Weber, but she remained the most influential member of the executive committee throughout the Republic. Her prestige grew as her colleagues resigned. By 1931 indeed she was the only remaining member who had served on the committee before the war. She was a member of the National Assembly, sat in the Reichstag throughout the Republic and held the high-ranking post of Ministerial Adviser *(Ministerialrätin)* in the Ministry of the Interior. She was the only bourgeois woman politician of any consequence in the Weimar

Republic. As time went on her liberalism became even more diluted. In 1930 she played a role in securing the merger of the DDP, to which she belonged, with a number of groups further to the right including the Young German Order (Jungdeutsche Orden), an organisation with strong völkisch, nationalistic and anti-Semitic tendencies.[18] Apart from Bäumer many other members of the women's movements were active in politics in the DDP during the Weimar Republic. Marie Baum and Marie-Elisabeth Lüders represented the party in the Reichstag. Others, such as Fried Radel in Hamburg, Regine Deutsch in Berlin, and Marie Stritt in Dresden, represented the party in local politics;[19] but these women no longer played an important part in directing the BDF's affairs by the end of the 1920s. By this time, in fact, the BDF leadership was a mixture of DDP, DVP and DNVP supporters. This pattern was repeated in the movement as a whole. In 1928 member associations were asked to suggest women candidates worthy of BDF support in the elections.[20] No SPD candidates were proposed, and only one each from the Catholic Centre and the Wirtschaftspartei, a bourgeois splinter-group. The candidates chosen were overwhelmingly from the three bourgeois parties to which the BDF leadership belonged: the DDP (29), the DVP (32) and the DNVP (21). The contrast with the pre-war situation was indeed striking.

Even more striking, perhaps, was the fact that two out of these three parties, the DVP and the DNVP, were actively hostile to women's rights. The fact was that − contrary to the expectations of both Gertrud Bäumer and Anita Augspurg before the enfranchisement of women − women voted for the whole range of political parties irrespective of each party's policies on women's rights. Indeed paradoxically, insofar as they voted for any parties to a greater extent than did men, it was for those which were most hostile to women's rights, the Catholic Centre and the DNVP. On the other hand, the parties that had been most inclined to favour women's rights, the DDP, and to a far greater extent the SPD, the USP and the KPD, received relatively little support from women at elections. This was perhaps the most unexpected development to which the women's movement had to adjust itself in the post-1918 era. Throughout the pre-war period it had relied largely on petitioning the Reichstag and other legislative bodies, and on trying to secure influence in a wide range of political parties, using as its only political weapon the claim that women of all classes and creeds held a large number of beliefs and desires in common, and that they were prepared to take political action in order to put them into effect. Now that belief was seen to be false. Women as a whole put party loyalty before their real or supposed interests as women, even, as we shall see, on issues that vitally affected these interests.[21] The BDF was therefore faced with the task of adjusting to the new political situation and manipulating the structure of party politics to the best effect if it was to see its goals realised. Despite its increase in size – by 1931 it claimed 1,500,000 members, and probably (allowing for the double counting which successive constitutional amendments failed to eliminate) numbered at least 750,000 women in its ranks – it could not employ the threat of using its membership against a government in the polls if that government failed to consult its interests. Instead it had to work indirectly, and here its ideological stance severely restricted the range of parties with which it could co-operate. A purely professional pressure-group such as the Civil Servants' League (Deutscher Beamtenbund) could have representatives in every party in the Reichstag from the Nazis to the Communists, but an organisation united around a *Weltanschauung,* such as the BDF, could only claim the support of a much narrower range of parties, and even here it had had to modify its doctrines until they ceased to provide any real representation of the interests of the group of people for whom it stood, before it could win the support of any political party to the right of the DDP.

The BDF may well have preserved its own existence by reducing its practical demands to a minimum and by refraining from indulging in politically controversial campaigns for the equality of the sexes. The adoption of the *Volksgemeinschaft* idea was evidence of the BDF's deeply felt need to place itself above the party-political struggle if it was to survive as an independent organisation and at the same time avoid being torn apart by the internal party-political dissensions that threatened to disrupt its unity now that women had the vote. The beginnings of this policy had been evident with the introduction of the *Reichsvereinsgesetz* in 1908. Moreover, added to this, the movement's inability to secure its aims had led it to modify its ideology to conform with the views of the ruling classes in the hope of gaining social and political respectability. However, the BDF achieved unity and respectability only at the price of political effectiveness. Because it abandoned many of the specifically feminist demands of the early 1900s, because it failed to find alternatives for those which had been achieved by the Revolution of 1918, it lost much of its raison d'être in the Weimar Republic. The interest groups which formed an ever-larger part of its membership could represent their economic interests best by dealing directly with employers and officials, and where legislative reform was their objective it would best be served by direct pressure upon the political parties in the Reichstag. There did not seem much left for the BDF to do.

The BDF's failure to find a role for itself in the Weimar Republic was reflected in its inability to extend the rights of women or to defend the interests of its members adequately. The Constitution of the Weimar Republic, of course, explicitly guaranteed female equality in good democratic fashion. Article 119 declared that 'marriage rests on the equality of rights of both sexes'. Article 128 opened all offices in the Civil Service to women. Above all Article 109 declared that 'men and women have basically the same rights and duties'. But the Weimar Constitution was in fact little more than a declaration of intent on such matters, and the nature of the new Republic, the fact that it rested behind a façade of democracy and progress on the same social, economic and institutional basis as the old Wilhelmine Empire, meant that much the same problems of female emancipation and equal rights remained to be solved after 1918 as had existed before. Article 119 remained a collection of empty phrases as long as no amendments were made to the Civil Code. Article 128 was a dead letter while the Civil Service remained dominated by conservative officials from Imperial days. Article 109 meant nothing because of the inclusion of the word 'basically', as the First Chamber of the national legislature – the Reichsrat – demonstrated in 1921, when it rejected the decision of the Reichstag to admit women to serve as lay assessors and jury members in courts, on the grounds that women were constitutionally incapable of performing this duty satisfactorily because they were too easily swayed by their emotions to be trusted to reach a fair verdict. 'Even if Article 109 of the Constitution gives men and women basically the same civil rights and duties and basically the same claim to admittance to public office', so the Reichsrat argued, 'nevertheless, according to Article 128, this admittance should only be granted to those who are capable.'[22] Given this situation, there remained all to fight for as far as middle-class women were concerned. The BDF, it is true, continued to demand in its programme the reform of the marriage provisions of the Civil Code, full equality for women in education and the professions and equal pay for equal work. But it never campaigned actively for these aims. Indeed to have done so would most probably have offended powerful member associations such as the Housewives' Unions. The BDF was thus unable to do anything to improve the position of women in Civil Law, education and the professions. Indeed, it was even unable to prevent the marked deterioration in opportunities for professional women that took place during the 1920s and early 1930s. The BDF of course took care to comment on the situation of women in these respects; but it clearly felt unable to mount campaigns of the sort that had taken place before the war, in the question of the Civil Code (1896) or the prostitution question (1902) or the suffrage (1910).[23]

The BDF itself was to some extent aware of its impotence, and as the 1920s wore on it began to search for ways of replacing the party-political system with a political structure which it hoped would be more amenable to pressure from the women's movement. Debate slowly grew within the BDF over the proposal that each party be requested or required to put forward separate lists of male and female candidates. Since elections combined direct voting for individual candidates with proportional voting for parties, this would guarantee at least a certain number of women in the Reichstag. The inclusion of women in parties' lists of candidates would no longer depend on the generosity of the (male) party leaderships. Even more fiercely debated than this proposal, however, was the idea of forming a separate women's party altogether, for which presumably women alone would be invited to vote. Frequently proposed and discussed within the women's movement during the 1920s, this idea represented an extension of the official BDF doctrine that it was up to women to lead the way in burying party political differences and create the longed-for organic national community; it also reflected a general tendency of interest-groups in the Weimar Republic to form their own small political parties rather than compromise their interests in the formation of larger ones — and there can be no doubt that the Frauenpartei, had it ever got off the ground (which is unlikely), would have been a very small political party indeed. From here it was only one step further to the demand made by the BDF in 1932 that the parliamentary system be replaced altogether by a Corporate State on the lines of Mussolini's Fascist Italy and that one of the 'corporations' should consist of women.[24]

Perhaps too this final proposal was a reaction to the virtual destruction in 1929-32 of the parties with which the BDF had the closest relationship. For in the years of the Depression in Germany, beginning in 1929, the urban and rural petty bourgeoisie deserted in their millions the parties to which they had given their electoral support during the Weimar Republic's years of prosperity. These parties included the DDP, DVP and DNVP, the parties to which the great majority of BDF members belonged. This shift to the right was followed by the BDF leadership, for at the same time as the bourgeois parties lost the bulk of their support the character of the BDF leadership also began to change. Between 1928 and 1932 the DVP moved over to the far right, losing some of its representatives from the BDF committee. More serious still, Marie Baum, Luise Kesselbach and Alice Bensheimer, all close to the DDP, were replaced on the BDF executive committee by women who stood further to the right such as Anne von Gierke (DNVP) and Lenore Kühn, who was strongly sympathetic to the Nazis. Thus the women's movement was beginning to lose its contacts with the liberal DDP as the DDP was itself declining in numbers; yet the parties further right were often openly hostile to women's rights, while the DDP itself, if not always favourable in practice, was at least sympathetic in theory. Clearly the political upheavals and economic crisis of the years 1929-32 were destroying the delicately balanced network of relationships between the BDF and the political parties through whose female Reichstag deputies it sought to exert its influence on the legislative process.

The Depression had equally serious effects on the internal structure and effectiveness of the BDF. To begin with, towards the end of the Weimar Republic the BDF's activities were more and more curtailed by financial weakness. Relatively well-off during the war, it had lost all its investments — government bonds — in the inflation of 1923; in February 1924 the Treasurer reported a balance of precisely 5 Marks and 14 Pfennigs. Added to this was the ever-mounting cost of the BDF's bureaucracy, particularly in the form of offices *(Geschäftsstellen)* in Berlin, Hamburg and Munich. For the rest of the Weimar Republic, these costs were barely covered by subscriptions; reserves, investments and donations remained negligible. In 1929/30 for example the BDF received 15,000 Marks in subscriptions, and very little else. The Berlin office alone cost 11,000 Marks to run, and the General

Assembly mounted that year cost 10,000 Marks all but 3,000 of this sum paid from a special ad hoc levy. It was not surprising that the BDF had to borrow on occasion, and was never able to build up satisfactory reserves. The situation became even worse with the onset of the Depression in 1929, and by 1931 the Treasurer was calling for economies. 'The General Assembly', she said, 'must be considerably more modest than that of 1929' – and this when she had already reduced the annual running costs of the Berlin office from 11,000 to 7,200 Marks.

The BDF could perhaps afford to stage a more modest General Assembly than was its custom. Much more serious, however, was the fact that lack of money obliged the BDF to curtail the pressure-group activities that were its raison d'être. Already in 1928 the Treasurer was obliged to make the following admission:

> With the help of the donations of 4200 RM. promised in (the) Eisenach (General Assembly), it was possible with the utmost frugality to bring the Federation through the last year. A number of tasks which fell within the Federation's area of competence could not be carried out; journeys by the Executive Committee were limited, and in part paid for by the Committee members themselves; there was no large conference at home or abroad which might have burdened us with greater expenditure. Special difficulties are faced by the Federation's funds in meeting the costs of all sorts of printed matter.

By 1931-32 the situation was considerably worse. The BDF's efficiency as a pressure-group, which depended to a great extent on its ability to circulate propaganda in the appropriate quarters and to send its leading members to put personal pressure on important individuals, was being seriously handicapped by the inadequacy of its funds.[25]

In the late 1920s and early 1930s too there was growing evidence that the leadership and membership of the BDF was becoming predominantly middle-aged. The younger generation was not joining the women's movement. As a leading newspaper, the *Vossiche Zeitung*, observed on 20 November 1932, 'almost all the meetings of women's organisations, whether the League of University Women or the Association of Women Citizens, show the same picture. At least three-fourths of the women present are over forty. The generation between twenty and thirty is almost completely lacking, that between thirty and forty is sparsely represented.' Other political organisations, notably the

SPD, were also ageing and losing their appeal to the younger generation. The BDF attempted to remedy the situation by encouraging the forma- tion of a women's youth organisation. Before long, however, this drifted rapidly away from the women's movement towards the Nazi girls' organisation, the Bund deutscher Mädel, with which it began to hold joint meetings. There seemed to be no escape from the fact that the women's movement had lost its appeal to youth by the end of the 1920s.[26] Moreover, as a German activist from the bourgeois women's movement later remarked from her exile in London in 1941,

> the German Women's Movement under the Republic had about it too elaborate an atmosphere of intellectual exclusiveness which, though un- intentional, precluded the broad masses of women from joining it . . . *Kleinbürgerfrauen* – the lower middle-class women – were noticeably scarce. As one of the American jouranlists commented: 'The German Women's Movement has rows of resplendent officers, but very few corporals and no privates . . .' At another of these meetings I had brought with me, in the hope of conversion, the quick-witted sceptical wife of my grocer. And it was all too plain that the speaker, a famous German feminist, was throughout our im- posing lecture speaking far above the head of my unacademic guest who was so urgently waiting to hear just how democracy and the vote for women were to fit into her everyday life of pushing groceries across the counter. The more the lecturer ranged through the high impersonal territories of history, eco- nomics and literature, the more bewildered, bored and angry grew my com- panion.[27]

The crisis into which Germany was descending at the very end of the 1920s quickly began to set the widely differing social and economic groups of which the BDF consisted at odds with one another. The predominantly professional and academic leadership was becoming in- creasingly unable to stop the Federation from falling apart at the seams. The younger generation of white-collar workers were not joining the movement; and as the crisis reached its height the largest constituent groups of the BDF, the Housewives' Unions, decided that their interests would no longer be served by remaining in the Federation.

In the summer of 1932 the smaller of the two Housewives' Unions, the 'rural' association, voted to leave the BDF, giving as its reason the financial impossibility of continuing to contribute to the BDF. Cer- tainly the Depression had made things more difficult; and one effect of the successive constituional amendments passed by the BDF in the Weimar period had also been to make the larger member organisations such as the Housewives' Unions pay higher subscriptions. According to the Constitution of 1924,[28] for example, the most any member union had to pay was 100 Marks a year, plus a maximum of 30 Marks for each of its member associations or branches joining separately. In the Constitution of 1929, however, unions over 128,000 members strong had to pay 900 Marks, plus a maximum of 40 Marks for each member association joining separately. These stipulations affected in the first place the 'urban' Housewives' Union which, with 200,000 members, was by far the largest member association of the BDF. The next largest member association, the Women's Groups of the Trade Union League of Salaried Employees (Frauengruppen des Gewerkschaftsbundes der Angestellten), had 100,492 members in 1931. The 'rural' housewives numbered perhaps 90,000 and formed the third largest association within the BDF. The 1929 Constitution had increased their contribution from 100 Marks to 650 or possibly even 750 Marks a year, even without counting in the individual contributions of the branches which belonged separately to the BDF.

Behind these financial reasons there also lay political motives that are hard to ascertain. There had long been a strong party within the Housewives' Unions in favour of leaving the BDF, and the withdrawal of the 'rural' housewives led the 'urban' Union to vote in favour of leaving the BDF by 587 to 478 votes at its next General Assembly. According to Agnes von Zahn-Harnack, the reasons were differences of opinion on the question of international disarmament, and the housewives' objection to the BDF's insistence that unmarried middle-aged women were entitled to be addressed as 'Frau' instead of 'Fräulein'. Lenore Kühn, a member of the BDF executive committee close to the NSDAP, declared that the real problem was that *Die Frau*, the BDF magazine, was not politically neutral, and was too inclined to favour liberalism against right-wing *völkisch* nationalism or National Socialism.[29] Certainly the Housewives' Unions were closer to the DNVP than to any other political party at this time. Indeed it was even claimed that the Nazis were behind the split. Whatever the cause, however, the BDF was completely surprised by the decision and quite unprepared for the housewives' withdrawal. In the last analysis the BDF leaders found it impossible to explain. Their helplessness and incomprehension at this major crisis in their affairs gave a foretaste of the attitude they were to display when confronted by the far more serious challenge of National Socialism in 1933.[30]

The defection of the Housewives' Unions dealt a very serious blow to the BDF. At a stroke its membership was reduced by nearly 300,000. The inadequacies of the BDF's membership statistics make it difficult to estimate how many women were left in the BDF after this blow, but it is unlikely − allowing for double-counting − that there were more than 500,000 and there might have been as few as 350,000. In other words, the BDF had lost between a third and a half of its entire membership as a result of the housewives' defection. In common with many other organisations the BDF was breaking up because of the growing opposition of economic interests between its constituent groups − an opposition of interests which not even the vague ideology developed by the BDF in the 1920s could hope to reconcile any longer.[31] At the same time as it lost the support of the Housewives' Unions, the BDF was still quite unable to protect the interests of its remaining members − the professional and white-collar workers − from attack in the economic crisis of the early 1930s. When the government proposed the dismissal of married women civil servants as a measure of alleviating male unemployment, neither the BDF nor its few remaining representatives in the Reichstag ventured to oppose the measure.

After 1930 in any case the BDF's room for manoeuvre was so restricted that it would have stood little chance of success even with a stronger organisation, more vigorous tactics and a more coherent ideology. Throughout the 1920s the presence of the Catholic Centre Party in government, even when it was in coalition with the SPD, ensured that feminist pressure would have to be very strong indeed before it had any effect. The likelihood of decisive measures being passed was further reduced by the fragility of most Weimar coalitions. And after 1930 even this small room for political manoeuvre disappeared as the government of the Catholic Centre politician Heinrich Brüning, lacking any positive parliamentary support, carried out its policies by issuing Presidential Decrees which the majority parties in the Reichstag, SPD, Catholic Centre and DDP *(Staatspartei)* were unwilling to overthrow for fear of playing into the hands of the extreme right and left by causing another election. Outside the Reichstag the catastrophic economic situation, with six million unemployed, removed from the BDF and its member unions the power of economic pressure, and led all political parties save the KPD to support the dismissal of married women workers in order to reduce unemployment among heads of families.[32] In these circumstances, to an even greater extent than in the circumstances of 1924-29, the BDF was forced into a wholesale surrender of women's rights by a combination of the inadequacy of its ideology, the ineffectiveness of its tactics and structure, and the sheer overwhelming strength of the political, social and economic pressures which it would have to overcome if it was to defend the interests of the women it represented.[33] By 1932 these pressures had become completely irresistible; and the BDF's capitulation on the issue of married women workers was only a foretaste of even more humiliating surrenders to come.

THE END OF THE WOMEN'S MOVEMENT, 1932-45

At the same time as it was suffering from the economic pressures generated by the Depression, the BDF also had to face a threat posed by the rapid growth of popular support for the Nazi Party, which by the summer of 1932 had won nearly 14 million votes and become the largest party in the Reichstag with 230 seats. The threat was initially twofold. First, the Nazis gained their support in large measure from middle-class, Protestant-based organisations like the BDF. The political parties with which the BDF was most closely associated, the DDP, DVP and DNVP, lost almost all their supporters to the Nazis between 1929 and 1933. Clearly the BDF was subject to the same kind of pressure, since it had proved no more capable than these parties of defending its members' interests in the crisis. Yet the legend that 'it was the women's vote that brought Hitler to triumph'[34] is quite false. The enfranchisement of women probably did little to help the Nazis. Certainly there were over a million more women voters than men voters in the Weimar Republic, but the difference was greatest in the older age groups, where female support for clerical and conservative parties was most overwhelming. This alone was enough to ensure that in the Presidential election of 13 March 1932 Hindenburg had many more women supporters than Hitler, both absolutely and relatively[35] a fact that gives the lie to the claim that Hitler exerted some kind of special fascination over women.[36] It was in the younger age groups, where the numbers of women and men were roughly equal, that Hitler's support was strongest; and it was here too, as we have seen, that the BDF was altogether failing to make an impact. The younger generation joined the Nazi women's organisation rather than the BDF. Moreover pro-portionately speaking, women had voted considerably less often than men in the 1920s; by 1932, however, the difference had disappeared, and most of these new voters supported the Nazis. In this category of Nazi voters, women were probably more numerous than men; but such women were unlikely to have been BDF members, since the BDF laid great stress throughout the 1920s on the duty to vote and in any case mainly relied on the most politically conscious groups of women for its membership. Nevertheless, it seems very likely that many BDF mem-bers did vote Nazi even if they did not actually leave the BDF itself.[37]

That this was so may seem surprising in view of the Nazis' reputation for antifeminism, but in fact the Nazis' policy towards women has long been misunderstood. It has often been dismissed as 'purely re-actionary',[38] a call for women to return to 'the bondage of pure housewifery'.[39] In reality, however, it represented a synthesis of re-actionary and progressive views that is characteristic of fascist ideology. The Nazis certainly regarded feminism as part of a Jewish conspiracy to undermine the German race, and they repeated the pre-war Anti-League's attacks on the women's movement for attempting to wipe out all differences between the sexes — an accusation that was even more absurd in 1932 than it was in 1912.[40] But the Nazis did not urge the total exclusion of women from the labour market, though they did demand their expulsion from political office.[41] Their real concern was with women as bearers of the future 'master race'; and here they urged (and after 1933 implemented) policies of eugenic selection and control that were close to those of the Mutterschutz League in 1908-1912, only with a stronger element of coercion and regimentation. These policies included not only legal abortion for 'unfit elements', but also equal status for unmarried mothers and improved maternity benefits.[42] Such ideas were considered very advanced before 1914. Hitler was careful too to stress that women were not inferior but rather, in their own way, equal. In fact he even availed himself of arguments devised by the women's movement itself, notably its attempt to argue that women were performing the equivalent of military service by risking their lives in childbirth.[43] It was not always easy therefore to describe the Nazis as a purely antifeminist movement.

The BDF's response to the Nazi threat strongly resembled its policy towards the Anti-League in 1912. This time, however, while it tried again to stress the common elements in the two ideologies, it refrained from openly criticising the views of its opponents. On 13 June 1932 the BDF executive committee met to discuss the attacks made by the Nazis on the women's movement. In the chair, the BDF President, Agnes von Zahn-Harnack, insisted that 'we are only interested here in policies towards women. To discuss an individual political party in any other sense would mean that we would be abandoning our party-political neutrality.' Else Uhlig-Beil, who urged the BDF to oppose Nazi anti-feminist policies, also added: 'National Socialism, insofar as it constitutes a system of belief, will be respected by us in the same way as every other party.' Although some members favoured an attempt to influence the NSDAP from within rather than attacking it from without, and all stressed the need to preserve the BDF's neutrality, the majority backed Emma Ender when she said: 'National Socialism has grown big in its fight against Jews and women. It will not give this fight up. Today I am for struggle'.[44]

The BDF was clear that this struggle against the Nazis was purely defensive. The apprehension it felt in taking this step, and its concern for its party-political neutrality, was clearly reflected in the cautious and timid form that the 'struggle' took. Apart from a few carefully worded articles in its periodicals it issued the so-called 'Yellow Leaves' (*Gelbe Blätter*), dry, factual pamphlets which reprinted Nazi and other attacks on the women's movement and added factual corrections. They were dull, and they were not distributed to press or public; they may indeed just have been intended to counter Nazi influence on BDF members. They were discontinued in April 1933.[45] By this time the BDF was being overtaken by events. Hitler had become Chancellor on 30 January and was rapidly bringing the country under total Nazi control by a mixture of pseudo-legality and violence. In an atmosphere of mounting Nazi terror an election was held in March; the BDF evidently thought that such elections still meant something, for it circularised all the parties asking them if they would recognise the political equality of women and put forward female candidates. Since it

added that it would use the answers for the political orientation of its
members, it is not surprising that those parties who replied did so in the
affirmative. Even the NSDAP, although it evaded the second question —
there were no women standing for the party — declared with breath-
taking effrontery that 'of course we unconditionally recognise women
as the completely equal companions of men in political life'.[46]

After the election, which gave the Nazis increased support (but still
no majority), Zahn-Harnack claimed that in circularising copies of the
completed questionnaire to BDF members she had undoubtedly made
it easier for women to vote Nazi.[47] Soon afterwards she reassured a
pro-Nazi member that 'all of us . . . can do nothing but approve of a
nationalist government and stand by it . . .' National Socialism did it
was true contain an element of 'manliness drunk with victory', against
which the BDF had to protect itself. 'Apart from this', she continued
however, 'it (the BDF) will do all it can to help us work together, and
will certainly take up personal contacts with the best women in
National Socialism'.[48] Already however there must have been an element of self-preservation at work in Zahn-Harnack's conduct, for the
Nazis were quickly moving to dissolve all independent associations,
including women's societies.

The first intimation that the BDF gained of the fate that was about
to overtake it was contained in a communication from the Baden
provincial union (Badischer Verband für Frauenbestrebungen). On 27
April 1933 it had received a curt note from Gertrud Scholtz-Klink — a
woman whose ruthless energy and unscrupulousness and total subservience to the Nazi leadership took her before long to the position of
leader of all the Nazi women's organisations in Germany[49] — informing
it that it was dissolved, and that she had assumed the leadership of all
women's activities in Baden. The BDF leadership was taken by surprise;
the process of *Gleichschaltung*, after all, had only just commenced and
had not yet begun to affect the bourgeois liberals.[50] The BDF executive committee drafted a letter to Dr. Frick, the Minister of the
Interior, requesting him to inform them what legal grounds there were
for Frau Scholtz-Klink's action. 'The Baden League for Women's Activities stands apart from all political activities', it wrote; 'in our
opinion, one cannot see in its activities, which confine themselves to
welfare and education, a danger to public safety and order.' The letter
went on to request the Minister to refrain from further intervention in

the member organisations of the BDF, especially as similar develop-ments seemed to be under way in other parts of the country. It was itself undertaking a reconstruction of the BDF which it hoped would make it more effective to fulfil its duties in 'the new Germany'.

The reply given by Lydia Gottschewski, leader of the Nazi Frauen-front, declared that the Baden League had been dissolved 'on the basis of the Law of the Revolution'. She further informed the BDF that its President, Agnes von Zahn-Harnack, had to submit herself and the BDF unconditionally to Adolf Hitler, providing the President with a form to that effect for her signature. The BDF was requested to expel all Jewish members from its committee and elect Nazi women to prominent positions, and to join the Frauenfront with all its constituent asso-ciations except the religious ones.[51] In view of the sensitivity of the religious question and the strength of religious feeling, these con-fessional women's associations were allowed to remain in existence for the time being. The Union of Catholic Women Teachers, for example, was not dissolved until October 1937,[52] the German-evangelical Women's League not at all. Lydia Gottschewski declared that these proposals could not be amended; if they were not agreed to before 16 May, the BDF would be immediately dissolved. The general committee of the BDF met on 15 May. It spent some time in discussing whether or not Section 726 of the Civil Code was applicable – a singularly futile exercise in the circumstances. Gertrud Bäumer favoured joining the Frauenfront, in the belief that the BDF could use its influence within this organisation to ensure the continuation of the 'idea' of the women's movement. However, the meeting came to the conclusion that since the BDF's constituent associations had in many cases already been dissolved, and the BDF constitution forbade it to join another organisa-tion, there was no alternative but to formally dissolve the BDF as well.[53]

The BDF did not dissolve itself as an act of ideological defiance. On the contrary, in its arguments with Gottschewski and other Nazi leaders it repeatedly insisted on its 'national' and its 'social' character, on the patriotic and chauvinistic tradition implied in the word *national,* on its concern for the welfare of 'woman as mother', and on its repudiation of the revolution of 1918 which was 'socialist in character', committed 'grave errors' and inflicted 'severe damage on the activities of voluntary associations'. It stressed as far as possible its affinities with and its approval of National Socialism.[54] The BDF President, Agnes von Zahn-Harnack, declared that 'the new Germany will undoubtedly have especial understanding for a whole series of tasks which the Federation believes to be urgent; in the first place a "biological policy" which supports the German family through economic and eugenic measures.' She pointed to the service the BDF had done the nation by holding meetings in Tilsit, Oppeln, Elster and the Saar to strengthen 'Germandom' in these 'border areas'. She expressed the hope that the NSDAP would introduce a 'Law of Preservation' such as had been advocated by the BDF for some years to 'preserve our people from asocial persons'.

The ambivalent way in which the women's movement approached National Socialism was not confined to the BDF and its leadership. Most of the BDF member associations shared in its attitudes.[55] The Women Teachers' Association for example, which regarded itself as the 'core' of the women's movement, was forced to dissolve on 7 May 1933; the Association's Committee recommended to its member associations that they should all join the new national organisation of men and women teachers being set up by the NSDAP. It declared that:

> The women teachers organised in the General German Women Teachers' Association are working with sincerity and with a genuine sense of responsibility to educate young people for the performance of their duties to the *Volk*. They are consciously placing themselves in the service of the growth of the *Volk (Volkwerdung)* and are working at this task with enthusiastic devotion in a national and social spirit. Teachers and educators, even more than other members of the *Volk*, must be required to consciously grasp the great national aims of the government and to offer themselves in its service.[56]

Nor was this statement merely lip-service designed to ingratiate the women teachers with the new régime, any more than was the case with the women's movement as a whole. The wider aims pursued by the Women Teachers' Association throughout the Weimar years had, like the aims pursued by the BDF, a great deal in common with National Socialist policy. Already in 1921 the Women Teachers had formulated a new programme which declared the 'basic and eternal' aims of their Association as follows:

> The German school must co-operate in the preservation and strengthening of the community of German people *(Volksgemeinschaft)*. It must bring up young people to have a strong character, a moral, religious and consciously German personality ... To the preservation of the national and cultural unity

of the school system as a whole, must be added for girls' schools the necessity of educating young girls to a deeper conception of the nature and value of womanhood, and of women's duties and responsibilities to the family and the *Volk*.[57]

Here too the influence of the idea that the task of the women's movement was to enlarge the 'female sphere of influence in society' is evident.

Clearly, the similarity between these ideas and much of what the NSDAP had to say about women was too striking to be overlooked. When Adolf Hitler declared that 'equal rights for women means that they experience the esteem that they deserve in the areas for which nature has intended them',[58] he could only be applauded by the women's movement. It had after all been saying the same thing for years. Whether as an upholder of aggressive and resentful German nationalism, as an opponent of parliamentarism, as an enthusiastic exponent of racialism determined to introduce a strong 'racial-biological' element into politics and preserve the race from 'inferior' elements, or as the harbinger of a new-found 'national community' transcending the barriers of class, creed and politics, the women's movement could do nothing but extend a warm welcome to Adolf Hitler and the Third Reich.

These ideological similarities were manipulated by the Nazis in the service of totalitarian power-politics. The women's movement may have approved of many of the Nazis' ideas; but it did not welcome its own dissolution. 'A wound has been inflicted upon us', wrote Agnes von Zahn-Harnack after the dissolution of the BDF, 'and we are hurt by it, and many of us, for whom the Federation was a kind of homeland, now feel that we have become rootless.'[59] At least one remnant of the women's movement survived, however, in the magazine *Die Frau,* the official organ of the BDF since 1921. It was considered sufficiently sympathetic to Nazi aims to be allowed to continue, still under Gertrud Bäumer's editorship, almost to the end of the Third Reich.[60] It thus remained the only means of communication between the old supporters of the BDF, and it continued to give them news such as the deaths of old members. For the most part it refrained from commenting on the position of women and discussing laws affecting them under the Third Reich. In effect indeed it withdrew entirely from the political scene. Had it not done so, it would hardly have been able to survive until

1944. Instead, the magazine devoted itself to the propagation of a vague Christian mysticism. In doing so Bäumer believed that she was contributing to the resistance against Nazi values by refusing to propagandise the ideas and policies of the Third Reich, particularly the worship of Hitler and attacks on the Jews, and by putting forward instead an alternative and superior set of beliefs. At the same time Bäumer devoted herself to much the same task in her own right by publishing a number of books and novels on mediaeval history, all breathing a strong spirit of religious enthusiasm.

These activities undoubtedly required courage. According to her own testimony, Bäumer was investigated several times by the Gestapo, and Himmler is said to have actually signed orders for her arrest, only to withdraw them later.[61] As a form of opposition to the regime, however, this did not go very far. It was not even comparable with the activities of those journalists who wrote newspaper articles condemning Attila the Hun, Genghis Khan and Robespierre with the purpose of condemning Hitler. Moreover, as Modris Eksteins has remarked of these newspapers, particularly the *Frankfurter Zeitung,* 'the mere survival of formerly democratic publications paid far greater dividends to the regime than to the cause of opposition and of German liberalism.'[62] Those who were able to gather from the inscrutable pages of *Die Frau* that it was offering a positive alternative to Nazi ideology must have been few indeed. Its stress on Christian mysticism, insofar as it was at all comprehensible, seemed to suggest withdrawal rather than opposition. Yet even *Die Frau* was not always aloof. On a number of occasions the magazine emphasised its positive support for policies of the Third Reich. In July 1933 indeed its readers were being told that the *Gleichschaltung* was far more than a mere formality affecting organisations and constitutions.

> The values of the women's movement (it declared) can (however) only become useful to the State if the leaders of the movement do not remain on one side in a critical and hostile spirit, but find their way on to an 'inner *Gleichschaltung'.*[63]

In the early stages of the war, when Germany was winning, it called for 'a new continental Europe with the Greater German Empire as its centre',[64] and writers such as Elly Heuss-Knapp enthused about the great future that awaited Germany after the conquest of France.[65]

Similarly, the Nazi scheme of compulsory service for women in the war effort was welcomed by Gertrud Bäumer herself as the fulfilment of the old idea of a 'Women's Year of Service' first mooted by the women's movement before the First World War.[66] The 'National Socialist Mother's Service'[67] and the Nazi Laws for the protection of mothers enacted in 1942 – 'epoch-making' according to Bäumer – were given a similar warm welcome.[68] Later on, when Germany began to lose, *Die Frau* played its part in keeping up the morale of the populace in the face of damaging bombing raids by the Allies. In an article entitled 'On the Dynamics of Evil', for example Bäumer attempted to argue that England alone was to blame for total war against civil populations.[69] It is hardly surprising, then, that when paper rationing was introduced in 1940, the Propaganda Ministry allowed *Die Frau* 80 per cent of its peacetime paper quota 'because the magazine', as Bäumer wrote, 'seems important to it'.[70]

The attitudes Bäumer adopted in *Die Frau* and in other publications she issued in the years 1933-45 got her into trouble with the Allies after the war ended. The British censors banned the publication of her books because of their militaristic nature.[71] The Americans attacked her in the *Neue Zeitung,* a newspaper they produced for the German population in the American Zone.[72] Her attempt to revive *Die Frau,* which had ceased publication in 1944, was rebuffed by the Allied authorities because the magazine was deemed to have been 'too political'. Bäumer replied to these and other criticisms with a strong defence of her record in the Third Reich. 'There is nothing in *Die Frau* that I do not agree with', she stated, and she claimed that she had used the magazine as an organ in her 'struggle' against the Nazis, in which she had attempted to 'maintain a positive counterbalance to the influence of National Socialism' by representing the religious values which she felt the Nazis rejected. She had, she maintained, fought against Nazism from the very beginning.[73] She claimed in addition that the campaign against her in 1946-48 was Communist-inspired.

In the growing atmosphere of Cold War the Allies gradually abandoned their campaign against former National Socialists and fellow-travellers. The British withdrew their censorship of Bäumer by the end of 1947, and by 1949 her troubles were over.[74] Once more, Bäumer prepared to take an active role in politics. She rejected, however, the idea that she should join the newly founded Free Democratic Party (Freie

Demokratische Partei or FDP), a liberal group; 'the FDP', she wrote in July 1946, 'is "liberal" here, you know, and conducts the election campaign with all the old platitudes and political tricks.'[75] Instead she participated, along with old followers from the women's movement such as Marie Baum, in the founding of the Christian-Social Union (Christlichsoziale Union, or CSU), a conservative party whose strength lay in South Germany.[76] She was now getting old, however, and her physical and mental health was rapidly declining. She soon retired from active life and died on 25 March 1954.[77]

The support given by Bäumer and her followers to the Third Reich may at first sight seem surprising. It appeared to run contrary to their own interests. Bäumer herself had been suspended from her post in the Ministry of the Interior on 27 February 1933, and was subsequently dismissed. On 7 April 1933 measures were enacted by the government which led to a whole series of similar dismissals, particularly of married women.[78] Even worse than this, from the point of view of the women's movement, many towns used the Nazi seizure of power to re-introduce regular police-controlled brothels.[79] The Nazis also took steps in 1933-35 to limit the access of women to universities and the professions and to ensure that women's education was strongly biased towards 'female' subjects.[80] Although their organisations and societies had been dissolved, however, their past vilified and some at least of their most cherished policies reversed under the Third Reich, the middle-class and professional women who had provided the support for the women's movement in the Weimar Republic were not in fact behaving in a wholly irrational manner in offering their support to the Third Reich. For after the initial turmoil of 1933-35 the government was gradually forced by the demands of the revived and expanding economy to ignore earlier Nazi policies and admit a growing number of women to the professions and also, therefore, to the universities and training institutions. The NSDAP had only seriously opposed female employment during the crisis of unemployment in 1930-34; once this was over, its opposition faded away. By 1938 a position had actually been reached in which women were being officially encouraged to train for a professional career, and the Nazis were claiming to take up the heritage of Helene Lange (perverted, they argued, in the later phase of the women's movement) in pressing for the admission of women to the universities.[81] The result of five years of Nazi rule was that middle-class women at least gained 'a new status of relative if unconventional equality'.[82]

The professional and middle-class women who had supported the women's movement before 1933 thus tolerated the Third Reich because, in the last analysis, it was in their interest to do so. It was not surprising that Gertrud Bäumer defended the Nazis' record in this respect against criticism from abroad.[83] Five years of Nazi rule did more in some ways to help professional women than a decade of feminist pressure in the Weimar Republic. This was because the position and status of women reflected not the totalitarian power politics of the Nazi regime, but the social and economic realities of class struggle and capitalist economy which the Nazi regime was not able to manipulate or banish from the scene. Professional, middle-class women did very well out of the economic and social struggles of the later 1930s.[84] Once again it was economic and social change, and not the doctrines and dogmas of feminists and anti-feminists, that determined the position and status of German women and sealed the fate of German feminism.

The lot of those remaining in Germany under the Third Reich was very different from that of radicals such as Anita Augspurg, Lida Gustava Heymann and Helene Stöcker. Augspurg, Heymann and Stöcker had cut off all contact with the mainstream of the women's movement after 1918, and throughout the Weimar Republic they devoted their energies to the small, radical bourgeois pacifist movement. Their magazines – *Die Frau im Staat* (Augspurg/Heymann) and *Die Neue Generation* (Stöcker) – and their organisations – the Women's League for Peace and Freedom and the Mutterschutz League – combined their old feminist objectives with their more recently developed pacifist ideals. They stood on the far left of the political spectrum, courageously opposed militarism, chauvinism and anti-democratic institutions in the Weimar Republic and declared their sympathy with the Societ Union.[85] Augspurg and Heymann were on holiday in Italy at the time of the Nazi seizure of power, convinced somewhat prematurely after the Nazi losses in the elections of November 1932 that the danger was over. After Hitler became Chancellor, however, they felt unable to return home to Bavaria and arrived in Geneva, the headquarters of the Women's International League for Peace and Freedom, on 7 April 1933.

Aged 75 and 65 respectively, Augspurg and Heymann felt themselves too old and too notorious to be able to return to Germany and take up illegal resistance work. For years they had been known as bitter opponents of everything Hitler stood for. They were certainly not prepared to stand idly by without protesting against Nazi outrages. In Geneva Frida Perlen and Gertrud Baer, who had also left the country, persuaded them that it was dangerous for them to return. Proof that this advice was correct came when they discovered that their possessions including all their papers, both personal and pertaining to their activities in the feminist and pacifist movements, had been confiscated by the Nazis. Supported by friends and sympathisers, they lived in Zürich, established a 'German section in exile' of the Women's International League for Peace and Freedom, and attempted as best they could to combat the Third Reich by using their international connections and by engaging in polemical journalism. In the early years of the Second World War they wrote their memoirs. Augspurg was now too old to complete the task herself, and the bulk of the work was done by Heymann. The book, which remained unpublished until 1972, is a story of continuous and unrelieved failure. Remarkably, it retains much of the energy and optimism that characterized these two women throughout their careers.[86] Augspurg and Heymann lived on for two years after completing the book, but they did not survive to see the final defeat of Hitler. Heymann died on 31 July 1943 and Augspurg followed her on 20 December.[87]

A similar fate befell the other surviving leader of the radical feminist movement, Helene Stöcker. In 1930 and 1932 she had suffered a series of heart attacks, and was already a sick woman when Hitler became Chancellor on 30 January 1933. For a short while she remained in Germany, too ill to travel, but on hearing of the arrest of one after another of her friends and associates in the pacifist movement she decided to leave. On 28 February 1933, immediately on hearing the news of the burning of the Reichstag which heralded a new wave of repressive measures and arrests, she travelled to a clinic in Theresienbad (Czechoslovakia). From there, still chronically ill, she moved via Prague and Vienna to Switzerland. Because of her illness she had left without her personal papers and manuscripts, which were subsequently thrown away as rubbish by order of the Nazi authorities when the attic of her house in Berlin was cleared in the course of air-raid precautions.

Although she was not made welcome by the Swiss, to whom she had referred in 1926 as 'the most backward people on Earth',[88] she stayed there until 1938, continuing her work in the pacifist movement as best she could. As war approached she left for London, then in 1939 travelled to Stockholm, resting there for a short while before going through Russia and Japan to the USA, where she died on 24 February 1943. Stöcker too began to write her memoirs, but this task had to be done almost entirely from memory and what remains is little more than a series of impressionistic sketches.[89] It can have been small comfort to Helene Stöcker that her former rival Adele Schreiber, who had been a member of the SPD during the Weimar years, was also obliged to emigrate in 1933. She spent the war years in London and after 1945 became Vice-President of the International Council of Women; she lived in Zürich until her death in 1957.[90] The removal of feminism from the German political system thus found its final expression in the physical separation of the leading radical feminists from their homeland. They had long been swimming against the political tide; now it carried them away from Germany's shores altogether.

CONCLUSION

Throughout this book, we have seen that the history and development of feminism in Germany cannot be understood unless we pay close attention to the political and social conditions under which it sought to achieve its aims. These conditions were, of course, operative for other movements of social reform and political emancipation. It should not be cause for surprise, then, that the development of other social movements in Germany over this period shows a close resemblance to the development of the feminist movement. German feminists frequently compared their own movement with the movements that grew up at the same time to emancipate two other large groups of the oppressed: youth and workers. While the youth movement did bear some resemblances to the women's movement, however, particularly in its independence from political and confessional ties, its emphasis on self-discipline and its eventual espousal of right-wing doctrines, it was never aimed at political or legislative reform, and this fact alone makes any real comparison between the two movements difficult if not impossible.[91] Far more striking, in fact, are the parallels between the women's movement and the working-class movement, both of which aimed at a combination of legislative reform and social emancipation.

The situation of the women's movement and the workers' movement under Wilhelm II was similar in a number of important respects. Their problems derived from the dilemma which faced all reformers under Wilhelm II: real reforms were impossible without a democratisation of the political structure; the democratisation of the political structure was impossible without a social revolution; the need for a social revolution made the demand for reform self-defeating. There was no clear solution to this dilemma, and it is not surprising that both movements were divided over the policies to be adopted — divided into radical, moderate and right-wing groups. Further parallels came too from the fact that both the SPD and the women's movement before the First World War were politically disfranchised — the one through the Prussian three-class suffrage and the impotence of the Reichstag, the other through the complete absence of political rights. They both formed what Peter Nettl has called 'inheritor parties';[92] they would only come into their own when the Wilhelmine system collapsed. Condemned to ineffectiveness within the existing political system, they tended more and more to look inwards. This in turn was a reason for the continuing internal struggles that beset both organisations; the party or movement became a political activity in itself. Within the SPD the mass basis of the party proved a restraining influence; within the women's movement, and in particular within its radical wing, the absence of a mass basis opened the way to even sharper internal conflicts.

Yet this isolation from the mainstream of politics was not welcomed by all. The growth of revisionism in the SPD can be seen as an attempt to reopen the Party's contacts with the political system through participation. Similar motives were behind the emphasis placed by the moderates within the women's movement on social welfare work. Indeed, not only did the moderates in the SPD believe in gaining power through participation in the political system as a whole; they also advised the SPD women to do the same in relation to the party when they joined it as full members in 1908. 'Should narrow-mindedness and prejudices on the part of men make themselves felt anywhere as a divisive element and lead to intolerance towards women party members' declared the party newspaper *Vorwärts*, 'the best course to take in most cases is to be calm and reticient. Instead of relying on the strength of the party card, women should as far as possible compel recognition of their equality through hard work and co-operation in the party.'[93]

As time went on more and more bourgeois feminists came to adopt similar views with regard to their own relations with the State. The most rapid strides in this development were made during the First World War. Here, many feminists thought, was a real chance to gain power through participation. The Kaiser's statement that he knew no parties, only Germans, fell on ready ears; so powerful was the sense of national unity indeed that even women such as Minna Cauer succumbed:

It is well known (she wrote in 1915)[94] that one party within the women's movement has always laid great stress on the development of the individual personality . . . (but now) the intervention of the State in personal relationships and the regulation of the use of things that had previously been freely at our disposal, have had an excellent educational effect. The necessity of subordinating oneself for the sake of the generality has made it clear to women for the first time that they belong to a greater whole, that a higher and stronger power has the right to exercise compulsion over them . . . This means a step forward from a purely individual egotism, which only allows validity to the individual's own needs, to a higher development as a member of the State . . .

This was a fundamental negation of the basic principles of liberal individualist feminism, just as the revisionist doctrine was a negation of revolutionary socialism; that it came from someone as generally radical as Minna Cauer made it all the more convincing.

In both movements the shift away from the politics of isolationism involved certain structural adjustments by which the party or movement came to duplicate the structure of the Empire on a smaller scale. This was evident in the growth and progress of the regional unions within the BDF and in the division of the Suffrage Union after 1908 into regional unions, of which the Prussian was by far the most influential, just as it was evident in the process by which the big cities, politically isolated in the Wilhelmine system which was dominated by an essentially preindustrial elite, became progressively more under-represented in the SPD. It was evident in the replacement of leaders whose essential role was to keep open the channels of communication between radicals and moderates or revolutionaries and revisionists, and to maintain a balance between the two wings, by leaders who were fundamentally opposed to all forms of radicalism. August Bebel played much the same role within the SPD, mediating between radicals and moderates, as Marie Stritt did within the women's movement; the replacement of these leaders in the last years before the outbreak of the First World War by Friedrich Ebert and Gertrud Bäumer respectively had a similar effect upon the organisations involved. In both cases it signalled the defeat of the radicals and meant that their complete exclusion from the movement was now only a matter of time.[95]

Most of all, however, it was evident in the role of the General Assembly within the two movements. Between 1898 and 1908 the General Assembly of the BDF was frequently referred to as a 'women's parliament' (*Frauenparlament*). It was no surprise that, as Helene Lange observed, the radicals went to the assembly hall early in the morning to reserve the left-hand seats for themselves, and that during this period the debates were accompanied by cries from the radicals of 'oho! ' or 'hear-hear! '[96] The 'slavish imitation of parliamentary forms' which the radicals introduced into the deliberations of the General Assembly[97] carried with it a determination that the Assembly should be the forum for real debates and decisions on vital issues. By 1908, however, it is significant that the shouts were all being uttered by the right wing. It was indeed the last Assembly in which real noises of dissent were to be heard. Under the leadership of Gertrud Bäumer the General Assembly was stage-managed from behind the scenes so as to give the appearance of unanimity. Thus, as we have seen, no discussion or debate was allowed on the official speech on the declining birth-rate at the 1914 General Assembly because the leadership did not wish to give the supporters of the Mutterschutz League the chance to air their opinions.[98] The behind-the-scenes stage-management of the Assembly corresponded to the measures taken by the SPD to ensure that its own party congresses fulfilled the role of inspiring and encouraging party workers and delegates rather than deciding upon great issues of principle. Just as the Reichstag itself was held in check by an irresponsible government, so the General Assemblies and Congresses of these various organisations were effectively muzzled by the executive organs whose policies in theory they were supposed to determine.

If the state of political isolation in which the women's movement and the SPD found themselves under Wilhelm II was already becoming less extreme in the years before 1914, the co-operation of both organisations in the war effort signified their conversion from 'inheritor parties' to pressure-groups. In the case of the women's movement, as we have seen, this was reinforced by the structural changes that took place in the organisation during the 1920s. Nevertheless, neither the SPD nor the women's movement managed to shed itself entirely of the ideology and attitudes of the 'inheritor party' era. The SPD, inured to perpetual opposition under Wilhelm II, was both unwilling and unable to play the role of a governing party in the Weimar Republic with the self-confidence necessary for real success. Its years of political opposition had left it unprepared for the situation of being in government. The women's movement was, as we have seen, even less able than the SPD to come to terms with the new political structure of Germany after 1918. Both groups had been in the process of evolving methods of dealing with, and ultimately perhaps of alleviating the situation in which they found themselves under Wilhelm II: revisionism in the case of the SPD, the ideology formulated by Gertrud Bäumer in the case of the women's movement. As a result, when the Weimar Republic came, neither movement was able to make full use of the opportunities offered it. Despite the tenacious survival of old institutional and social structures in the Weimar Republic, both movements had the chance of real power after 1918; but neither knew how to grasp it. Both were imprisoned in the web of an ideology developed to deal with a situation of political impotence.

These parallels between two movements which, despite their common desire to emancipate very large, politically and socially oppressed sectors of the community, diverged sharply in their social basis and in their political ideology, indicate the enormous influence that the antiquated political and social structure of the *Kaiserreich* exerted on every kind of social movement long after the *Kaiserreich* itself had disappeared. They provide further support for the assertion with which this book began – that the status of women, the nature of their subjection and the extent to which they are able to emancipate themselves, can only be properly understood in the context of the particular social and political structures within which they live. However, the relationship of the liberal women's movement and the Social Democratic Party was a more complex and subtle one than that of a simple parallel development. For if the aims and beliefs of the radical feminists corresponded to those of any political group, it was in fact to those of the Social Democrats. Nearly every point on the feminist programme was also to be found in the list of the Social Democratic Party's demands. Before the First World War the SPD was the only party in German politics to demand universal suffrage for both sexes and equality of opportunity for women in education, employment and the professions. It was the only party in German politics that gave any countenance at all to ideas of sexual freedom and their practical concomitants of legalised abortion, freely available contraceptives and legal equality for 'free marriages', unmarried mothers and illegitimate children.[99] In the debates on the Civil Code in 1895-96 it was the only party to argue consistently for full equality to be granted to women within marriage and the family.[100] Throughout the period, it was untiring in its exposure of the evils of State-regulated prostitution.[101] Its leader, August Bebel, was the author of a best-selling book on the emancipation of women.[102] It had a large and well-organised women's movement of its own.[103] The fact that it supported many if not most of the reforms demanded by the radical feminists, meant that the feminists were often regarded as being politically closer to Social Democracy than to liberalism. Many of the measures urged by the SPD and the radical feminists had political implications far beyond their immediate area of application. To demand universal suffrage for men and women in all elections was to challenge the three-tier property franchise in Prussia, which was one of the main props of the régime of Wilhelm II. To attack the State regulation of prostitution was to challenge the police, another principal support of the Wilhelmine system, the instrument through which the SPD was kept under a strict control and constantly reminded of its exclusion from political and social respectability. When the feminists went beyond this to attack the moral and political practices of the ruling class itself, they were in effect aligning themselves with the SPD's demands for a fundamental revolution in the social structure of the political system. The liberal parties, fearful for their own position in view of the growing strength of the SPD, were not prepared to participate in an attack on the political and social status quo.

The German feminists were thus left with the fact that their only support lay in the Social Democrats. No doubt the close proximity of their demands accounts to some degree for the fact that feminists sometimes employed a rhetoric tinged with Marxism when they launched their attacks on the rulers of the country. This was particularly true of feminists active in the Abolitionist movement, who often protested that while poor prostitutes were frequently subjected to gross indignities at the hands of the police 'the men of the upper 10,000 who patronise them', as Lida Gustava Heymann said, were not: 'the police do not ask themselves whether the upper 10,000 engage in prostitution.'[104] In 1906 the periodical *Der Abolitionist* went beyond the usual Abolitionist condemnation of prostitution as primarily a result of the male domination of society to argue, in terms redolent of Social Democratic rhetoric, that:

> The Regulation of Prostitution is symptomatic of the fact that our public life rests on a false system, the system of the double standard which creates a class of pariahs from the ranks of the economically dependent female sex, and makes it alone pay the debts of the whole community, in order to allow the ruling male sex the irresponsible and unbridled satisfaction of its sexual instincts. Regulation is therefore only possible in a class state, in which the upper classes and the propertied classes are in a position to exert capitalist exploitation of the lower classes and the propertyless classes, and in which, moreover, the female sex is deprived of all public rights.[105]

In the early propaganda of the Suffrage Union attacks on the upper classes were quite explicit. Anita Augspurg declared at a suffragist meeting in Hamburg in 1903 that 'the agrarians and heavy industrialists exploit the people'. They were 'enriching themselves at the cost of the people' through heavy duties on foodstuffs and − a typical radical feminist point − 'sugar premium concessions to distillery owners'.[106] The suffragists, indeed, campaigned actively against proposals to increase import duties in 1903, and their predecessors in the Frauenwohl did the same in 1901. Although they made no positive statements in favour of free trade, there can be little doubt that their inclinations were as much in its favour as they were against State intervention in society. As far as education was concerned, Augspurg also wished 'not only to reform schools, but to revolutionise them, so that the individuality of the child is no longer destroyed by the levelling process of examinations and other tasks the schoolchildren are set.'[107]

Yet the views of the radical feminists were in reality far removed from those of the Social Democrats. Liberal individualism, not Marxian socialism, was their creed.[108] The ultimate aim of the radical feminists was to secure the self-determination of the individual woman. Self-help and self-discipline were seen as the way to a perfect society and the full realisation of the female personality. In order to achieve this, it was essential to give women the same rights as men; a career open to the talents had to be open to the talents of women as well as men; a nation governed by elected institutions had to ensure that women as well as men had the right to vote; a society that rejected State control and State paternalism had to remove the State from interference in the private morality of women as well as the public affairs of men. Women had to have the right of free disposition over themselves, their bodies and their personal development. Only in this way could social justice be achieved. This was an ideology that was well-suited to the frontiers of America and Australasia or the liberal society of Victorian England, where feminism gained some of its most striking successes, but it was ill-equipped to survive in the hostile atmosphere of Wilhelmine Germany. Liberal individualism had never taken root in Germany; the tradition of State intervention was generally accepted, and the fragmented collection of small and declining political parties that constituted the remains of German liberalism by the turn of the century was no exception to this rule. Only Eugen Richter, the leader of the Liberal People's Party, had any claim to represent the legacy of classical liberalism, and long before his death in 1906 he was generally felt to have lost touch with the political views of the mass of his followers. The feminists looked to his party for support and worked for it at election-time, but it never reciprocated this goodwill. Nor did the Progressive Party, founded in 1910, accept the feminists' demands. The very nature of feminist ideology was alien to the dominant spirit of German liberalism; the necessary objects of the feminists' attack were subject to political assault only from the Social Democrats. Caught between a liberalism that was too conservative to accommodate their programme, and a socialism that could only treat their policies as half-hearted bourgeois reformism, the radical feminists were suspended for the brief period of their existence in a political vacuum where the different pressures of middle-class liberalism and working-class socialism, acting on them from opposing sides, were bound in the end to tear them apart. The radical feminists represented, often in person, a minority tradition within German liberalism, a tradition of liberal individualism, a tradition that — tenuous though it was — can be traced from the democrats of 1848 to the pacifists of the Weimar Republic. Both the leaders of the radical feminist movement — women such as Anita Augspurg, Lida Gustava Heymann and Helene Stöcker — and the movement's closest and most enthusiastic supporters — men such as Hellmuth von Gerlach and Rudolf Breitscheid — belonged to this tradition. It was never dominant either in German liberalism or in German feminism; and indeed perhaps the most striking thing about the radical feminists is the nearness of their failure to capture the women's movement as a whole in the early 1900s; they came, after all, surprisingly close to success.

The truth is, however, that whether we regard the emergence and advance of radical feminism in Germany around the turn of the century as evidence of a revival of liberal and democratic politics, as part of a realignment of the centre in response to the regrouping of the right in the *Sammlungspolitik,* as part of the educated middle class's reaction to the new social problems posed by the transition to a mature industrial economy, or as an inevitable consequence of the changing economic status and widening professional and educational opportunities of the middle-class woman, the rise of radical feminism was less significant in the long run than its downfall. Whatever the situation in 1900, ten years later the German women's movement was in full retreat from the conventional doctrines of bourgeois feminism. It was in these last few years before the outbreak of the First World War that the decisive developments occurred; it was then that *völkisch* and proto-fascist ideas became institutionalized within the framework of the feminist movement, fatally weakening its commitment to liberal values.

Many historians have argued that this was indeed the crucial period in which the ground was laid for the triumph of Nazism in the 1930s.[109] While this is in general confirmed by the evidence reviewed in the present work, it is perhaps necessary however to add a few qualifications. In the first place, as we have seen, many of the influences which reinforced the trend to the Right within the BDF were operative in the case of the women's movement alone. The removal of legal barriers to female activity in politics in 1908, in particular, had an incalculable effect on the defeat of radical feminism. The mass of middle-class women were probably conservative all along; and the rightward drift of the women's movement was to some extent indeed a kind of historical optical illusion, as it were: as soon as the BDF ceased to be an unrepresentative minority movement and began to gain a measure of mass support, it ceased to be truly feminist. In addition, though it is possible to see in the programme of the pre-war BDF many protofascist ideas, it is not possible to see them all; outright opposition to women engaging in politics, for example, was clearly not a feature of pre-1914 BDF policy. Moreover, in the case of some of these ideas – notably Social Darwinism – it is often hard to disentangle the genuinely liberal from the potentially totalitarian. Also, even if the German women's movement had largely succumbed to the protofascist ideas by 1914, this did not make it inevitable that it would support the advent of genuine fascism in 1930-33. As we saw in Chapter 8, other developments – reaction to the 'disorder' of the 1918 Revolution, structural changes in the 1920s, weaknesses engendered by the Depression, and so on – had to intervene before the potentialities inherent in the situation of 1914 could be made actual. Finally, it should be borne in mind that feminist movements in other countries were also turning to the right at much the same time, and that elsewhere too there was a general retreat from liberalism in the 1920s. These developments, then, were not confined to Germany, even if the form they took there was rather different from – and ultimately much more violent and destructive than – the form they took in other countries.

Perhaps the conclusion to be drawn from all this is basically a negative one: that in investigating the longer term origins of the Nazi seizure of power, we need now to adopt a rather different approach from the essentially political and organisational one represented by the present work.[110] The evidence presented here will, of course, it is to be hoped, illuminate a number of aspects of the Nazi seizure of power that urgently need analysing; among them, the overlap between the ideas of the Nazis and those of other groups apparently opposed to them, the complex issue of antifeminism, the political and social timidity of the *Bildungsbürgertum,* the extent of continuity from the late 19th century to the 1930s, the conservative nature of German liberalism, above all, perhaps, the attitudes of the neglected larger half of the German population, without a full consideration of whom no work on the major trends in recent German history can be considered adequate.

Yet there are risks in generalizing about an entire class – still more about an entire sex – from the organisations which claimed to represent it, for in some ways at least (even if only in their willingness to take action) the members of political organizations and social movements are atypical of the larger social groups from which they come.[111] There are also risks in confining our attention to Germany alone. What we need now are more studies of the grass roots of German social and political opinion, a more genuinely social history centred on the German people rather than on their organisational and political life. We urgently need, too, to place German history more firmly in a comparative and international context, in order to bring out more clearly the peculiarities which distinguished Germany from other contemporary industrialised countries.[112] That such peculiarities did indeed exist however is quite beyond doubt; they affected every sector of German life, including that of German women, who, in the Western half of the country at least, had to wait until the passage of the Equal Rights Act (leichberechtigungsgesetz) in 1956 before they could enjoy many of the basic rights possessed by women in the bourgeois democracies since before the First World War.

NOTES

1. For the programme of 1907, see Chapter 5, above. The Revolution pushed the BDF further to the right once more.

2. The following account of the structure and ideology of the BDF in the 1920s is based on *JB* 1919, 1920, 1921, 1927, 1928 and 1932. For a general survey of the efforts of German liberalism to adjust to the new conditions of the Weimar Republic, see Lothar Albertin, *Liberalismus und Demokratie an Anfang der Weimarer Republik. Eine vergleichende Analyse der Deutschen Demokratischen Partei und der Deutschen Volkspartei* (Beiträge zur Geschichte des Parlamentarismus und der politischen Parteien, Bd. 45, Düsseldorf, 1972).

3. *JB 1921,* 9-10.

4. Jill R. Stephenson, *Women in German Society 1930-40* (unpublished Ph.D. thesis, Edinburgh, 1974), 22-23. Cf. Remme, op. cit.

5. (My underlining).

6. *JB 1919, 1920,* etc., 'Programm'. For the way in which this ideology underlay even such apparently feminist demands as full access for women to universities and the professions, see Michael H. Kater, 'Krisis des Frauenstudiums in der Weimarer Republik', *Vierteljahrschrift für Sozial- und Wirtschaftsgeschichte* 59/2, 1972, esp. 226-8, 244.

7. See Kurt Sontheimer, *Antidemokratisches Denken in der Weimarer Republik. Die politischen Ideen des deutschen Nationalismus zwischen 1918 und 1933* (4th ed., Munich, 1962), 308-317.

8. *JB 1920,* Gertrud Bäumer, 'Die Einheit der Nation und die Einheit der Frau' 58 ff.

9. ABDF 8/1, 2, 3; *Reichsgesetz zur Bekämpfung der Geschlechtskrankheiten ... mit Einleitung und Erläuterungen von Dr. jur. Waldemar Adler* (Munich, 1929).

10. Cf. the similar situation of the Catholic Centre Party: Rudolf Morsey, *Die Deutsche Zentrumspartei 1917-23* (Düsseldorf, 1966). The Party also opposed divorce reform, equal status for illegitimate children and coeducation.

11. Agnes von Zahn-Harnack, op. cit., 55-7.

12. For Augspurg and Heymann, see their journal, *Die Frau im Staat,* and their memoirs (*Erlebtes-Erschautes,* op. cit.). For Stöcker, brief mentions in Heinz Habedank, *Der Feind steht rechts. Bürgerliche Linke im Kampf gegen den deutschen Militarismus* (Berlin, 1965). I hope to analyse her career in greater detail elsewhere. Minna Cauer did not support pacifist feminism, and moved further to the right towards the end of her life. She died on 3 August 1922, aged 81 (Else Lüders, *Minna Cauer. Leben und Werk ...* op. cit., 272-300).

13. The Imperial Union for Women's Suffrage dissolved itself on 5 October 1919 (*SB* 8/1, April 1919, 4, 10-12; 8/4-5, July/Aug. 1919, 39-40; 8/7 Oct./Nov. 1919, 57-60, 61-2, 66). The *Zeitschrift für Frauenstimmrecht,* organ of the German Women's Suffrage League, ceased to appear after 1 Jan. 1919 and the last issue of *Die Frauenbewegung,* the major radical journal, was published on 15 December 1919.

14. The figure given in *JB* 1932 is 46,202. This covers roughly half the member associations. See Regine Frankenfeld, *Der Deutsche Landfrauenverband e. V. Fakten und Daten* (Hamburg, 1969).

15. *Kaufmännischer Verband für weibliche Angestellte.* The rapid expansion in numbers of the female salaried clerks since the turn of the century was a major social development; it urgently needs detailed investigation by historians.

16. See Krüger, op. cit.

17. Biographical details in ABDF 2/I/2, 3, 4.

18. Karl Dietrich Bracher, *Die Auflösung der Weimarer Republik. Eine Studie zum Problem des Machtverfalls in der Demokratie* (Schriften des Instituts für politische Wissenschaft, Bd. 4, 4th ed., Villingen, 1964), 335-358. Membership in the party formed by the merger (*Staatspartei*) was refused to members of the German Peace Society. See also Erich Matthias and Rudolf Morsey, 'Die Deutsche Staatspartei', in Matthias/Morsey (eds.), *Das Ende der Parteien 1933* (Bonn, 1960), 31-72.

19. ABDF 2/I/2, 3, 4. Marie Stritt died in 1928 at the age of 72.

20. *JB 1932.*

21. Gabrielle Bremme, *Die politische Rolle der Frau in Deutschland* (Göttingen, 1953), and Hans Berger, *Die Frau in der politischen Entscheidung* (Stuttgart, 1933), for female voting patterns in the Weimar Republic.

22. *JB 1927*, 48-50.

23. Michael H. Kater, art. cit., for the failure of women's position to improve in education; for the professions, cf. Renate Bridenthal, 'Beyond *Kinder, Küche, Kirche:* Weimar Women at Work', *Central European History,* June 1973.

24. Agnes von Zahn-Harnack, 'Schlussbericht über die Arbeit des Bundes Deutscher Frauenverene', *DF* 40/9, 554.

25. ABDF 5/I/2: Kassenberichte 1897-1932.

26. Clifford Kirkpatrick, *Nazi Germany: Its Women and Family Life* (New York, 1938), 36. See also the complaints in the report of the BDF's activities in *JB 1932.* Cf. Richard N. Hunt, *German Social Democracy 1918-1933* (London, 1964).

27. Katherine Thomas, *Women in Nazi Germany* (London, 1943), 20.

28. i.e. the first stipulation on subscriptions after the great inflation of 1923 had made previous rulings meaningless.

29. ABDF 16/II/5: Sitzung des engeren Vorstandes, 13/16 June 1932.

30. Cf. Kirkpatrick, op. cit; ABDF 16/II/5: Sitzung des engeren Vorstandes, 13/16 June, 1932.

31. A similar process of disintegration occurred in other middle-class organisations at the same time. See for example Larry Eugene Jones, 'Between the Fronts: the German-national Union of Commercial Employees (DHV) from 1928 to 1933' (Internationale Konferenz: 'Industrielles System und politische Entwicklung in der Weimarer Republik', June 1973, Bochum, typescript). I am grateful to Stephen Hickinbotham for the loan of the typescript. See also Larry Eugene Jones, 'The "Dying Middle": Weimar Germany and the Fragmentation of Bourgeois Politics', *Central European History* V (1), 1972.

32. For the BDF's decision not to oppose these measures, see ABDF 16/II/5: Sitzung des engeren Vorstandes, 21 Jan. 1932. For the general background, see Jill Stephenson, 'Women in German Society 1930-1940' (unpublished Ph.D. thesis, Edinburgh, 1974), and Jill R. McIntyre, 'Women and the Professions in Germany, 1930-1946', in *German Democracy and the Triumph of Hitler* (ed. Anthony Nicholls and Erich Matthias, St. Antony's Publications No. 3, London 1971), 175-80.

33. For the persistence of antifeminism among civil servants, university teachers, students, the Press and women themselves during the Weimar Republic, see Michael H. Kater, art. cit., 219-26.

34. Hermann Rauschning, *Hitler Speaks. A Series of Political Conversations with Adolf Hitler on His Real Aims* (London, 1939), 259.

35. K. D. Bracher, *Die Auflösung der Weimarer Republik* (op. cit.), 476, n.132.

36. J. C. Fest, *The Face of the Third Reich* (London, 1972), 400-1.

37. For a detailed discussion, see Bremme, op. cit., and Hans Berger, op. cit.

38. Richard Grunberger, *A Social History of the Third Reich* (London, 1974), 322.

39. R. Bridenthal, 'Beyond *Kinder, Küche, Kirche:* Weimar Women at Work', *Central European History,* June 1973, 148-166.

40. Kirkpatrick, op. cit., 110. See also George L. Mosse (ed.), *Nazi Culture* (New York, 1966), 298-319.

41. David Schoenbaum, *Hitler's Social Revolution. Class and Status in Nazi Germany 1933-39* (London 1967), 189-90.

42. Stephenson, op. cit., Ch. 2.

43. Grunberger, op. cit., 323.

44. ABDF 16/II/5, 13 June 1932.

45. ABDF 1/A/2: Gelbe Blätter.

46. ABDF 1/A/2: BDF circular, 13 Feb. 1933.

47. ABDF 1/A/2 Mitteilung an die dem Bund Deutscher Frauenvereine angeschlossenen Verbände, 29 Mar. 1933, Anlage 1.

48. ABDF 16/II/5: Zahn-Harnack to Kühn, n.d. (late April 1933).

49. See Stephenson, op. cit., 350-66, for an account of the ousting of Gottschewski and the installation of Scholtz-Klink as *Reichsfrauenführerin.*

50. Karl Dietrich Bracher, Wolfgang Sauer, Gerhard Schulz, *Die national-sozialistische Machtergreifung. Studien zur Errichtung des totalitären Herrschaftssystems in Deutschland 1933/34* (Schriften des Instituts für politische Wissenschaft, Bd. 14, 2nd ed., Köln/Oplden 1962), 169-219.

51. This step was taken by many conservative associations no longer affiliated to the BDF, including the German-evangelical Women's League and the two Housewives' Unions (Kirkpatrick, op. cit., 57).

52. Jill McIntyre, loc. cit., 106, n.2.

53. ABDF 1/A/2: 'Vertraulich! Gesamtvorstandssitzung des Bundes Deutscher Frauenvereine, den 15. Mai 1933'; Zahn-Harnack to Gottschewski, 14 May 1933.

54. ABDF 1/A/2: 'Vertraulich! Gesamtvorstandssitzung des Bundes Deutscher Frauenvereine, den 15. Mai 1933'; ibid. Zahn-Harnack to Gottschewski, 14 May 1933; ibid.; Mitteilung an die dem Bund Deutscher Frauenvereine angeschlossenen Verbände, Anlage 1, 29 April 1933..

55. For material on the *Gleichschaltung* of the *Rechtsschutzvereine,* see BA Koblenz, NL Camilla Jellinek, Pak. 2, Vol. 4, NS-Frauenschaft (Baden) to Frau Endemann, 12 May 1933, et.seq.. For other women's organisations, see also Stephenson, op. cit. 33-7.

56. In doing this they were following Bäumer's advice. Cf. Bäumer to Beckmann, 13 April 1933, in *Des Lebens Wie der Liebe Band. Briefe von Gertrud Bäumer,* (ed. Emmy Beckmann, Tübingen, 1956), 50.

57. Emmy Beckmann, 'Die Auflösung des Allgemeinen Deutschen Lehrerinnenvereins', *DF* 40/9, June 1933, 547-49.

58. Quoted in Schoenbaum, op. cit., 189-90.

59. Agnes von Zahn-Harnack, 'Schlussbericht über die Arbeit des Bundes Deutscher Frauenvereine', *DF,* 40/9, June 1933, 551. Gertrud Bäumer, however, thought that the dissolution signified the fact that 'a new, spiritually different

phase of the women's movement is coming'. 'I want', she added, 'to join in it, as far as is possible for one of my generation.' (Bäumer to Beckmann, 13 April 1933, in Beckmann (ed.), op. cit., 50).

60. Cf. Bäumer's description of Gertrud Baumgart's Nazi apologia for the work of the old BDF – 'strong propaganda for *Die Frau,* headed with a swastika', in Beckmann (ed.), op. cit., 34, Bäumer to Beckmann, 30 June 1935. At this stage, Bäumer seems to have thought that the Nazi women's organisation would simply be a new version of the old BDF, a striking indication of her perception of the ideological similarities between the two movements (see also Beckmann (ed.), op. cit., 50-51, 68).

61. Ibid., 339-43; Gertrud Bäumer, 'In Eigener Sache' (Auszug).

62. Modris Eksteins, 'The *Frankfurter Zeitung:* Mirror of Weimar Democracy', *Journal of Contemporary History,* 6/4, 1971, 9, n.6.

63. Ingeborg Lorentzen, 'Gleichschaltung', *DF,* 40/10, July 1933, 629.

64. Else Ulich-Beil, 'Die Zerstörung Europas Durch Versailles', *DF* 48/2, Nov. 1940, 35-40.

65. Elly Heuss-Knapp, 'Rheinüberwärts', *DF,* 48/2, Nov. 1940, 45-46.

66. Gertrud Bäumer, in *DF,* 48/1, Oct. 1940.

67. By Elisabeth Lippsert, in *DF,* 48/No. 1, Oct. 1940, 15.

68. Gertrud Bäumer, in *DF,* 50/1/2, Oct./Nov. 1942.

69. Gertrud Bäumer, 'Zur Dynamik des Bösen', *DF,* 51/7-9, April-June 1944, 73-78.

70. Beckmann (ed.), op. cit., 136: Bäumer to Beckmann, 18 June 1940.

71. '. . . Ihre besondere Wertschätzung soldatischer Lebenshaltung und -gesinnung . . .' (quoted in H. Exenberger, 'Das Beispiel Gertrud Bäumer', *Die Weltbühne,* 2/19, Oct. 1947, 843-5).

72. *Die Neue Zeitung,* 4 March 1948 (copy in ABDF files).

73. Gertrud Bäumer, 'In Eigener Sache (Auszug)', in Beckmann (ed.), op. cit., 339-343. Cf. her statement to Helene König that National Socialism was 'correct in essence' but involved 'an impossibly improper way of dealing with people' (*Unanständigkeit der Menschenbehandlung*); ibid., 63, Bäumer to König, July 1933.

75. Ibid., 321: Bäumer to Marie Baum, 19 July 1946.

76. Cf. I. Geiss und V. Ulrich (eds.), *Woher kommt die CDU?* (Reinbek bei Hamburg, 1971).

77. Hans Georg Wieck, *Christliche und Freie Demokraten in Hessen, Rheinland-Pfalz und Württemberg, 1945/46* (Beiträge zur Geschichte des Parlamentarismus und der politischen Parteien, Bd. 10, Düsseldorf, 1955), 128, 133.

78. Jill McIntyre, loc. cit.

79. ABDF, 'I.A. Föderation (separate, not indexed): Mitteilungen der Arbeitsgemeinschaft für Volksgesundung, e.V., No. 16, 6 July 1934, No. 23, 30 Sept. 1934, No. 2, 20 Jan. 1937, No. 10, 5 April 1937, No. 17, 14 April 1937.

80. Stephenson, op. cit., Ch. 4-5.

81. McIntyre, loc. cit., 212, Stephenson, op. cit., 231.

82. Schoenbaum, op. cit., 201.

83. Gertrud Bäumer, 'Zur Berufsgeschichte der deutschen Akademikerin',

DF, June 1939, 453.

84. For the miserable position of working-class women, on the other hand, cf. Grunberger, op. cit., 244.

85. Heinz Habedank, *Der Feind Steht Rechts. Bürgerliche Linke im Kampf gegen den deutschen Militarismus* (East Berlin, 1965). See also Stephenson, op. cit., for documentation of their continued adherence to feminist ideals of sexual, economic, social and political freedom (esp. 22-26). The Nazis regarded the Mutterschutz League as a KPD front organisation. (ibid., 87).

86. Heymann/Augspurg, *Erlebtes-Erschautes,* 268-310.

87. 'Lida Gustava Heymann', *Die Frau in Leben und Arbeit,* Sept. 1943, Vol. 15, No. 9, 5; 'Anita Augspurg zum Gedächtnis', ibid., Vol. 16, No. 2, Feb. 1944, 8; 'Lida Gustava Heymann', *Schweizerisches Frauenblatt,* 1943; 'Dr. Anita Augspurg', ibid.; Gertrud Baer, 'Eine Kämpferin fur Frieden und Freiheit', *National Zeitung* (Basel) March 1968; Gertrud Baer, 'Anita Augspurg zum Gedenken ihres 100. Geburtstages', *Schweizerisches Frauenblatt,* 27 Sept. 1957; 'Lida Gustava Heymann', *National Zeitung* (Basel), No. 361, 8 August 1943; Elisabeth Rotten, 'Eine Kämpferin für den Weltfrieden', *Die Friedenswarte,* Vol. 43, No. 6, 1943, 328-330. I am grateful to the Schweizerisches Sozialarchiv, Zürich, for supplying this documentation.

88. SCPC Swarthmore, NL Helene Stöcker, 3: Stöcker to Springer, 3 Sept. 1926.

89. Ibid., 1/2: Selbstbiographie (B), 18, passim.

90. H. A. L. Degener (ed.), *Wer Ist's? Unsere Zeitgenossen* (Leipzig, 1957).

91. Walter Laqueur, *Young Germany* (London, 1962).

92. J. P. Nettl, 'The German Social Democrats as a Political Model', *Past and Present,* 30 (April, 1965), 65-95.

93. StA Hbg, PP, S8897/III: *VW,* 23 Sept. 1908.

94. *FB* 21/8, 29.

95. Previous to this it was the right wing in each case – the revisionist group in the SPD and the German-evangelical Women's League in the BDF – that had been most likely to break away from the parent body. See Dieter Groh, *Negative Integration und revolutionärer Attentismus. Die deutsche Sozialdemokratie am Vorabend des Ersten Weltkrieges* (Berlin/Frankfurt, 1973).

96. ABDF 16/I/1: Generalversammlung 1900.

97. Helene Lange, in *DF* 8/2, Nov. 1900, 65-67.

98. See 196-200 above.

99. Ulrich Linse, 'Arbeiterschaft und Geburtenentwicklung im Deutschen Kaiserreich von 1871', *Archiv für Sozialgeschichte* XII (1972).

100. RT, 9 Leg. Per., 4 Sess., Vol. 4, 25 June 1896, 2916-2938.

101. Cf. Urban, op. cit., passim.

102. August Bebel, *Die Frau und der Sozialismus* (64th ed., East Berlin, 1964).

103. See Werner Thönnessen, *The Emancipation of Women. The Rise and Decline of the Women's Movement in German Social Democracy 1863-1933* (London, 1973); Jacqueline Strain, *Feminism and Political Radicalism in the German Social Democratic Movement 1890-1914* (Ph.D. Diss., University of

California, 1964); Jean Quataert, *The German Socialist Women's Movement 1890-1918: Issues, Internal Conflicts, and the Main Personages* (Ph.D. Diss., University of California, 1974).

104. StA Hbg, PP, SA593/I, 240-241, Versammlungsbericht, 18 April 1902.

105. *Der Abolitionist*, 5/2, 1 Feb. 1906, 13.

106. StA Hbg, PP, S9001/1: *HE,* 12 May 1903.

107. StA Hbg, PP, S5466/I: *HE,* 12 May 1911.

108. Cf. the feminists' attempts to give working women the means of self-improvement: StA Hbg, Senat, Cl. VIII, Lit. Rf, Nr. 344, Vol. 1; HStA Stuttgart, E151 c II Nr. 238.

109. Mosse, *Crisis of German Ideology* (op. cit.), Pulzer, op. cit., Stern, op. cit., etc.

110. When I began research for this book in 1970, studies of this sort were thin on the ground. In the intervening five years, however, a number of excellent organisational histories have appeared in print. Important studies, of relevance to the present book but published too late to be taken into consideration in its preparation, are Roger Chickering, *Imperial Germany and a World Without War: The Peace Movement and German Society, 1892-1914* (Princeton, 1975), and Karl Holl, Gunther List (eds), *Liberalismus und imperlialistischen Staat. Der Imperialismus als Problem liberaler Parteien in Deutschland 1890-1914* (Göttingen, 1975). More general, but also flawed: Walter Struve, *Elites against Democracy: Leadership Ideals in Bourgeois Political Thought in Germany 1890-1933* (New York, 1975).

111. I hope in a forthcoming work to discuss this atypicality on the basis of an analysis of the collective biography of the leadership of the German women's movement.

112. For an excellent discussion of the problems of research into the long-term origins of the Nazi seizure of power, see 'The Coming of the Nazis', *Times Literary Supplement,* No. 3752, 1 Feb. 1974, 93-96.

BIBLIOGRAPHY

This Bibliography lists only materials used in the preparation of the present work. It is not intended to be a comprehensive guide to the sources for the history of German feminism. Readers who seek a critical survey should consult my article 'Feminism and Female Emancipation in Germany 1871-1975: Sources, Methods and Problems of Research' (forthcoming). A comprehensive list of the printed sources is to be found in the standard bibliography compiled by Agnes von Zahn-Harnack and Hans Sveistrup and listed below.

I. UNPUBLISHED SOURCES

A. Deutsches Zentralarchiv Potsdam

1. *Reichskanzlei*

2266   Frauenbewegung

2. *Reichsamt des Innern*

12295-6   Die pazifistische Bewegung

3. *Fortschrittliche Volkspartei*

20	Parteitag Mannheim 1912
21	Parteitag Eisenach 1914
26	Preussentag 1917
26/1	Preussentag 1917
36/1	Geschäftsführender Ausschuss: Protokolle 1910-18
37	Zentralausschuss: Protokolle 1910-17
49	Frauenrechtskommission
50	Gemeindewahlrechtskommission
54	Liberale Frauenpartei

4. *Nachlässe*

Friedrich Naumann   59   Wahlverein der Liberalen

B. Bundesarchiv Koblenz

1. *Nachlässe*

Bauer	Nr 1c, 1d	Kritik an der Frauenbewegung (MSS.)
Gothein	Nr 14	Erinnerungen (MS.)
C. Jellinek	Pak. 1-2	Briefe und Bücher
Koch-Weser	Nr 36	Tagebuch
Schreiber	Pak. 1	Mutterschutzbund: Briefe B268-B367, Berichte etc.
	Pak. 2	Mutterschutzbund: Briefe B1-B267, Satzungen, Gerichtsverhandlungen
	Pak. 3	Mutterschutzbund: Protokolle P1-P183, Berichte, Gründung des Bundes
	Pak. 4	Mutterschutzbund: Briefe, Artikel, Gerichtsverhandlungen 1914
	Pak. 5	Mutterschutzbund: Briefe, Artikel
	Pak. 16	Briefe bis 1902
	Pak. 25	Zeitungsausschnitte 1897-1912

2. *Kleine Erwerbungen*

Nr 258-1	Briefe von Gertrud Bäumer an Marianne Weber

3. *Zeitgeschichtliche Sammlung*

ZSg 1-165/1	Deutscher Verband für Frauenstimmrecht
ZSg 1-228/1, 2, 3, 6	Deutschnationaler Handlungsgehilfenverband

C. Bayerisches Hauptstaatsarchiv München

1. *Allgemeines Staatsarchiv*

M Inn 66132	Friedensbewegung
MK 11116	Frauenstudium-Universitäten

2. *Geheimes Staatsarchiv*

Gesandschaft Bern, Kriegsakten 8 Rückreise von Frauen aus Frankreich
MA 92765 Bayerischer Verein für Frauenstimmrecht

D. Württembergisches Hauptstaatsarchiv Stuttgart/Ludwigsburg

1. *Hauptstaatsarchiv Stuttgart*

E151 cII Nr 238 Konferenzen zur Förderung der Arbeiterinneninteressen
Nachlass Haussmann   Nr 30   Verfassungsausschuss 1917
                       Nr 52   Friedensvermittlungsversuche 1914-18

2. *Heeresarchiv Stuttgart*

Kriegsministerium M1/4 Nr 1727 Zivilbevölkerung-Aufklärung

Stellvertretende Generalkommando
               XIII. Armeekorps Bund 93 Nr 54   Vereine und Versammlungen
                                 Bund 99   Bureau für Sozialpolitik

3. *Staatsarchiv Ludwigsburg*

F201 Bü 653   Deutsche Friedensgesellschaft

E. Niedersächsisches Hauptstaatsarchiv Hannover

Hann. 122a Nr 348   Wohltätigkeit anlässlich des Krieges
            Nr 365   Stimmung der Zivilbevölkerung während des Krieges

F. Staatsarchiv Hamburg

1. *Sensatsakten*

Cl. I.Lit. T.   Nr. 7, Vol. 6,   Fasc. 9, Inv. 6a Prostitution-Beschwerde der L.
                                                      Heymann
Cl. VII. Lit. Lb. Nr. 28c, Vol. 14, Fasc 7   Beschwerde der L. Heymann
                            Fasc 9   Reichsvereinsgesetz von 1908
Cl. VII. Lit. Rf. Nr. 29, Vol. 41   Bund Deutscher Frauenvereine
                  Nr. 166, Vol. 35   International Freidenskonfer-
                                                     enz Haag 1899
                  Nr. 344, Vol. 1   Verband für Handwerksmäss-
                                                     ige und fachgewerbliche Aus-
                                                     bildung der Frau

2. *Senat-Kriegsakten*

AII p 47 Nr. 5815 Überwachung weltbrüderlicher Friedensbestrebungen

3. Politische Polizei

S3502 Bd. I-II	Wohltätige Frauenvereine zu Hamburg
S4930	Deutsche Friedensgesellschaft
S5466 Bd. I-III	Verein 'Frauenwohl'
S5808 Bd. I-II	Allgemeiner Deutscher Frauenverein, Ortsgruppe Hamburg
S7484	Internationale Frauenkongresse 1899-1918
S8004	Lida Gustava Heymann
S8326	Deutsch-evangelischer Frauenbund
S8897 Bd. I-V	Sozialdemokratische Frauenbewegung
S9000 Bd. I-II	Verband Fortschrittlicher Frauenvereine
S9001 Bd. I-IV	Deutscher Verband für Frauenstimmrecht
S9168	Verband norddeutscher Frauenvereine
S14139	Anita Augspurg
S14459	Adele Schreiber
S18848	Deutscher Bund zur Bekämpfung der Frauenemanzipation
S19031	Deutscher Männerbund für Frauenstimmrecht
S19925	Deutscher Frauenstimmrechtsbund
S20214	Deutscher Bund für Mutterschutz, Ortsgruppe Hamburg
SA593 Bd. I-II	Hamburg Zweigverein der Internationalen Abolitionistischen Föderation
SA1023	Jüdischer Frauenbund
SA1767	Norddeutscher Verband für Frauenstimmrecht-Bezirksverein Hamburg-Altona und Umgegend
V858	Verein zur Beschränkung der Frauenarbeit im Handelsgewerbe
V1047	Hamburger Landesverein für Frauenstimmrecht

4. Amtsgericht-Vereinsregister

B1953-52	Hamburg-Altonaer Verein für Frauenstimmrecht

G. Staats-und Universitätsbibliothek Hamburg

Handschriften-Abteilung: Dehmel-Archiv

Autographen: Vera Tugil-Dehmel:
Schriftwechsel Ida-Dehmel-Alice Bensheimer

H. Internationaal Instituut voor Sociale Geschiednis Amsterdam

1. Nachlass Vollmar

3156	Verein für Fraueninteressen (München)

2. *Collection Henriette Fürth*

Briefe an Henriette Fürth von Helene Stöcker.

I. Friedrich Ebert Stiftung/Archiv der Sozialen Demokratie Bonn-Bad Godesberg

Nachlässe

Emil Barth	I	Nr. 97	Protest der Kellnerinnen
	II	Nr. 269	Protest der Heimarbeiterinnen
Gerda Weyl		Nr. 19	Lebenserinnerungen von Klara Weyl

J. Universitätsbibliothek Rostock

Nachlass Käthe Schirmacher (ungeordnet)

K. Swarthmore College Peace Collection, Swarthmore, Pennsylvania, USA

Helene Stöcker Papers

Box 1 folder 2	Manuscripts of Dr. Stöcker's autobiography (incomplete): Copy B
Box 3	Personal Letters 1913-1926
	Kriegstagebuch
	Miscellaneous personal letters

L. Archiv des Bundes Deutscher Frauenvereine Berlin

1/A/2	Satzungen und Geschäftsordnungen; Auflösung des Bundes
2/I/1	Der Bundesvorstand (Internes aus seiner Geschichte)
2/I/2	Lebensbilder engerer Bundesvorstandsmitglieder
2/I/3	Lebensbilder von Gesamtvorstandsmitglieder
2/I/4	Lebensbilder einzelner Persönlichkeiten der Frauenbewegung
2/III/3	Rechtskommission 1894-1906
2/III/4	Rechtskommission 1907-1910
3/4	Deutsch-evangelischer Frauenbund
4/1	Stimmrechtsbewegung
4/2	Gegnerschaft des Bundes
4/3	Internationale Friedensbestrebungen
4/4	Der linke Flügel
5/I/2	Kassenberichte 1897-1932

5/II/1	Älteste Bundesbriefe 1894-1897
5/II/2	Älteste Bundesbriefe 1898
5/II/4	Älteste Bundesbriefe 1899-1902
5/IV/1	Anschreiben an den engeren Bundesvorstand, 1906-1908
5/IV/2	Anschreiben an den engeren Bundesvorstand, 1909
5/IV/5	Anschreiben an den engeren Bundesvorstand, 1912
5/VIII/1	Anschreiben an den Gesamtvorstand 1907-1913
5/VIII/2	Anschreiben an den Gesamtvorstand 1914-1915
5/VIII/3	Anschreiben an den Gesamtvorstand 1916
5/VIII/5	Anschreiben an den Gesamtvorstand 1918
5/XII/1	Briefe von Auguste Schmidt
5/XII/4	Briefe von Hanna Bieber-Böhm
5/XII/5	Briefe von Ika Freudenberg
5/XII/6	Briefe von Katharina Scheven
5/XII/7	Briefe von Anna Pappritz
5/XIII/4	Briefe von Alice Bensheimer
5/XIII/5	Briefe von Elisabeth Altmann-Gottheiner
5/XIV/1	Briefe von Marie Stritt 1895-1907
5/XIV/2	Briefe von Marie Stritt 1908 ff.
5/XV/1	Briefe von Gertrud Bäumer 1910-1911
5/XV/2	Briefe von Gertrud Bäumer 1912
5/XVI/1	Briefe von Gertrud Bäumer 1913
5/XVI/2	Briefe von Gertrud Bäumer 1914
5/XVI/3	Briefe von Gertrud Bäumer 1915 ff.
8/1	Sittlichkeitsfragen – Allgemeines
8/2	Bekämpfung der Prostitution
8/3	Kampf gegen Schund und Schmutz
9/1	Hygienische Fragen
16/I/1	Generalversammlungen 1896-1900
16/I/2	Generalversammlung 1902
16/I/5	Generalversammlung 1908
16/I/8	Generalversammlung 1919
16/II/1	Vorstandssitzungen 1896-1906; Sitzungen des Gesamtvorstandes 1907-1911
16/II/2	Sitzungen des Gesamtvorstandes 1912-1920
16/II/4	Sitzungen des engeren Vorstandes 1906-1928
16/II/5	Sitzungen des engeren Vorstandes 1928-1933

Frankfurter Ortsgruppe des Allgemeinen Deutschen Frauenvereins (not indexed)
I.A. Föderation (not indexed)
Documentation on Gertrud Bäumer 1945-7

M. Helene Lange Archiv Berlin

For this archive I have used the pencilled numbers on the new boxes rather than the original scheme of classification.

16	Schriften von Anna Pappritz
17	Briefe an Anna Pappritz
18	Sittlichkeitsfragen
50	Frauenstimmrecht in Deutschland
57	Stellung und Mitarbeit der Frau in der Politik (bürgerliche Parteien)

N. Archiv des Allgemeinen Deutschen Lehrerinnenvereins Berlin

1/2   Korrespondenz 1894-1895

L, M, and N are at present housed in the Deutsches Zentralinstitut für Sociale Fragen in the care of the Berliner Frauenbund von 1945 e.V..

O. Archiv des Deutsch-evangelischen Frauenbundes Hannover

A14	(Verhältnis zum Bund Deutscher Frauenvereine)
A14b	Vorgänge anlässlich der Bundestagung Heidelberg 1910
A14c	Vorgänge anlässlich der Bundestagung Gotha 1912
A14d	Schriftliche Abstimmung betr. Austritt des Deutsch-evangelischen Frauenbundes aus dem Bund Deutscher Frauenvereine
A14e	Austritt des Bundes und Vorgeschichte
B1	Material über die Gründung des Deutsch-evangelischen Frauenbundes und seine Entwicklung bis 1934
Q1	Anteilnahme der Frau am Staatsleben

P. Schweizerisches Sozialarchiv Zürich

Documentation on Anita Augspurg and Lida Gustava Heymann

II. PUBLISHED SOURCES

A. Periodicals

Centralblatt des Bundes Deutscher Frauenvereine 1899-1913
Der Abolitionist 1902-1914
Die Frau. Monatsschrift für das gesamte Frauenleben unserer Zeit 1893-1944
Die Frauenbewegung 1895-1919

Die Frauenfrage 1913-1920
Die Gleichheit 1891-1923
Die Neue Generation 1908-1919
Die Staatsbürgerin 1914-1919
Evangelische Frauenzeitung 1907-1918
Frauenstimmrecht! Monatshefte des Deutschen Verbandes für Frauenstimmrecht
1912-1914
Mitteilungen des deutschnationalen Handlungsgehilfenverbandes 1894-1914
Mutterschutz. Zeitschrift zur Reform der sexuellen Ethik 1905-1907
Zeitschrift für Frauenstimmrecht. Beiheft der 'Frauenbewegung' 1907-1918

B. Books and Pamphlets

W. Adler (ed.), *Reichsgesetz zur Bekämpfung der Geschlechtskrankheiten*
(Munich, 1929)
Allgemeiner Deutscher Frauenverein: *Die Tätigkeit des Allgemeinen Deutschen
Frauenvereins, Hamburg, 1896-1921* (Hamburg, 1921)
Allgemeiner Deutscher Frauenverein: *Die Tätigkeit des Allgemeinen Deutschen
Frauenvereins, Ortsgruppe Hamburg, nebst Zweigvereinen, 1909-1911* (Hamburg, 1911)
Jenny Apolant, *Das kommunale Wahlrecht der Frauen in den deutschen Bundesstaaten* (Leipzig/Berlin, 1918)
Minna Bahnson, *Ist es wünschenswert, dass der §3 aus den Satzungen des
Deutschen Verbandes für Frauenstimmrecht gestrichen wird?* (Bremen, 1912)
Rita Bardenheuer, *Woher und Wohin. Geschichtliches und Grundsätzliches aus der
Geschichte der deutschen Frauenbewegung* (Berlin, n.d.)
Gertrud Bäumer, *Lebensweg durch eine Zeitenwende* (Tübingen, 6th ed., 1933)
Gertrud Bäumer and Helene Lange (eds.), *Handbuch der Frauenbewegung* (5
vols., Berlin, 1901-1906)
Emmy Beckmann (ed.), *Des Lebens wie der Liebe Band. Briefe von Gertrud
Bäumer* (Tübingen, 1956)
Hanna Bieber-Böhm, *Vorschläge zur Bekämpfung der Prostitution* (Berlin, 1895)
Hans Blüher, *Der bürgerliche und der geistige Antifeminismus* (3rd ed., n.d., c.
1920)
Hans Blüher, *Frauenbewegung und Antifeminismus* (Lauenburg a.E., 1921)
Lily von Gizycki (i.e. Lily Braun), *Die Bürgerpflicht der Frauen* (Berlin, 1895)
Lily Braun, *Memoiren einer Sozialistin* (2 vols., Munich, 1908 and 1909)
Toni Breitscheid, *Die Notwendigkeit der Forderung des allgemeinen, gleichen,
geheimen Wahlrechts* (Berlin, 1909)
Bund Deutscher Frauenvereine: *Die Stellung der Frau in der politisch-sozialen
Neugestaltung Deutschlands* (1917)
Minna Cauer, *25 Jahre Verein Frauenwohl, Gross-Berlin* (Berlin, 1913)
H. A. L. Degener *et al.* (eds.), *Wer Ist's? Unsere Zeitgenossen* (Leipzig, 1909 ff)
Regine Deutsch und Francis Sklarek (eds.), *Zur Krise im Bund für Mutterschutz*
(Berlin, 1910)

(Die) Deutschen Frauen und die Hamburger Bordelle. Eine Abrechnung mit dem Syndikus Dr. Schäfer, Hamburg, wegen seiner Reichstagsrede am 28. Januar 1904. Referate in der Protestversammlung des Deutschen Zweiges der 'Internationalen Föderation' am 12. Februar 1904 in Berlin (Pössneck i.Th., n.d.)

Deutscher Bund für Mutterschutz. Bericht über die praktische Arbeit 1908-1910 (Berlin, 1910)

W. Deist (ed.), Militär und Innenpolitik im Weltkrieg 1914-1918 (Quellen zur Geschichte des Parlamentarismus und der politischen Parteien, 2. Reihe, Bd. 1, 2 vols., Düsseldorf, 1970)

Deutscher Verband für Frauenstimmrecht. Arbeitsberichte über die Geschäftsperiode . . . (Munich, 1907 ff)

Hans Exenberger, 'Das Beispiel Gertrud Bäumer', Die Weltbühne, 21, 19. Oct. 1947

(Die) Geburtenrückgang in Deutschland. Seine Bewertung und Bekämpfung. (im Auftrage Seiner Exzellenz der Herrn Ministers des Innern, herausgegeben von der Medizinal-Abteilung des Ministeriums, Berlin, 1912)

Grundlagen des Stimmrechts (Frauenstimmrechtsverband für Westdeutschland, Solingen, 1911)

Werner Heinemann, Die radikale Frauenbewegung als nationale Gefahr! (Hamburg, 1913)

Lida Gustava Heymann, Gleiches Recht, Frauenstimmrecht! (Munich, 1907)

Lida Gustava Heymann, in Zusammenarbeit mit Dr. jur. Anita Augspurg, Erlebtes-Erschautes. Deutsche Frauen kämpfen für Frieden, Recht und Freiheit 1850-1940 (ed. Margrit Twellmann, Meisenheim am Glan, 1972)

(Lida Gustava Heymann) Völkerversöhnende Frauenarbeit während des Weltkrieges (Munich, 1920)

(Der) Internationale Kongress für Frauenwerke und Frauenbestrebungen in Berlin, 19. bis 26. September 1896. Eine Sammlung der auf dem Kongress gehaltenen Vorträge und Ansprachen. Herausgegeben von der Redaktions-Kommission: Rosalie Schoenfliess, Lina Morgenstern, Minna Cauer, Jeannette Schwerin, Marie Raschke (Berlin, 1897)

International Woman Suffrage Alliance, Conference Reports (1906 ff.)

Jahrbuch der Frauenbewegung (from 1927: Jahrbuch des Bundes Deutscher Frauenvereine), ed. E. Wolff (1-3), E. Altmann-Gottheiner (4-10), and E. Uhlig-Beil (11-12), (Leipzig/Berlin, 12 Vols., 1912-1932)

Auguste Kirchhoff, Zur Entwicklung der Frauenstimmrechtsbewegung (Bremen, 1916)

Auguste Kirchhoff, Warum muss der Deutsche Verband für Frauenstimmrecht sich zum allgemeinen, gleichen, geheimen und direkten Wahlrecht bekennen? (Bremen, 1912)

Hanna Krüger, Die Unbequeme Frau. Käthe Schirmacher im Kampf um die Freiheit der Frau und die Freiheit der Nation 1865-1930 (Berlin, 1936)

Helene Lange, Lebenserinnerungen (Berlin, 1921)

Helene Lange, Kampfzeiten. Aufsätze und Reden aus 4 Jahrzehnten (2 vols., 1928)

Helene Lange, Die Frauenbewegung in ihren modernen Problemen (Leipzig, 1908)

Ludwig Langemann, Helene Hummel, *Frauenstimmrecht und Frauenemanzipation* (Berlin, 1916)

Frieda Ledermann, *Zur Geschichte der Frauenstimmrechtsbewegung* (Berlin, 1918)

Lexicon der Frau (Zürich, 2 vols., 1953)

Maria Lischnewska, *Die deutsche Frauenstimmrechtsbewegung zwischen Krieg und Frieden* (Berlin, 1915)

Maria Lischnewska, *Unser praktischer Mutterschutz. Bericht, erstattet auf der 1. Generalversammlung des Bundes für Mutterschutz . . .* (Berlin, 1907)

Else Lüders, *Minna Cauer. Leben und Werk. Dargestellt an Hand ihrer Tagebücher und nachgelassenen Schriften* (Gotha, 1925)

Else Lüders, *Ein Leben des Kampfes um Recht und Freiheit. Minna Cauer zum 70. Geburtstag* (Berlin, 1911)

Else Lüders, *Der 'linke Flügel'. Ein Blatt aus der Geschichte der deutschen Frauenbewegung* (Berlin, n.d.)

Wilhelm Lührs, (ed.), *Bremische Biographie, 1912-1962* (herausgegeben von der Historischen Gesellschaft zu Bremen und dem Staatsarchiv Bremen. In Verbindung mit Fritz Peters und Karl H. Schwebel bearbeitet von Wilhelm Lührs, Bremen, 1969)

Max Marcuse, *Aus unseren bisherigen Erfahrungen und Erfolgen. Rückblick auf das 1. Jahr des Bundes für Mutterschutz: Jahresbericht des Vorsitzenden* (Frankfurt am Main, 1906)

Erich Matthias and Rudolf Morsey (eds.), *Die Regierung des Prinzen Max von Baden* (Quellen zur Geschichte des Parlamentarismus und der politischen Parteien, 1. Reihe, Bd. 2, Düsseldorf, 1961)

Heinrich Meyer, *Das Christentum und die Neue Ethik* (Berlin, n.d.)

John Stuart Mill, *The Subjection of Women* (London, 1929)

Susanne Miller and Heinrich Potthoff (eds.), *Die Regierung der Volksbeauftragten 1918/19* (Quellen zur Geschichte des Parlamentarismus und der politischen Parteien, 1. Reihe, Bd. 3, Düsseldorf, 1969)

Paula Müller, *Die 'Neue Ethik' und ihre Gefahr.* (Berlin, 1908)

Neue Deutsche Biographie (Historischer Verein bei der Bayerischen Akademie der Wissenschaften, Berlin, 1956 ff)

Anna Pappritz, *Einführung in das Studium der Prostitutionsfrage* (Leipzig, 1919)

Frieda Radel, *Warum fordern wir das Frauenstimmrecht?* (2nd ed., Gautzsch bei Leipzig, 1910)

Hermann Rauschning, *Hitler Speaks. A Series of Political Conversations with Adolf Hitler on his Real Aims* (London, 1939)

Max Rosenthal, *Zur Geschichte des Deutschen Bundes für Mutterschutz* (Breslau, 1912)

Max Schwarz, *MdR. Biographisches Handbuch der Reichstage* (Hanover, 1965)

Toni Sender, *Die Frauen und das Rätesystem* (Berlin, 1919)

Statistik der Frauenorganisationen im Deutschen Reiche (1. Sonderheft zum Reichsarbeitsblatte, Berlin, 1909)

Statistisches Jahrbuch für das Deutsche Reich (Berlin, 1908-9)

Stenographische Berichte über die Sitzungen der Bürgerschaft zu Hamburg

Stenographische Berichte über die Verhandlungen des deutschen Reichstages
Helene Stöcker, *Krisenmache. Eine Abfertigung* (The Hague, 1910)
Helene Stöcker, *Lieben oder Hassen?* (Breslau, 1915)
Helene Stöcker, *Die Liebe und die Frauen* (2nd ed.), Berlin, 1908)
Helene Stöcker, *Liebe* (Berlin, 1922)
Alfred Urban, *Staat und Prostitution in Hamburg von Beginn der Reglemen-
tierung bis zur Aufhebung der Kasernierung* (Hamburg, 1927)
Verein für Fraueninteressen, München. Berichte über die Generalversammlungen
(Munich, 1895 ff, from 1928 typescript, Stadtarchiv München)
L. Weber, *Lebenserinnerungen* (Hamburg, n.d.)
Marianne Weber, *Ehefrau und Mutter in der Rechtsentwicklung* (Tübingen, 1907)
Hedwig Weidemann, *Frauenstimmrecht! Vortrag* (Hamburg, n.d. prob. 1908)
Marie Wegner, *Merkbuch der Frauenbewegung* (Leipzig/Berlin, 1908)
Agnes von Zahn-Harnack, Hans Sveistrup, *Die Frauenfrage in Deutschland.
Strömungen und Gegenströmungen 1790-1930. Sachlich geordnete und er-
läuterte Quellenkunde* (2nd ed., Tübingen, 1961) (and supplements to 1960)
U. Zeller, *Conrad Haussmann. Schlaglichter. Reichstagsbriefe und Aufzeich-
nungen* (Frankfurt am Main, 1924)

III. SECONDARY WORKS

Lothar Albertin, *Liberalismus und Demokratie am Anfang der Weimarer Repub-
lik. Eine vergleichende Analyse der Deutschen Demokratischen Partei und der
Deutschen Volkspartei* (Beiträge zur Geschichte des Parlamentarismus und der
politischen Parteien, Bd. 45, Düsseldorf, 1972)
J. A. and Olive Banks, *Feminism and Family Planning in Victorian England*
(Liverpool, 1964)
Richard Barkeley, *Die deutsche Friedensbewegung (1870 bis 1933)* (Hamburg,
1948)
Helmut Beilner, *Die Emanzipation der bayerischen Lehrerin, aufgezeigt an der
Arbeit des bayerischen Lehrerinnenvereins (1898-1933). Ein Beitrag zur Ge-
schichte der Emanzipation der Frau* (Miscellanea Bavarica Monacensia, H. 40;
Neue Schriftenreihe des Stadtarchivs München, Bd. 57), (Munich, 1971)
Hans Berger, *Die Frau in der politischen Entscheidung* (Stuttgart, 1933)
V. R. Berghahn, *Germany and the Approach of War in 1914* (London, 1973)
Rudolf Binion, *Frau Lou. Nietzsche's Wayward Disciple* (Princeton, 1968)
Gundula Bölke, *Die Wandlung der Frauenemanzipationstheorie von Marx bis zur
Rätebewegung* (Berlin, c.1970)
H. Boog, *Graf Ernst zu Reventlow, 1869-1943* (Phil. Diss., Heidelberg, 1965)
Karl Erich Born, *Staat und Sozialpolitik seit Bismarcks Sturz* (Wiesbaden, 1957)
Karl Dietrich Bracher, *The German Dictatorship* (London, Eng. trans., 1972)
Karl Dietrich Bracher, *Die Auflösung der Weimarer Republik. Eine Studie zum
Problem des Machtverfalls in der Demokratie* (Schriften des Instituts für

politischen Wissenschaft, Bd. 4, 4th ed., Villingen/Schwarzwald, 1964)

Karl Dietrich Bracher, Wolfgang Sauer, Gerhard Schulz, *Die nationalsozialistische Machtergreifung. Studien zur Errichtung des totalitären Herrschaftssystems in Deutschland 1933/34* (2nd ed., Schriften des Instituts für politische Wissenschaft, Bd. 14, Köln/Opladen 1962)

Gabrielle Bremme, *Die politische Rolle der Frau in Deutschland* (Göttingen, 1956)

Renate Bridenthal, 'Beyond *Kinder, Küche, Kirche:* Weimar Women at Work', *Central European History,* June 1973

Martin Broszat, *Zweihundert Jahre deutsche Polenpolitik* (2nd ed., Frankfurt am Main, 1971)

Gertrude Bussey and Margaret Tims, *Women's International League for Peace and Freedom 1915-1965. A record of fifty years' work* (London, 1972)

F. L. Carsten, *Revolution in Central Europe 1918-1919* (London, 1972)

Georges Castellan, *L'Allemagne du Weimar* (Paris, 3rd ed., 1972)

Peter T. Cominos, 'Late-Victorian Sexual Respectability and the Social System', *International Review of Social History,* 1963

George Dangerfield, *The Strange Death of Liberal England* (London, 1936)

Istvan Déak, *Weimar Germany's Left-Wing Intellectuals. A Political History of the Weltbühne and its circle* (Berkeley/Los Angeles, 1968)

Carl N. Degler, 'What Ought to Be and What Was: Women's Sexuality in the Nineteenth Century', *American Historical Review,* Dec. 1974.

Modris Eksteins, 'The *Frankfurter Zeitung:* Mirror of Weimar Democracy', *Journal of Contemporary History,* Vol. 6, No. 4, 1971

Ludwig Elm, *Zwischen Fortschritt und Reaktion. Geschichte der Parteien der liberalen Bourgeoisie in Deutschland, 1893-1918* (East Berlin, 1968)

R. J. Evans, *The Women's Movement in Germany 1890-1919* (D.Phil. thesis, Oxford, 1972, unpublished)

Gerald D. Feldman, *Army, Industry and Labor in Germany, 1914-1918* (Princeton, 1966)

Joachim C. Fest, *The Face of the Third Reich* (London, 1972)

Fritz Fischer, *Krieg der Illusionen. Die Deutsche Politik von 1911-1914* (Düsseldorf, 1969)

Abraham Flexner, *Prostitution in Europe* (New York, 1912)

Regina Frankenfeldd, *Der Deutsche Landfrauenverband e.V.. Fakten und Daten* (Hamburg, 1969)

Dieter Fricke, *1830-1945, Die Bürgerlichen Parteien in Deutschland, Handbuch, Vol. 1:* (Historisches Institut der Friedrich-Schiller-Universität, Jena; Leipzig, 1968)

Walter Gagel, *Die Wahlrechtsfrage in der Geschichte der Deutschen Liberalen Parteien, 1848-1918* (Beiträge zur Geschichte des Parlamentarismus und der politischen Parteien, Bd. 12, Düsseldorf, 1958)

Daniel Gasman, *The Scientific Origins of National Socialism. Social Darwinism in Ernst Haeckel and the German Monist League* (London, 1971)

Peter Gay, *Weimar Culture. The Outsider as Insider* (London, 1969)

Imanuel Geiss and Volker Ullrich (eds.), *Woher kommt die CDU?* (Reinbek bei Hamburg, 1970)

294 The Feminist Movement in Germany 1894-1933

Robert Gellately, *The Politics of Economic Despair: Shopkeepers and German Politics 1890-1914* (Sage Studies in 20th Century History, Vol. I, London 1974)

Ursula von Gersdorff, *Frauen im Kriegsdienst* (Beiträge zur Militär- und Kriegsgeschichte, herausgegeben vom Militärgeschichtlichen Fortschungsamt, Vol. 11, Stuttgart, 1969)

Alan P. Grimes, *The Puritan Ethic and Woman Suffrage* (New York, 1967)

Patricia Grimshaw, *Woman Suffrage in New Zealand* (Wellington, 1972)

Dieter Groh, *Negative Integration und revolutionärer Attentismus. Die deutsche Sozialdemokratie am Vorabend des Ersten Weltkrieges* (Berlin/Frankfurt, 1973)

Richard Grunberger, *A Social History of the Third Reich* (London, 1971)

Heinz Hadedank, *Der Feind steht rechts. Bürgerliche Linke in Kampf gegen den deutschen Militarismus* (Berlin, 1965)

Amy Hackett, 'The German Women's Movement and Suffrage, 1890-1914: A Study in National Feminism', in Robert J. Bezucha (ed.), *Modern European Social History* (Lexington, Mass., 1972)

Iris Hamel, *Völkischer Verband und nationale Gewerkschaft. Der Deutschnationale Handlungsgehilfenverband 1893-1933* (Frankfurt am Main, 1967)

Brian Harrison, 'For Church, Queen and Family: 'The Girls' Friendly Society 1874-1910', *Past and Present* 61, Nov. 1973

Holger H. Herwig, *The German Naval Officer Corps. A Social and Political History 1890-1918* (Oxford, 1973)

Theodor Heuss, *Friedrich Naumann. Der Mann, das Werk, die Zeit.* (2nd ed., Tübingen, 1949)

Hajo Holborn (ed.), *Republic to Reich. The Making of the Nazi Revolution* (New York, 1972)

R. J. Hollingdale, *Nietzsche* (London, 1974)

E. R. Huber, *Deutsche Verfassungsgeschichte seit 1789. Vol. 4. Struktur und Krisen des Kaiserreichs* (Stuttgart, 1968)

Richard N. Hunt, *German Social Democracy 1918-1933* (London, 1964)

Larry Eugene Jones, 'Between the Fronts: The German-national Union of Commercial Employees (DHV) from 1928 to 1933' (*Internationale Konferenz: 'Industrielles System und politische Entwicklung in der Weimarer Republik'*, Bochum, June 1973 — typescript) (published 1974, ed. Hans Mommsen)

Larry Eugene Jones, 'The "Dying Middle"; Weimar Germany and the Fragmentation of Bourgeois Politics', *Central European History* V (1), 1972

Michael H. Kater, 'Krisis des Frauenstudiums in der Weimarer Republik', *Vierteljahrschrift für Sozial und Wirtschaftsgeschichte* 59/2, 1972

Eckart Kehr, *Der Primat der Innenpolitik. Gesammelte Aufsätze zur preussischdeutschen Sozialgeschichte im 19. und 20. Jahrhundert* (ed. H. -U. Wehler, Berlin, 1965)

Clifford Kirkpatrick, *Nazi Germany: Its Women and Family Life* (New York, 1938)

Martin Kitchen, *The German Officer Corps, 1890-1914* (Oxford, 1968)

Viola Klein, *The Feminine Character. The History of an Ideology* (London, 1946)

John E. Knodel, *The Decline of Fertility in Germany, 1871-1939* (Princeton, 1974)

Jürgen Kocka, *Unternehmensverwaltung und Angestelltenschaft am Beispiel Siemens* (Stuttgart, 1969)

Jürgen Kocka, 'The First World War and the "Mittelstand": German Artisans and White-Collar Workers', *Journal of Contemporary History*, Vol. 8, No. 1, Jan. 1973

Jürgen Kocka, *Klassengesellschaft im Krieg. Deutsche Sozialgeschichte 1914-1918* (Göttingen, 1973)

Aileen Selma Kraditor, *The Ideas of the Woman Suffrage Movement 1890-1920* (New York, 1965)

Werner Krause, *Werner Sombarts Weg vom Kathedersozialismus zum Faschismus* (East Berlin, 1962)

A. Krekel-Wissdorf, *50 Jahre Deutscher Hausfrauen Bund* (Hanover, 1965)

Jürgen Kuczynksi, *Die Geschichte der Lage der Arbeiter unter dem Kapitalismus. Bd. 18: Studien zur Geschichte der Arbeiterin in Deutschland von 1700 bis zur Gegenwart* (Berlin, 1965)

Walter Laqueur, *Young Germany,* (London, 1962)

Herman Lebovics, *Social Conservatism and the Middle Classes in Germany, 1914-1933* (Princeton, 1969)

R. J. V. Lenman, 'Art, Society and the Law in Wilhelmine Germany: the Lex Heinze', *Oxford German Studies,* Vol. 8 (1973)

Ulrich Linse, 'Arbeiterschaft und Geburtenentwicklung im Deutschen Kaiserreich von 1871', *Archiv für Sozialgeschichte* XII (1972)

Jill R. McIntyre, 'Women and the Professions in Germany, 1930-1940', in *German Democracy and the Triumph of Hitler,* ed. Anthony Nicholls and Erich Matthias (St. Antony's Publications, No. 3, London, 1971)

Frances Magnus-von Hausen, 'Ziel und Weg in der deutschen Frauenbewegung des XIX. Jahrhunderts', in *Deutscher Staat und Deutsche Parteien: Festschrift für Friedrich Meinecke,* ed. Paul Wentzke (Munich/Berlin, 1922)

Erich Matthias and Rudolf Morsey (eds.), *Das Ende der Parteien 1933* (Kommission für die Geschichte des Parlamentarismus und der politischen Parteien in Bonn, 1960)

Wolfgang J. Mommsen, *Max Weber und die deutsche Politik 1890-1920* (Tübingen, 1959)

Barrington Moore, Jr., *Social Origins of Dictatorship and Democracy. Lord and Peasant in the Making of the Modern World* (Boston, 1966)

Rudolf Morsey, *Die Deutsche Zentrumspartei 1917-1923* (Beiträge zur Geschichte des Parlamentarismus und der politischen Parteien, Bd. 32, Düsseldorf, 1966)

George L. Mosse, *The Crisis of German Ideology. Intellectual Origins of the Third Reich* (London, 1966)

George L. Mosse, *Nazi Culture* (New York, 1966)

Hans Muthesius, *Alice Salomon, Die Begründerin des Sozialen Frauenberufs in Deutschland. Ihr Leben und ihr Werk* (Köln/Berlin, 1958)

J. P. Nettl, 'The German Social Democrats as a Political Model', *Past and Present* 30 (April 1965)

Peter Oertzen, *Betriebsräte in der Novemberrevolution* (Düsseldorf, 1963)

W. L. O'Neill, *The Woman Movement; Feminism in the United States and England* (London, 1969)

Richard V. Pierard, 'The Transportation of White Women to German Southwest Africa, 1898-1914', *Race,* XII, 13 Jan. 1971

Hartmut Pogge-von Strandmann, 'Domestic Origins of Germany's Colonial Expansion under Bismarck', *Past and Present,* Feb. 1969

F. K. Prochaska, 'Women in English Philanthropy 1790-1830', *International Review of Social History,* XIX/3, 1973

Hugh Wiley Puckett, *Germany's Women Go Forward* (New York, 1930)

Martin D. Pugh, 'Politicians and the Women's Vote, 1914-1918', *History,* 59/197, Oct. 1974

P. J. G. Pulzer, *The Rise of Political Anti-Semitism in Germany and Austria* (New York, 1964)

Jean Quataert, *The German Socialist Women's Movement 1890-1918: Issues, Internal Conflicts, and the Main Personages* (Ph.D., University of California, 1974)

Joachim Reimann, *Ernst Müller-Meiningen Senior und der Linksliberalismus seiner Zeit* (Miscellanea Bavaria Monacensia – Neue Schriftenreihe des Stadtarchivs München, Nr. 11, Munich, 1968)

Irmgard Remme, *Die Internationalen Beziehungen des deutschen Frauenbewegung vom Ausgang des 19. Jahrhunderts bis 1933* (phil. Diss., West Berlin, 1955)

Eric Richards, 'Women in the British Economy Since About 1700: An Interpretation', *History,* 59/197, Oct. 1974

Ingeborg Richarz-Simons, *Zum 100. Geburtstag von Dr. phil. Helene Stöcker* (Typescript, Munich, 1969)

S. T. Robson, *Left-Wing Liberalism in Germany, 1900-1919* (D.Phil. thesis, Oxford, 1966, unpublished)

J. C. G. Röhl, *Germany without Bismarck. The Crisis of Government in the Second Reich, 1890-1900* (London, 1967)

R. Rürup, 'Problems of the German Revolution, 1918-1919', *Journal of Contemporary History* (1968)

Ruth Schlette, 'Neue Veröffentlichungen zur Geschichte der Frauenbewegung', *Archiv für Sozialgeschichte* 1974, pp. 631-6

David Schoenbaum, *Hitler's Social Revolution. Class and Status in Germany, 1933-1939* (London, 1967)

Carl. E. Schorske, *German Social Democracy 1905-1917. The Development of the Great Schism.* (New York, 1955)

James D. Shand, 'Doves among the Eagles: German Pacifists and their Government during World War I', *Journal of Contemporary History,* 10/1 Jan. 1975

James J. Sheehan, 'Liberalism and the City in Nineteenth-Century Germany', *Past and Present,* No. 51, May 1971

Kurt Sontheimer, *Antidemokratisches Denken in der Weimarer Republik. Die politischen Ideen des deutschen Nationalismus zwischen 1918 und 1933* (4th ed., Munich, 1962)

Dirk Stegmann, *Die Erben Bismarcks. Parteien und Verbände in der Spätphase des Wilhelminischen Deutschlands* (Köln/Berlin, 1970)

Jonathan Steinberg, *Yesterday's Deterrent. Tirpitz and the Birth of the German Battle Fleet* (London, 1965)

Jill R. Stephenson, *Women in German Society 1930-1940* (unpublished Ph.D. thesis, Edinburgh, 1974)

Jill R. Stephenson, 'Girls' Higher Education in Germany 1930-40', *Journal of Contemporary History*, Jan. 1975

Fritz Stern, *The Politics of Cultural Despair* (Berkeley/Los Angeles, 1961)

Jacqueline Strain, *Feminism and Political Radicalism in the German Social Democratic Movement 1890-1914* (Ph.D. Diss., University of California, 1964)

Michael Stürmer (ed.), *Das Kaiserliche Deutschland. Politik und Gesellschaft 1870-1918* (Düsseldorf, 1970)

'The Coming of the Nazis', *Times Literary Supplement*, 3, 572, 1 Feb. 1974

Gertrud Theodor, *Friedrich Naumann oder der Prophet des Profits* (East Berlin, 1957)

Katherine Thomas, *Women in Nazi Germany* (London, 1943)

Werner Thönnessen, *The Emancipation of Women. The Rise and Decline of the Women's Movement in German Social Democracy 1863-1933* (London, 1973)

Louise Tilly and Joan Scott, 'Women's Work and the Family in 19th Century Europe', *Comparative Studies in Society and History*, Jan. 1975

Margrit Twellmann, *Die Deutsche Frauenbewegung im Spiegel repräsentativer Frauenzeitschriften. Ihre Anfange und erste Entwicklung, 1843-1889.* (Marburger Abhandlungen zur Politischen Wissenschaft, Vol. 17/1-2 (2 vols.) Meisenheim am Glan, 1972)

Julie Vogelstein, *Lily Braun. Ein Lebensbild* (Berlin, 1922)

Konstanze Wegner, *Theodor Barth und die Freisinnige Vereingung. Studien zur Geschichte des Linksliberalismus im Wilhelminischen Deutschland (1893-1910)* (Tübingen, 1968)

Hans-Ulrich Wehler, 'Sozialdarwinismus im expandierenden Industriestaat', im Imanuel Geiss and Bernd-Jürgen Wendt (eds.), *Deutschland in der Weltpolitik des 19. und 20. Jahrhunderts. Festschrift für Fritz Fischer* (Düsseldorf, 1973)

Hans-Ulrich Wehler, *Das Deutsche Kaiserreich 1871-1918* (Göttingen, 1973)

Klaus Wernecke, *Der Wille zur Weltgeltung. Aussenpolitik und Öffentlichkeit im Kaiserreich am Vorabend des Ersten Weltkrieges* (Düsseldorf, 1970)

Hans-Georg Wieck, *Christliche und Freie Demokraten in Hessen, Rheinland – Pfalz und Württemberg, 1945/46* (Beiträge zur Geschichte des Parlamentarismus und der politischen Parteien, Vol. 10, Düsseldorf, 1955)

Agnes von Zahn-Harnack, *Die Frauenbewegung-Geschichte, Probleme, Ziele* (Leipzig, 1928)

Hans-Günter Zmarzlik, 'Der Sozialdarwinismus in Deutschland als geschichtliches Problem', *Vierteljahreshefte für Zeitgeschichte*, Vol. 11, No. 3, July 1963; trans. as 'Social Darwinism in Germany, seen as a Historical Problem', in Hajo Holborn (ed.), *Republic to Reich. The Making of the Nazi Revolution* (New York, 1972)

INDEX

Richard J. Evans was born in 1947. From 1966 to 1969 he was Open Scholar in Modern History at Jesus College, Oxford, and from 1969 to 1972 he held a Studentship at St. Antony's College, Oxford. In 1969 he was awarded the Stanhope Historical Essay Prize. In 1970 he became Hanseatic Scholar at the University of Hamburg. He took his B.A. in 1969, and his M.A. and D.Phil. in 1973. From 1972 to 1976 Dr. Evans taught at the University of Stirling. In 1976 he was appointed to a post in the School of European Studies at the University of East Anglia, Norwich. Dr. Evans has published articles in scholarly journals, and is at present completing further research in the fields of women's history and German social history.